THE MUSIC OF THE TROUBADOURS

J

MUSIC: SCHOLARSHIP AND PERFORMANCE

THOMAS A. BINKLEY, FOUNDING EDITOR;
PAUL HILLIER, GENERAL EDITOR

Willi Apel. *Italian Violin Music of the Seventeenth Century.*

A. Peter Brown. *Performing Haydn's* The Creation.

David Ledbetter. *Harpsichord and Lute Music in 17th-Century France.*

George Houle. *Meter in Music, 1600–1800.*

Meredith Little and Natalie Jenne. *Dance and the Music of J.S. Bach.*

Timothy J. McGee. *Medieval Instrumental Dances.*

Timothy J. McGee, with David N. Klausner and A. G. Rigg, eds.
Singing Early Music.

Betty Bang Mather, with Dean M. Karns. *Dance Rhythms of the French Baroque.*

Nigel North. *Continuo Playing on the Lute, Archlute and Theorbo.*

Jason Paras. *The Music for Viola Bastarda.*

Dolores Pesce. *The Affinities and Medieval Transposition.*

Sandra Rosenblum. *Performance Practices in Classic Piano Music.*

Beverly Scheibert. *Jean-Henry D'Anglebert and the
Seventeenth-Century Clavecin School.*

Jeremy Yudkin. *De musica mensurata.*

THE
MUSIC
OF THE
TROUBADOURS

Elizabeth Aubrey

*Indiana
University
Press*

BLOOMINGTON AND INDIANAPOLIS

This book is a publication of

Indiana University Press
601 North Morton Street
Bloomington, IN 47404-3797 USA

http://www.indiana.edu/~iupress

Telephone orders 800-842-6796
Fax orders 812-855-7931
Orders by e-mail iuporder@indiana.edu

The paper used in this publication meets the minimum
requirements of American National Standard for Information Sciences—Permanence of Paper for Printed Library
Materials, ANSI Z39.48-1984.

Manufactured in the United States of America

Library of Congress Cataloging-in-Publication Data

Aubrey, Elizabeth, date
The music of the troubadours / Elizabeth Aubrey.
p.   cm. — (Music—scholarship and performance)
Includes bibliographical references and index.
ISBN 0-253-33207-9 (cl : alk. paper)
1. Troubadours. 2. Music—500–1400—History and criticism.
I. Title.   II. Series.
ML 182.A78 1996
782.4'3'0944809021—dc20   96-10358

ISBN 0-253-21389-4 (pbk : alk. paper)

2   3   4   5   6   05   04   03   02   01   00

CONTENTS

ACKNOWLEDGMENTS

This book has been over nine years in the making, and the assistance and encouragement that I have received along the way from individuals, institutions, and agencies have played a major role in its evolution. Grants from the National Endowment for the Humanities and the American Council of Learned Societies made it possible for me to travel to France, Italy, and England for research and consultation with colleagues. The staffs of the Bibliothèque nationale (particularly Patricia Stirnemann and François Avril), the Bibliothèque de l'Arsenal, the Biblioteca Ambrosiana, the Biblioteca Apostolica Vaticana, the British Library, the Institut de Recherche et d'Histoire des Textes of the C.N.R.S. (especially Geneviève Brunel-Lobrichon and Claire Maître), the Library of Congress, and the University of Iowa Libraries made available to me every resource possible during the course of my research.

Several colleagues graciously sacrificed many hours to read and comment on all or parts of earlier drafts of this book, and I credit each of them with helping me focus my thinking and clarify my language. They include Margaret L. Switten, who meticulously read the first draft and made invaluable observations, nearly all of which have influenced the final version; Elizabeth W. Poe, who reviewed a penultimate version; Anne Stone, who read and helped me rework several chapters; and Rebecca A. Baltzer, whose keen eye caught several incongruities and ambiguities, and who helped sharpen some of my arguments. The input both direct and indirect of Hendrik van der Werf has contributed much to the development of my research in general and to the shape of this book in particular. Although I have found occasion to disagree with him on some points, I have never lost my respect for the enormous contributions that he has made to our understanding of the songs of the troubadours, and I have benefited from his critique of my work.

To Professor Lowell Cross, Director of the Recording Studios of the University of Iowa, I owe an incalculable debt. He painstakingly read the entire book and made numerous insightful suggestions on content, organization, and wording. Lowell and his wife, Nora, both provided support and encouragement in countless intangible and tangible ways, not least in a ready bottle of *vin de pays d'oc*. My mother, father, sister, and other family members have been as constant in their tolerance of so many years of my seemingly endless preoccupation with this project as in their intolerance of any obstacle that threatened its ultimate realization.

Another author who has had the good fortune to have published with Indiana University Press assured me beforehand that Natalie Wrubel was a "dream" editor, and she has more than lived up to the billing. To the extent that my text is characterized by lucidity and consistency, this is largely owing to her calm and careful emendations, and I offer her my heartfelt thanks. The musical examples were expertly typeset by Christopher Preissing of cp Music Engraving, and the neume font of Examples 2–1, 2–2, 2–3, 2–6, 4–4, 7–1, and 7–5 was created by David Bohn.

Finally, I tender my deepest gratitude and and highest homage to the general editor and visionary of this series, the late Thomas Binkley. His extraordinary insights, so economically expressed, have guided this book from its beginning, and they continued to have an uncanny influence on its consummation even after his tragic death. At my first meeting with him in 1986, during which I described a project that I had in mind (not this one), Tom informed me, "What you really want to write is a book about the music of the troubadours." I smiled politely, wondering how he could presume to know what I wanted to do; I realized several months later that he was exactly right. Eight years later, after his first encounter with an early draft of the book, Tom told me that I needed to cut it down by about a third. Once again I responded politely, thinking that this was neither possible nor desirable; I realized several months later that once again he had been exactly right. I would never have started this work without his shrewd discernment of how my efforts were best spent, nor would I have finished it without his singular perception of what the final product should look like. I dedicate this book to his memory.

Aquest bon libre es fenitz,
Dieus en sia totz temps grazitz.
—Anonymous, the romance of *Jaufre*, twelfth century

GLOSSARY

ALBA. A lyric genre in which the coming of the dawn, usually signaled by a friend, brings to an end a tryst between lovers.

CAESURA. A syntactic pause with accent in the middle of a verse of six or more syllables, most commonly found after the fourth syllable of a verse of eight to ten syllables.

CANSO. A lyric genre on the subject of love.

COBLA. Stanza.

COBLAS CAPCAUDADAS. Literally "head-to-tail," a device in which the final verse of each stanza ends with a word or rhyme sound that recurs as the word or rhyme sound of the first verse of the following stanza.

COBLAS CAPFINIDAS. Literally "head-to-end," the repetition of the final word in each stanza as the first word (not the rhyme word) of the following stanza.

COBLAS DOBLAS. Stanza-linking device whereby the rhyme sounds change every two stanzas.

COBLAS REDONDAS. Stanza-linking device in which the rhyme scheme of the final stanza is linked to the rhymes of the first stanza, bringing the verse and stanza structure full circle.

COBLAS RETROGRADADAS. Stanza-linking device in which the rhymes or rhyme words are given in reverse order in alternating stanzas.

COBLAS SINGULARS. Device in which each stanza has different rhyme sounds, but usually following the same scheme.

COBLAS TERNAS. Stanza-linking device whereby the rhyme sounds change every three stanzas.

COBLAS UNISSONANS. Literally "stanzas with single sounds," a poem in which every stanza uses exactly the same rhyme sounds in the same pattern.

DANSA. A lyric genre of the late thirteenth century, usually on the subject of love, which begins with a *respos* of one or more verses whose rhyme scheme matches that of the opening verses of the stanzas; this *respos* might have been repeated like a refrain at the beginning of every stanza; the melodic structures of the extant *dansas* reflect this rhyme scheme and are often seen as an incipient *virelai* form.

DESCORT. A lyric genre on the subject of love, defined in a late twelfth century treatise as "a song having different sounds"; the subject matter might express some "discord" on a topical level, or have unusual or unmatching rhymes, verse structure, or language; sometimes the melody changes with each stanza or pair of stanzas.

ENUEG. A lyric genre, a type of *sirventes* that expresses annoyance or worry, usually in a long list of complaints.

ESTAMPIDA. A lyric genre on the subject of love that sometimes has a structure of paired verses in rhyme and melody; it is associated with a very vigorous type of dancing.

EXTRINSIC VARIANT. A difference between two concordant versions of a melody.

HEMISTICH. The portion of a verse before or after a *caesura*; sometimes (more loosely) the first or second part of a verse whether or not a *caesura* is present.

INTRINSIC VARIANT. A difference between repeated phrases or motives within a melody.

LAI/LAY. A long love song, sometimes on a didactic or religous theme; each stanza usually consists of a group of two or more versicles that are linked by rhyme and syllable count, which usually change with each new stanza; the melody is nonstrophic, changing with each new stanza.

LAISSE. An irregularly structured poetic unit in epic poetry that links verses by rhyme or assonance.

OXYTONIC RHYME. A rhyme whose accent occurs on the final syllable (sometimes called a "masculine" rhyme).

PAROXYTONIC RHYME. A rhyme whose accent occurs on the penultimate syllable (sometimes called a "feminine" rhyme).

PARTIMEN. A lyric genre, a type of *tenso* that consists of a debate between two speakers on a question that has only two possible answers.

PASTORELA. A lyric genre that narrates the story of the attempted seduction (usually unsuccessful) of a peasant girl or shepherdess by a lord or knight, sometimes told in dialogue but usually related in the first person by the male.

PLANH. A lyric genre that laments the death of a loved one, usually a lord or patron.

RAZO. From Latin *ratio:* 1. in poetic theory, the theme or subject matter of a song; 2. an anecdote about a song, often derived from the text of the song itself, possibly told in conjunction with a performance of the song.

RETRONCHA. A late thirteenth century lyric genre on the subject of love whose last verse or verses serve as a poetic refrain in all stanzas.

RIMS DERIVATIUS. A poetic device wherein some or all of the rhyme words are derived grammatically from other rhyme words, usually resulting in a change from oxytonic to paroxytonic rhymes or vice versa.

RIMS ESTRAMPS. A rhyme sound that does not rhyme with any other rhyme sounds within the stanza, but with the rhymes of corresponding verses in other stanzas.

SENHAL. A pseudonym used by a poet for a patron, lady, *joglar*, or another troubadour.

SESTINA. A rare lyric genre in which all the rhyme sounds change from stanza to stanza; more specifically it has six verses (*sest*) and six rhyme words, which are used in all the stanzas but in a different order.

SIRVENTES. A lyric genre on the subject of politics, religion, morality, or the like rather than love; the poetic structure is often borrowed from a preexisting song, usually another *sirventes* or a *canso*, and presumably the earlier melody could also "serve" the new song.

TENSO. A lyric genre consisting of a discussion between two or more speakers, often two poets, on a philosophical or political question.

TORNADA. A truncated stanza of two, three, or four verses at the end of a poem; these verses match the syllable count and rhyme scheme of the corresponding verses at the ends of the other stanzas; the verses sometimes sum up the theme of the preceding stanzas, or are addressed directly to a lady, a patron, another troubadour, or a *joglar*.

SIGLA AND ABBREVIATIONS

MANUSCRIPTS

C   Paris, Bibliothèque nationale, f. fr. 856

F   Florence, Biblioteca Laurenziana-Medicea, Pluteus 29.1

G   Milan, Biblioteca Ambrosiana, S. P. 4 (*olim* R71 sup.)

Hu   Burgos, Monasterio de las Huelgas, unnumbered codex

Mo   Montpellier, Faculté de Médecine, H. 196

O   Paris, Bibliothèque nationale, f. fr. 846

R   Paris, Bibliothèque nationale, f. fr. 22543

V   Venice, Biblioteca Marciana, fr. App. cod. XI

W   Paris, Bibliothèque nationale, f. fr. 844

W2   Wolfenbüttel, Herzog-August Bibliothek, Helmst. 628 (*olim* 677)

X   Paris, Bibliothèque nationale, f. fr. 20050

m   Paris, Bibliothèque nationale, f. fr. 12615

k   Rome, Biblioteca Apostolica Vaticana, Reg. 1659

SECONDARY LITERATURE (FULL CITATIONS GIVEN IN BIBLIOGRAPHY)

BS   Boutière, Jean and A.-H. Schutz. *Biographies des troubadours*, 2nd edition

GRLMA   *Grundriss der romanischen Literaturen des Mittelalters*, ed., Erich Köhler, Ulrich Mölk, and Dietmar Rieger

MW   Mölk, Ulrich and Friedrich Wolfzettel. *Répertoire métrique de la poésie lyrique française*

PC   Pillet, Alfred and Henry Carstens. *Bibliographie der Troubadours*

RS   Spanke, Hans, ed. *G. Raynauds Bibliographie des altfranzösischen Liedes*

INTRODUCTION

During the last several decades many studies and editions of the poetry of the troubadours have been published. During the same period, three editions of the melodies have appeared (Friedrich Gennrich, *Der musikalische Nachlass der Troubadours*, 1958–65; Ismael Fernández de la Cuesta, *Las Cançons dels Trobadors*, 1979; and Hendrik van der Werf, *The Extant Troubadour Melodies*, 1984), each quite distinct in its methods and goals. Several studies have examined the melodies of the troubadours as part of a larger body of medieval monophony (in particular van der Werf, *The Chansons of the Troubadours and Trouvères*, 1972; Christopher Page, *Voices and Instruments of the Middle Ages*, 1986; and John Stevens, *Words and Music in the Middle Ages*, 1986), and a few studies of a single composer's works also have been published. But since the early part of the twentieth century, no comprehensive critical study of the music of the troubadours in its own right has appeared. This book is intended to address that need.

The books by van der Werf, Page, and Stevens, as well as the entry by Stevens and Theodore Karp in *The New Grove Dictionary of Music and Musicians* (1980), demonstrate that it is common today to discuss the melodies of the troubadours and the trouvères together. Some studies even defer to the trouvère melodies over those of the troubadours because many more of them survive (over 2,000), and of this number, a vast majority are extant in more than one reading. The contrastingly small number of troubadour melodies that survive has made many skeptical of any hope of systematic or thorough analysis.

This attitude was not prevalent in the earlier years of the twentieth century, when formidable scholars such as Jean-Baptiste Beck, Pierre Aubry, and Friedrich Gennrich so appreciated the wealth of available material that they devoted entire volumes to analysis of the music of the troubadours. Certainly these earlier musicologists also accorded attention to other monophonic repertoires, and the virulent arguments over rhythm in which they all were intensely engaged subsumed the troubadours, the trouvères, and the Minnesinger. Yet they regarded the troubadour corpus as significant enough to deserve separate investigation. The first half of Beck's study of 1910 discusses the music notation of the principal troubadour manuscripts and surveys the genres of troubadour song.[1] Although Gennrich's edition of 1958–60 is of limited use because of his heavy-handed imposition of modal rhythms and his Lachmannian (but largely unexplained) text-critical method, it is supplemented with detailed structural analyses of the melodies.[2]

In writing this book, I have drawn upon materials offered in all of these important earlier studies and editions. By exploring what we know, acknowledging what we do not know, and suggesting what we may know better, I have striven for three goals: to place the music of the troubadours in its historical and theoretical context; to elucidate the respective contributions of composers, singers, and scribes to the music as it survives; and to propose new ways of analyzing the extant melodies. To approach these goals, I have used the complexities of the interrelationships between the melodies and the poems as a framework for my inquiry.

The melodies of the troubadours constitute one of the earliest repertoires of vernacular music to be preserved, and in terms of quality it is one of the most significant. Some 315 discrete musical settings for 246 poems survive.[3] There is no preceding body of comparable music that anticipates the sudden appearance of so large a corpus—certainly no trivial matter. The survival of these songs with their music is astounding in view of the fact that the extant chansonniers all were produced after the terrible devastation of the Albigensian Crusade and during a period of great social and political unrest punctuated by repeated inquisitions. How the poetry and music of such an oppressed culture survived, thrived, and found their way to *scriptoria* is evidence of the vitality of and widespread acclaim for the works. Although few concordant readings of these melodies have reached us (only 51 of the 246 poems have more than one melodic reading), the paucity of multiple readings can be seen as a clue to the nature of the repertoire itself.

During the twelfth and thirteenth centuries counterpoint, notation, theoretical constructs, compositional techniques, and genres and forms of music underwent astonishing and rapid development. This was the age of Aquitanian and Notre Dame polyphonies, modal and mensural notations, *versus* and *conductus*, *organum*, *discant*, and motet, all developed evidently by and for a learned and mainly clerical establishment.[4] Music theorists began to focus as much on the study of music as a practical art as they did on its philosophical location in the *quadrivium*.

The art of the troubadours was spawned in the same environment that led to the development of a new style of Latin paraliturgical song, the *versus* that are associated with the school of St. Martial de Limoges in Aquitaine.[5] The earliest troubadours lived and worked in this northwestern part of the Midi, and it is quite likely that they were familiar with the sacred literatures of their day. New principles of prosody, articulated later in the thirteenth century by poetic theorists like Geoffroi de Vinsauf and Jean de Garlande, were practiced by both clerics and troubadours in Limousin. There is some evidence that there were borrowings between the Latin and the Occitanian repertoires. But the exact relationship between the songs of the troubadours and the products of the Aquitanian clerics remains an open question, especially because few troubadour melodies of this early period survive.

By the early thirteenth century the center of new musical developments had taken root in Paris and its environs. But the music of the troubadours appears to have had little direct connection with these northern innovations, especially those in polyphonic sacred music. Although many practitioners of the *art de trobar* had ecclesiastical ties, they created their songs within traditions quite different from the liturgical and theoretical ones that gave rise and justification to the new musical practices in the Church that were described by Johannes de Garlandia, Anonymous IV, the Anonymous St. Emmeram, Franco of Cologne, and the other important theorists of the Notre Dame era. The troubadours looked south and east.

The radically different states of survival of the troubadour and the trouvère melodies are a clear indication of differences between the northern and the southern repertoires. The northern political and economic climate was comparatively stable, making production and conservation of music manuscripts much easier. Something about the aesthetic in which the production of the songs of the trouvères was valued seems to have fostered their dissemination and preservation in a form that ensured their stability; this aesthetic ultimately diverged rather significantly from the one in which the songs of the troubadours were created. Furthermore, the close relationship of trouvère music with emerging polyphony, which also helped ensure the preservation of many songs within that tradition, was not enjoyed by the troubadour melodies.

The language of the troubadours, *langue d'oc*, often called Old Provençal but now more commonly referred to as Old Occitan, is one of the Romance languages, a sister tongue to Old French (the *langue d'oïl*), Italian, Spanish, Catalan, and Galician-Portuguese. The *langue d'oc* as it appears in thirteenth- and fourteenth-century manuscripts is not necessarily a simple, easily identifiable *koïne*. Linguistic studies of the last several decades have localized many dialects, ranging from Limousin-influenced northern strains, to Catalan- and Gascon-tinged southern varieties, to Italianate southeastern dialects; these differences are even detectable in manuscripts, whose scribes' own dialects colored the texts. The troubadours did not comprise a single national group but reflected the variety of this large and linguistically disparate area. But as a *koïne*, Old Occitan became the vehicle for the development of the earliest significant vernacular lyric poetry in western Europe. Over 2,500 poems are extant, and they are extraordinarily diverse in content, structure, and style.

This book begins with the premise that the melodies of the troubadours are autonomous entities. They are in a sense mobile, most obviously in the existence of *contrafacta*—different texts that use the same melody. But even internally they are mobile—one tune serves five, six, or more discrete stanzas of a poem. At the very least this suggests that specific notes are not wedded to specific words, and that the collections of pitches that constitute a melody are governed by cohering principles of a purely musical nature. Thus while a basic tenet here is that the music of the troubadours cannot be fully understood apart from the poetry, and indeed that the poetry cannot be fully understood apart from the music, I will argue that their inseparability cannot necessarily be recognized word by word and note by note, but rather through larger constructs of theme, structure, and style. The interaction between poetry and music is most effective when the poem achieves excellence in the disposition of its poetic materials, and when the melody achieves a similar excellence in its disposition of musical materials. The poem is heard once during a performance, while the melody is repeated five or six times, both together creating a multi-layered texture of meaning.

Chapter 1 provides a brief historical context within which the troubadours must be viewed, along with sketches of what is known today about the lives of the 42 composers whose music survives. Like the trouvères, the troubadours were a diverse group of men and women active through at least 175 years of turbulent times. Some troubadours stayed in one place all their lives—in Languedoc or Provence, Auvergne, Catalonia, or Limousin. Others traveled extensively, throughout the Midi, to France, Aragón, Italy, the Holy Roman Empire, and the Holy Land. Some seem to have been virtually untouched by events around them; others responded directly and even vigorously to current happenings, such as the Dominican Inquisition in the thirteenth century and various crusades to the Holy Land. Some were polylingual, familiar enough with other Romance languages to handle them as easily as their own; others restricted themselves to some variety of the *langue d'oc*.

The chansonniers that transmit the songs are of widely diverse origins—some from the south in Languedoc and Provence, some from northern France, some from Catalonia, and many from Italy. All the manuscripts are relatively late (mid- to late thirteenth and early fourteenth centuries), and the contents of each of them span many decades and regions; their scribes inevitably reflected aesthetics and practices of their own eras and places. Only four of the major sources transmit music, and only one of these was produced in Occitania. The problem of attribution is acute in this repertoire. Some of the manuscripts upon which we rely do not identify the authors of poems at all, so that many *unica* remain of doubtful authorship. Conflicting, erroneous, or questionable attributions by the scribes are not uncommon.

Chapter 2 demonstrates that there were many people involved in the transmission of the melodies of the troubadours. Composers, singers, and scribes all played a part in the life of a song—its generation, performance, dissemination, and preservation. Oral and written traditions interacted in ways that are still difficult to sort out. Evidently the functions of composer (*trobador*) and performer (*joglar*) were not sharply delineated, and both functions were important in meridional society. As for scribes, it is difficult to detect what their sources were or how closely the melodies they recorded reflect the practices of the composers or of the singers.

The vagaries of the manuscript tradition, along with some uncertainty about how to define the art of the troubadours, has left the exact number of extant melodies by troubadours in some dispute. One goal of Friedrich Gennrich was to demonstrate the wide influence of the troubadour tradition, so he proposed the creation of some *contrafacta* after the manner of what he (and others, notably Hans Spanke) supposed was medieval practice; he included these modern fictions in his edition, in effect broadening the corpus. On the other hand, van der Werf chose to exclude many songs from his edition, those that he believed survive only in "late" readings (i.e., late thirteenth-century and early fourteenth-century), or whose formal structures betrayed late or external influence.

I have chosen to reject such presuppositions and to include in this book all lyric works in the *langue d'oc* that are extant with music in thirteenth- and early fourteenth-century medieval chansonniers. I do not consider an early fourteenth-century source or an unusually regular structure to be too late to transmit some reflection of the music of the troubadours.

Courtly lyric, never well defined in the Middle Ages, requires a fluid definition today as well. Literary genres fall into different categories, but there is not universal agreement on how to delineate the categories. To some, a genre is in a "High Style" or a "Low Style,"[6] or occupies an aristocratic register or a popular register; while to others the most significant distinction is between lyric and non-lyric genres.[7] Implicit in these delineations is an evaluation not only of differences in forms, styles, and language, but also of sociological function and cultural worth: where a song was performed, by whom, and for whom, are increasingly appreciated as factors in a song's definition.

Contemporary theorists described the poetry of the troubadours, the *art de trobar*, in the context of the art of rhetoric, one of the language arts of the *trivium*, whose concern was to teach how to move an audience, by means of the most eloquent expression, to a specific response, such as joy, pathos, sympathy, or anger. Chapters 3 and 4 of this book explore this theoretical environment and the way it affected the music. In lyric poetry, different genres were developed to embody specific themes, such as love of a lady in the *canso*, lament over a loss in the *planh*, satire or complaint in the *sirventes*, a love dialogue in a rural context in the *pastorela*, and philosophical dialogue in the *tenso*. Theorists discussed how poets should craft their poems to express these themes, and they appear to have assumed that music worked along with the text to convey the message of the song.

The versification schemes of the troubadours' poems were nearly as numerous as the songs themselves. The poets devised limitless ways of combining rhyme schemes, verse and stanza structures, and strophic interrelationships. The style of language, too, enjoyed great creativity. Some early troubadours, the most famous being Arnaut Daniel, composed very obscure poetry, known variously as *trobar clus*, *trobar ric*, or *trobar car*, using esoteric rhymes, made-up words, and inscrutable imagery. Others, like Bernart de Ventadorn, excelled in writing clear but elegant poetry in the more accessible *trobar leu*, sometimes called *trobar plan*.

Partly because of the great sophistication and wide stylistic variety among the poems of the troubadours, it has been easy to believe that in one way or another the tunes were, if not inferior, at least subordinate to the texts. This view was common until recently, when various authors suggested a more equitable view: John Stevens, for instance, has made an enormous contribution to our understanding of medieval monophony by showing specific ways in which the melodies are more than just vehicles for their texts.[8] But even as he defended the autonomy of both melody and text, he offered a theory of the songs' performance—isosyllabism—that forces the melodies to fit the structure of the texts, arguing that in order to avoid violating the irregularly placed text stresses, the music should have no rhythmic shape of its own. Others have recently attempted to demonstrate how the texts and music interact, sometimes on the level of structure, sometimes of sense. Such work goes a long way toward according to the music greater respect, but too often it does not appreciate the integrity of a melody as melody, apart from its text.

As with the poems, describing the style and structure of the music of the troubadours in general terms is nearly impossible. Numerous melodies are through-composed. It is widely believed that many melodies adhere to some kind of ABABx—or even simpler, AAB—structure. A majority of trouvère melodies have this form, but fewer than half of the extant troubadour melodies do, and even they exhibit astonishing variations of the structure, made even more numerous by differences among variant versions of the same tune. An analysis of the repetition schemes of the extant melodies, which is undertaken in Chapter 5, reveals that no two melodies among the 315 extant have precisely the same melodic form—even among supposed concordant readings of the same melody.

But structure encompasses more than simple repetition schemes. It can include the uses of phrase incipits and cadential figures, pitch goals and the contour of phrases, and tonal centers. Poetic structure can interact in subtle and complex ways when articulated through these elements of musical structure, which is the subject of Chapter 5. Even more variety emerges upon an examination of stylistic features in the music, such as range, texture (between notes and syllables), interval content, and motivic repetition and manipulation. Chapter 6 examines such characteristics and discusses ways in which they reflect features of poetic style. Some melodies are quite free and unpredictable in their use of these elements, while others are marked by more regularity or simplicity. Chapters 5 and 6 also identify various structural and stylistic musical features with succeeding generations of composers, although again generalizations are difficult and dangerous.

The discussions of transmission, style, structure, and interaction between the poetry and the music all have a bearing on the final chapter, which takes up the most controversial issues in the study of troubadour songs, those having to do with their performance. Some of the problems concerning rhythm, instrumental accompaniment, and the extent to which performers altered the melodies perhaps can be clarified, and our understanding deepened, in the context of the ideas developed in this book. A fuller appreciation of the exigencies of the melodies' transmission, and of the ways in which the composers, singers, and scribes approached the songs as poem and melody together, sheds new light on the way they may have sounded. Performance, after all, is the actualization of the song itself, the final realization of an idea born in the imagination of the composer.

THE MUSIC OF THE TROUBADOURS

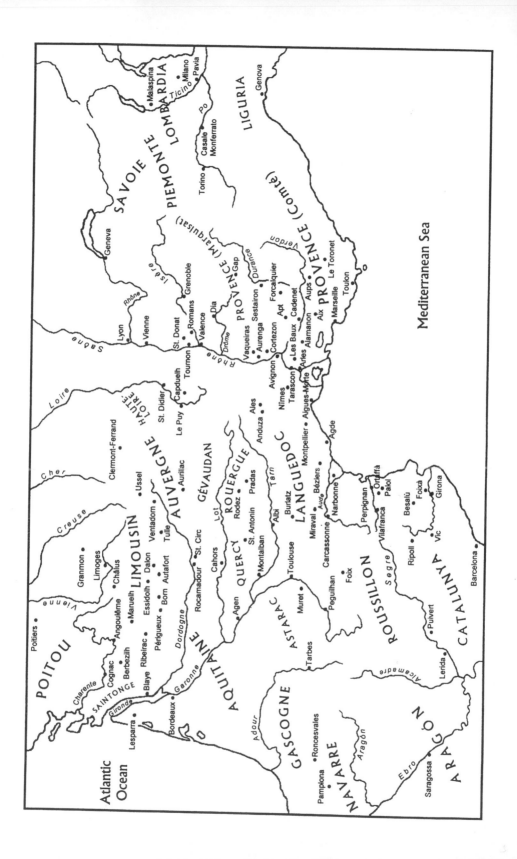

Atlantic Ocean

Mediterranean Sea

POITOU
SAINTONGE
LIMOUSIN
AUVERGNE
HAUTE-LOIRE
GÉVAUDAN
ROUERGUE
QUERCY
AQUITAINE
GASCOGNE
ASTARAC
NAVARRE
ARAGÓN
CATALUNYA
ROUSSILLON
LANGUEDOC
PROVENCE (Marquisat)
PROVENCE (Comté)
SAVOIE
PIEMONTE
LOMBARDIA
LIGURIA

Poitiers
Granmon
Limoges
Angoulême
Châlus
Cognac
Berbezilh
Ribeirac
Blaye
Bordeaux
Lesparra
Périgueux
Marueth
Dalon
Ussel
Ventadom
Tulle
Essidolh
Born Autafort
Clermont-Ferrand
Aurillac
Rocamadour
St. Circ
Cahors
Agen
Muret
Toulouse
Montalban
St. Antonin
Rodez
Pradas
Albi
Burlatz
Peguilhan
Tarbes
Roncesvalles
Pamplona
Saragossa
Lerida
Barcelona
Vic
Puivert
Foix
Foixà
Girona
Palol
Ripoll
Besalú
Ortaffa
Perpignan
Vilafranca
Narbonne
Béziers
Miraval
Carcassonne
Aude
Agde
Montpellier
Aigues-Motte
Nîmes
St. Didier
Le Puy
Capdueth
Anduza
Ales
Tarascon
Arles
Les Baux
Cortezon
Avignon
Aurenga
Vaqueiras
Tournon
St. Donat
Lyon
Vienne
Valence
Romans
Dia
Sestairon
Grenoble
Geneva
Torino
Casale
Monferrato
Milano
Pavia
Malaspina
Genova
Gap
Forcalquier
Apt
Cadenet
Alamanon
Aups
Aix
Marseille
Le Toronet
Toulon

Rhône
Saône
Loire
Cher
Creuse
Vienne
Charente
Gironde
Garonne
Dordogne
Lot
Tarn
Aude
Segre
Alcamadre
Ebro
Aragón
Adour
Isère
Drôme
Durance
Verdon
Ticino
Po

ONE

HISTORICAL BACKGROUND

The Midi in the Twelfth and Thirteenth Centuries

The *art de trobar* flourished between 1100 and 1300 in the Midi, or Occitania, the area encompassing Aquitaine, Périgord, Limousin, Auvergne, Gascony, Languedoc, and Provence in the south of present-day France. Troubadours were also found in northeastern Spain and northern Italy, and a few went on crusade to the Holy Land.[1] The poet-composers worked within a system that was loosely feudal, but without a centralized authority until the second half of the thirteenth century, when it succumbed to French domination. There was regular trade and academic intercourse between meridional cities and other towns in Europe. Commerce flourished among Marseille, Toulouse, Arles, and Genoa, for example, and Bologna had close ties with Toulouse, Marseille, Montpellier, Narbonne, and Carcassonne. The first several decades of the era of the troubadours were relatively stable and prosperous in the Midi.[2]

The kings of France were nominal overlords of much of the area south of the Loire and west of the Rhône, including Aquitaine, Limousin, Poitou, Auvergne, and Gascony; but throughout most of the twelfth century their influence was limited mainly to northeastern France. For much of the century they were overshadowed by one of their vassals, the duke of Normandy, who was also king of England. Henry II of England (r. 1135–1189), among whose seigneurial titles were count of Anjou, count of Poitou, duke of Normandy, and duke of Aquitaine (by marriage to Aliénor of Aquitaine, granddaughter of the troubadour

Guilhem IX), was much more powerful in the west and southwest of France than was the French king.

But regional counts, viscounts, and lords in the south were unwilling to yield actual power to a distant feudal liege-lord, whether French or English. Henry II faced rebellion throughout France for much of the 1150s through 1180s, spearheaded on many occasions by his own sons, the "Young" Henry, Richard Coeur-de-Lion, Geoffrey of Brittany, and John Lackland. And when Richard eventually became king, even his Aquitanian fidelities were not enough to insulate him from the scorn of his vassals in the south throughout his short reign (1189–1199). The various squabbles among Henry II, his sons, and the French kings kept the south relatively safe from interference during the twelfth century.

The art of the troubadours developed first in this west-central area: Limousin, Auvergne, Périgord, Poitou, and Gascony. Some poet-composers took a role in the political events of the time, while others managed to avoid the conflicts. Many troubadours were fairly well off, owning property or businesses, and some were members of the minor nobility. Those without independent means attached themselves to whatever powerful figure was willing to support them. In the second half of the twelfth century the literature took root further south in Languedoc and had begun to spread east to Provence.

The most powerful figure in Languedoc during the twelfth century was the count of Toulouse, who was a regular patron of the troubadours. The counts were vassals of the king of France and liege-lords of, among others, the counts of Angoulême, the lords of Montpellier, and, after the partition of Provence in 1125, the marquis of Provence, who occupied the area east of the Rhône and north of the Durance. Toulouse's power was constantly challenged—by England, France, Aragón, or the counts of Provence (south of the Durance)—but the county escaped serious intervention during the twelfth century.

Troubadours also found employment in Iberia, especially in the kingdom of Aragón, which ruled Catalonia and the area south of the Pyrenees east of Navarre and northeast of Castile.[3] The counties of Barcelona and Provence had been united in 1112, and Provence was added to Aragón's possessions by 1137. In Castile, whose rulers had familial connections with Aragón, a major preoccupation during the twelfth century was the attempt to recapture from the Moors cities and territories south of Toledo. The Reconquista of the late Middle Ages, sometimes reinforced by papal calls to crusade, involved an extended series of campaigns by Castile, Aragón, Navarre, León, and Portugal, occasionally joined by nobles from Toulouse, Aquitaine, Poitiers, and Provence.[4] Bit by bit the Almoravide dynasty's holdings were reduced to a sliver of territory around Granada by the end of the thirteenth century.

During the twelfth century the towns and cities of northern Italy gradually gained economic power by virtue of their strategic locations near trade routes through the Alps. By late in the century the regions of Piemonte, Lombardy, Liguria, the Veneto, and Tuscany had become the battleground for the competing expansionist ambitions of Holy Roman Emperor Friedrich I Barbarossa (r. 1152–1190) and the papacy. The marquisats of Monferrato, Malaspina, and Este and the city-states of Padua, Verona, Milan, Treviso, Pavia, Modena, and Parma were forced to side with either the imperial Hohenstaufen cause (*ghibelline*) or the papal cause (*guelph*), all the while attempting to remain independent of any external rule. The Peace of Constance of 1183 guaranteed the Lombard cities the right to self-rule, and it was about this time that troubadours began journeying in large numbers to the courts of northern Italy.[5]

The thirteenth century saw the dramatic rise of the French monarchy as a political power. As the twelfth century came to a close, Philippe II Auguste (r. 1180–1223) began to exert his feudal authority in the English holdings in Champagne, Burgundy, and Flanders. He encouraged the rebellion of Henry II's sons and later fomented local dissatisfaction with Richard Coeur-de-Lion. In 1204 Philippe succeeded in regaining Normandy from a weak King John, and during the next ten years he captured control of most of the other English fiefs on the Continent, consolidating his power at the Battle of Bouvines in 1214.

Gascony and parts of Aquitaine resisted French inroads, however, and the county of Toulouse remained autonomous. But with his northern realm stable, Philippe was now powerful enough to look southward, and the Church had given him an ideal excuse for doing so in the Albigensian Crusade (1209–1229). In 1215 he sent his son, the future Louis VIII, to join Simon de Montfort and the French forces in their quest to subjugate the Midi. By 1259, after several decades of battle and inquisition, the French monarchy controlled all of southern France west of the Rhône. (See further below on the Albigensian Crusade.)

Pedro II (r. 1196–1213) of Aragón attempted to provide support to the count of Toulouse during the Albigensian Crusade, but he was killed at the pivotal Battle of Muret in 1213, and thereafter Aragón ruled only in Catalonia. The county of Provence fell to imperial rule in 1212, and it along with the cities of northern Italy became subject to intense jockeying among France, Emperor Friedrich II (r. 1211–1250), and popes Innocent III and Gregory IV. The city leagues and marquisats of Lombardy and Tuscany once again were forced to defend their communal republics; they were saved from imperial domination only because of the strong support of Pope Innocent IV. Ultimately Charles of Anjou, brother of Louis IX of France, succeeded in bringing Provence into the French orbit. The troubadours were buffeted by all this turmoil in Occitania and Italy, and their art suffered in both quantity and quality.[6]

Several troubadours participated in crusades to the Holy Land during the twelfth and thirteenth centuries. The Second Crusade (1147–1149), preached by Bernard of Clairvaux, involved most of the important rulers of Europe, including Louis VII of France and his then wife, Aliénor of Aquitaine; the count of Toulouse; and Emperor Konrad III; troubadours Jaufre Rudel and Marcabru may have joined them (see below). Jerusalem fell in 1187 to Saladin, to loud and widespread dismay, and many troubadours added their voices to the call to arms for its liberation. The Third Crusade (1189–1192), an attempt to retake Jerusalem, was taken up by Friedrich I Barbarossa, Philippe II Auguste, and Richard I Coeur-de-Lion; and Guiraut de Bornelh, Gaucelm Faidit, and possibly Peire Vidal participated in this campaign at some point. The Fourth Crusade (1202–1204) was an enterprise led by Count Baldwin of Flanders, Marquis Bonifacio of Monferrato, and a number of French nobles, and once again Gaucelm Faidit, along with Raimbaut de Vaqueiras and Peirol, appears to have gone with them. The crusaders stopped at Constantinople before ever reaching Palestine. The Fifth Crusade (1228–1229), led by Friedrich II, landed at Acre and retook Jerusalem; Pons de Capduelh may have been there. The Sixth (1248–1254) and Seventh (1270) crusades of Saint Louis IX, directed against Egypt, were disastrous for the Europeans; Louis, along with many other crusaders, died of the plague at Tunis in 1270.

The clerical establishment in the Midi, as in most other parts of Europe, had lost much of its moral authority by the twelfth century. Some cynicism, combined with a rather libertarian view of religion, provided fertile ground for an antisacerdotal attitude. The Catharist heresy, which spread through Occitania in the twelfth century, was a Manichean faith evidently imported from eastern Europe.[7] It included belief in two equally powerful gods (one good and one evil), in the absolute corruption of this world and the necessity to subdue the flesh under rigorous constraints, and in physical reincarnation until the soul achieved perfection. The teachings had apparently arrived in Limousin by 1020, and practitioners enjoyed the protection of Guilhem IX of Poitiers. Toulouse was especially receptive to the doctrine, and in 1119 an ecclesiastical council there resulted in orders to the nobility to quell the heresy.

The number of true believers—the "Cathars" or "perfecti"—was relatively small (significantly, nearly 70 percent of them were women[8]). But most people, including nobles, bourgeois, some troubadours, and even a few bishops, who resented papal interference and the hauteur of the Pope's legates to the region, were at least sympathetic to the anticlerical cast of the doctrine, and it eventually became impossible to ignore. Pope Innocent III attempted at first to intervene peacefully. He replaced several bishops, including Raimon de Rabasteus, bishop of Toulouse, who was succeeded by Foulque, the erstwhile troubadour Folquet de Marselha.[9] Innocent adjured vigorous preaching of orthodox

Christianity in the region. One who responded was a young Spanish Augustinian canon, Dominicus of Caleruega; eventually, with Bishop Foulque's sanction, he founded the Order of Friars Preachers (the Dominican rule) in Toulouse. But the preaching was not effective in converting most of the heretics, so when the papal legate, Peire of Castelnau, was assassinated in 1208, ostensibly by a retainer of Raimon VI of Toulouse, Innocent called a crusade to wipe out the heresy. This bloody campaign came to be called the Albigensian Crusade.

Various northern French nobles, led by Simon, Lord of Montfort, answered the call. Persons of property and position, including some troubadours, were forced to choose sides. Control of towns and territories shifted back and forth, and the resulting economic, political, and cultural chaos devastated Languedoc and Provence. The Battle of Muret in 1213 was disastrous for Raimon VI and his allies; and at the Lateran Council of 1215, Raimon was dispossessed of his county. Fighting continued for many years, though, as meridional cities and principalities refused to bow to the invaders. The northern forces, in a final brutal and destructive push from 1226 to 1229, succeeded in subduing their opposition. Although the Treaty of Paris in 1229 forced the count of Toulouse to cede permanently much of his territory to the French crown, the heresy itself was not so easily conquered. An inquisition, begun by Bishop Foulque of Toulouse in 1229, given papal sanction in 1231, and led by Dominicans, resulted in persecutions and stake-burnings throughout the rest of the century.

The 1229 treaty also provided for the establishment of the University of Toulouse, endowing salaries for four masters of theology, two masters of canon law, six masters of liberal arts, and two masters of grammar. One of these grammarians was a young English scholar at the University of Paris, named Jean de Garlande.[10]

The nobles of the Midi eventually abandoned—publicly, at least—their support of Catharism, and the troubadours who depended on their patronage followed suit. While the literary culture had enjoyed a brilliant flowering in the decades leading up to the crusade, in the decades that followed there was a startling decline in poetic activity. The very identity of the *langue d'oc* came under stress, and the second half of the thirteenth century witnessed some self-conscious attempts to preserve the *art de trobar*, in the form of grammars, rhyme-dictionaries, and the art of poetry, especially in Catalonia. But the golden age had passed.

The Troubadours

The lives and chronology of works of individual troubadours can be pieced together, to some extent, using a wide variety of sources.[11] The references in the poems are sometimes overt and unambiguous, but they often require extensive digging and creative reasoning to reveal their meanings. Intertextual studies of poems that seem to be related by imitation, homage, and direct exchange have revealed relationships among troubadours that also help establish dates and places. Many troubadours used pseudonyms (*senhals*) for patrons, ladies, *joglars*, and other troubadours in their poems, and editors have often succeeded in divining the identities of the objects of many of the *senhals*. Much information can be gleaned from historical allusions to places, persons, and events in the literary works, and from the thirteenth- and fourteenth-century biographies and anecdotes (*vidas* and *razos*). These prose works were derived largely from details in poems, and they are not always reliable as histories, since their purpose, like that of the poems, was to entertain.[12] But in many cases their testimony has proven to be valid.

Of surprising significance is the amount of archival material that has been uncovered, which has provided a glimpse of the activities, social and economic status, loyalties, and even occasionally the personalities of many troubadours. These documents include records of feudal and property transactions, wills and testaments, civic and ecclesiastical proceedings, and chronicles. Troubadours were frequently witnesses or even principals in such affairs. Often the evidence afforded by these documents corroborates or clarifies references in the poems, *vidas*, and *razos*, although frequently it reveals those references—or modern interpretations of them—to be erroneous, misleading, or fantasied. The existence of such materials indicates that a number of these composers were persons of some consequence during their day, including minor nobles, knights, retainers of aristocratic figures, and clerics. Those who had no standing left very little independent testimony of their activities other than their literature.

Of about 460 named troubadours (including *trobairitz*, the women poet-composers) whose poems survive, the music of only 42 are extant. They include most of the poet-composers whose work is considered significant today. The following discussion briefly locates each of these troubadours in time and place, and divides them roughly into generations.[13]

The music of the earliest known troubadour, GUILHEM DE PEITIEU (i.e., Poitiers; VII Count of Poitiers and IX Duke of Aquitaine, 1071–1126), is known to us only by a fourteenth-century fragment of one melody, actually a *contrafactum*. It is set to a text modeled on one of his poems, but is too meager to afford an impression of his musical style. A slightly later period, however, from c. 1120 to 1150, is represented by two important and quite distinct figures, Jaufre Rudel and Marcabru. Both worked in the region around Poitou, although Marcabru was from the southern region of Occitania.

JAUFRE RUDEL (fl. 1125–1148) was a man of means, heir to the title "Blaviensium princeps" ("princes de Blaia" in his *vida*).[14] The fiefdom of Blaye, on the Gironde north of Bordeaux and southwest of Angoulême, was at the extreme southern end of the county of Poitou, and Jaufre probably encountered Count Guilhem VII shortly before the latter's death. The first documentary reference to Jaufre is in a feudal transaction dated 1125. In 1147–1148, Jaufre appears to have accompanied Count Guillaume VI Taillefer of Angoulême, Count Alphonse-Jourdain of Toulouse, and other southern nobles on the Second Crusade to Acre; the evidence for his participation in this expedition is in his *vida*, in some references in his poems, and in a *tornada* of a poem by Marcabru that names "Jaufre Rudel oltra mar"—across the sea.[15] There is no trace of Jaufre after 1148, and the account in the *vida* that he perished in the Holy Land (if not its assertion that he died in the arms of the countess of Tripoli) is plausible. Jaufre's extant output includes six *cansos*, all treating the theme of courtly love. His famous song of "distant love" (PC 262,2) and three other *cansos* survive with melodies.

Jaufre's contemporary MARCABRU (fl. 1129–1149), in contrast, was an unpropertied man who evidently depended entirely on the largesse of others. His Gascon origins are attested in his *vida* and in distinctive linguistic elements in his poems.[16] He and his slightly older compatriot Cercamon, with whom he may have apprenticed, were patronized by Count Guilhem VIII of Poitiers, son of the troubadour Guilhem VII. After the death of Guilhem VIII en route to Compostela in 1137, Marcabru unsuccessfully appealed for support to the kings of France and Portugal, the count of Toulouse, and the count of Barcelona and Provence; he finally found a ready patron in King Alfonso VII of Castile. He may have composed his crusade song "Pax in nomine Domini" (PC 293,35) in connection with the Iberian Reconquista of the late 1130s and early 1140s, in which Alfonso VII played a major role,[17] or for the Second Crusade to the Holy Land in 1148–1149.[18] Marcabru returned to Aquitaine, possibly by 1145.[19] One of his last songs mentions the defeat of Count Raimon-Berengar IV of Barcelona at Lérida in October 1149.[20] Marcabru's language is often acerbic and moralizing, and sometimes obscure.[21] Of 44 extant songs, four (a crusade song, a *pastorela*, a *sirventes*, and a *canso*) survive with melodies.

The second generation of troubadours, c. 1140–1175, boasts several extraordinarily talented authors, including the universally acclaimed Bernart de Ventadorn, as well as Rigaut de Berbezilh, Peire d'Alvernhe, and Raimbaut d'Aurenga. The first three, like composers of the earlier period, worked mainly in the west, including Limousin, Poitou, Périgord, and Auvergne, but this generation also produced the first composer, Raimbaut, from the eastern region of the Midi, Orange (Aurenga) in Provence.

RIGAUT DE BERBEZILH (fl. 1140–1162), may well have known Jaufre
Rudel, who almost certainly was a distant cousin of his through
the house of Angoulême, and some of his songs echo the poetry of
Marcabru. A "Rigaudus de Berbezillo" appears in documents between
1140 and 1163 from the Saintonge and Cognac region south of the
Charente River, north of Blaye.[22] He evidently was a knight whose
family had been agents or deputies of the lord of the castle of Berbezilh.
Rigaut was probably the younger of two sons, and he married into a
fairly well-off Angoumais family. There is no firm evidence that Rigaut
strayed far from the region south of Angoulême. An undated document
(probably after 1157) states that he took the monk's habit. A few of
Rigaut's songs achieved long-lasting fame, such as his "Atressi com
l'orifans" (PC 421,2), whose melody survives in three manuscripts
and whose text appears in a late thirteenth-century Italian *novellino*.[23]
Rigaut's output includes one *planh* and ten *cansos*. His poetic imagination produced figures of beasts, birds, stars, and other natural objects, as
well as allusions to Ovid and the Perceval tale. Two of the bestiary
cansos, the Perceval *canso*, and a more traditional love song survive with
melodies.

PEIRE D'ALVERNHE (fl. 1149–1170) might have been the "Petrus
d'Alvengue" or the "Petrus de Alvernia" mentioned in two Montpellier
documents dating from 1148.[24] His career apparently began just as that
of Marcabru, who parodied one of Peire's songs, was ending.[25] Although Montpellier's *seigneurs* were nominally vassals of Toulouse,
they were allied with Barcelona and Aragón during this period, and
some allusions in Peire's poems to the counts of Barcelona and Provence
suggest that the troubadour sought their patronage. Peire also appears
to have curried the favor of an adversary of Barcelona and Provence,
Raimon V of Toulouse.[26] Peire composed a famous *sirventes*, "Chantarai
d'aquest trobadors" (whose melody unfortunately does not survive),
which satirizes a number of his contemporaries, including Raimbaut
d'Aurenga, Guiraut de Bornelh, and Bernart de Ventadorn. The song
must predate 1173, when Raimbaut d'Aurenga died (see below), and
probably postdates 1165.[27] The Monk of Montaudon later composed a
parody of this satire, probably between c. 1192 and 1194 (see below). No
firm dates can be assigned to Peire after 1170. Evidently well educated,
Peire composed about 24 poems, often in an esoteric and complex idiom
akin to that of Marcabru. Only two of his melodies survive, a *tenso* and
a *canso*.

RAIMBAUT D'AURENGA (fl. 1162–1173), like Jaufre Rudel, was a
member of the aristocracy. He is one of the best-documented troubadours.[28] He was a vassal of the *seigneurs* of Montpellier and also had
connections with the lords of Baux, who were vassals of Aragón in the
county of Provence south of the Durance. He spent his career east of the

Rhône, as lord of Omelas in the Marquisat of Provence north of Avignon, and of the castle at Cortezon, between Orange and Avignon. After reaching his majority in 1163, Raimbaut seems to have maintained a fairly lavish court at Cortezon, where he may have hosted Marcabru, Guiraut de Bornelh, and Peire d'Alvernhe, as well as Levet, a *joglar* mentioned in some of Raimbaut's poems and in his testament. Raimbaut died at Cortezon in 1173. Citations in his and others' poems indicate that he was acquainted at least with the works of Marcabru, Guiraut de Bornelh, and Bernart de Ventadorn. His poetry contains allusions to French literature, Ovid, rhetoric, and other learned matters, using recondite versification schemes, a style known as *trobar ric*. He left behind at least 40 lyric poems, but surprisingly only one *canso* melody, and that one in a northern French source.

BERNART DE VENTADORN (fl. 1147–1180), among the most celebrated troubadours in his day and ours, may have been the son of servants in the castle of Eble II, viscount of Ventadorn, which was north of the Dordogne, southeast of Limoges. This is the description that Peire d'Alvernhe gives in his famous satire, an account echoed in Bernart's *vida*. Eble, who died in 1147, was himself celebrated as a *cantator* in the contemporary chronicle of Geoffroi de Vigeois,[29] and his court attracted Marcabru and others besides Bernart.[30] There are references in Bernart's poems to personages in Narbonne and Toulouse. But there is no independent corroboration of several other notions commonly believed about Bernart, such as the statement in his *vida* that he went to the court of Aliénor when she was duchess in Normandy, or that he accompanied her to England.[31] The *vida* says that he ended his days in the Cistercian monastery of Dalon (see Bertran de Born, below).

It had been assumed that Bernart stopped composing about 1180, but William Paden recently advanced a new hypothesis that the "Bernardus de Ventedor" who was elected abbot of the Benedictine monastery of Saint-Martin de Tulle in 1210 was the troubadour,[32] that he was a member of the Ventadorn family (son of Eble III), and that his poetic activity took place c. 1170–1200, a generation later than generally believed. Although this suggestion has yet to be tested, Paden points out that the only authorities for the earlier chronology are not necessarily trustworthy: a poem whose purpose is satire, and a *vida* composed several decades later. If this theory proves correct, it would necessitate a reevaluation of Bernart's place in the history of Occitan song. His extant output includes at least 39 securely attributed *cansos* and two *tensos*, all on the theme of courtly love in the straightforward style known as *trobar leu*; eighteen of the *cansos* are transmitted with music.[33]

The third generation, c. 1160–1210, saw an explosion of poetic activity, the beginning of a "golden age" for the troubadours. It encompasses the relatively peaceful and prosperous decades leading up to the Albigensian Crusade. Most of these composers were natives of the western and central part of Occitania, although a few came from the extreme east in Provence, and one was from Roussillon. Originating in the western region were Jordan Bonel, Bertran de Born, Guiraut de Bornelh, Guilhem de Saint Didier, Arnaut de Maruelh, Arnaut Daniel, Gaucelm Faidit, and Gui d'Ussel. From the central and southern portion came Berenguier de Palol, Raimon Jordan, and Peire Vidal. From Provence came Folquet de Marselha, Raimbaut de Vaqueiras, the Comtessa de Dia (the most prolific of the *trobairitz*, and the only one for whom any music survives), and Guilhem Magret. Several of these persons worked in northern Italy, including Gaucelm Faidit, Raimbaut de Vaqueiras, and Peire Vidal; and some went on the third or fourth crusade: Guiraut de Bornelh, Gaucelm Faidit, Raimbaut de Vaqueiras, and possibly Peire Vidal.

Almost nothing is known for certain about JORDAN BONEL (fl. second half of the twelfth century) except that he seems to have been a contemporary of Bertran de Born. His *vida*, which says he was from Saintonge, appears to borrow details from a *razo* about one of Bertran de Born's songs.[34] One known *canso* is almost certainly by Jordan, and at least two others with conflicting attributions might be his as well. The uncontested song is the only one with an extant melody.

GUIRAUT DE BORNELH (fl. 1160–1200) was evidently of low birth, without title or property. His origins were in Limousin, near the town of Essidolh (Excideuil) south of Limoges and northwest of Autafort (Hautefort).[35] Guiraut enjoyed the companionship and esteem of some of the era's notables, including Raimbaut d'Aurenga, whose court at Cortezon in Provence he may have visited and for whom he composed a *planh* in 1173. He probably spent time in Spain at the court of Alfonso II of Aragón, and he may also have had connections with Alfonso VIII of Castile and Fernando II of León. Guiraut joined the Third Crusade in late 1191 at the siege of Ascalon, and he claims in one poem to have visited the Holy Sepulchre. His *planh* on the death of Richard Coeur-de-Lion (PC 242,64) takes his productivity at least to 1199; no firm dates can be assigned to him after that. Guiraut's *vida* calls him *maestre dels trobadors*, which may indicate that he was a teacher of the arts of rhetoric and poetry.[36] Guiraut composed at least 76 songs, in which he demonstrated his mastery of a wide range of topics, techniques, and styles. Only four songs—a *sirventes*, a *canso*, an *alba*, and a *tenso*—survive with music.

BERENGUIER DE PALOL (fl. 1160–1209), the first major troubadour from Catalonia, evidently was from a family of some property in the fief of Palol or Palou (Occitan Palazol), just west of Elna in Roussillon.[37] He was no doubt the "Berengarius de Palatiolo" mentioned in five documents of Roussillon dating from 1196 to 1209. He was a vassal of Jaufre III, Count of Roussillon, from 1113 to 1164, whom he mentions in several poems.[38] Raimbaut de Vaqueiras used one of Berenguier's *cansos* as a model for a *sirventes* dated 1196.[39] Twelve *cansos* are attributed to Berenguier, all commentaries on courtly love; eight survive with melodies.

GUILHEM DE SAINT DIDIER (fl. 1165–1200) was *seigneur* of Saint Didier, a town east of the Loire,[40] and a vassal of the viscounts of Polinhac. A papal bull dated July 1165 mentions a "W. Sancti Desiderii" in the bishopric of Le Puy, and another document of 1171 lists "Guillelmo de Sancto Desiderio" among the episcopat's vassals. One of Guilhem's poems mentions a count "Raimon," almost certainly Raimon V of Toulouse, who was overlord of Le Puy and Velay. Other documents suggest that Guilhem had died by 1200. The Monk of Montaudon gave Guilhem prominent place in his satire on Peire d'Alvernhe's famous panoply of troubadours of 1192–94 (see below). Thirteen poems on themes of courtly love can be attributed securely to Guilhem, of which only one survives with music.

Only literary works yield any information about ARNAUT DE MARUELH (fl. 1171–1195). According to his *vida*, he was from "a castle named Maruelh," presumably Mareuil-sur-Belle, which lies about halfway between Angoulême and Périgueux. He evidently did not have independent means and was forced to seek patronage. Most of his love songs are addressed to Azalais of Burlatz (south of Albi and east of Toulouse), daughter of Count Raimon V of Toulouse and wife of Viscount Rogier II Taillefer of Béziers and Carcassonne.[41] Arnaut also was satirized in the Monk of Montaudon's poem of 1192–94, so he was active at least until then.[42] His poetry suggests that he had connections with Alfonso II of Aragón and with Seigneur Guilhem VIII of Montpellier. The *vida* of the *joglar* Pistoleta (see below) identifies Pistoleta as Arnaut's "singer," but none of Arnaut's texts mention the employment of Pistoleta or any *joglar*, and Arnaut's impecunious condition casts some doubt on the *vida*'s account.[43] His output includes at least 25 *cansos*, five love letters, and a long *ensenhamen* (a didactic poem) on the subject of courtesy, which betray familiarity with a wide range of classic and contemporary texts and topoi. Six of the *cansos* survive with melodies.

A cartulary from Obazine abbey in Limousin mentions that GAUCELM FAIDIT (fl. 1170–1202) and his family sold land to the abbey in 1197–98.[44] This record implies that Gaucelm was a member of the landed nobility and not as poverty-stricken as his *vida* portrays him. His use of the *senhal* "Linhaure," by which Guiraut de Bornelh referred to Raimbaut d'Aurenga (d. 1173), suggests that Gaucelm was composing at least by the early 1170s. His early years were spent in Limousin, probably under the influence of the school of Ventadorn; he dedicated at least thirteen songs to Maria de Torena, viscountess of Ventadorn.[45] He exchanged a *partimen* (a poetic dialogue) with Count Geoffrey Plantegenet, brother of Richard Coeur-de-Lion, alternating stanzas in the *langue d'oc* and the *langue d'oïl*. Gaucelm soon began to travel extensively—to Provence, where he may have encountered Raimbaut d'Aurenga personally; further east to the county of Apt; and past the Alps to Lombardy, where he formed an attachment to Marquis Bonifacio I of Monferrato, his "bel Thezaur." Gaucelm accompanied the French and Italian nobles on the Third Crusade, probably between 1190 and 1192. One of his crusade songs is composed entirely in the *langue d'oïl*, evidently for the benefit of the predominantly French-speaking crusaders.[46] In 1199 Gaucelm composed his most famous song, the *planh* on the death of Richard Coeur-de-Lion at Châlus in Limousin (PC 167,22). He apparently departed for the Fourth Crusade after this, and there is no trace of him after 1202. By his own account Gaucelm was obese, for which he was teased by his fellow poets. He and Guiraut de Bornelh were the most prolific of his generation, Gaucelm leaving behind at least 65 songs, including eight *partimens* with some of his younger contemporaries (Aimeric de Peguilhan, Peirol, Perdigon), and two crusade songs. He emulated Raimbaut d'Aurenga's *trobar ric* style in some songs, the more direct style of Bernart de Ventadorn in others. Thirteen *cansos* and the *planh* are transmitted with melodies.

BERTRAN DE BORN (fl. 1175–1202; d. 1215), *seigneur* of Autafort (Hautefort) south of Limoges, was deeply embroiled in political and military affairs during the turbulent years of conflict among Henry II of England and his sons. Numerous documents record his activities and status as a member of the lesser nobility, with a large household, an entourage of several knights, and extensive properties.[47] As a vassal of the duke of Aquitaine, Bertran owed fealty to the Plantegenet king of England, but he joined the rebellion of the Young Henry against the king; he thereby lost his castle at Autafort, but he regained it after currying the king's favor. He made frequent donations to the Cistercian abbey at Dalon, which he finally joined as a lay monk in 1196. In 1215 Bertran bequeathed a votive candle to be burned in his memory at St. Martial in Limoges, leading scholars to date his death around that time. Bertran appears to have had contact with the trouvère Conon de Béthune, and he exchanged poetic contrivances with Guiraut de Bornelh, Guilhem de Saint Didier, Peire Vidal, Arnaut Daniel, and Raimon de Miraval, among others. His extant output includes at least 39 songs, many ringing with military language and with references to the political events of his day; only one of his works, a *sirventes*, survives with music; its melody was borrowed by the Monk of Montaudon (see Chapter 4).

RAIMON JORDAN (fl. 1178–1195) was a member of the family of the viscounts of Saint-Antonin, a town in Quercy southeast of Cahors, in the county of Toulouse.[48] Although his *vida* calls him "vescoms," Raimon appears never to have held the title himself. A feudal document of 1178 containing the name of Raimon Jordan as a witness has led to the assumption that his poetic activity started about this time. Little other evidence has been located about Raimon, but he was celebrated by the Monk of Montaudon in his poem of 1192–94, so he probably was still active then. The viscounts of St.-Antonin embraced Catharism, which had made inroads in Rouergue and Quercy by the 1140s; their heresy eventually cost them their *seigneurie*, when Simon de Montfort took Saint-Antonin in 1212, and their title, which they had ceded to Louis IX of France by 1247. A detail in one version of Raimon Jordan's *vida*, impossible to verify, indicates how much the Albigensian movement seems to have been a part of the social fabric. The author of the *vida* links Raimon with the viscountess of Pena (a fortress near Saint-Antonin), who entered *en l'orden dels ereges*—an order of the heretics—on news of Raimon's death.[49] Raimon left at least thirteen songs; two *cansos* are given melodies in the chansonniers.

FOLQUET DE MARSELHA (fl. 1179–1195, d. 1231) was a member of a Genoese banking family named "Anfos" that took up residence in Marseille in the twelfth century. The name "Fulco Anfos," generally thought to refer to the troubadour Folquet, is found in a list of Marseillais bourgeois in 1178,[50] and the grammarian Jean de Garlande calls him *joculator, civis et inde Marsiliae*[51] (a *joglar*, citizen and native of Marseille), all suggesting that Folquet supported himself by maintaining his father's business operations. Although some of his poems allude to rulers of Aragón, Toulouse, Montpellier, Castile, and Aquitaine, there is no firm evidence that he was financially dependent as a composer on any nobility. He did direct special approbation to Raimon Gaufridi Barral, viscount of Marseille (r. 1188–1192), the same "En Barral" celebrated by several other troubadours, and he supported Alfonso II of Aragón in his dispute with Raimon V of Toulouse, a harbinger of Folquet's later opposition to the counts of Toulouse during the Albigensian crusade. Folquet earned a stanza in the Monk of Montaudon's satire of 1192–94, and he received poetic compliments from Peire Vidal, Pons de Capduelh, and, very late in his life, Aimeric de Peguilhan.

Folquet's poetic activity appears to have ended about 1195, when he, like Bertran de Born, joined a Cistercian abbey (Toronet in Provence). He entered it with his wife and two sons and probably brought material wealth to the abbey, which might explain his quick elevation to abbot in 1201. In 1205 he was appointed bishop of Toulouse, taking him across the Rhône, and thereafter he began his leading role in the crusade to quell the heresy that by that time was rooted firmly in the region. He supported Dominic and the foundation of the Order of Friars Preachers at the Lateran Council of 1215, and he enlisted the help of Simon de Montfort against Toulouse. Folquet was roundly condemned in the epic *Chanson de la croisade albigeois* for his merciless pursuit of the heretics.[52] But his motivation may have been more spiritual than political; some of the poems he had composed in the 1190s have a very pious and moralizing tone.[53] One tradition suggests that Folquet deeply rued the worldly and irreligious content of his earlier poems.[54] He evidently had a hand in founding the University of Toulouse in 1229, and he died shortly thereafter, in 1231. His poetry is in a learned style, influenced perhaps by the rise of scholasticism, and includes 24 songs; thirteen *cansos* have melodies.

Despite Dante's approbation in *Purgatorio*, we know very little about ARNAUT DANIEL (fl. 1180–1200). His *vida* tells us that he was born at Ribeirac, a castle in northern Périgord, west of Bertran de Born's home of Autafort. In one of his poems Arnaut claims to have attended the coronation of Philippe II Auguste, on 29 May 1180.[55] Arnaut is the subject of one stanza in the Monk of Montaudon's poem of 1192–94, so by then he evidently was known. Some versions of his *vida* claim that Arnaut became a *joglar*, and an amusing *razo* tells of his theft of a song from another *joglar* during a competition at the court of Richard Coeur-de-Lion.[56] Whether seen as a *trobador* or a *joglar* (and the distinction was not necessarily great), Arnaut was unquestionably a poet of great learning and subtlety. He was a chief proponent of the *trobar clus*, using obscure structures and language; his sophisticated devices, including those in his famous *sestina* (PC 29,14; see Chapter 5), betray a scholar's mind. Arnaut's surviving works include eighteen songs; only two melodies survive, for the celebrated *sestina* and for a *canso*.

RAIMBAUT DE VAQUEIRAS (fl. 1180–1205) was a native of the area of Aurenga (Orange); the castle of Vaqueiras belonged to the Baux family. Raimbaut was probably of humble origins, but he was well schooled, and he quickly attached himself to powerful rulers.[57] He divided his time between his native Provence and northern Italy, and was among the first troubadours to spend significant time across the Alps. Raimbaut became closely attached to Marquis Bonifacio I de Monferrato, who knighted him in return for his military service. His well-known *estampida* "Kalenda maia" was composed in honor of Beatriz, Bonifacio's daughter. Raimbaut also had contact with the Malaspina family at Genoa, and he participated in some of the struggles between the papacy and the Holy Roman Empire. He evidently joined Bonifacio on the Fourth Crusade in 1202. His last datable song (PC 392,24), a *sirventes* that survives with music, was probably composed in Salonika in 1205. He may have died with Bonifacio in 1207 in a battle against the Bulgarians. Raimbaut was adept in several languages, as evidenced in a polylingual *descort* with stanzas in Occitan, Italian, French, Gascon, and Galician-Portuguese. He had contact with Peire Vidal, Gaucelm Faidit, Arnaut Maruelh, and Perdigon, and with the trouvère Conon de Béthune, who also went on the Fourth Crusade. Raimbaut's output includes 26 extant poems, of which five *cansos*, a crusade song, and the *estampida* have melodies.

The poems of PEIRE VIDAL (fl. 1183–1205) are full of allusions to people, places, and events. A Toulousain document of 1164 that refers to a merchant named "Petrus Vitalis" supports the implication in his *vida* that Peire came from the bourgeois class in Toulouse, and several poems refer to Count Raimon V.[58] Peire's earliest poetry can be dated to c. 1183–84, and he earned a place in the Monk of Montaudon's satire of 1192–94.[59] Peire spent a great deal of his career in Provence at the court of En Barral of Marseille and at the court of Alfonso II of Aragón. He devoted two songs, which survive with music, to Alfonso and to his queen (PC 364,40 and 364,42).[60] His poetry also mentions Alfonso IX of León, Alfonso VIII of Castile, Pedro II of Aragón, the count of Forcalquier, and Lord Uc des Baux. He apparently made a pilgrimage to the Holy Land shortly before the Third Crusade (c. 1187), and he worked briefly in Lombardy at the Monferrato court. One of his poems was composed in Hungary at the court of King Aimeric, whose wife was a daughter of Alfonso II of Aragón. There is some indication that Peire was in the retinue of Count Enrico Pescatore of Malta, c. 1204–1205. Peire's poems contain allusions to works of Bertran de Born and Folquet de Marselha. At least 45 poems are attributed to Peire, and twelve melodies, all *cansos*, survive.

The "COMTESSA" DE DIA (fl. end of the twelfth century or beginning of the thirteenth) is a mysterious figure historically. Scholars have disagreed on her identity, since the details given in her *vida* do not neatly match historical data known from other sources; none of the chansonniers gives this "countess" a first name. The *vida* says she was the wife of "Guillem de Poitiers" and was in love with Raimbaut d'Aurenga (who died in 1173; see above). But no documents record any Guillem de Poitiers who was married to a woman who held the title of "countess" of Dia, a city on the Drôme north-northeast of Aurenga in the marquisat of Provence. Many scholars believe that she may have been Beatriz, daughter of the dauphin of Viennois and wife of a Guillem de Poitiers, count of Valentinois from c. 1163 to 1189; this Guilhem controlled properties in the area of Dia, but he never held the title of count of Dia.[61] A more likely theory is that she was another Beatriz, daughter of Count Isoard II of Dia, cited as "Beatrix comitissa" in a document of 1212 from Châtillon; she may have become the second wife of Guilhem de Poitiers, count of Viennois, but retained her title as countess of Dia.[62] This second Beatriz, however, would have been rather young in 1173, when the troubadour Raimbaut d'Aurenga died, so the declarations of the *vida* remain problematic, and the "comtessa's" identity is still uncertain. Singing in the feminine voice of courtly love, she composed one *tenso* and four *cansos*,[63] one of which survives with music.

GUI D'USSEL (fl. 1195–1209) was evidently the youngest of three sons in a family of nobles who owned a castle at Ussel in Limousin, northeast of Ventadorn. Gui and his two brothers, Eble and Peire, and their cousin Elias are all called troubadours in a single *vida*,[64] which says that Gui was a canon of Montferrand (now Clermont-Ferrand) and Brioude, south of Montferrand. No documents support this claim, although one of 1195 names "Eblo Usseli" and his brother "Guido" as donors of land to the abbey of Bonaigue.[65] Gui mentions only a few known personages in his works; they include Maria de Ventadorn, who is the object of several of his songs, and the king of Aragón, presumably Pedro II. Reference to the "queen of Aragón" in a *razo* for the latter song, which survives with music (PC 194,19), suggests a date of 1204 for its composition, since Pedro was not married until then.[66] The *vida* says that Gui acceded to an injunction by the papal legate to stop composing, possibly as early as 1209.[67] None of his extant works can be dated after this, nor is there any mention of the crusade in his poems, so it is plausible that he obediently took the safe course. Gui left behind twenty poems, and four *cansos* survive with melodies.

GUILHEM MAGRET (fl. 1195–1210?) is not mentioned in any known documents, but editor Fritz Naudieth has dated one of his songs to 1196 because it refers to the death of Alfonso II of Aragón and the accession of his son Pedro II in that year.[68] Another song celebrates the coronation of Pedro II by Pope Innocent III in Rome, which took place in November 1204. Guilhem's *vida* says he was a *joglar* from Vienne (south of Lyon on the Rhône), and he appears to have had relations with the house of Aragón, which ruled Provence in that period. A *tenso* created with Guilhem Rainol d'Apt—which indicates he was still alive during that composer's life (the first third of the thirteenth century)—calls Guilhem *joglar vielh, nesci, badoc* (an old, silly, stupid *joglar*); and his *vida* tells the pathetic story of his ultimate deprivation because of gambling and drink. He was said to have ended his days in a hospital in Spain. He left behind eight works, of which a *sirventes* and a *canso* have surviving melodies.

The fourth generation of troubadours, c. 1180–1240, spans the Albigensian Crusade and the Inquisition, which continued for some years afterward. While it was a period of great upheaval, it saw a continuation of the spectacular level of productivity established by the previous generation. Ironically, most of these troubadours were natives of the center and west, the region at the heart of the Albigensian controversy. They include the Monk of Montaudon, Peire Raimon de Tolosa, Peirol, Perdigon, Aimeric de Peguilhan, Raimon de Miraval, Guilhem Ademar, Uc Brunenc, and Pons de Capduelh. A few came from Provence, including Albertet, Pistoleta, Cadenet, and Guilhem Augier Novella. Many of these troubadours traveled to Catalonia, Spain, and Italy.

The exact identity of the MONGE (MONK) DE MONTAUDON (fl. 1180–1210) is not certain. His *vida* claims that he was a member of a minor noble family of Vic, a town northeast of Aurillac in Auvergne, and that he became a monk in the Benedictine abbey at Aurillac, whose library had been enriched with masterworks of antiquity (especially of rhetoric) in the tenth century.[69] The *vida* also says that the monk requested and received the benefice of a priory named Montaudon, whose location is uncertain, but it may have been near a little hill named Mons Odonis, a short distance southeast of Clermont.[70] His earliest datable song alludes to the captivity in Austria of Richard Coeur-de-Lion from 1192 to 1194. The monk traveled widely throughout Auvergne, Périgord, Languedoc, and Catalonia, judging from places mentioned in his poems; and he was patronized by Dalfi d'Alvernhe, Maria de Ventadorn, and possibly Alfonso II of Aragón.[71] According to his *vida* he became "lord" of the Puy-Sainte-Marie, the court at Velay that recognized a *canso* by Rigaut de Berbezilh (see above). The monk's best-known song is a parody of Peire d'Alvernhe's famous satire on his contemporaries, "Pos Peire d'Alvernh' a chantat." Composed c. 1192–94, it levels irreverent comments at Guillem de Saint Didier, Raimon Jordan, Peirol, Raimon de Miraval, Gaucelm Faidit, Guilhem Ademar, Arnaut Daniel, Arnaut de Maruelh, Folquet de Marselha, and Peire Vidal.[72] The monk may have ended his days at the Benedictine priory of Sant Pere de Bell-loc, near Vilafranca in Roussillon. His extant works include sixteen songs; four are *enuegs* (for one of which he borrowed a melody by Bertran de Born),[73] which are lists of complaints about various social irritations. Only one melody, for a *canso*, by the monk himself survives.

PEIRE RAIMON DE TOLOSA (fl. 1180–1221) was, according to his *vida*, the son of a merchant. Rubrics refer to him as *lo viellz* and *lo gros* (the old and the fat), although some scholars believe that these appelations may refer to two different persons.[74] The name "Petrus Raimundus" appears in Toulousain charters of 1182 and 1214.[75] Peire's *planh* composed on the death of the Young Henry, who died in 1183, may be his earliest datable song. The troubadour evidently worked at the courts of Raimon V or VI of Toulouse, Alfonso II of Aragón, Guilhem VIII of Montpellier, and Tomas I of Savoie. In Italy he spent time with Guillermo Malaspina and at the Este court of Azzo VI, whose daughter Beatriz he addressed in one song. Peire often used nature themes, sometimes composing in a hermetic style; Bertran de Born imitated one of his poems. He left eighteen songs, of which one *canso* survives with music.

PEIROL (fl. 1185–1221) appears to be the surname of a family of lesser nobles in Auvergne in the late twelfth century. The poet who is known by that name in the chansonniers evidently began composing shortly before the Third Crusade in 1189, when he produced a *tenso* that refers to the campaign against Saladin, although there is no evidence that Peirol actually joined this crusade.[76] Peirol worked at the court of Dalfi d'Alvernhe, count of Clermont and Montferrand, whose wife provided a small bequest in her will to a "Peyro servienti Dominae Comitissae."[77] His *vida* says he became a *joglar* after falling out of favor with Dalfi, and a *tornada* in a poem by Albertet (de Sestaro) calls him a fiddler and singer. A crusade song that he composed during the return journey from the Fourth Crusade in 1221 seems to place Peirol in Italy to witness the vow of Emperor Friedrich II to take the cross. Peirol cannot be traced after this. He was known and admired in Italy, judging from homage by Francesco da Barberino and other poets.[78] His output included 32 poems; seventeen *cansos* survive with melodies.

RAIMON DE MIRAVAL (fl. 1185–1229) belonged to a family of minor lords, proprietors of a castle at Miraval north of Carcassonne, vassals of the viscount of Béziers and Carcassonne. The Miraval name figures often in Languedocian documents of the twelfth and thirteenth centuries, and a document of 1213 records a land transaction in which the troubadour took part.[79] The Miraval castle, which Raimon bemoaned in song, fell to crusaders in the earliest stage of the Albigensian campaign, before the disastrous Battle of Muret in 1213.[80] Raimon enjoyed the sponsorship of Raimon VI of Toulouse, to whom he addressed at least seventeen songs. A stanza in the satire by the Monk of Montaudon is devoted to Raimon, who, in turn, mentioned various nobles in his songs, including lords of Foix, Carcassonne, and Béziers, Pedro II of Aragón, and Alfonso VIII of Castile. His *vida* says he died at the Cistercian monastery of Sancta Clara in Lérida, Catalonia, and a 1229 land sale document locates a "Raimundo de Miravals" near Lérida.[81] His works include at least 44 poems; 22 of the *cansos* have melodies.[82]

The biography of PERDIGON (fl. 1190–1212) presents a formidable puzzle; details in his *vida* contrast sharply with historical allusions in his poems.[83] The report in the *vida* that he was a *joglar* and a fine fiddler is corroborated by manuscript illustrations showing him holding a fiddle and by allusions to his fiddling skills in his and others' poems.[84] A wide traveler, Perdigon enjoyed the patronage of Dalfi d'Alvernhe, the lord of Les Baux (probably Guillem), Pedro II of Aragón, and En Barral of Marseille, for whom Perdigon composed one of the *cansos* that survives with music (PC 370,14), before Barral's death in 1192. The *vida* claims that Perdigon took up the anti-heretical cause in the Albigensian

Crusade, an unpopular thing to do in the Midi, and that he eventually died in a Cistercian monastery. Nothing in his poetry unequivocally supports this report, though, and indeed the wide respect in which the poet-*joglar* was held is demonstrated by the inclusion of many of his songs in the chansonniers and the citation of his works by his contemporaries.[85] Fourteen of his songs survive, and three of the *cansos* have melodies.

AIMERIC DE PEGUILHAN (fl. 1190–1225) was probably from the town of Peguilhan west-southwest of Toulouse just north of the Pyrenees, and he may have been member of a bourgeois Toulousain family.[86] From references in his poems it appears he had visited Catalonia by the early 1190s and had contact with the Castile and Aragón royal families and with various vassals of Aragón.[87] The texts indicate that he traveled then to Italy, where he addressed songs to Marquis Guglielmo IV of Monferrato and composed *planhs* on the deaths of Marquis Azzo VI d'Este (1212), Bonifazio de Verona (1212), and Marquis Guglielmo of Malaspina (1220). Several of his songs, including the *descort* "Qui la ve en ditz" (PC 10,45), which survives with two different melodies, allude to "Beatritz d'Est," undoubtedly the daughter of Azzo VI.[88] Several other songs can be dated after the coronation of Friedrich II as Holy Roman Emperor in Rome in 1220. Aimeric was a prolific composer, for whom at least 49 poems survive, including the two *descort* melodies and four *canso* melodies.

One document has been uncovered that bears the name of Uc BRUNENC (fl. 1190–1220), dated c. 1190. It relates how "Lord Ugo Brunenc" and the monks of the abbey of Bonnecombe (in Rouergue south of Rodez) settled their differences over Uc's demand to be provided lodging for himself, five of his knights, and a servant.[89] Among his patrons were Alfonso II of Aragón, Dalfi d'Alvernhe, and Bernart VII d'Anduza in Provence, who also patronized Pons de Capduelh and Gaucelm Faidit.[90] A *planh* on Uc's death composed by his younger compatriot Daude de Pradas suggests that Uc was active until at least the second decade of the thirteenth century. Daude claims that Uc was a fine singer, but his *vida* says that he did not compose music. If that is true, one wonders who composed the melody given in one manuscript with one of his six poems.[91]

PONS DE CAPDUELH (fl. 1190–1237) was from the Haute-Loire, probably the minor lord "Pontius de Capitolio" mentioned in documents of 1189–1220. This Pontius married a woman whose dowry included the castle of Vertaizon, a feudal holding of the bishop of Clermont.[92] Pons composed a crusade song dated 1213 that probably refers to the Battle of Muret. His *vida* says he went on crusade to the Holy Land, but this cannot be confirmed. His last datable song is a *planh* composed on the death of Azalais, daughter of Bernart d'Anduza, who died in 1237.[93]

Pons composed at least 26 songs, and four of the *cansos* survive with music.

GUILHEM ADEMAR (fl. 1190–1217) was called a "bad *joglar*" by the Monk of Montaudon.[94] His *vida* claims that he was a poor knight from the castle of Mayrueis in Gévaudan; and several documents of the area between 1192 and 1217 mention a minor noble named "W. Ademars" or "Azemars," although none can be securely identified with the troubadour.[95] There are references in his poems to his overlord Raimon VI of Toulouse, to a "rey Fernando" (probably Fernando III), and to Alfonso VIII of Castile; Guilhem may have been in Spain while Raimon VI helped in the crusade of 1212 against the Moors.[96] His *vida* says that he entered "the order of Granmon," presumably the Benedictine abbey there, but this is not independently confirmed. Of his sixteen extant poems, one *canso* survives with music.

ALBERTET (fl. 1194–1221) was a well-respected *joglar* who lived and worked in Provence and Italy. His *vida* declares that his best work was music—as a singer as well as a composer—and that his poems were not of outstanding merit. A poem by Uc de Lescura echoes the *vida* in praising Albertet's musical skills, specifically his *votz a ben dir* (well-spoken-of voice.)[97] Three manuscripts refer to him as "Albertet de Sestaro," and his *vida* says that he ended his days in the Provençal town of Sestairon, but that his origins were in Gapenses (Gapençais), further north in the county of Forcalquier. References in his songs locate him west of the Rhône at Montferrand, where he had contact with Dalfi d'Alvernhe, Gaucelm Faidit, and Peirol, and as early as 1210 at the courts of Savoie, Monferrato, Malaspina, Genoa, and the d'Este in Ferrara, where he probably encountered Aimeric de Peguilhan, Aimeric de Belenoi, Peirol, and Guillem Augier Novella. In one famous satire Albertet praises seven celebrated ladies of the day, including "comtessa" Beatritz, wife of Raimon-Berengar IV of Provence.[98] His output includes 21 songs, of which three *cansos* have melodies.

"PISTOLETA" (fl. 1205–1228), literally "small letter," was the name of a shadowy figure, evidently from Provence. According to his *vida* he was Arnaut de Maruelh's singer (*cantaire*), although nothing in the works or known activities of Arnaut confirms such a connection (see above).[99] The *vida* says that Pistoleta composed songs *com avinens sons* (with pleasing melodies).[100] Some poems attributed to him suggest that he made a youthful visit to Limousin and Languedoc and encountered Maria de Ventadorn, wife of Eble V.[101] He also had connections with Pedro II of Aragón and Alfonso VIII of Castile, both of whom were active in Languedoc during this period. He returned east of the Rhône, perhaps coming into contact with Count Tomas I of Savoie.[102] A *tenso* with Lord Blacatz, a generous patron of several troubadours, mentions the "emperaire," doubtless Friedrich II, who was crowned Emperor in

1220 and hence became overlord of Provence.[103] Pistoleta's *vida* says that he became a wealthy merchant in Marseille, enabling him to abandon his court-hopping, but no other documents confirm this. Of the eleven songs by Pistoleta that survive, only one *sirventes* melody is extant (in two rather different versions).

CADENET (fl. 1204–1238) was from a knight's family who owned a castle at Cadenet, just north of the Durance River, south of Apt. Cadenet's *vida* says that the castle was laid in ruins (which still remain today) by forces from Toulouse, probably in 1165 during struggles among the counts of Provence, Forcalquier, and Toulouse for hegemony in the region.[104] Cadenet was taken as a young child from Provence to Toulouse by a knight named Guillem de Lantar, a retainer of the count of Toulouse.[105] While in Languedoc, Cadenet composed songs for Countess Mathilda of Angoulême and for Elionor, the daughter of Alfonso II who married Count Raimon VI of Toulouse in 1204. Cadenet ultimately returned to Provence, where he found favor with the beneficent Lord Blacatz. He may also have gone to Italy and come into contact with Bonifacio I of Monferrato.[106] His *vida* says that Cadenet died after entering the order of the Hospitalers; this claim is reinforced by a document of 1239 listing one "frater Cadanetus, miles," or knight, as witness to a donation of property to the Hospitalers in Orange. On conventional themes, Cadenet's poems were imitated by Peire Cardenal, Peire Raimon de Tolosa, and Gui d'Ussel. Twenty-four poems survive, one of which is an *alba* with its melody.

GUILHEM AUGIER [Novella] (fl. 1209–1230) was a *joglar* from the small town of St. Donat, south of Vienne in northern Provence. Rubrics in the chansonniers give different versions of his name: Ogier, Guillem Augier, Ogiers Novella, and Ugiers de Viena; the epithet "Novella" was probably added during his Italian travels.[107] Guilhem found his way to the court of Béziers in Languedoc, where he debated in a *tenso* with another *joglar* on the question of whether it was more dishonorable to be a *joglar* or a robber.[108] Guilhem lamented the death of Count Raimon-Roger II of Béziers in a *planh* of 1209, at the beginning of the Albigensian Crusade. Afterwards Guilhem fled to northern Italy, where he found quarter with Marquis Bonifacio II of Monferrato. He also mentions Emperor Friedrich II, both before and after the latter's coronation in 1220.[109] Guilhem evidently returned to his native Provence before his death. His extant works include nine songs, of which one *descort* has an extant melody.

Perhaps because most of the troubadours in the previous generation got their start before the Albigensian Crusade began, they were able to continue their craft despite its difficulties. But the few decades after the beginning of the crusade were lean ones for the troubadours, and only a few melodies survive from the period 1210–1255. These troubadours, including Pons d'Ortaffa, Aimeric de Belenoi, Uc de Saint Circ, and Blacasset, worked mainly in the center, south, and east, and some traveled to Spain and Italy.

PONS D'ORTAFFA (fl. 1217–1240) apparently was a minor noble from Roussillon, from a family that contributed several clerics to the regional ecclesiastical establishment. The town of Ortaffa was a few kilometers southwest of Perpignan, the same region that produced Berenguier de Palol; Pons may have had contact with the earlier troubadour.[110] Two documents locate Pons in time: one of 1217 lists him among lords who attested to a peace with Nunyo Sanchez, governor of the county of Roussillon under Jaime I of Aragón; the other is his testament dated 1240.[111] One of the two extant *cansos* by Pons (PC 379,2, whose melody survives) mentions a lady of Narbonne, suggesting that Pons ventured north from his homeland.[112] This text also indicates that Pons contemplated becoming a "monge de Jau" because of his broken heart, evidently referring to the Cistercian abbey of Jau.[113] Of Pons's two surviving *cansos*, one has a melody.

The output of AIMERIC DE BELENOI (fl. 1215–1242) includes fifteen securely attributed songs; seven more, one of which survives with music, were credited to him by some scribes. Aimeric's *vida* says that he was from Bordelais, specifically a castle at Lesparra, north-northwest of Bordeaux.[114] Aimeric's poetry contains allusions to personages at the courts of Toulouse, Provence, and Italy.[115] Sometime after his stay in Italy Aimeric evidently went to Castile, and the *vida* says that he ended his days in Catalonia, where he composed a *planh* on the death of Nunyo Sanchez, governor of Roussillon, in 1242.[116] The song whose melody survives (PC 9,13a) addresses "comtessa Beatris" and "senher N'Imo," that is, the wife of Count Raimon-Berengar IV of Provence and her brother Aimon, children of Count Tomas I of Savoie;[117] these two persons are mentioned in other songs that are accepted as part of Aimeric's oeuvre. The work is attributed in most manuscripts to Raimbaut de Vaqueiras, but his authorship has been doubted on stylistic grounds and on the basis of its references to persons not otherwise found in Raimbaut's works.[118] Three manuscripts attribute the song to Aimeric de Belenoi, although the manuscript in which its melody is given ascribes it (uniquely) to Peirol, who like Aimeric and Raimbaut worked in northern Italy.

UC DE SAINT CIRC (fl. 1217–1253) apparently was from a castle at Saint-Circ near Rocamadour in Quercy.[119] It is generally believed that Uc was author of at least some of the *vidas* and *razos* of other troubadours, although he takes credit for only one, that of Bernart de Ventadorn.[120] His own *vida* claims that his family sent him to Montpellier to study for an ecclesiastical post, but that he devoted his time instead to studying vernacular literature. It appears that he spent a decade or so in Languedoc, then traveled to Provence.[121] He evidently became a companion of the troubadour and warrior Savaric de Mauleon, who was active on the anti-French side in the Albigensian Crusade.[122] Uc's activities in northern Italy from c. 1220 to 1253, especially in association with the Malaspina and da Romano families, are clear from numerous references in his works. Uc appears to have been a *guelph*, a partisan of the papacy against Emperor Friedrich II.[123] Forty-four songs and an *Ensenhamen d'onor* survive; only three *canso* melodies are extant.

BLACASSET (fl. 1233–1242) was probably the son of Blacatz (fl. 1194–1236), lord of Aups in eastern Provence and generous benefactor of several other troubadours.[124] A document of 1238 identifies the sons of this older troubadour as "Blacacius, B. Blacacius, and Boniffacius," one of whom was likely to have been called by the diminutive name "Blacasset."[125] Blacasset appears not to have been a professional, but an amateur like his father. He left at least eleven songs, with only one *canso* melody.

The last generation of troubadours, who worked mainly during the second half of the thirteenth century, labored to keep alive a tradition that had been sorely tested during the first half of the century. Peire Cardenal, Daude de Pradas, Guiraut d'Espanha, and Guiraut Riquier, like composers of the previous generation, were concentrated in the central and eastern part of the Midi, and they too had considerable contact with Italy and the Iberian peninsula.

PEIRE CARDENAL (fl. 1205–1272) was a member of a minor noble family in Puy-en-Velay, where the Cardenal family name appears in several documents during the thirteenth and fourteenth centuries. Peire was destined for an ecclesiastical post, but his education led him instead into vernacular poetry,[126] and he sought patronage first at Toulouse, where a "Petrus Cardinalis" is mentioned in a 1204 charter as a scribe to Count Raimon VI.[127] Peire became known at the courts of Les Baux, Rodez, Auvergne, Vienne, Foix, and probably Alfonso X of Castile; he was on good terms with Jaime I of Aragón. His poems refer to several *joglars* by name, suggesting that they accompanied him on his travels; he probably encountered Raimon de Miraval, Aimeric de Peguilhan, and Aimeric de Belenoi, and he paid homage to Cadenet in one of his songs. In his earlier poetry Peire expressed outrage against the French and the clergy over the Albigensian Crusade; later he seemed reconciled to French domination. He evidently died in Montpellier, at an age well beyond the average. Most of his surviving 96 songs are satirical, moralizing *sirventes*. Three of his songs survive with music, but two of them, a *canso* and a *sirventes*, are on borrowed melodies (by

Guiraut de Bornelh and Raimon Jordan respectively); the third melody, another *sirventes*, does not have an extant model, and perhaps is in fact by Peire.

DAUDE DE PRADAS (fl. 1214–1282) is identified in documents of Rodez between 1214 and 1282 as "Deodatus de Pradas" or "Pratis," and was referred to as *magister*, probably because he was a canon at Santa Maria in Rodez.[128] He kept company with the counts and bishops of Rodez, and in 1266 he was named vicar general by the pope. He composed a *planh* on the death of Uc Brunenc, also a native of Rodez (see above), and he referred to Gui d'Ussel in a *tenso*. Like Peire Cardenal, Daude lived an extraordinarily long life. His clerical position implies that he maintained an anti-heretical attitude, but this is not directly evident in his poetry. He composed at least seventeen songs, a poetic treatise on birding, and a didactic poem on the four virtues; only one *canso* melody survives.

GUIRAUT D'ESPANHA (fl. 1245–1265) is said in one manuscript rubric to have been "de Tholoza,"[129] but little else is known of him beyond the few references in his songs. He appears to have been close to Charles of Anjou, who became count of Provence by his marriage to Beatriz, daughter of Raimon-Berengar IV; Guiraut addressed many of his songs to this Beatriz. He composed ten *dansas* (one of which survives with music), a *pastorela*, and a *balada*.

The life of GUIRAUT RIQUIER (fl. 1250–1292) is documented in an unusual way, through dated rubrics in two manuscripts that transmit his works, including manuscript R,[130] which transmits his melodies.[131] He may have been born into the merchant class in Narbonne, but in 1254 he found his way to the court of Viscount Amalric IV of Narbonne.[132] He appears to have traveled to Montpellier, where he encountered Jaime I of Aragón. By 1270 he was in Toledo at the court of Alfonso X "el Sabio" of Castile, where he stayed for several years, undoubtedly encountering there the remarkable repertoire of the "cantigas de Santa Maria."[133] Guiraut returned to Languedoc in 1279, visiting the courts of Astarac and Rodez (where he may have met Peire Cardenal and Guiraut d'Espanha), before settling in Narbonne once again. He evidently died there, sometime after 1292. Guiraut is represented in the manuscripts by 87 poems, sixteen poetic letters, and other longer works. His poetry explores new techniques in genre, metrics, structure, and subject matter; he composed a number of hymnlike religious songs, several on Marian themes. More melodies (48) by Guiraut Riquier survive than by any other troubadour.[134]

Thirteen songs by anonymous composers survive with their melodies. One troubadour of the early fourteenth century, Matfre Ermengau (1280–1322), the author of nine poems and an encyclopedia, the *Breviari d'Amor*, is represented in the sources by one melody. He is not included in this study.

The troubadours were a peripatetic and diverse group of men and women. Some traveled widely, while others stayed close to their native regions. All were involved to some degree with important figures of their day, and all interacted with other poet-composers. They came from all strata of the social fabric: upper and lower nobility, the clergy, knights, the bourgeois, and unpropertied classes. All were educated to some degree, at least in the vernacular literature of their day, and many were also acquainted with Latin texts both contemporary and classic, epic and lyric works, and scholastic documents including dialectic and rhetoric. Some were amateurs, while others made their sole living as composers. Some were better regarded as poets, some as musicians, some as singers, some as composers. A few were extraordinarily prolific and creative, while many produced works that followed the conventions of poetic style and structure without great creativity. Some explored sophisticated, obscure, or novel styles, genres, and structures; others kept within predictable and sometimes narrow norms. They were not a uniform group of artists, and the works they produced reflect the diversity of their origins, environs, and activities.

T𝔴O

TRANSMISSION

Oral and Written Traditions

The transmission of a troubadour's song began at the moment of its creation, continued through each performance, and included at some stage its written preservation. A troubadour composed for a hearing; the instant of composition itself probably coincided with a performance, whether before an audience or not, and whether written down or not. As long as a song was sung, it obviously had an oral tradition; the written tradition began when a scribe translated the words into letters and the music into neumes on parchment—perhaps contemporaneously with the troubadour, perhaps later.[1] Composing, performing, and writing probably did not follow a diachronic sequence, one after the other, but were somehow synchronous.[2] Each song had a unique life of creation and dissemination, involving both oral and written stages, and we do not know how long (or whether) a given song existed before it was written down, how performance and writing interacted, in what order they occurred, or what stage was more influential in the formation of the song that we have finally received.

About forty manuscripts and fragments transmit Occitanian literature of the twelfth and thirteenth centuries, including didactic, epistolary, and epic texts, and over 2,500 lyric poems, most of them in more than one reading.[3] Only two of these manuscripts transmit music. More than half of the surviving manuscripts were produced not in southern France, but in Italy. None of them can be dated securely before the fourth decade of the thirteenth century, and almost half were copied in

the fourteenth century. Many sources survive in fragmentary or mutilated condition. The processes of compilation, including *mise en page*
and order of the entry of the texts, decoration, and music, as well as the
hierarchy and sectionalization of contents, differ radically not only
from source to source but often even within a manuscript. Rubrics with
composer attributions are often lacking, erroneous, or conflicting; and it
is impossible to be certain that these rubrics refer to the melodies as well
as the poems.

Both the immediate and the more distant exemplars for the extant
texts and melodies are shrouded in mystery. Manuscripts have been
lost, some perhaps as a result of the Albigensian Crusade, whose ill
effects may have stifled the very craft of producing manuscripts in
Languedoc and Provence. Each chansonnier that survives appears to
have had several exemplars, both for texts and for music, and there are
few clear-cut filial or lateral relationships among the large collections.
Some songs probably had short and uncomplicated lives, while others
traveled a serpentine path to reach the extant codices; the history of a
chansonnier must be the sum of the histories of every song it contains.

For many years it was believed that the texts were written down
from the very beginning, following the lead of Gustav Gröber, who in
1877 developed a system for explaining the intricate relationships
among all of the troubadour sources known to him.[4] His "tree" of
transmission placed hypothetical rough drafts of single poems, bits of
parchment that he called *Liederblätter*, at the root. They were anteced-
ents of what he called *Liederbücher*, autonomous collections of one
author's works, which then became part of larger compendia, or *Gele-
genheitssammlungen*, assembled at random by patrons, *joglars*, or scribes.
These collections, in Gröber's view, became the direct exemplars of
many of the main extant codices.[5] Gröber did not deal with the melodies, but suggested that oral transmission played a much greater role in
their preservation than it did for the texts.[6] In 1961 D'Arco Silvio Avalle
accepted much of Gröber's system, but integrated into it more fully the
influence of oral tradition.[7] Avalle also devoted more attention to the
presence of music in some of the chansonniers.

Although the sophistication of the poetry's structure and style
makes it tempting to believe that the poets composed with the aid of
writing, scholars are increasingly grappling with these issues, finding
Gröber's system and its presuppositions too simple. While many continue to believe that writing and reading played an important role in
composition and transmission,[8] others have begun to assert that troubadours composed the songs (text and music) orally.[9] Poetic texts that
mention writing (*escriure*), reading (*lire*), listening and hearing (*escoutar*
and *auzir*), and other suggestive words have been variously interpreted,
but the wide array of extant variant textual and musical readings

unequivocally evidences the fluidity (or *mouvance*, using Paul Zumthor's term[10]) of a song during its transmission, whether written or oral, or both. Textual differences include transpositions of words, phrases, verses, and stanzas; omissions of stanzas or inclusion of extra ones; orthographic peculiarities; syntactical and lexicological distinctions; and even rhyme-word variations. Some variants are due to scribal errors, but others might be evidence of the ambivalence of a composer toward his or her work, as a song by Cercamon suggests:[11]

Plas es lo vers, vauc l'afinan	The song is plain, and I perfect it
ses mot vila, fals, apostitz;	without a vile, false, bastardized
et es totz enaissi noiritz	word; and it has been worked over
c'ap motz politz lo vau uzan;	to the point that I practice it with
e tot ades va.s meilluran	polished words; and it still continues
s'es qi be.l chant ni be.l desplei.	to improve if there's one to sing or
	perform it well.

One could easily believe that composers modified their songs for a second or third hearing, perhaps to suit a patron or a lady, or as here, to "improve" it. The last verse of this stanza implies that such creative reworking could apply to the melody as well, and it even suggests some give and take between composition and performance.

The music seems to have been transmitted differently, at least in part, than the texts. Paleographical traits in the manuscripts (most spectacularly, the numerous empty staff lines above poetic texts) suggest that scribes often drew on certain exemplars for the melodies and on others for the poems.[12] Even more striking is that only two extant southern chansonniers (manuscripts R and G) contain music, a misfortune only slightly mitigated by the fact that a few troubadour melodies are found in two northern trouvère chansonniers (manuscripts W and X). Most of the compilers of troubadour songs never intended to include music in their manuscripts and therefore did not provide space for it, as they did for rubrics and decorated initials. The lack of surviving music in general thus appears to be no accident. Only one other chansonnier, produced in Catalonia in 1268 (manuscript V), was measured and ruled for musical staves, although music was never entered.[13]

Nonetheless, most of the music in the surviving codices appears to have been copied from other written sources, and there is some evidence that music-writing was taking place at least by the early thirteenth century. The *vida* of Elias Cairel (fl. 1204–1222), for instance, refers to his skill at writing (as distinct from composing) both texts and melodies:[14]

E fetz se joglars e anet gran temps per lo mon. Mal cantava e mal trobava e mal violava e peichs parlava, e ben *escrivia* motz c sons.

And he became a joglar and traveled for a long time around the world. He sang badly, composed badly, played the fiddle badly, and spoke still worse, but he *wrote* words and melodies well.

One of the northern chansonniers that contains some troubadour songs (manuscript X) was copied perhaps a decade before the middle of the thirteenth century. Musical exemplars for this manuscript presumably were produced earlier.

Variants among different readings of a troubadour melody are in the main more pronounced than those in the texts, involving sometimes significantly different contours, pitch levels, textures (number of notes per syllable), interval content, and structures. Some poems are given altogether different melodies in different sources. As with the texts, some musical variants are attributable to medieval scribes, who not only made mistakes but also corrected, added to, omitted from, regularized, and otherwise changed the melodies in their received exemplars[15] (see below).

These musical variants are taken as the principal evidence of a long oral tradition for the melodies. This view has been articulated most forcefully by Hendrik van der Werf, who has argued that the melodies of the troubadours were composed and transmitted orally almost exclusively until about the middle of the thirteenth century, when a written tradition began, shortly before the earliest extant codices themselves were copied.[16] Deliberate or unconscious changes made during the course of performance would produce variants that different scribes at different times and places captured on parchment. The oldest melodies, those with a longer oral tradition, presumably changed more during the course of transmission than those that were written down during the composers' lifetimes.

If earlier songs lived only because they continued to be performed, then the snapshots of the songs that scribes eventually wrote down would, unless they themselves changed them, reflect that performing tradition. There is no reason to think that a melody that a scribe wrote would have been fundamentally or conceptually different from the melody that a singer sang on the same day. Recent research has suggested that writing may well have been just one more tool in the service of memory, no different in aim than encoding a melody in the mind's eye.[17] So unless the art of the troubadours itself changed, the written form of a song may well have mirrored the aesthetic of the composer, whether Marcabru or Gaucelm Faidit, even if the initial set of pitches and rhythms had changed.

But other recent studies have argued that the new "book culture" of the second half of the thirteenth century—with its proliferation of written texts—did change the aesthetic surrounding the songs, from *mouvance* to fixity.[18] According to this view, later scribes imposed new values, such as regularization of form or of pitch sets, and mensural notation, on songs that previously had not had such features, so these written versions do not necessarily reflect faithfully either the compositional or the performance style of earlier decades, or even of contemporary composers, since the scribes themselves were "performers."

Unfortunately, it is nearly impossible to test this view of transmission, since if it is true, the evidence for it has been obliterated by scribes who were under no compulsion to preserve the musical features of earlier songs, or even of songs sung during their own day. Thus we cannot judge whether differences or similarities we detect between earlier melodies and later ones are a result of scribal tampering or of a real change in compositional or performance style during the thirteenth century. If a new aesthetic created within the scribal culture brought about a transformation in the art of the troubadours—composition and performance as well as preservation—then while we may be able to rely on the extant sources to give us a faithful glimpse of the art of the late troubadours, the earlier style is lost to us. If, on the other hand, the art itself did not change, then the scribes essentially ignored what composers and singers were doing and became composers themselves, making melodies work according to their own notions of pitch, structure, and rhythm. In the first case, scribes exercised enormous power over the way composers composed and singers sang. In the second case, scribes ignored what composers composed and singers sang.

It seems likely that the truth lies somewhere in the middle, that composition and performance began to change gradually; that composers, singers, and scribes affected one another reciprocally; and that the manuscripts transmit evidence of the newer styles as well as the older ones.[19] Both writing and oral transmission wrought changes in an individual song over time—this much is certain. Just like singers and composers, scribes reprocessed the songs as they translated them to a written state, but this might have been similar in style and nature to the re-creation worked by singers. As written texts led to more written texts—i.e., when a written tradition supplanted or eclipsed the oral one—the songs perhaps became more fixed, and their nature may have changed. Even though there is evidence that melodies were being written down by the early thirteenth century, as van der Werf has pointed out, there is little evidence of a systematic transmission from one written copy to another until the end of the century. So whatever changes that a "book culture" may have worked on the melodies would not be realized until the time when the art of the troubadours and the trouvères was coming to a close.

Furthermore, because the texts may have had a longer written tradition than did the melodies, the preserved poems may be more distant than the preserved melodies from the actual performed tradition of the troubadours who composed them. The extant melodies, then, might represent more closely the ways in which the earlier troubadours composed and sang than has been thought. In this way, there is a significant difference between the troubadour and the trouvère repertoires, since in the latter the melodies were recorded earlier and more numerously.

Underlying all these issues, of course, are two questions: Why did the scribes write down the melodies? Who used the completed chansonniers? If singers used the books, they probably treated a song that they read there in the same way as a melody that they heard. One cannot assume that seeing music as neumes imprinted a melody more exactly in a singer's mind than hearing it as aural pitches.[20] Indeed, the neumes that scribes wrote down conveyed only one dimension of the song; they lacked indications of rhythm, phrasing, tempo, dynamics, and rhetorical inflection—all the elements of music other than relative pitches. The singer had to supply all these things on his or her own.

A striking feature of oral repertoires, including epic French narrative and plainchant, is the similarity among readings, even more than the disagreements.[21] Works transmitted orally depend on some kind of organization of the material transmitted, whether it is prose, poetry, or music. Something about the content remains the same from one performance to the next. For a poetic text, formulas and motives, syntactical units, themes or topics, and versification help provide the framework for the subject matter.

Epic narratives, which it is generally agreed were transmitted orally in the main, are nonstrophic. They proceed by irregularly structured *laisses* that depend at least as much on assonance as on rhyme; they are structurally quite distinct from the lyric poetry of the troubadours.[22] The function of the narrative is to tell a story, and the progression of the plot in the text is of utmost importance. The texts are full of formulas, and the music also probably was necessarily simple and repetitive (perhaps the reason none of it survives). A complicated melody might not only detract from the narrative nature of the text but also make an already long poem even longer.

Lyric songs tend to be more personal than epic narratives: except for the *pastorela*, lyric poems do not relate a series of events so much as express a subjective point of view.[23] In addition to using commonplace formulas, they treat commonplace themes with multifarious expressions, language, and constructions. The poetic structures depend on a regularity of verse and rhyme scheme. The order of the stanzas (which often differs from manuscript to manuscript[24]) is less important than consistency of versification among them, which had to be carefully worked out by the composer, either mentally or with the help of writing.

Like their complicated texts, the surviving melodies for the troubadours' poems are generally not formulaic, simple, or syllabic. There is great structural subtlety and stylistic variety among them. The delivery of epic songs was probably rapid and dramatic, while that of lyric songs could be somewhat more leisurely and personal; a singer had more time to linger over a sophisticated melody of a troubadour song than over a tune of a *chanson de geste*.

Similar distinctions can be seen in comparing the lyric songs of the troubadours with plainchant. Chant had a long history of oral creation and transmission, and notwithstanding the differing versions, a significant portion of the chant repertoire was transmitted fairly uniformly.[25] Toward the end of the several centuries during which notation was being developed and liturgical practices were standardized, much of the chant repertoire had become more stable and uniform. Other factors played an important role, but it was at least partly through the writing process and the dissemination of manuscript copies that the corpus became more settled.

The songs of the troubadours do not resemble early plainchant any more than they do epic songs. Except for hymns and sequences, most of the texts of chant are prose or nonstrophic poetry, and most are anonymous. The function of plainchant was to direct the attention of the hearers to God, while lyric songs were intended to draw attention to themselves or to their authors (or perhaps ladies or patrons). Lyric poem and melody presumably were created together, by the same author, in a relatively short space of time. Formulas and formulaic systems are found in a large body of plainchant, and only in the hymns, sequences, and relatively late chants can one generally isolate a "melody" apart from its liturgical placement or text.

The songs of the troubadours existed as definite "pieces" whether in written form or not. In most cases where there are two or more readings of a troubadour's melody, they share elements that enable us to recognize in each a version of the same melody.[26] Scribes and singers evidently retained some core or essence that constituted the actual melody. Such melodic stability derives at least in part from the coherence and consistency designed by the composer. The musical elements that make stability possible are difficult to identify, since the nature of the variants does not permit a simple reduction to some skeletal form. But they are the elements that both restricted variation by scribes and singers whose aim was to transmit the essential song, and freed them to recreate the songs without fear of losing that essence.

Did the singers use the manuscripts to learn or sing the songs? William Paden has suggested that "most *joglars* were illiterate."[27] But the line between troubadour and *joglar* as "professions" was not very marked;[28] besides, the composers themselves sang their own songs, even if they employed other singers to do so as well. Most troubadours were probably able at least to read, if not to write.[29] Manuscript illuminations show singers holding scrolls.

But this iconographical evidence does not prove that the singers were reading during an actual performance, or that they were reading music and not just the poetry. Rather than sing from a book or a leaf of parchment, performers probably memorized both the music and the poetry. There is some indirect evidence of the importance of memory in the transmission of troubadour songs. Many song texts mention "learning" (*aprendre*) or "remembering" (*sovenir*) a song—implying a process whereby a stable work of art, with a certain identity, was instilled in the singer's mind.[30] In the famous *razo* about Arnaut Daniel (cited in Chapter 1), in which the troubadour steals an itinerant *joglar*'s song by listening to the *joglar* sing it to himself over and over during the night, the central object is a definite song. According to the story, the *joglar* was singing the song not to perfect it, as the poem by Cercamon cited above describes, but to learn it.[31] A similar story about the famous "Kalenda maia" of Raimbaut de Vaqueiras claims that the tune existed in an instrumental version which Raimbaut heard, learned, and provided with a text.[32]

"Memorization" should not necessarily be understood as exact imprinting on the mind of details from which one must not waver, as we tend to think of it today.[33] A singer could retain the important features of a song that gave it its identity, while allowing some details to change. For the poem, its features of versification (rhyme, verse length and number) were the most compelling elements and allowed for little modification. But individual words, short phrases, and order of stanzas could diverge without losing the essence of the text. For the music, there must be similar elements—perhaps the contour, range, tonal orientation, intervallic structure—that a singer retained in the memory, while allowing details to change.

While complex and often nonrepetitious internally, the melodies were fairly short and were repeated, strophe after strophe, during a performance. Neither the simplicity nor the complexity of a melody as it now survives can be taken by itself as evidence of oral transmission. A melody first designed as melismatic, through-composed, and unpredictable would be difficult to learn and remember, and a singer might very well have simplified it, just as a scribe zealous for clarity and uniformity might have regularized it. On the other hand, a melody first designed as simple, predictable, and repetitive might have been embellished by a singer or mangled by a scribe. Again, the singers received a song, either by ear or by eye, and they appropriated that song into their own repertoires, retaining its essence, but reconstructing it according to their own performing style.

A song may not have received a large number of hearings. Many of the occasional pieces that provide so much of our biographical information probably had comparatively short lives; thus while they were performed orally, they may not have had an oral *tradition* per se. Singers' repertoires probably included a number of their own songs (assuming the performer was a composer) plus a few "great hits"— perhaps a dozen or so at any given point.[34] The songs that survive may represent only a fraction of those that were composed and sung; they are the ones that were kept alive, for some reason, even after the deaths of the troubadours who produced them.

Thus we see that transmission was not a unidimensional or unidirectional process. The texts and melodies in the manuscripts represent a synthesis of the input of composers, singers, and scribes. Oral and written traditions interacted synchronically. The orality of the repertoire affected composers, singers, and scribes; but, conversely, writing may not have had as much influence on composers and singers. The melodies retained some stability in transmission, but the variant readings are testimony to their fluidity.[35] The variants should be evaluated in the context of several factors: 1. the style of other extant melodies by the troubadour; 2. the distance in time and place between a composer and the manuscript; 3. the likelihood that the composer sang the song himself or herself; 4. the frequency with which a song was likely to have been sung; 5. the paleographical and codicological features of each manuscript that transmits it and the habits of individual scribes; and 6. the type of person for whose eyes a manuscript was intended. The rest of this chapter discusses the manuscripts themselves and what they can tell us about their scribes and about the readings of the melodies found in them.

The Manuscripts

The four manuscripts that transmit troubadour melodies could not be more different from one another in provenance and date, layout, contents, dialectal/orthographical pecularities, and the procedures followed for entering text, decoration, and music. None is a polished, complete chansonnier overall, and each has some musical lacunae.

Manuscripts W and X are important collections of trouvère songs with discrete sections of songs in Old Occitan that clearly betray a

French linguistic influence.[36] The earlier of the two, manuscript X (also known as trouvère manuscript U, and as the chansonnier "St.-Germain-des-Prés," because it was owned in the eighteenth century by the abbey of St.-Germain[37]) is a small book. Except for a few melodies its Lothringian neumes appear to be the work of one music scribe.[38] It contains 352 songs, with no composer attributions. As the notator entered the music, he made some corrections to the text, both within the main body and occasionally in the margin. The calligraphic style of the corrected text appears to be identical to that of the text itself, so it seems quite possible that the main music scribe also wrote the texts.

A provenance of Lorraine[39] seems to be confirmed by the orthography of the texts, reinforced by the fact that the codex was owned by the bishop of Metz in the eighteenth century. The manuscript has several text hands, but some features suggest that it was the product of a single scriptorium and not the result of several decades of accumulation by different persons in different places, as Julius Brakelmann argued in 1868.[40] Madeleine Tyssens' analysis of the structure of the gatherings, which are quaternions, shows that the scribe who produced the manuscript's index added most of the foliation to the following gatherings.[41] (This theory is reinforced by the presence of gathering cues that appear to be contemporary with the main text hand at the end of almost every gathering, a detail not mentioned by Tyssens.) Tyssens further shows that the careers of some of the trouvères represented in the manuscript did not begin before about the second third of the thirteenth century, and thus places a *terminus a quo* for at least the largest, first section of the codex (where all of the music was written), at 1240.[42] The fact that no troubadours active after c. 1240 are represented in manuscript X suggests a *terminus ad quem* of shortly before mid-century.

The first twelve gatherings that constitute the large first section have a unified appearance, with a single column on each page and the music placed above the first stanza, as was customary. Space for musical staves was measured as the text was being written, and the staff lines seem to have been entered uniformly throughout the section. The text proceeds without a break from the verso of the last leaf of each gathering to the recto of the first leaf of the next, often in the middle of a song.

But the music was not entered consistently in all gatherings. The songs in gatherings 2, 8, 9, and 12 (the last of which contains most of the troubadour songs) were entirely notated, while gatherings 3, 7, and 11 have a few empty staves, gatherings 5 and 10 have only empty staves, and gatherings 4 and 6 have only a few melodies. Tyssens suggests that this inconsistency of entry may mean that some gatherings never went to the music scribe, while others might reflect exemplars that lacked music.[43]

Several other features of the codex support the impression that it was produced as a cooperative effort among several laborers, and that they worked by gatherings. The text and music scribes and the decorator (perhaps more than one person, who colored initials red at the beginnings of poems and highlighted the first letters of interior stanzas with a red mark) seem to have passed gatherings and leaves back and forth inconsistently. In most gatherings the stanza highlights were entered after the text, then the staves, then the notation, and finally the larger red initials (all clearly seen where ink or paint lies atop or under the other media). Gathering 8 was not given to the highlighter until after the notator had entered the melodies. Gathering 4 received only one melody by the main notator, some time after the red initials were drawn; another notator wrote in two melodies on the opening of fol. 22v–23.

In one case the notator evidently received a gathering without its outer bifolio. The first leaf of gathering 6, fol. 36, has no melodies on recto or verso, while the next six leaves (fol. 37–42v) do. A melody that was begun at the bottom of fol. 42v was left incomplete at the top of fol. 43, the last leaf of the gathering, which also has no music on its verso. For some reason the notator evidently never had an opportunity to enter the missing melodies on the outer bifolio.

The second section of the codex, fol. 92–173, is decidedly more haphazard in its format than the first, and is apparently the work of several scribes working from several exemplars. Tyssens has suggested that these gatherings constitute a "rough draft."[44] A striking feature here is that there are no staff lines filling the spaces measured out by the text scribes. The possibility that these gatherings were an earlier stage in the preparation of a more complete collection, coupled with the lack of staves and melodies, suggests that the scribes expected to locate sources for the music separate from their text exemplars.

The troubadour melodies occupy fol. 81–91v, the last five leaves of gathering 11 and all of gathering 12. Four Occitan songs begin the section, followed by two Old French songs to end gathering 11.[45] The bottom half of fol. 83v, which ends the gathering, is blank; and the beginning of gathering 12 begins anew with Occitan songs. All of the melodies appear to have been written by the main notator of the codex, except for the first melody in the section.[46] He evidently forgot to turn fol. 89 over (perhaps waiting for the ink to dry) to finish the melody at the top of fol. 89v.

The geographical and chronological spread of the troubadours in manuscripts X, W, G, and R is shown in Table 2–1. The earliest songs in manuscript X are by Jaufre Rudel and Rigaut de Berbezilh, the latest by Pons de Capduelh, Pistoleta, Peirol, and Albertet. Most of the troubadours found in X were active in the northwestern region, including Auvergne, Aquitaine, Limousin, and Périgord. Only a few were Languedocian; none were from Gascony; some worked in Provence, Spain, and Italy. The inclusion of one melody by Raimbaut d'Aurenga, who

TABLE 2–1. Troubadours Represented in Manuscripts
X, W, G, and R, by Generations

The first column following a troubadour's name gives the number of melodies by that troubadour in the manuscript; the second shows the total number of melodies that are extant; and the asterisks in the last seven columns indicate in which areas he or she worked.

A = Auvergne, Aquitaine, Limousin, Périgord, Poitou, Quercy, Velay
T = Toulousain, Languedoc, Rouergue, Gévaudan
G = Gascony
S = Aragón, Catalonia, Roussillon, Navarre
P = Provence, Viennois
I = Italy
H = Holy Land

MANUSCRIPT X

	Melodies	Extant	A	T	G	S	P	I	H
I. 1120–1150									
Jaufre Rudel, 1125–1148	1	4	*	*					*
II. 1140–1175									
Rigaut de Berbezilh, 1140–1163	2	4	*						
Peire d'Alvernhe, 1149–1170	1	2	*			*	*		
Raimbaut d'Aurenga, 1162–1173	1	1					*		
Bernart de Ventadorn, 1147–1180	2	18	*						
III. 1160–1210									
Gaucelm Faidit, 1170–1202	7	14	*			*	*	*	
Peire Vidal, 1183–1205	2	12		*		*	*	*	*
IV. 1180–1240									
Peirol, 1185–1221	1	17	*				*	*	
Perdigon, 1190–1212	1	3	*		*	*			
Pons de Capduelh, 1190–1237	1	4	*						*?
Albertet, 1194–1221	1	3	*			*	*		
Pistoleta, 1205–1228	1	1	*	*		*	*		

MANUSCRIPT W

	Melodies	Extant	A	T	G	S	P	I	H
II. 1120–1150									
Jaufre Rudel, 1125–1148	1	4	*	*					*
Marcabru, 1129–1149	2	4	*	*	*	*			
II. 1140–1175									
Rigaut de Berbezilh, 1140–1163	3	4	*						
Peire d'Alvernhe, 1149–1170	1	2	*			*	*		
Bernart de Ventadorn, 1147–1180	8	18	*						
III. 1160–1210									
Jordan Bonel, 2d half 12 cent.	1	1	*						
Gaucelm Faidit, 1170–1202	3	14	*			*	*	*	
Raimon Jordan, 1178–1195	2	2		*					
Folquet de Marselha, 1178–1195	4	13				*	*		
Peire Vidal, 1183–1205	2	12	*		*	*	*	*	

TABLE 2–1. (continued)

	Melodies	Extant	A	T	G	S	P	I	H
Comtessa de Dia, end 12 cent. /beg. 13 cent.	1	1	*?			*?			
Gui d'Ussel, 1195–1209	1	4	*						
Guilhem Magret, 1195–1210	2	2					*	*	
IV. 1180–1240									
Aimeric de Peguilhan, 1190–1225	1	6		*	*		*		
Pons de Capduelh, 1190–1237	1	4	*						*?
Albertet, 1194–1221	2	3	*				*	*	
Guilhem Augier, 1209–1230	1	1		*			*	*	
V. 1210–1255									
Blacasset, 1233–1242	1	1					*		
VI. 1230–1300									
Daude de Pradas, 1214–1282	1	1		*					
Guiraut d'Espanha, 1245–1265	1	1		*		*			

MANUSCRIPT G

	Melodies	Extant	A	T	G	S	P	I	H
II. 1140–1175									
Rigaut de Berbezilh, 1140–1163	2	4	*						
Bernart de Ventadorn, 1147–1180	10	18	*						
III. 1160–1210									
Guilhem de Saint Didier, 1165–1200	1	1	*						
Arnaut de Maruelh, 1171–1195	2	6	*	*		*			
Gaucelm Faidit, 1170–1202	11	14	*				*	*	*
Folquet de Marselha, 1178–1195	13	13					*	*	
Arnaut Daniel, 1180–1200	2	2	*						
Peire Vidal, 1183–1205	5	12		*		*	*	*	*
Gui d'Ussel, 1195–1209	3	4	*						
IV. 1180–1240									
Peire Raimon de Tolosa, 1180–1221	1	1		*		*	*	*	
Peirol, 1185–1221	14	17	*					*	*
Raimon de Miraval, 1185–1229	4	22		*	*				
Perdigon, 1190–1212	3	3	*			*	*		
Aimeric de Peguilhan, 1190–1225	6	6		*	*		*		
Pons de Capduelh, 1190–1237	2	4	*						*?

evidently never left Provence (X is the only source for Raimbaut's melodies), and two by Peire Vidal, who traveled almost everywhere *except* the northwestern area that is closest to France, is evidence for the popularity of their songs apart from their persons. The largest number of melodies by one troubadour is seven, by Gaucelm Faidit, who may have traveled to France (some of his poems are in French). He was probably Limousain by birth, and he spent many years in Limousin. He composed the famous *planh* on the death of Richard Coeur-de-Lion.

	Melodies Extant	A	T	G	S	P	I	H
V. 1210–1255								
Uc de Saint Circ, 1217–1253	3 3		*		*	*	*	

MANUSCRIPT R

	Melodies Extant	A	T	G	S	P	I	H
I. 1120–1150								
Jaufre Rudel, 1125–1148	4 4	*	*					*
Marcabru, 1129–1149	2 4	*	*	*	*			
II. 1140–1175								
Peire d'Alvernhe, 1149–1170	1 2	*			*	*		
Bernart de Ventadorn, 1147–1180	13 18	*						
III. 1160–1210								
Guiraut de Bornelh, 1160–1200	4 4	*			*			*
Berenguier de Palazol, 1160–1209	8 8				*			
Guilhem de Saint Didier, 1165–1200	1 1	*						
Arnaut de Maruelh, 1171–1195	4 6	*	*			*		
Gaucelm Faidit, 1170–1202	9 14	*				*	*	*
Bertran de Born, 1175–1202	1 1	*	*					
Folquet de Marselha, 1178–1195	10 13				*	*		
Raimbaut de Vaqueiras, 1180–1205	7 7				*	*	*	
Peire Vidal, 1183–1205	9 12	*			*	*	*	*
IV. 1180–1240								
Monge de Montaudon, 1193–1210	1 1	*	*	*				
Peirol, 1185–1221	4 17	*					*	*
Raimon de Miraval, 1185–1229	22 22		*	*				
Aimeric de Peguilhan, 1190–1225	2 6		*	*	*			
Uc Brunenc, 1190–1220	1 1	*	*					
Pons de Capduelh, 1190–1237	1 1	*						*?
Guilhem Ademar, 1195–1217	1 1		*	*				
Cadenet, 1204–1238	1 1		*		*			
V. 1210–1255								
Pons d'Ortaffa, 1217–1240	1 1		*	*				
Aimeric de Belenoi, 1215–1242	1 1	*	*		*	*	*	
VI. 1230–1300								
Peire Cardenal, 1205–1272	1 1	*	*		*	*		
Guiraut Riquier, 1254–1292	48 48		*	*				

Manuscript W (known also as trouvère manuscript M) is difficult to study. It suffers from lacunae caused by the excision of a number of its miniatures and the loss of several leaves (resulting in the fragmentation of some songs) as well as a seriously garbled gathering structure.[47] The codex as it is now bound probably started as at least two separate compendia (both made up of quaternions), one an anthology of lyric songs and motets, the other a *libellus* (the "chansonnier du roi") of 60 songs by Thibaut de Champagne, king of Navarre.[48] The first section, including the motets, is in one text hand, while the Thibaut collection has the same format but was written by a different scribe.

In their facsimile edition of 1938, Jean and Louise Beck speculated that the manuscript was prepared for Charles d'Anjou, fourth son of Louis VIII of France;[49] Charles married Beatriz, daughter of Raimon-Berengar IV of Provence, became count of Provence upon Raimon-Berengar's death in 1245, and was crowned king of Naples and Sicily in 1265. Beck's *terminus a quo* of 1254 for the manuscript is certainly accurate, since it contains a chanson composed by the count of Bar during his captivity in Germany in 1253. A *terminus ad quem* is more difficult to establish, but a dating of its latest songs suggests that it had been copied by c. 1280. Mark Everist has offered the theory that it was produced in Artois.[50]

The main anthology originally contained 428 trouvère songs, most of which have their melodies, grouped by authors proceeding from nobles to non-nobles. Rubrics at the beginnings of sections announce the authors of the songs to follow. The next two gatherings contain 61 troubadour songs, of which 51 are notated; a section of two- and three-voice French motets; and finally one French and two Occitan *lais*. Composer attributions, often in conflict with those in most other sources, precede the first few troubadour songs, but the second gathering lacks them altogether. The first leaf of the Occitan section was mutilated by the excision of the large initial in the top of the left column, which also removed any rubric that might have been there.

The text scribe of the anthology seems not to have had access to the full texts of all of the songs he was copying, and he often left space in the columns at the ends of songs, presumably so that more stanzas could be added. Sometimes he gave only the first stanza, and some of his exemplars themselves may have been *florilegia* that contained only a single stanza, and perhaps also the melody, because he often left space for subsequent stanzas, as if he expected to supply them from other sources.

The compilers of the anthology and the Thibaut *libellus* spared no expense, indulging in the luxuries of wide margins and elaborate decoration that included painted initials, miniatures, and colored line endings. If these collections had been left in their original states, they would be magnificent. The songs are arranged in two columns; four-line staves are provided for the first strophe of each song. The gatherings are usually self-contained, each beginning with a new song and often a new composer with a large historiated initial. Columns and even entire leaves were left blank at the ends of many gatherings. As in manuscript X, the gatherings of W appear to have been exchanged randomly among notators, decorators, and rubricator, suggesting that music and texts were readily available to the compiler and were entered contemporaneously. Close inspection of the inks and colors reveals that in some gatherings the notation was the last element to be entered, while in others the rubrics or decoration were last. In at least two gatherings the decorator did his work even before the staves were drawn, while in most of the codex the staves were entered just after the texts were written in.

The quadratic music notation appears to be in two hands, one compressed and quite black, the other larger and more watery, with longer note tails, squarer C-clefs, and a more casual *ductus*. These two scribes appear to have been working contemporaneously, perhaps one as an apprentice of the other. One entered melodies in the first two gatherings, leaving only three melodies unnotated. The other hand appears first in the third gathering, and then intermittently throughout the rest of the codex up to the two gatherings of troubadour melodies, which were notated by the first scribe. As in the trouvère gatherings, some of the poems here lack some of their stanzas, and several leaves are missing. All the motets in the next gathering are in the first music hand; music is missing for some of the tenors, which being liturgical perhaps were considered gratuitous. The Occitan *lais* of the final gathering of the anthology are in the first music hand, while the French *lai* that follows them is in the second hand.

As Table 2–1 shows, Jaufre Rudel is the earliest troubadour represented in manuscript W. The inclusion of two songs by the Gascon Marcabru gives this manuscript a slightly wider geographical distribution than manuscript X. The chansonnier contains songs by a larger number of troubadours who worked in Provence as well, including Folquet de Marselha, the Comtessa de Dia (the only source for her one extant melody), and Guilhem Magret. The Provençal Raimbaut d'Aurenga, on the other hand, is not represented, as he was in X. Daude de Pradas, who probably worked into the third quarter of the thirteenth century, is the latest troubadour found in the original layer of W.

This sumptuous and carefully designed collection was not allowed to remain in its pristine state for long. Within a few years more scribes had filled in the empty columns and pages, mostly with anonymous lyric songs, but also with several untexted pieces, notably the famous *estampies royales*. Ten Occitan songs were added at four locations, and although none of them is attributed in the manuscript, the composers of four songs have been tentatively identified.[51]

fol. 1v/B3v, two anonymous *dansas*, "Donna pos vos ay chausida" (PC 461,92) and "Pos quieu vey la fualla [sic]" (PC 461,196)

fol. 117–117v/B109–109v, an anonymous *descort*, "Bella donna cara" (PC 461,37)

fol. 185–187v/B170–170ᵗᵉʳv, three *descorts*, Aimeric de Peguilhan's "Qui la ve en ditz" (PC 10,45), the anonymous "Sill ques caps e guitz" (PC 461,67a), and Guilhem Augier's "Sens alegrage" (PC 205,5); and two *dansas*, Guiraut d'Espanha's "Ben volgra s'esser poges" (PC 244,1a), and the anonymous "Amors mart con fuoc am flama" (PC 461,20a)

fol. 78v/BXXIv, an anonymous *dansa*, "Tant es gay es avinentz" (PC 461,230), and a *canso* by Blacasset, "Ben volgra quem venques merces" (PC 96,2).

Aimeric de Peguilhan, Guilhem Augier, Guiraut d'Espanha, and Blacasset were not known to be active any farther north than Languedoc, so their addition to this northern manuscript is a curiosity and suggests a written tradition for their songs. The so-called *descorts* have paired-versicle textual structures, but only "Sens alegrage" has a paired-versicle musical structure; the other melodies are through-composed. The two *lais* that are part of the original layer of the anthology have paired-versicle structures in both text and music.[52] Blacasset's *canso* has only one strophe. The remaining five works are dance songs; all five have a large-scale ABA structure that seems to be incipient *virelai* form. Guiraut d'Espanha's *dansa* has three stanzas plus three *tornadas* whose rhymes match the rhymes of the refrain. Two of the anonymous *dansas* have two stanzas, the other two only one (making identification of a refrain impossible). Chapter 4 includes a discussion of these refrain types.

These songs were added by a variety of hands, probably by the end of the thirteenth century or very early in the fourteenth.[53] The first two were written on the blank verso of the leaf immediately preceding the first trouvère *chansons*. Five-line staves were drawn in a single column across the page, and then the two texts were added in a late thirteenth-century script. The notation is Franconian, with ligatures *cum opposita proprietate* and occasional semibreves. The first melody shifts between rhythmic modes 1 and 2. It has many more semibreves than the second melody, which is in mode 1. There two songs were probably entered by different scribes.

The next Occitan addition, an anonymous *descort*, is found in the middle of gathering 14. The scribe here used four-line staves in two columns, as in the manuscript's first layer, but with a larger rastrum, drawn down the entire page instead of within a measured space for a single stanza. The calligraphic style of the text is very close to that of the main text hand and is probably only slightly later. The notation is Franconian, very similar in appearance to the notation of the second added song on fol. 1v/B3v, except that it has an occasional rising *plica*, sometimes notated with two stems and sometimes with one on the right side. The melody is in mode 1.

The next five added songs fill in space left on five and a half leaves at the end of the first Occitan gathering. As on fol. 117/B109, the added four-line staves fill two columns the entire length of the pages; for the *dansa* by Guiraut d'Espanha the scribe wrote the second and third stanzas and the *tornadas* between the lines of the staves. The text hands are late thirteenth century. The Franconian notation was probably entered by the same scribe for the first four songs, and it is strikingly similar to that of the added song on fol. 117/B109. The fifth song added here, in the right column on the verso of the last leaf in the gathering, uses staves that were probably added at the same time as the others, but different scribes, of perhaps the same period as those found on fol. 1v/B3v, added the text and the Franconian notation.

The last two added songs, on the verso of the last leaf of the Thibaut collection, appear to have a slightly later calligraphic style than that of the other Occitan additions, but its Franconian notation is not significantly different. Most of these additions clearly display some of the new musical characteristics of the second half of the thirteenth century, specifically in their refrain structures and in the Franconian notation. They are so distinct, in fact, from the troubadour music in the rest of the codex, that they might be taken as evidence against the theory of the general imposition of a late scribal aesthetic discussed earlier in this chapter.

The two southern manuscripts, R and G, are a few decades later than X and W, and they seem to have been prepared for bibliophiles who wished to own a manuscript devoted exclusively to Occitanian works. Manuscript G, copied in the late thirteenth century, contains 235 lyric poems with 81 melodies; empty staves are scattered randomly throughout the quaternions, but become much more frequent from the middle of gathering 7 to the end.[54] The marked italianate spellings and grammatical constructions indicate that the text scribe was a northern Italian, probably from Lombardy or Veneto.[55] The calligraphic style places the manuscript at the very end of the thirteenth century or perhaps the first decade of the fourteenth.

Manuscript G is not elegantly decorated, but it was begun with a design, starting with a large section of songs that are carefully arranged by author, then alphabetically within each author group by the first letter of each text. Every song in this first section was provided with space for its melody on five-line staves. After this come ten leaves devoted to *tensos*, without staves. Then follows another section of songs grouped by author and containing music staves, all of which remain empty. Gathering 15 has space measured for the staves, but no lines were ever drawn in. The gatherings up to this point are not self-contained as they are in manuscript W; in G, texts continue from the verso of one gathering onto the recto at the beginning of the next. The lyric songs come to an end in the middle of gathering 15, and then begins a collection of *ensenhamens, saluts, coblas,* and other nonstrophic works. Gatherings 17 and 18 are of slightly smaller dimensions than the preceding gatherings, and they contain the *Ensenhamen d'onor* of Sordello in a text hand later than that in the main body of the codex; these gatherings were probably bound in at some later date.

The music notator's ink, blacker than the (now) brownish ink used for the texts, changes appearance, sometimes looking very faint and thin, sometimes quite black with broader strokes. It might appear that two notation hands were at work, but the clefs and neumes are quite similar throughout, and it seems more likely that the observable differences are due to a change in the size of the pen nib, suggesting different stages in the entry of the melodies.

The chansonnier is distinguished by some idiosyncrasy in the layout of its texts. In gathering 1 the text scribe copied the poems so that each verse begins at the left margin, as in a manuscript of narrative poetry, resulting in a few millimeters of wasted space at the ends of many lines. Above each verse of the first stanza and, from fol. 2, also above the first verse of the second stanza, he measured room for staves. He also began all subsequent stanzas for the songs at the left margin, sometimes even beginning each individual verse at the left margin, leaving blank whatever space was left at the ends of verses. It appears that he began by counting the verses in each stanza, measuring the space to correspond to this number for each song, then writing in the text. After seeing how much parchment this wasted at the right margins, on fol. 3v he began attempting, inconsistently, to compress the text by erasing some of the words he had already written and moving them up to fill empty lines, even occasionally erasing unnecessary musical staves at the ends of the first stanzas. But because he had already copied the beginning of the second stanza below a space he had previously measured for musical staves, these attempts at compression were fruitless. With the second gathering, starting on fol. 9, he abandoned his habit of counting out the verses and measuring the space before writing, as well as the format of allowing one full line for each verse. Instead, he simply wrote the text as it came, measuring as he went along. He continued to provide space for music above the first verse of the second stanzas (although for the first song on fol. 9, for some reason he drew staves above the entire second stanza, not just the first verse).[56]

After the texts were entered, and before the manuscript was decorated or rubricated, the notator entered music, jumping from one section to another depending upon which songs he had sources for. The provision of staves for the incipits of second stanzas offers us a rare opportunity to observe a music scribe at work. He accommodated the peculiarities left behind by the text scribe, writing in musical notes wherever there were staves, mostly repeating the first notes of the melody for the second stanzas (occasionally with slight variations, providing some insight into the kinds of changes a scribe or a singer might make upon repetition). Once (fol. 64v–65) he copied the wrong incipit for stanza II, taking the first few notes of a song that appears on the opposite folio rather than the one he had just finished (a circumstance that points to his use of a written exemplar, at least for this song). The notator was creative, varying the notational forms in such a way that betrays a breadth of aptitude and cognizance of the notator's craft. But he was careless in at least one respect: the alignment of syllables with neumes, sometimes obscuring the lengths of the musical phrases. This practice suggests that he was unfamiliar with the tunes he was copying, that he was not writing them down from memory or dictation, and that the music was not found in the same exemplars from which the texts were copied.

The overall impression created by these features is that the procedures of the text scribe varied according to the way things appeared after he had written them down and with the availability of materials at any given time. The manuscript begins with large collections of songs by important composers: Folquet de Marselha, Bernart de Ventadorn, Gaucelm Faidit, and Peire Vidal, most of whose songs are provided with melodies. Perhaps the scribe had collected these songs in loose gatherings or leaves, quite likely with melodies in some sources and not in others, and he envisioned a large canzoniere into which to copy them. After he had exhausted his first supply of materials, he added whatever songs he could lay his hands on, often without their melodies. By gathering 7 he had long since settled on the page format, but his sources were becoming less coherent, and he was finding fewer and fewer melodies. He interrupted his design in gathering 12 to enter a varied collection of *tensos*, for which he had no melodies (and for which he expected to find none—signalling something about the aesthetic and perhaps performance practice of this genre by the end of the thirteenth century). He attempted to return to his original plan in gathering 13, with sizable collections of songs by Cadenet, Gausbert de Poicibot, Bertran de Born, and Guillem de la Tor, again providing space for music; but here his sources were bereft of music altogether.

As Table 2–1 shows, manuscript G transmits a significant number of the extant melodies of troubadours who had strong ties to Italy, including Gaucelm Faidit, Folquet de Marselha, Peire Vidal, Peire Raimon de Tolosa, Peirol, Aimeric de Peguilhan, and Uc de Saint Circ. The earliest generation of troubadours is not represented; that is not surprising for a codex that was prepared at least 150 years after the careers of Marcabru and Jaufre Rudel had ended. The greatest concentration of troubadours is from the middle generations, spanning the Albigensian Crusade, a period when many poet-composers sought refuge in Italy. The latest troubadour whose music survives in G is Uc de Saint Circ, who worked until at least c. 1253. The codex also contains poems (without music) by Daude de Pradas, who was active in the 1280s.

Manuscript R is the largest repository of Occitanian melodies and the only music source produced in Languedoc, perhaps in or near Toulouse.[57] Its provenance tempts us to trust its readings more than those of the others. However, like G, it is quite late, no earlier than 1292 (since one rubric in the codex gives that date), and perhaps a decade or so later.[58] François Pirot has suggested that one of R's exemplars was a book prepared for Enric II, count of Rodez (1274–1302), to whom Folquet de Lunel (late thirteenth century) dedicated a *roman* found in the nonlyric section of the manuscript.[59] The possibility of a Rodez connection may be reinforced by some marginalia found on several leaves, *manchettes* of five fingers that point to certain songs, a common motif in medieval manuscripts. One such song is Uc Brunenc's *sirventes* "Conplidas razos novelas e plazens," written with its melody on fol. 66, to which not one but three *manchettes*, each accompanied by the word "nota," draw attention. Uc was a native of Rodez in the late twelfth century and had strong ties to the family of the count; stanza V of this song mentions the death of *los comtes*.[60]

Manuscript R was not carefully planned from its inception, and its contents are more varied than those of the other manuscripts.[61] The first gathering, a quinternion like most of the others, consists of a collection of 27 *vidas* and *razos*. These are followed by 947 lyric songs, of which 160 have melodies, several short sections containing 146 *coblas triadas esparsas* by Bertran Carbonel and Guilhem Olivier d'Arles, letters by Guiraut Riquier (including the famous "exchange" with Alfonso X of Castile concerning the words *trobador* and *joglar*[62]), the *Tezaur* of Peire de Corbian, *ensenhamens* and other didactic works, and finally a few more lyric songs. None of these collections occupies a self-contained gathering or gatherings; there is one hand throughout almost the entire manuscript, and it appears that this scribe worked straight through from beginning to end, adding a new section as he completed the previous one. Sometimes he entered a poem that he had already copied on an earlier leaf, having not collated his sources thoroughly (if at all). Throughout the text there are many blank spaces, ranging in length from one word to an entire verse or stanza, suggesting that the scribe was unable to decipher his exemplar or that the exemplars themselves had blank spots. Some of the blanks were filled in later, by the original scribe or by someone else.

The lyric songs and the *coblas* are arrayed in two columns per page, and in general the scribe provided space for the melody above the first stanzas of the songs (but not for the *coblas*). The compiler did not envision adding melodies from the beginning, however. Like most other extant troubadour chansonniers, R was begun as a collection of poetry, without musical staves. Only where the melody was readily available did the text scribe provide space for it. In the first gathering, staves for music were provided for only ten of 72 poems; seven of those ten received melodies.[63]

From the second gathering on, however, the scribe allowed space for the four-line musical staves for nearly every poem, although most of them remain blank. The change of procedure appears to have come about because of an oversight on fol. 8, where the scribe entered the text without musical staves for a song by Guiraut de Bornelh in the left column, then entered another song, then in the right column reentered the first stanza of the earlier song *with* staves and the melody. If the scribe had had both the melody and the text before him to begin with, he would have allowed space for the melody the first time, rather than having to enter it again. Evidently he was using one exemplar for the texts and came across the melody in a different source.[64] Once he realized his mistake, he decided to leave space for the melodies all the time, whether they were immediately available or not. Evidence that the text scribe entered the poems with little regard for the spatial requirements of the music notation is also found in songs where the notes of the melody must be severely crowded to fit.

There is one main music hand in the codex, but several other scribes added melodies here and there throughout the leaves; empty staves occur in all gatherings.[65] In a few places where textual emendations have been made, they appear to have been added while the melodies were being written in; and there are more such emendations in the songs with melodies—suggesting again that there were separate sources for text and music, allowing the compiler to double-check his texts.[66] There are obvious notational errors as well, such as a misplaced clef, and the notators sometimes corrected their own work. In one instance an entire melody was written and then erased so that a completely different one could be entered. This musical *palimpsest* is the only one of its kind in the troubadour manuscripts, and the erased melody (which is still readable) does not correspond to any other extant melodies.[67]

The somewhat haphazard entry of texts and melodies in R suggests that songs were added as they became available, and that there were several exemplars for both the texts and the music. In contrast to most of the manuscript, though, one section is so complete and self-contained as to appear to have been copied from a single unified exemplar which contained full texts, melodies, and rubrics: the Guiraut Riquier *libellus* that occupies the second half of gathering 12 and the first three leaves of gathering 13.[68] Among the 53 poems in this collection, all but five have melodies, and all but nine are preceded by a rubric that gives the genre and, surprisingly, a date of composition. While written in the same hand, these rubrics are unlike the others in R, which for the most part give only the composers' names. The melodies are unique to this source. The section also manifests an exception to the general disregard on the part of the text scribe for the horizontal space required to enter the music. One melody has a verbal canon describing a musical structure that is unique in the extant troubadour repertoire. The structure described by the canon will be discussed in Chapter 5 (see Example 5–14); it is worth observing here that a written antecedent of this song had to have consisted of both text and melody together.[69]

The music notators of R used a uniform style, suggesting that all the melodies were entered within a short period of time. In some places it seems that the music scribe acted as an editor, regularizing the musical structures, shapes of phrases, and so forth, in ways not as obvious in the other manuscripts. One scribe, perhaps the main music scribe, used a notation with clearly distinguished longs and breves for a few melodies.[70] This notation is not consistently mensural as in the Franconian melodies added to manuscript W, but its presence in a source that otherwise uses nonmensural quadratic notation raises performance practice questions that will be revisited later in this book.

Of the four music codices, R contains the largest number of extant troubadour melodies and is the most diverse in chronological and geographical range (see Table 2–1). Marcabru and Jaufre Rudel represent the earliest generation; important collections of melodies by Berenguier de Palol, Bernart de Ventadorn, Folquet de Marselha, Arnaut de Maruelh, Guiraut de Bornelh, Raimbaut de Vaqueiras, Gaucelm Faidit, Peire Vidal, and Raimon de Miraval represent the mid- to late-twelfth century; the thirteenth century is represented by Peire Cardenal and Guiraut Riquier. Manuscript R contains music for 25 of the 42 troubadours for whom music survives. It is the sole source for music by Guiraut de Bornelh, Berenguier de Palol, Bertran de Born, Raimbaut de Vaqueiras, the Monge de Montaudon, Uc Brunenc, Guilhem Ademar, Cadenet, Pons d'Ortaffa, Aimeric de Belenoi, Peire Cardenal, and Guiraut Riquier.

The music scribes of these codices were educated and skilled notators. Some appear to have modified the melodies as they wrote. Some may have been composers or musicians themselves, or had an acquaintance with music theory (particularly the ones who used mensural notation), and this may have affected their work. Some made errors in copying that they (or someone else) later rectified. Other errors remain uncorrected, however, suggesting that the scribes were not always familiar with the music itself, with the texts or the language (especially the French and Italian scribes), or with the style of the repertoire.

All indications are that many if not all of the immediate exemplars for the melodies were widely divergent in content, format, provenance, and date. The numerous empty staves indicate that the scribes relied on written exemplars for the melodies and that they were unable to locate sources for many of them. Some of the melodies may represent creations by the scribes themselves—either adaptations of melodies they knew or had copied elsewhere, or altogether new tunes that they composed on the spot.

The scribes and compilers attempted to produce well-organized, broadly inclusive anthologies; their intelligence and instincts for systematization are likely to have influenced their attitudes toward the songs they were writing. The scribes played an active, not simply a passive, role in their transmission. Many of the possibilities of scribal intervention suggested here are revealed in the paleographical features on the leaves of the manuscripts. Further light is shed on this by a comparison of the variant readings.

Concordances

The incidence of a melody in more than one of these chansonniers is relatively rare. Of the 246 poems that are provided with melodies, and counting each of the musical readings as an autonomous version, the four manuscripts (including two melodies found in manuscript m) transmit a total of 315 melodies.[71] Of the 246 poems, 195 have only one version of a melody extant (see Table 2-2). Fifty-one texts survive with more than one musical reading (see Table 2-3).[72]

These numbers are not as straightforward as they first appear. Of the 195 melodic *unica*, six represent *contrafacta*, one melody attached to two different poems, and thus only three distinct melodies: PC 80,37=305,10; 242,51=335,7; and 335,49=404,11. Fourteen of the "concordances" actually involve two different nonconcordant musical settings

TABLE 2–2. Manuscripts and Number of *Unica* Melodic Readings

Manuscript	Number of Melodies	Unica	Percentage of Unica
X	21	5	24%
W	51	32	63%
G	81	39	48%
R	160	119	74%

TABLE 2–3. Manuscripts and Number of
Concordant Melodic Readings

Manuscript	Concordances
G, R	19
G, W	3
R, X	5
G, X	3
R, W	1
G, R, W	10
G, R, X	5
G, W, X	2
R, W, X	1
W, m	2

(discussed below). So only 37 songs plus the three *contrafacta*—a total of 40—transmit concordant melodies. The 192 *unica*, 51 concordant melodies, fourteen nonconcordant melodies, and three *contrafacta* make a total of 260 distinct melodies; only 16 percent of them are found in more than one reading.

In addition to these variants, which I will call extrinsic, many melodies contain one or more repeated phrases or motives internally, which often manifest some variants that I will call intrinsic. An examination of the extrinsic and intrinsic variants can help us discover what kinds of changes might have occurred during different stages in the lives of the melodies. Although not every variant can be traced unequivocally to a composer, a singer, or a scribe, such an examination might uncover something about the compositional conventions and methods of the troubadours, about the performing techniques and aesthetics, about the talents and habits of the scribes, and about the nature of the songs themselves.

The differences among the variant readings of the melodies are more difficult to evaluate than those of the texts, because the syntax and vocabulary of the music are not as definable as in the poetry. Most of the concordant melodies are the same in overall shape, but nearly all of them are marked by differences within short musical figures, often occupying the space of a single text syllable. Small-scale differences might involve the number of notes or their alignment with the text, the contour or content of a motive, or pitch goals.[73] Other variants are more substantial, involving such elements as mode and structure.

Composers probably made some variations deliberately, such as developing, relocating, or recombining motives; articulating the struc-

ture by changing the phrase ending or by slightly modifying the contour of a repeated phrase; transposing a phrase; or shifting the modal
orientation. Other variants can be seen as conscious or unconscious
alterations made by performers as they sang, such as ornaments, chromatic inflections, and passing tones. Still other variants appear to have
resulted from scribal editing or error, such as regularization of form,
omission of syllables, realignment of notes with syllables, improper clef
placement, changing of ligature shapes, and different interval content
within motives or phrases.

The rest of this chapter will explore some of the variants for evidence of scribal habits and errors. Later chapters will take up the
variants as they relate to composing and performing practices.

Example 2–1 shows the first verse of stanzas I and II of a song by
Folquet de Marselha, as written by the Italian scribe of manuscript G.
Note the use of two different forms of two-note neume on the seventh
syllable, both obviously meaning the same two notes, G–A. It is a small
point, but it illustrates that the scribe of G, or of his exemplar, used these
two shapes interchangeably.

Example 2–2 offers a glimpse of the way the same scribe tried to
make the best of a confusing situation. In general he was rather careless
about aligning the notes above the proper text syllables, and here he got

EX. 2–1. Folquet de Marselha. PC 155,21, stanzas I and II, verse 1. G fol. 3.

I. 1. Sui tot me sui a trat a - per - cen - buz.

II. 1. Ab bel sen - blan qe fals a - mors a - duz.

EX. 2–2. Bernart de Ventadorn. PC 70,17, verses 1–4. G fol. 69.

1. In con - si - rer 'l en es - mai. 2. sui d'un a - mor qi.m la - ça e.m te.

3. qe tan no vai ni ça ni lai. 4. q'a - des no.m te - gna en son fre....

himself into trouble right away by assuming an elision between tironian "and" (which presumably would be "e" in Italian) and the word "en" in verse 1. Verse 2 continues with no problem, but in verses 3 and 4, which probably should be a repetition of the music, he tried to shift the notes back to their proper positions, but overcompensated on "qades nom tegna," so that he had to add an extra note at the end of verse 4.

Example 2–3 demonstrates the same tendency on the part of R's scribe to substitute one neume form for another—compare the descending ligatures at the ends of verses 1 and 3, and of 2 and 4. Both scribes also substituted a *plica* for a single note, in G verses 1 and 3 and R verses 2 and 4. But more important is the jarring difference between the two readings of G and R—they are a whole tone apart, the one in G beginning with a rise of a fourth through a minor third, the one in R rising through a major third. The melodic differences become even more pronounced after verse 4. If the clef in R were a C-clef instead of an F-clef, the intervals in these four verses would be exactly the same. This can only mean error on the part of the scribe of R or of his source. Such a variant is more likely to have come about within a written rather than an oral tradition.

If the scribe of G was somewhat careless as a technician, knowledgeable but not always precise, the scribe of R appears to have been

EX. 2–3. Raimon de Miraval. PC 406,7, verses 1–4. R fol. 88; G fol. 69.

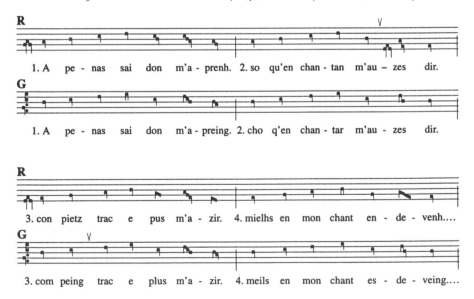

almost as much a pedant as an editor. In Example 2–4, the melody given
in G is characterized by subtle variation among its phrases—note the
open/closed relationship between verses 2 and 4, and the variation in
verse 6 of the previous phrase. In contrast, the reading in R begins to
sound monotonous, verses 1, 3, 4, 5, and 6 all beginning with the same
three notes. The open ending has been eliminated in verse 2, verses 5

EX. 2–4. Bernart de Ventadorn. PC 70,6. R fol. 57v; G fol. 13v.

EX. 2–5. Pons de Capduelh. PC 375,27, verses 1–5. X fol. 90v; R fol. 55v.

and 6 are identical, and it is not until the end of the penultimate verse that we hear any new material.

Example 2–5 shows the same proclivity for standardization in R. The variations that occur in the reading in X are nowhere to be found in R. Both readings have open and closed endings on verses 2 and 4, but the end of verse 4 in X is marked by an astonishing downward leap of a minor sixth, from C to E. The E is unlikely to be an error, or the scribe would have corrected it when he moved on to the next verse, which begins on E. In fact, he may have been reflecting a performing practice in which a singer linked one phrase to the next with a smooth progression of pitch (see Chapter 5). R's scribe brings the melody down to a close on C, also perhaps a performing practice (perhaps a later one?) that lays more stress on return to a tonal center at the ends of phrases.

Example 2–6 also suggests that the scribe of R—and not his exemplars—was the agent of such musical redactions. Note here that the

EX. 2–6. Bernart de Ventadorn. PC 70,1, verses 1–4. W fol. 194/B202;
R fol. 57; G fol. 9v.

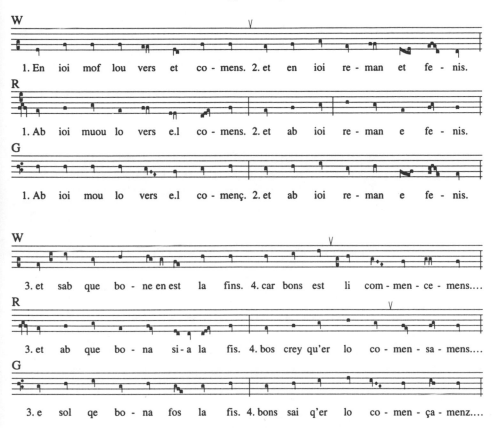

reading in W (the earliest of these three manuscripts) contains the least repetition of musical material, its verse 4 being unrelated to any earlier phrase. G's version is a bit more regular, in that verse 4 begins like verse 3. The scribe of R has given a clear-cut ABAB form, with only slight modifications (note the consternation caused by the word "sia" in verse 3, which made it necessary for him to distribute his neumes and *plicas* differently). But the most obvious trait in R's melody is the radical paleographical regularization represented by the rhythmic notation—something that occurs only in R.

The fourteen poems that survive with two different melodies reveal much about scribal practices. It is sometimes difficult to be certain whether different melodies for a single poem exist because the composer gave the poem two musical settings, or a singer created a new melody in place of the composer's, or a scribe provided a new melody for a poem for which he could not find music. But again, it is manuscript R that seems most often to transmit a melody that does not match those found in other sources.

Several songs transmitted in both R and X have divergent melodies. Peire d'Alvernhe's "Dejosta.ls breus jorns" (Example 2–7) has the same overall formal design in both manuscripts, and both melodies have numerous melismas that tend to occur on the same syllables and move in the same direction; but the similarities between the two melodies end there. The second and fourth verses in X repeat the music of the first and third phrases exactly. In R, however, verses 2 and 4 begin a third higher than the corresponding verses 1 and 3, and verse 4 continues a third higher than verse 2 to its cadence. Verse 3 waffles on the second syllable to just a step higher than in verse 1, and it remains a step higher to its

EX. 2–7. Peire d'Alvernhe. PC 323,15, verses 1–5. X fol. 86; R fol. 6.

cadence. Scribal error or adaptation of some sort is almost certain at this point. An unmistakable scribal error occurs in verse 5 in R, which is broken at the end of a line in the middle of the diphthong "fuelhs." The text scribe split the word across the two lines, "fu-elhs"; though paleographically this split is not atypical, it caused the music scribe to construe the word as two syllables, for which he provided two notes.[74]

Two more songs with nonmatching melodies in R and X are by Gaucelm Faidit, "Si tot ai tardat mon chant" (PC 167,53) and "Mon cor e mi e mas bonas chansos" (PC 167,37). Both melodies are through-composed in X, while in R verses 3 and 4 repeat the music of 1 and 2. Furthermore, the phrase contours, tonal centers, and interval content of the two melodies in each case are quite distinct. The second of these two songs in R (Example 2–8), in addition to repeating entire phrases, reuses motivic material, a feature that appears in other tunes in the codex as well. See, for example, the first six syllables of verse 6, whose descending G–F–E–D figure is repeated quickly (without the G), and then recurs in verse 8 on syllables 1–3 and 6–8. (The same notes constitute the cadences at the ends of verses 1, 2, 3, and 4.) One begins to suspect that the scribe of R was fond of melodic repetition.[75]

Peire Vidal's "Anc no mori per amors" (Example 2–9) is found in X, R, and G; again the R version diverges from the other two. The melody in G is a fourth lower than that in X and R, but the interval content of the versions in X and G is quite close, as are the contours and structures. The melody of R appears rather close in its contour, but the half and whole steps occur in quite different places than in X and G. While the melody in X and G is through-composed, in R verse 6 is a slight variation of verse 3. The number of syllables in verse 6 is one short of the necessary ten, and the music scribe adjusted the notes from verse 3, compressing the pitches that would have fallen on verses 7 and 8 into one syllable (G–F–E). This sort of adaptation, and the different modal quality of the melody in R because of its different interval content, point away from an oral source and toward a written exemplar (which the scribe may have misread) or a scribal composition. Gaucelm Faidit's "Lo jent cors onratz" (PC 167,32) also appears in X, R, and G, and all three versions diverge significantly from each other after verse 5.

The two readings of Bernart de Ventadorn's "Pus mi prejatz senhor" (PC 70,36) in manuscripts R and G begin alike, and both melodies have repetition, although R's is a great deal more regular:

R: A   B   A'   B   C   D   C   D   C'
G: A   B   A'   C   D   C'   D   C'   E

Perhaps the scribe of G misread his source and skipped the music for verse 4, and running out of music at the end, composed a new phrase for

EX. 2–8. Gaucelm Faidit. PC 167,37. X fol. 84; R fol. 44.

the last verse. The lack of any variation in the repetitions in R (except on the last verse, which consists simply of a different pitch at the beginning and again at the end of the phrase) is something we begin to expect from this scribe.

The two melodies for Folquet de Marselha's "Amors, merce, no mueyra tan soven" (Example 2–10) found in R and G are radically different. While the contours are roughly similar, the specific starting

EX. 2–9. Peire Vidal. PC 364,4. X fol. 85v; R fol. 46v.

and ending pitches of the phrases and the intervals (especially whole steps and half steps) do not coincide, internal motives move in different directions, and the ranges (much wider in R) contrast sharply. The scribe of R made an adaptation in verse 6, where he ignored the omission of three syllables by the text scribe, and simply wrote in enough notes to fit the words that were there.

Besides the differences in contour, note groupings, and intervals,

EX. 2–10. Folquet de Marselha. PC 155,1, verses 5–7. R fol. 42v; G fol. 1v.

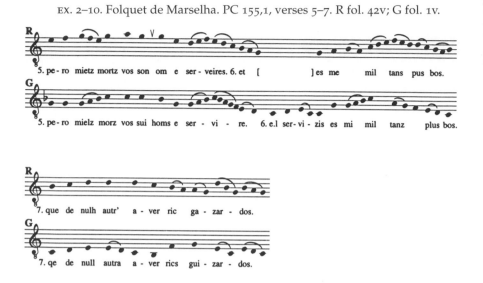

G's version of Raimon de Miraval's "Aisi com es gensers pascors" (Example 2–11) has more structural regularity than R's:

R: A   B   A'   B'   D   E   F   B"   G
G: A   B   A   B   A'   C   B'   D   E

There is a discrepancy in syllable count in verses 7 and 8.[76] Verse 7 in R has eight syllables, and verse 8 has seven; the opposite obtains in G. The scribe of G used a variation of verse 2 for verse 7 and gave verse 8 entirely new music, ignoring what should have been an elision between "q'avia" and "en." The scribe of R, on the other hand, began verse 7 with six repeated notes, a unique occurrence in the repertoire. He then reused the music of verse 2 for verse 8, varying it slightly. One cannot escape the impression that R's musical exemplar was somehow deficient at verse 7, and rather than improvise more creatively, the scribe simply wrote six A's in a row.

Gaucelm Faidit's "Tant ai sufert longuamens greu afan" (PC 167,59) is notated with a C-clef in manuscript G, and it is a half step lower than R's reading. The resulting interval differences between the two versions give decidedly different modal sounds to the two melodies, which are unlikely to have occurred within an oral tradition. The scribe of R began with an F-clef, changed several times between F- and C-clefs, and also changed their placement on the staff. These shifts—more frequent here than generally found in R—signal some attention on the scribe's part to

EX. 2–11. Raimon de Miraval. PC 406,2, verses 1–2, 7–8. R fol. 85v; G fol. 68.

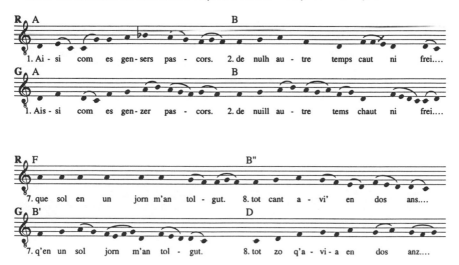

the correct placement of the notes and perhaps some uncertainty on that point in his exemplar.

R is set apart once again in three songs with melodies in W, R, and G: Bernart de Ventadorn's "Eras no vei luzir solelh" (PC 70,7), Gaucelm Faidit's "No.m alegra chan ni critz" (PC 167,43), and Peire Vidal's "Cant hom es en autrui poder" (PC 364,39). The versions of Bernart's song in W and G are quite close in intervallic content, although W's version is slightly more florid. The melody in R, however, has a different structure, largely because of the reiteration of a four-note descending motive in six of the eight verses; often the direction of individual phrases is the opposite of that in W and G.

The three manuscripts transmit strikingly different melodies for Gaucelm's song (Example 2–12). The W and G versions seem close to each other in phrase contours. But although both are rather florid, they do not agree on which syllables receive three, four, or five notes, and which are undecorated—possibly reflecting different ways of ornamenting the melody in performance. The two melodies are a third apart from verse 6 through the first part of verse 9, perhaps through a scribal error. R's melody for this poem is much simpler. It is mainly syllabic and conjunct, lacking the wide leaps of fourths, fifths, sixths, and octaves found in W and G. Hardly surprising, R's melody features phrase repetition that is entirely missing from the other versions. The ABAB structure of the first four verses would not be possible were it not for an error in the text in verses 4 and 5. The rhyme scheme and syllable count

EX. 2–12. Gaucelm Faidit. PC 167,43. W fol. 194/B202; G fol. 30; R fol. 43v.

for the first five verses, as attested in other versions of this song, should be a7–b7–b7–b3–c7'. In R, however, while the rhyme scheme is correct, verse 4 has three extra syllables, while verse 5 has one syllable too few. The music scribe did not correct this error but accommodated the seven-syllable phrase of verse 2 to the six of verse 4 by omitting a repeated G on the fifth syllable.

For Peire Vidal's song notated in W, G, and R, W's melody is a fifth higher than G's, giving it a different intervallic content, which might have been modified in performance by means of *musica ficta* (see Chapter 7 for a discussion of this issue). Once again, R's melody is quite distinct. Some of its pitch goals at the ends of phrases coincide with the same ones in G, but other than that it moves in entirely different directions and through different intervals.

Aimeric de Peguilhan's "Qui la ve en ditz" (PC 10,45) has a parallel-verse structure that is associated with the *lai* and the *descort*, but it also has three stanzas of identical structure (only two in W), hence there is some perplexity today about its genre. The scribe of R treated the song as a *canso*, giving it a melody that must be repeated for all three strophes; this melody, though, has a paired structure, overall AA'BB'CC', which precisely matches the poetic scheme. In W, only two of the stanzas found in R (and nine other manuscripts) are given, and they are followed by two more with the same structure, which many believe to be an imitation by an unknown author of Aimeric's poem (PC 461,67a). The melody in W is through-composed and the notation is mensural (see Example 4–7). The melody for these two stanzas plus that for the next two added stanzas in W are stylistically similar enough to suggest the same composer, possibly the scribe himself.[77] W does not transmit any other melodies by Aimeric, which are found mainly in manuscripts G and R, and the poem is not attributed to any author in W. The musical regularity is to be expected of the scribe of R; but the irregularity of the melody in W is surprising, given that it is in mensural notation in a northern source of the second half of the thirteenth century, when more and more secular songs were taking on clear-cut repetition schemes.

The final song transmitted with two different melodies is Bernart de Ventadorn's "Non es meravilh s'eu chan" (Example 2–13). The scribe of G copied out the melody twice, for the first two stanzas. W's melody is a fifth higher than G's, and their contours are quite similar at the beginning. They diverge quickly, though, moving with different intervals and tonal centers, coming closer together in the final two verses. The two stanzas notated in G suffer from misalignment in one stanza or the other (it is difficult to tell which is correct, although it appears that the scribe attempted some adaptation in the second strophe to make up for an omission of two neumes in verse 4), a problem made more difficult by errors in the text.[78] The music scribe does not appear to have attempted to reconcile the two stanzas until the end, where he ran out of music and simply repeated the notes of the last three syllables to finish stanza II.

EX. 2–13. Bernart de Ventadorn. PC 70,31. W fol. 191/B182; G. fol. 9.

Examination of these manuscripts reveals that the scribes were active agents, either consciously or unconsciously, in recording the melodies of the troubadours. The main music scribe of R, who entered all the melodies discussed in this chapter, appears to have manipulated, adapted, and regularized the melodies. The scribe of G gives all the appearance of being more careless than others, while the scribe of W sometimes seems to have been ignorant of the repertoire he was copying. The nature of the intervention of the scribes must underlie any inquiry into the compositional process and the performance practice of the troubadours' songs, since no melody that survives escaped it.

Thꝛee

POETICS
AND MUSIC

The Medieval Arts of Poetry and Prose

The troubadours were engaged in a very pragmatic occupation, that of producing songs for an audience. But while they were not theoreticians, they were learned and familiar with many of the texts of their contemporaries and predecessors, and often with a wider range of literature, including epic narratives and classical Latin works. Even if an individual troubadour did not study poetics systematically, much of the poetry appears to have been shaped at least indirectly by the late medieval arts of poetry and prose, whose roots lay in the classical disciplines of grammar and rhetoric developed during the first centuries B.C. and A.D.

Cicero's *De inventione* (c. 100 B.C.), the anonymous *Rhetorica ad Herennium* (c. 100 B.C.), portions of Quintilian's *Institutio oratoria* (c. A.D. 92), and Horace's brief *Ars poetica* (23–13 B.C.) were widely known and portions of them were translated into various vernaculars during the later Middle Ages.[1] In classical theory, rhetoric involved inventing persuasive public orations within the judicial (forensic) and political (deliberative) spheres especially, and also the epideictic sphere, "praise or censure of a particular individual."[2] Within one of these three broad subjects (the *materia*), a discourse focused on a specific "issue" or question to be argued,[3] and this issue was expressed by means of arguments (*loci* or *topicii*).[4] The classical authors described multifarious *loci* or *topicii*, inventing countless examples to illustrate their points; Boethius (early sixth century) devoted an entire treatise to it, *De differentiis topiciis*. The category of praise and blame eventually was broadened to encompass the subject matter of poetry in the Middle Ages.

An argument was designed mentally before the actual formulation of the speech, during *inventio,* the first of five stages or "parts" of rhetoric. Once the issues and arguments were determined by the orator, he could set about arranging the components of the speech (*dispositio*), fashioning the specific words that he wished to use (*elocutio*), fixing the speech in his memory (*memoria*), and finally executing the oration (*pronuntiatio*):

> Invention is the discovery of valid or seemingly valid arguments to render one's cause plausible. Arrangement is the distribution of arguments thus discovered in the proper order. Expression is the fitting of the proper language to the invented matter. Memory is the firm mental grasp of matter and words. Delivery is the control of voice and body in a manner suitable to the dignity of the subject matter and the style.[5]

The arrangement, expression, and delivery of the speech fell into one of three "styles" according to the type of language used, ranging from the impressive and ornate to the colloquial: grand or high (*gravis* or *grandiloquus*), middle (*mediocris*), and simple or low (*adtenuata* or *humilis*).[6] To express these styles, the orator learned to use figures of thought and of speech (*colores* or *figurae*), and the creative orator could vary styles within a speech.[7]

The mechanics of poetry, in particular metrics and versification, eventually came to be understood as falling within the province of grammar. In classical theory, grammar entailed the correct use of language (*recte loquendi*), which was learned principally by imitating master authors (later "interpreting the poets," *enarratio poetarum*). Horace's *Ars poetica*, which touches on poetic meter, is in this tradition.[8] Donatus' *Ars minor* (c. A.D. 350) deals with the parts of speech, but also appropriates from rhetoric instruction in how to use certain figures and tropes in the service of speaking not only correctly but also effectively. Priscian (fl. c. 510) treats the parts of speech, letters, syllables, diction, sentence construction, etc., in the *Institutiones grammaticae*; and in another treatise he discusses the poetic meters of classical Latin, with Virgil as the supreme model.

The Venerable Bede (673–735), in *De arte metrica,* signaled the existence of a new type of Latin versification, in which verses were ordered not by classical quantitative meters, but by *rithmus,* or syllable-counting, "as in the songs of the vernacular poets."[9] Gradually the art of versification began to include instruction not only in counting syllables, but also in rhyme, stanza construction, and qualitative or accentual meters that eventually supplanted quantitative meters. Even though Latin poetry, including hymns, had departed significantly in style, content, and structure from its classical models, emulation of the masters remained paramount in the training of poets, who studied collections of *exempla* of the poetry of classical authors, imitated them, and drew from them lessons on language, style, structure, and content.[10]

The development of the system of liberal arts gradually provided a place for grammar and rhetoric, along with dialectic, in the *trivium*, the arts of language. But a demarcation between the two—the evident tidiness of the *trivium* notwithstanding—was not always very clear, especially because the figures and tropes were used by both orators and grammarians to arrange and embellish their speech. From a theoretical point of view poetry was still seen as imitation rather than creation, and hence was a grammatical rather than a rhetorical art. But by the late Middle Ages poetry increasingly received specific attention from theorists as an art distinct from both rhetoric and grammar.

Several well-known treatises on the arts of poetry and prose were produced between about 1170 and 1280: John of Salisbury's *Metalogicus* (c. 1159), Matthieu de Vendôme's *Ars versificatoria* (before c. 1175), Geoffroi de Vinsauf's *Poetria nova* (c. 1208–1213) and *Documentum de modo et arte dictandi et versificandi* (after 1213), Gervase de Melkley's *Ars versificaria* (c. 1208–1213?), Jean de Garlande's *Parisiana poetria* (after 1229), Évrard (Eberhard) l'Allemand's *Laborintus* (before 1280), and Brunetto Latini's *Li livre dou tresor* (c. 1260) and *Rettorica* (a translation of Cicero's *De inventione*, c. 1260). Their subject was mainly Latin poetry, although some of them acknowledge in one way or another the existence of vernacular literature.[11]

These authors were indebted to the traditions of both rhetoric and grammar. From grammar they adapted instruction on the correct use of language, the imitation and interpretation of poetry, and versification. Some, like Gervase and Jean, discussed all forms of verse-making, including classical quantitative meters, syllable-counting rhymed verse, and the more recent qualitative (accentual) type of poetry, such as the Aquitanian *versus*, with which many troubadours were probably familiar. From the realm of rhetoric they adopted the Ciceronian framework of the five parts—*inventio, dispositio, elocutio, memoria*, and *pronuntiatio*—devoting space to the subject matter of the composition, to its arrangement and delivery, and especially to the rhetorical *colores*, the tropes and figures taken from both rhetoric and grammar.

The "material" or subject matter of the poem was conceived in the imagination during *inventio*, and it played a part in defining a poem's genre.[12] The high, middle, and plain styles, which in classical *dispositio* and *elocutio* had been distinguished by the style and arrangement of language, now became important factors in *inventio* as well. The personages (nobles, bourgeois, peasants) by whom, about whom, or for whom a poem was composed distinguished a poem's "material style," along with its subject matter, its function, and its speaker.[13] The medieval Latin theorists sometimes categorized the tropes and figures as either *ornata difficultas (gravitas)* or *ornata facilitas (levitas)*, difficult or easy, which found a direct counterpart in the *trobar clus* and *trobar leu* (discussed below in Chapter 5) of some of the early troubadours.[14]

Geoffroi de Vinsauf's *Poetria nova* was glossed heavily and disseminated widely during the Middle Ages.[15] It relies on Horace, Cicero, and the author of the *Rhetorica ad Herennium*, all of whom it generously quotes. Geoffroi colorfully presents the paradigm of imagination in the process of fashioning a poem, urging careful contemplation as the first step, before taking up pen or opening the mouth:

> If a man has a house to build, his impetuous hand does not rush into action. The measuring line of his mind first lays out the work, and he mentally outlines the successive steps in a definite order. The mind's hand shapes the entire house before the body's hand builds it. Its mode of being is archetypal before it is actual. . . . Let the poet's hand not be swift to take up the pen, nor his tongue be impatient to speak; trust neither hand nor tongue to the guidance of fortune. To ensure greater success for the work, let the discriminating mind, as a prelude to action, defer the operation of hand and tongue, and ponder long on the subject matter. Let the mind's interior compass first circle the whole extent of the material. . . . As a prudent workman, construct the whole fabric within the mind's citadel; let it exist in the mind before it is on the lips.[16]

Once the subject matter has been invented and the poem mentally designed, then the steps of arranging the materials and choosing suitable words can take place: "When due order has arranged the material in the hidden chamber of the mind, let poetic art come forward to clothe the matter with words."[17] Subject and audience are both important in the determination of the style of the poem: "Regard not your own capacities, therefore, but rather his with whom you are speaking. Give to your words weight suited to his shoulders, and adapt your speech to the subject. . . . In a common matter, let the style be common; in specialized matters let the style be proper to each. Let the distinctive quality of each subject be respected."[18]

After treating the figures and tropes, Geoffroi makes traditional remarks about proper use of the voice in delivery, including an admonition to keep in mind the subject matter: "Modulate your voice in such a way that it is in harmony with the subject; and take care that voice does not advance along a path different from that which the subject follows. Let the two go together; let the voice be, as it were, a reflection of the subject."[19] In delivering a poem of anger, for instance, the performer is to "imitate genuine fury, but do not be furious." One should use a "caustic voice," "an inflamed countenance," and "turbulent gestures" (lines 2044–2049).

Jean de Garlande, perhaps today the most recognized among late medieval poetic theorists (but not of widest dissemination during the period), is of particular interest to students of Occitanian literature. As pointed out in Chapter 1, he was a *magister* of grammar at the University of Toulouse from 1229 to 1231. Educated at Oxford and Paris, Jean spent most of his professional career in Paris. Although he did not stay in Toulouse long, he took note of at least some musical practices in the city, as we know from a reference he later made to the performance of liturgical organum there in a tract that describes the Albigensian Crusade, *De triumphis ecclesiae* (c. 1252).[20] In his *Parisiana poetria* he demonstrates his familiarity with Boethian *musica speculativa*, at the same time drawing a direct connection between music and poetry, but the context seems to suggest a theoretical rather than a practical connection, the common element being mathematical proportion or counting:

> Rhymed poetry is a branch of the art of music. For music is divided into the cosmic, which embraces the internal harmony of the elements, the humane, which embraces the harmony and concord of the humors, and the instrumental, which embraces the concord evoked by instruments. This includes melody, quantitative verse, and rhymed verse. There is nothing here about the other branches; my present subject is rhymed poetry only.[21]

In his writings about poetry Jean is concerned with Latin literature, but he acknowledges some similarity between Latin versification and the versification of vernacular poetry.[22] He had a personal acquaintance with Bishop Foulque of Toulouse, the former troubadour, having assisted at the siege of Toulouse led by the bishop and Simon de Montfort in 1218.[23]

Jean's treatise on poetry is an ungainly hodge-podge of traditional and original material dealing with letter-writing, grammar, poetry, and rhetoric. *Inventio* has "five species: Where, what, what kind, how, and why."[24] "Where"—perhaps to be understood in the Ciceronian sense of "locus" or argument—concerns the characters treated by the poet, corresponding to three styles:

> Three kinds of characters ought to be considered here, according to the three types of men, which are courtiers, city dwellers, and peasants. Courtiers are those who dwell in or frequent courts, such as the Holy Father, cardinals, legates, archbishops, bishops, and their subordinates, such as archdeacons, deans, officials, masters, scholars; also emperors, kings, marquises, and dukes. City dwellers are count, provost, and the whole range of people who live in the city. Peasants

are those who live in the country, such as hunters, farmers, vine dressers, fowlers.[25]

"What" is the subject matter itself, which might be dependent on the persons involved. "What kind," or the "quality of the subject matter invented,"[26] is divided into honorable or disreputable—again determined by the subject matter and persons. "How" concerns the language used, especially tropes and figures.

The last species of invention, "to what end," has to do with the function of the work. In this respect and others, Jean betrays the influence of Aristotle on his thinking. He concludes his discussion of invention with the following:

> *A Way of Inventing Subject Matter.* Here is a device that is useful in certain kinds of writing; students particularly who aim to amplify and vary their subject matter may observe it. I mean they should not overlook the four principal causes—the efficient cause, and so on—of any subject proposed to them. Thus, suppose one of them is treating of his book. He might praise it or criticize it through the efficient cause, that is, through the writer; through the material cause, that is, through the parchment or the ink; through the formal cause, as through the layout of the book or the size of the letters; or through the final cause, by considering for what purpose the book was made, namely, that in it and through it the ignorant may be made more knowledgeable.[27]

Hence Jean claims as the purpose of invention, or its final cause, "to promote what is both useful and right."[28] The final cause includes the choice of persons and the subject matter:

> With persons there is always a pair of alternatives; as with kings: to rule the kingdom well, or to tear the kingdom to pieces like a tyrant; with prelates: to pursue divine contemplation, or to idle about in secular affairs; with city dwellers: to carry on the business of the city, to strengthen the republic, or to squander it; with peasants, it means sweating over rural duties, or giving up.[29]

To discuss the choice of words, Jean returns to the three styles—high, middle, and low—which he attributes to Virgil.[30] He identifies them respectively with soldiers and governers, farmers, and shepherds, and the styles appropriate for each are expressed in the language: "The level of style itself amplifies the material, when high sentiments are chosen for the high style, middling ones for the middle style, low ones for the low style—provided that in treating a low subject we be not too lackluster and unfigurative, confusing that style with inarticulateness. . . ."[31] Like other writers, Jean allows the poet to use "high" language for a "low" subject, and vice versa, if this serves a rhetorical purpose. "High matter can be lowered, in imitation of Virgil, who calls

Caesar—or himself—Tityrus and Rome a beech; and low matter can be exalted, as when in a treatment of a high subject women's distaffs are called 'the spears of peace'. . . .[32]

Jean provides definitions of words for narrative and poetic genres (*genera narrationum* and *genera carminum*, Chapter V), derived from classical catalogs of quantitative verse types.[33] He defines them according to the subject matter, or sometimes the speaker, and although the names do not usually appear in lists of genres of medieval lyric songs, some of the types he describes are certainly to be found among songs by the trouvères (and perhaps by troubadours) that he undoubtedly knew. The "Epichedion," for example, is "a plain song apart from a burial, that is, one that is composed for someone not yet buried,"[34] which has its parallel in the Occitan *planh*. A few years later Jean added to his treatise a section on *ars ritmica*, including discussion of versification and stanza structure.[35]

Thus in medieval Latin poetics, a conception of the subject matter of a song, which included the speaker, the topic, the function, the audience, and the specific points made about the topic, was the principal business of *inventio*. Arranging the parts, choosing the words, and uttering the song depended on the content determined in the mind at the outset, as did the "style" by which the poet arranged, expressed, and delivered the poem.

The Art de trobar *and the Art of Music*

Several treatises on poetry and language—the *art de trobar*—were written in the *langue d'oc* during the late twelfth through the mid-fourteenth centuries, all modeled to some degree on these classical and medieval texts on Latin grammar, rhetoric, and poetics. Most of them were written by and for Catalan patrons, amateurs, and beginners in the art of poetry, not for native speakers of the *langue d'oc* or for professional poet-composers.[36]

Two of these treatises were produced before the middle of the thirteenth century: Raimon Vidal's *Las Razos de trobar* (Catalonia, c. 1190–1213[37]) and Uc Faidit's *Donatz proensals* (Italy, c. 1225–45[38]). The latter, as its title implies, is mainly a treatise on grammar in the tradition of Donatus. The former is extant in several redactions, reflecting various stages of revision and probably scribal intervention.[39] It is a rather idiosyncratic and superficial prose tract mainly on Occitan grammar, despite its author's claims in the opening sentences that it offers a method for learning to compose poetry.[40]

Raimon follows the tradition in rhetoric and grammar of encouraging the emulation of great poets, quoting from Bernart de Ventadorn, Guiraut de Bornelh, Arnaut de Maruelh, Gaucelm Faidit, Bertran de

Born, Folquet de Marselha, Peire Vidal, Peire Raimon de Tolosa, Peirol, and Guilhem de Saint Didier.[41] He does not mention music, but of twenty poems that Raimon quotes, thirteen ultimately survived with melodies: seven by Bernart de Ventadorn, two by Folquet by Marselha, and one each by Guiraut de Bornelh, Arnaut de Maruelh, and Peirol.[42] Eight of these poems survive with melodies in at least two manuscripts, and four of the songs by Bernart[43] have three extant melodies each, in manuscripts W, R, and G; all are found in manuscript R except for the melody by Peirol.

Thirteen out of twenty citations is far out of proportion to the number of melodies that survive in the repertoire as a whole. Raimon clearly was highlighting songs that were part of a living tradition. All these troubadours probably were still alive when Raimon wrote his treatise, but more important, these particular songs were widely known (as far as Catalonia, anyway) and revered. And they remained part of a living tradition, in that their melodies as well as their texts were ultimately preserved in writing. Marshall postulates that Raimon may have been quoting many of his citations from memory; if so, the melody may have aided in this remembering.[44] Thus music may have played a role in the durability of certain songs, not just within the song tradition itself, but also in the theoretical and the written traditions.

Several decades later, after the "classical" period of the troubadours was past, two more Catalan treatises appeared, one definitely by Jofre de Foixà, the *Regles* [*de trobar*] (c. 1286–91), and the other probably by Jofre, the *Doctrina de compondre dictats*. The *Regles* is extant in two manuscripts, with differences between them significant enough to lead Marshall to postulate some active scribal intervention in both versions.[45] Jofre relied somewhat on Raimon Vidal's treatise in producing an elementary Occitan grammar for his lay Catalan audience.

Although like Raimon, Jofre does not refer to music in the *Regles*, he gives some basic information on versification and quotes from eleven poems, including works by Bernart de Ventadorn, Gaucelm Faidit, Bertran de Born, Folquet de Marselha, and Aimeric de Peguilhan. Five of the eleven songs from which Jofre quotes are extant with music: two by Gaucelm and one each by Bernart, Folquet, and Aimeric.[46] Four of these melodies are found in both manuscripts R and G; one of Gaucelm's two melodies[47] is found only in manuscripts X and G. Here again, the theorist cites many songs whose melodies ultimately survived. Besides possibly quoting from memory, Jofre may have had access to poetic readings that were related to those found in the Languedocian sources C and R.[48]

The *Doctrina de compondre dictats* is a short exposition on the versification and subject matter of the different genres of troubadour poetry; it is the earliest thorough description of these poetic genres and represents a crystallization that was not as strict in the earlier period.[49] The text is found in only one manuscript, and Marshall considers it to be "the concluding section of the *Regles de trobar*" of Jofre, erroneously separated from it by an inattentive scribe.[50] The details of structure given for some of the genres do not square with many earlier Occitanian examples of them, and the discussion of some genres betrays its author's Catalan background.[51] The inclusion of rather dogmatic instructions on the structural features appropriate to each genre may reflect the later thirteenth-century taste for defining types by form as much as (or more than) by subject matter. As will be discussed in Chapter 4, the author of the *Doctrina* alludes to the musical style and structure of the music suited to the various genres,[52] which seem tied to the poem's material or content.

Although these poetic theorists gave little attention to music, their remarks and their treatment of song in general suggest that they were aware on some level of how critical music was to the essence of the songs. They certainly knew that the texts were sung; indeed their own acquaintance with particular songs may have been through the medium of music (as opposed to written texts). As we shall see in the next chapter, they seemed to assume that a "song" was words and music together, and that text and melody were in a certain sense both products of a common purpose.[53] At the very least, the theorists knew that musical and textual structures must match numerically—verse and stanza lengths must coincide. Although they did not have the vocabulary to express it, one senses that these theorists knew that the melodies of the best songs were as much a feature of their essence as were the rhyme schemes and stanza structures, and that in some way the poet-composers conceived the poems and melodies together.

The poetic theorists probably did not have any formal musical training beyond a fundamental, probably Boethian, education in music as an art of the *quadrivium*. Until the late Middle Ages, many authorities considered poetry to fall under the rubric of Musica, from at least as early as the fourth century.[54] That this philosophical tradition survived in the late Middle Ages is evident from the passage in Jean de Garlande's treatise (quoted above): "Rhymed poetry is a branch of the art of music."[55] But by the twelfth and thirteenth centuries, as we have seen, the art of poetry had been taken over largely by rhetoricians and grammarians, and their writings seem to imply a new practical and theoretical relationship between music and text. Poetry now was treated less as a subcategory of music than as an art in its own right, which operated with its own rules, in cooperation with music. Music itself was seen in a much more pragmatic light than in the early Middle Ages. From a song's initial conception, at least, poet and composer were the same person (except for cases of borrowing, as in the *sirventes*). As the twelfth and thirteenth centuries progressed, poets and composers developed, and theorists articulated, rules for poetry and rules for music that resulted in increased separation between the two arts. The poetry and the poetic rules took new directions and became extraordinarily sophisticated. The music and music theory also veered into radical new areas.

Just as a practical theory of poetry and a practical theory of music developed along parallel but largely distinct paths, the songs themselves embraced the autonomy of each art, treating them as equal but separate partners. The music of the troubadours was not dependent on poetry for all of its coherence or meaning; yet it was in its essence "poetic" in the sense that it relied on the poetry for its structure and was wedded to the text in its delivery. A poem, in its turn, was governed by complex processes of invention, arrangement, and style, yet it was "musical" in that it relied on music for its performance.[56]

The art of poetry of the twelfth and thirteenth centuries can be seen as a bridge, both theoretical and practical, between rhetoric in the *trivium* and music in the *quadrivium*. By the end of the period, though, music and poetry began to diverge altogether, and poet and composer need not be the same person. While at the beginning of the fourteenth century Dante could call poetry "rhetorical invention set to music,"[57] he could also presage a type of poetry that was not dependent on music for its delivery, or even conceived with a melody at its outset.

The music treatises that began to appear in the second half of the thirteenth century reflected enormous practical, theoretical, and philosophical changes in music. As in other scholastic disciplines, the position of music began to shift from its neo-Platonic foundations to an Aristotelian framework.[58] Practically, music was emerging from its function as a servant of the liturgy or of the art of poetry. Music theorists increasingly concerned themselves with exciting developments in notation and rhythmic systems, techniques, and genres. *Discantus, organum, conductus*, and especially the motet represented novel ways of organizing music; innovations occurred in the use of music in the liturgy; and in particular new attitudes arose about the place of music in the larger, secular, world.[59] Canon, hocket, voice-exchange, and other contrapuntal devices enriched the harmonic and melodic vocabularies. Musical structures that were dependent less on text and more on repetition schemes and counterpoint began to overshadow the texts that originally generated the music. And theorists began discussing instrumental music—music without text—as a species of "art" music.

Northern France was the center of these scholastic and practical developments. Secular music in the second half of the thirteenth century, like poetry, began to manifest its own signs of a changed aesthetic, especially in the appearance of structural schemes based on repetition that matched the rhyme scheme of the poetry. Where genres earlier had been defined by subject matter, they now began to be defined by musical and poetic structure—*rondeau, ballade, virelai.*[60] Melody began taking on an autonomous identity, less tied to a text or to a theme. While music was becoming less dependent on the text for its nature, poetry was at least in a structural sense becoming more "musical."

The Parisian Johannes de Grocheio in some ways expressed the expansion of music beyond the *quadrivium* and the liturgy better than any other late medieval music theorist, by treating vocal and instrumental secular music on a par with liturgical chant and polyphony. He appears to have been the first theorist to give untexted music serious attention. Grocheio also was the first to discuss vernacular music systematically. He has long been consulted for insight into French monophony of the twelfth and thirteenth centuries, but it has been pointed out recently that Grocheio, writing c. 1300, expressed many of the new aesthetic ideals of the late thirteenth century.[61]

Yet at the same time that Grocheio expounds ideas that are proper to the late thirteenth century, he also articulates some concepts that seem relevant to music and poetry of the earlier period. Despite the fact that the late thirteenth-century music theorists did not devote much attention to the intricacies of poetry and prose, they certainly did not ignore the presence of texts in the music they discussed. Indeed, it is a constant undercurrent in their expositions on music for the liturgy, in discussions of such things as ligatures and their relation to syllables, and in descriptions of styles of music appropriate to particular genres— defined by the content of their texts. Grocheio and other music theorists no doubt were familiar with the same theoretical traditions that served as background for Jean de Garlande, Geoffroi de Vinsauf, Raimon Vidal, Jofre de Foixà, and other grammarians and rhetoricians. The connection between Paris and Toulouse, exemplified by the early thirteenth-century career of Jean de Garlande, implies an intellectual atmosphere common to the south and the north.

The concepts in Grocheio's treatment of vernacular song concerning the interconnection between words and music are very similar to those found in poetic treatises that deal with courtly lyric.[62] Grocheio views text and melody as together constituting a song's substance, and he uses the Aristotelian concepts of *forma* (music) and *materia* (words) to convey this idea.[63] Each element serves its own function, one to express the theme of the song, the other to give it tangible shape, and the composer must consider both in the process of composing. These ideas are found also in the art of rhetoric. The "material" is created by the composer in the first stage of *inventio,* and is then given "form" in the steps of *dispositio* and *elocutio*—all perhaps mentally.[64] To Grocheio, the music is what ultimately gives the song its form; in other words, it is not actuated, or realized, until it is sung aloud, the rhetorical stage of *pronuntiatio*.[65]

Like the poetic theorists, Grocheio asserts that an author must take into account the subject matter of the song he is composing before he can arrange his materials accordingly. Grocheio discusses the differences among types of secular song, which are determined in part by subject matter, style, function, audience, and performance style.[66] He further implies that the music must be appropriate for the text, since together they serve a common function. He suggests that certain guidelines must be followed in devising an appropriate melody for a song. Grocheio's discussion of melodic form, while intricate and in some respects apparently contradictory, nonetheless reflects his view that, as in poetry, the way in which the elements of a melody are arranged is a factor in the song's success. Like the poet, the musician has certain means of moving the audience.

Poetic and music theorists, then, were concerned that poets and composers utilize the tools of their respective arts appropriately and effectively. Theorists of both disciplines insisted that text and music complement each other in theme, structure, style, and performance. According to the art of poetry, an author first had to determine what type of song he wished to compose; that is, he had to determine its theme, expressed by the Occitan word *razo*. A general idea of the character of the poem and of the melody took shape in the composer's mind, even if the exact words and notes had not. The melody is as much bound by the theme, or *razo*, as is the poem.

To what extent can we take these theorists' remarks to explain how troubadours composed? They almost certainly did not learn their craft by studying these pedagogical tracts.[67] They were more likely to have learned by hearing, memorizing, perhaps reading, and imitating poetry—the ancient ones, as well as more recent *exempla*, including Latin hymns and *versus*.[68] It is conceivable that some chansonniers were intended as pedagogical aids, repositories of *exempla* for instruction in the Occitanian *art de trobar*, not only for the patrons and amateurs who would never excel beyond an elementary level of composing but perhaps also for some (late) troubadours.

But did the poet-composers see words and music as equal partners as they imagined or created their songs? Given the common practice of sharing melodies among poems, as well as the presence of phrase repetition within a song and the reuse of the melody for several stanzas, it is obvious that the words of a particular text and the notes of a particular melody were not inextricably and exclusively linked.[69] However, in a larger sense, the troubadours seemed to see their task as forging a song out of words and music—*motz e son*, in a formula commonly found in the poems. For example, Bernart de la Fon uses the phrase in an explanation of his compositional process:

Leu chansonet' ad entendre	An easy little song to understand,
ab leu sonet volgra far,	with an easy little tune, I want to
coindet' e leu per apendre	make, graceful and easy to learn and
e plan' e leu per chantar,	smooth and easy to sing, for the
quar leu m'aven la razo,	subject came to me easily, and the
e leu latz *los motz e.l so*.[70]	words and melody lie easy.

In a song that uses the same rhymes and verse structure as Bernart's poem, Uc de Saint Circ describes the kind of song that pleases him most, one in which words and music fulfill their proper roles in expressing the song's *razo*, or theme:

Chanzos q'es leus per entendre	The song that is easy to listen to and
et avinenz per chantar,	graceful to sing, so that no one can
tal qu'om non puescha reprendre	reprove the words or correct the
los motz ni.l chant esmendar,	singing [or melody], and which has
et a douz e gai lo son	a sweet and happy melody and a
e es de bella *razon*	beautiful theme and is graceful in
ed avinen per condar,	measure, pleases me and I wish to
mi plai e la voil lauzar	praise it to whomever criticizes it,
a qi la blasm'e defendre.[71]	and to defend it.

Both of these texts describe the words and the melody in terms that place them on a par, and also declare that the performance itself—the singing, the learning, and the hearing—is critical to an appreciation of the song. Together the words and the melody convey the song's theme, its *razo*. (Neither of these poems, unfortunately, survives with a melody, although since they share the same versification scheme, they may have been sung to the same tune.[72])

These passages suggest that the troubadours imagined their texts and melodies as cohesive parts of a whole, and that they understood the peculiar capacity of each to convey what they intended. They also imply that the troubadours, whether or not they saw their songs in Aristotelian terms, assumed that the fullest realization of a song could come about only through performance.

The structure, style, and delivery of both text and melody were governed to some degree by the song's subject matter. Several genres were associated with a particular broad subject (*materia*), including the love song (*canso*), dawn song (*alba*), lament (*planh*), moral or political commentary (*sirventes*), debate (*tenso*), and pastoral scene (*pastorela*). But within a genre the topics could vary widely. *Cansos* could be simple expressions of adulation or unmitigated complaints about the beloved's cruelty. A *planh* might celebrate the lamented one's life, or describe the miseries of the abandoned. A *tenso* could be about any question whatever, so long as there were at least two protagonists to argue it. A *sirventes* likewise could draw on an extraordinary range of issues.

During the process by which the words and notes actually took shape and style, the troubadour to some extent had to deal with poem and music separately, since each followed different rules: rhyme scheme, verse and strophe scheme, vocabulary, syntax, etc., for the former; melodic contour, tonal orientation, intervallic and motivic content, incipits and cadences, etc., for the latter. These issues are explored in detail in later chapters. But even though poetic and musical style and structure were devised according to the tools particular to each art, they must have interacted to some degree because the troubadours composed with the delivery of a song very much in mind. The processes involved in conceiving, arranging, and expressing one's ideas through words and music may have been so intertwined at the moment of performance that they occurred almost simultaneously. As suggested in Chapter 2, the stages in composition, performance, and dissemination are difficult to separate diachronically. For the troubadours there was no sharp dividing line separating the mental conceptualization and the oral actualization of a song.

It is difficult to say to what extent the troubadour was conscious of following any particular steps while composing. But what does seem certain is that while melody and poem were separate in following their own rules, the two elements must be understood as equal parts of a whole, and that to understand fully a troubadour's melody we must examine its pitches, its structure, and its style along with the words, structure, and style of its text, and both within the context of the song's performance.

CHAPTER

FOUR

GENRE

Theories of Genre

Poetry theorists of the second half of the thirteenth and the early fourteenth centuries evinced a penchant for codification and conventionalization by defining genres in specific terms, especially according to their subject matter and versification, which eventually resulted in a system of "genres."[1] Scholars today are as eager as their medieval predecessors to codify the "genres" of troubadour song.[2] But it is problematic to assign generic names to many of the troubadours' songs because of the loose mixing of themes and personages, the diverse structural characteristics, and the many styles of discourse. A song that some might see as a *sirventes* because of its moralizing theme, for example, for others might fall in the category of a *canso* because it is about love—spawning a hybrid modern term, *sirventes-canso*.[3] In the *lay* and the *retroncha* the structure rather than the theme seems to be the defining characteristic, even though the subject matter might also be love, as in the *canso*. Sometimes the style of the language—*trobar clus* or *trobar leu*, for instance, or a particularly colorful metaphor—is the most striking feature of a song, rather than its theme or its form.

In 1960 Roger Dragonetti published a study that placed trouvère song within the tradition of classical rhetoric and the medieval art of poetry.[4] He coined a phrase to refer to courtly trouvère love song, *le grand chant courtois*, which has been widely adopted. Dragonetti placed *le grand chant courtois* within the medieval rhetorical tradition of the three styles (*grandiloquus, mediocris, humilis*), which were distinguished by language, poetic voice, and the social status of speaker, subject, and audience. He likened the style of the trouvère chanson to the *stylus grandiloquus*. While Dragonetti pointed out that for medieval poets the "high style" was rooted in the personages, themes, and language of the songs, he was careful not to call the courtly love song a "genre" per se. Rather, his discussion focused on the stylistic features of the songs that mark them as "high."

Dragonetti's approach to the study of rhetoric in trouvère song has carried much weight in subsequent examinations of French and Occitan literature and music. While Dragonetti himself discussed only the courtly songs of the trouvères and did not deal with any medieval literatures that might parallel the other two styles, others have posited the existence of two distinct styles or categories of medieval literature, courtly trouvère poetry on the one hand and popular types such as dances and *pastourelles* on the other. These two classes of literature have been called also *troubadouresque* and *jongleuresque*,[5] or aristocratic and popular.[6] Christopher Page carried the courtly-popular dichotomy a step further.[7] He elevated Dragonetti's *grand chant courtois* to the status of a genre, applying to it the term "High Style," in contrast to the "Low Style" genre that includes dance songs, *pastourelles*, and songs with refrains. This dichotomy served as a framework for Page's theory of the use of instruments in vernacular vocal music.

Another way of classifying medieval vernacular literature depends primarily on structure. Structural features of the music have been used to define genres, including especially the presence of a refrain or a repetition pattern to distinguish one type from another, although this method of analysis has limitations with respect to secular monophony before the late thirteenth century.[8] Another way of classifying by structure is suggested by Pierre Bec, who has argued that more important than theme or language in distinguishing registers or styles is the overall form of the text—lyric or nonlyric. He asserts that both registers can use either plain or sophisticated language.[9] Lyric, strophic genres include both aristocratic works (like *cansos* and *sirventes*) and works with more popular origins (like *dansas* and *pastorelas*), while nonlyric poetic genres such as the epic and the romance often use an elevated level of discourse. Douglas Kelly provides historical and theoretical support for the dichotomy between lyric and nonlyric by arguing that the arts of poetry and prose—that is, the treatises that define them— spring from two different contemporary traditions, one derived from the southern aristocratic literature of short lyric genres, the other from the northern tradition that included narrative poetry (romances, *chansons de geste*, etc.) and shorter works produced within a bourgeois, urban culture.[10]

Neither theorists nor works of art make the task of sorting out the ambiguities about typology easy. Repeated attempts to make sense of the system of genres articulated by Johannes de Grocheio, for example, demonstrate how frustrating it is to match a theorist's descriptions with surviving pieces.[11] Undoubtedly well versed in poetical doctrines, Grocheio spoke of three categories of "vulgar" (vernacular) music, mixing the various "genres" among them. According to Grocheio, a *chanson de geste*, with its high social class of personages and its often tragic subject, occupied one of the most honored places in vernacular literature. Yet to us, an epic narrative's *laisse* structure and its presumably improvised formulaic melody are not overly sophisticated.

Students of medieval lyric are becoming more reluctant to succumb to the proclivity to pigeonhole. While today we find genres, classes, and registers of medieval literature useful analytical tools, they are very inexact concepts if examined through the eyes of a medieval poet. The troubadours themselves made fewer distinctions among the kinds of literature they composed and performed than did theorists, early or late, who attempted to codify that literature.[12] The poets used words like *canso*, *vers*, and *lay* to refer to their songs in contexts that tell us no more about the specific type of poetry than references to *corn* and *flautella* tell us about specific musical instruments.[13] Furthermore, before the middle of the thirteenth century, poetry theorists like Raimon Vidal spoke of the subject matter, persons, function, and language of poems without suggesting an ossification of these characteristics into a system of genres.

The troubadours were enormously creative in mixing themes, personages, topics, arguments, styles of language, and structures. A strophic courtly lyric might be characterized by an elevated level of structural complexity and a carefully composed melody, yet it might relate a bawdy or even obscene topic and be sung by a low-class *joglar*. A serious love song by Bernart de Ventadorn was likely to have a straightforward, plain style of language (*trobar leu*), while one by Arnaut Daniel could have obscure, esoteric expressions and structures (*trobar clus*). A *pastorela* by Marcabru, consisting of peasant subject matter, has quite subtle expressions and creative imagery that clearly were thought out carefully by the composer. The *pastorela* as a genre may have had roots in an oral and popular tradition, but by the middle of the twelfth century such popular songs could be and were treated as lyric songs comparable to the courtly *canso* and *planh*.

The concept of "genre," as problematic as it is, can be helpful in classifying the subject matter of a troubadour song, and in certain cases its structure and its performance, and for this reason I accept it in this study. To me it is not compelling to equate "genre" with a style of language, since high and low (or "grand" and "simple") styles of expression are found across genres that are defined by theme or form. In the medieval art of poetry, the different "styles" do not themselves define genres, but are techniques of composition applied after the theme of a song has been decided. Structure, language, and delivery are described as having different "styles," and a song's subject matter might or might not dictate what that style should be. The choice of a theme was among the first steps, perhaps a fundamental step, in the compositional process. It led to a much broader process, that of developing the "material style" of a song, including its personages (audience and speaker), function, and language, and choosing and arranging the issues and topics to be developed, as discussed in the preceding chapter. If we use a specific generic term for a song, we must recognize the elements that define it as such, and these can include its theme, structure, function, and performance. We must also realize that the troubadours were not so concerned with the generic designation as they were with these practical features of their songs.

We must also ask to what extent the music contributes to or is affected by the genre of the poem or by its theme, structure, function, and performance. While it is dangerous to argue that troubadours made direct connections between poetic elements and musical elements, it does stand to reason that a common aesthetic guided the composition of both poem and melody. As the poet manipulated topics, language, and structure to achieve the most compelling expression of the song's theme, the composer manipulated motives, intervals, contours, and textures to produce a melody that would be effective in conveying the poem.[14]

Several problems make it difficult to test this theory. First of all, as argued in Chapter 2, we cannot be certain that the melody given with a poem in an extant manuscript is the one composed by the poet; it may represent modifications that occurred during oral and written transmission. However, if transmission did retain some semblance of the "essence" of a melody, then exploring how an extant poem and its extant melody worked together as a song might reveal something about that essence and hence something about how the composer conceived the song. Poetic variants, especially differences in the stanza order, also indicate differences in transmission. But here, too, the essence of the text is maintained because the stanzas all address the song's theme in one way or another (see below).[15]

Further, even if we can define a poem as a *canso*, there is not necessarily anything inherent in the melody that defines *it* as a *canso*. This is evident in the practice of borrowing a melody of one song for another. Rather than look at detailed connections between words and pitches, we should examine larger features, like the progression of the poem through its arguments as related to the progression of a melody through its contours, tonal goals, and motivic development. Two different *cansos* that share a melody might have different arguments and structures, but they may be organized and presented in similar ways, and this organization may be reflected in the music.

Finally, the medieval evidence for the definition of genres in the treatises is relatively late, and it is very vague on the subject of music. But as argued in Chapter 3, even if the troubadours themselves were not governed by the rules laid down by the theorists, the treatises provide a framework for analysis, and they are offered here as a starting point for our examination of different types of songs.

Genre in the Art de trobar

What Occitanian theorists say on the subject of genre is within the prevailing rhetorical tradition.[16] Raimon Vidal, in his *Razos de trobar*, does not discuss genres systematically but suggests that the *art de trobar* involves different social classes of audiences and performers, a variety of topics, and various circumstances of performance:

Totas genz cristianas, iusieuas et sarazinas, emperador, princeps, rei, duc, conte, vesconte, contor, valvasor, clergue, borgues, vilans, paucs et granz, meton totz iorns lor entendiment en trobar et en chantar, o q'en volon trobar o q'en volon entendre o q'en volon dire o q'en volon auzir; qe greu seres en loc negun tan privat ni tant sol, pos gens i a paucas o moutas, qe ades non auias cantar un o autre o tot ensems, qe neis li pastor de la montagna lo maior sollatz qe ill aiant an de chantar. Et tuit li mal e.l ben del mont son mes en remembransa per trobadors. Et ia non trobares mot [ben] ni mal dig, po[s] trobaires l'a mes en rima, qe tot iorns [non sia] en remembranza, qar trobars et chantars son movemenz de totas galliardias.[17]

All good Christians, Jews and Saracens, emperor, prince, king, duke, count, viscount, commander, vassal, cleric, citizen, and peasant, small and great, daily give their minds to composing and singing, by either inventing or listening, speaking or hearing; no place is so isolated or solitary that, as long as there are a few or many, you will not hear singing either by a single person or by many together; even the shepherds in the mountains know of no greater amusement than song. All good and evil things in the world are commemorated by the troubadours. Indeed there is no [good] or evil saying put into rhyme by a troubadour, that is not remembered every day, because inventing and singing are the driving force behind all valor.

Raimon mentions some specific lyric genres in a well-known comment about the suitability of the *langue d'oc* (which he refers to as the language of Limousin) to shorter strophic types, opining that French is the proper language for longer epic works:

| La parladura francesca val mais et [es] plus avinenz a far romanz et pasturellas, mas cella de Lemosin val mais per far vers et cansons et serventes.[18] | The French language is more worthy and suitable for composing romances and *pastourelles*, but that of Limousin is better for making *vers* and *cansos* and *sirventes*. |

Raimon does not specify what the themes of a *vers*, *cansos*, or *sirventes* should be, but toward the end of his treatise he offers an observation about the composition of a poem in accordance with an appropriate and unified sentiment throughout, or in Occitan, *razo* (from Latin *ratio*). This notion of unity of subject matter becomes axiomatic for later theorists who do define genres by their themes.[19] Raimon also warns against using "low discourse," probably meaning a base or faulty style of expression that would belie the eloquence of the theme:

| Per aqi mezeis deu gardar, si vol far un cantar o un romans, qe diga rasons et paraulas continuadas et proprias et avinenz, et qe sos cantars o sos romans non sion de paraulas biaisas ni de doas parladuras ni de razons mal continuadas ni mal seguidas.[20] | One also should take care, if he wants to compose a song or a romance, that he arranges its theme and discourse continually and properly and pleasingly, and that his song or romance not be of low discourse or of two [different] dialects or of a theme badly continued or badly pursued. |

Later in the thirteenth century Jofre de Foixà's *Regles* [*de trobar*] echoes Raimon's comments about the unity of a song's theme and further implies that the *rayso* is important in the concept of genre:

| Rayso deu hom gardar per ço cor la mellor causa que ha mester totz cantars es que la rasos sia bona e que hom la vage continuan, ço es a entendre que de aquella rayso que començara son cantar, perfassa lo mig e la fi. Car si tu comences a far un sirventesch de fayt de guerra o de reprendimen o de lausors, no.s conve que.y mescles raho d'amor; o si faç canço o dança d'amor, no.s tayn que.y mescles fayt d'armes ne maldit de gens, si donchs per semblances no o podiets aportar a raho.[21] | One should take care with the theme, for the most important thing that all songs require is that the theme be good and that one continue with it, so it is understood that this theme which begins the song be achieved in the middle and the end. For if you begin making a *sirventes* about deeds of war or about reproof or about praise, it is not appropriate to mix in a theme of love; or if you make a *canso* or a *dansa* about love, it is not appropriate to mix in deeds of arms or men's slander, if it does not resemble or communicate [carry] the theme. |

The *Doctrina de compondre dictats* gives the earliest detailed descriptions of the genres of troubadour poetry. It also mentions the poems' melodies, relating them to the song's theme, structure, function, or performance.[22] The theorist differentiates among some genres according to their *razos* (e.g., love or grief) or their functions (e.g., a debate), but he mentions other details that help elucidate the way music played a role. For example, he says that some songs, such as the *canso, vers, dansa, estampida, retroncha, descort,* and *alba,* require a newly composed melody. Others, including the *sirventes, planh, pastorela, tenso,* and *lay,* can use a borrowed tune, and for these the author suggests certain structural or stylistic interrelationships between the poem and the melody. Some genres are at least partially defined by their structures, like the *dansa* and the *retroncha.* The *dansa, estampida,* and *pastorela* are so much defined by their function and mode of delivery that the performance itself is at least as important as the theme and the form.

The theme, or *razo,* be it love, moralization, lament, or conflict, takes pride of place in this theorist's definition of genres. The *canso, retroncha, dansa, pastora, planh, alba,* and *descort* all treat the subject of love. According to the theorist, the theme may be approached from any point of view in the first three types, while in the latter four types the love theme has a particular slant. The *pastora* involves wooing a shepherdess; the *planh* deals with the loss of a loved one; the *alba* has at its center the coming of the dawn, which brings to an end a tryst; the *descort* deals specifically with unrequited love.

The majority of extant troubadour songs are classified today as *cansos,* and the styles and contents of their melodies and texts cover a broad range, making generalizations impossible. This variety suggests that it is more than the general theme that helps determine the character of the melody, but perhaps something about the arrangement of the specific music materials. The melody of a *canso* is supposed to be "as beautiful as possible," musical qualities that reflect an aesthetic that is only dimly evident to us today. But the theorist's discussion suggests that this beauty in the melody is in keeping with the instructions that the poem should "speak pleasingly of love":

E primerament deus saber que canço deu parlar d'amor plazenment, e potz metre en ton parlar eximpli d'altra rayso, e ses mal dir e ses lauzor de re sino d'amor. Encara mes, deus saber que canço ha obs e deu haver cinch cobles; eyxamen n'i potz far, per abeylimen e per complimen de raho, .vj. o .vij. o .viij. o .ix., d'aquell compte que mes te

And first you should know that a *canso* must speak pleasingly of love, and you can put in your poem examples of other themes, but without speaking evil, and praising nothing but love. Furthermore, you should know that a *canso* needs and must have five stanzas; but to ornament and perfect the theme, you may give it six or seven or eight or

placia. E potz hi far una tornada o
dues, qual te vulles. E garda be que,
en axi com començaras la raho en
amor, que en aquella manera
matexa la fins be e la seguesques. E
dona li so noveyl co pus bell poras.[23]

nine, as many as you please. And
you can give it one or two *tornadas*,
as you wish. And take care that you
continue and finish with the same
theme with which you began. And
give it as beautiful a new melody as
you can.

Taking the *razo* of love, a composer developed the topoi and arguments that illuminate some aspect of the theme, arranged them, and
devised expressive language to convey them. In a *canso* by Bernart de
Ventadorn, perhaps the most highly regarded composer of love songs,
one might see some parallels between the progression of the theme's
arguments in the poem and the contours of the melody. As it is transmitted in manuscript R (with only five of the seven extant stanzas and no
tornada), "La dossa votz ai auzida" (Example 4–1) begins with a nature
topos, moves from hope (stanzas I–II) to despair, bitterness, and treachery (stanzas III–IV) to resolution (stanza V). The contrasts in this progression from hope to despair to resolution are reflected in the melody,
verses 5 and 6 of which have a higher range characterized by leaps and
descending cadences, compared to the more conjunct motion of the
surrounding phrases. Verses 1, 2, 3, 4, and 7 of the melody all begin with
F–G–A, a motive found in other songs by Bernart that begin with a
nature theme; here it provides a sense of return and unity.

The cadence on E at the end of the melody is unexpected, and it
sounds incomplete. It is possible that this is a scribal error, since in the
other extant version (manuscript X) the cadence is a step lower and ends
on D. But the cadence in R might be the one that was sung at the end of
every stanza except the last, so that it leads by a half-step directly into
the first note of the next stanza.[24] The last stanza of the song then might
have concluded with a different pitch, perhaps D or F (this idea will be
explored more in Chapter 5). Such a lead-in from the end of one stanza
to the next heightens the sense of movement from idea to idea, stanza to
stanza.

The melody of this *canso* inhabits a layer superimposed over the
poem, both developing from a point, to a distant point, and a return. But
the melody's progress occupies much less time, one stanza in contrast to
the five of the poem, and it is reiterated with each new stanza; it is in a
sense a microcosm of the poem. The many repetitions of the melody, as
the topoi of the poem develop one by one at a more leisurely pace, create
a texturing effect in performance that reinforces the progression of the
thematic material (both poetic and musical), foreshadows a sense of
completion and resolution even while the poem continues through its
emotional journey, and allows singer and listener to reinterpret the
melody for each new stanza. Even a different analysis of the motivic,

EX. 4–1. Bernart de Ventadorn. PC 70,23. R fol. 57v.

1. La   dos - sa   votz   ay   au - zi - da.

2. del   ros - si - nho - let   sal - va - tge.

3. que   m'es   dins   lo   cor   sa - lhi - da.

4. si   que   tot   lo   cos - si - ri - er.

5. e.l   mal   tratz   c'a - mors   me   do - na.

6. me   leu - ja   e   m'as - sa - zo - na.

7. et   au - ri - a.m   be   mes - tier.

8. au - tre   joi   a   mon   damp - na - tje.

cadential, intervallic, and directional musical materials does not change the fact that the melody moves through time at a pace different from that of the poem, and that its effect changes with the changing text.[25]

Bernart's famous *canso* "Can vei la lauzeta mover" (Example 4–2) is about unrequited love. Its stanzas proceed through envy, despair, renunciation, another cycle of despair and renunciation, and finally reproach (of both the lady and the poet). The stanza order of this song varies quite a bit among the manuscripts. The order given here is found in manuscript G and in four other manuscripts, all Italian in provenance. In other sources, stanzas III and V occur later in the song, while IV and VI occur earlier.[26] The final stanza here, with its expression of self-reproach, occurs after stanza III or IV in several other manuscripts, which conclude instead with the despair of stanza IV or the renunciation of stanza V. The *tornada* reiterates the topos of renunciation, echoing the mood of stanza V.

I. La dossa votz ay auzida
del rossinholhet salvatge,
que m'es dins lo cor salhida
si que tot lo cossirier
e.l maltratz c'amors me dona
me levia e m'assazona;
et auria.m be mestier
autre joi a mon dampnatie.

I have heard the sweet voice of the
wild nightingale, and it has so
pierced my heart that it has lifted
and softened all the worry and
mistreatment that love gives me.
And I will very much need another
joy in my sorrow.

II. Ben es totz hom d'avol vida
c'ap joi non ha son estatie,
e qui vas amors non guida
son cor e son dezirier;
e per tot non l'abandona
vals e refrims critz non sona,
pratz e deves e vergiers,
combas e plas e boscatie.

Any man who does not dwell with
love has a truly miserable life, he
who does not steer his heart and his
desire toward love. For everything
must surrender to it, and the cry of
the birds must resound, likewise the
field and pasture and garden, dale
and plain and forest.

III. Una falsa descauzida
e razitz de mal linhatge
m'a trait e es traida
a culhit so ab que.m fier;
e cant autre la razona
d'eys lo sieu tort l'ochazona;
et an ne mais li derrier
qu'ieu que n'ay fag lonc badatge.

A false, base woman, sprung from
evil lineage, has betrayed me, yet
she herself is betrayed to the same
measure with which she struck me.
And when others speak to her, she
accuses them of her own faults. But
the worst ones get more from her
than I, who have waited so long.

IV. Mout l'avia gen servida
tro ac vas mi cor volatie;
e pus ilh no m'es cobida
fols serai si mais li quier;
servir c'om non gazardona,
et esperansa bretona,
fa del senhor escudier
per costum e per uzatie.

I have served her so well that her
heart is fickle towards me; and since
she will not reconcile with me, I will
be a fool if I ask it anymore. Service
that is not rewarded, and the Breton
hope, make a lord into a squire in
custom and in practice.

V. Pus tant es vas mi falhida
aisi lais son senhoratge,
e no vuelh que.m si' aizida
ni ja mais parlar no.n quier;
ab tot neis don m'en somona,
car non es maneira bona
ans par com guizardon quier
qui trop tem mal dig coratge.

Since she has so abandoned me, I
desert her sovereignty, and I do not
want to serve her or to seek any
more speech with her. Yet she still
summons me, for it is not good
manners for someone who once
sought recompense as her companion to fear malicious speech too
much.

EX. 4–2. Bernart de Ventadorn. PC 70,43. G fol. 10.

I. Qan vei la laudeta mover
de joi sas alas contra.l rai,
per la dolçor q'el cor li vai
s'oblida e.s laisa cader,
ha las, com grand enveia.m ve
de cui que veia jaucion;
meraveillas ai car dese
lo cor de desirer no.m fon.

When I see the lark beating its wings
for joy against the sun, and for the
sweetness that comes to its heart it
forgets and lets itself fall: alas, then
what great envy comes over me, of
those whom I see rejoicing. I marvel
that my heart does not melt immediately from desire.

II. Ha las, qant cuiava saber
d'amor e tant petit en sai,
qeç eu d'amar no.m pos tener
cella dund ja pro non aurai;
tolt m'a mon cor e tolt m'a me
e si meteissa e tot lo mon;
e cant si.m tolc, no.m laisa re
mas desirer e cor volon.

Alas, I thought I knew so much about
love, but I know so little about it, for I
cannot keep myself from loving her
from whom I shall have no favor. She
owns all my heart, and all of myself,
and even herself and all the world.
And when she took herself away from
me, she left me nothing but desire and
a willing heart.

III. De las domnas mi desesper;
ja mais en lor no.m fiarai;
c'aisi com las sol captener
enaissi las descaptenrai;
pois vei c'una pro no mi te
veis lei qi.m destrui e.m confon,
tutas las dompt' e las mescre
qe ben sai q'altretals se son.

IV. Merces es perduy et es ver,
et eu non o saubi anc mai;
qar cel qe plus en degr'aver
no.n a ges, et on la qerrai?
ha, co mal çembla, qi la ve
a seis oillç chaitis jauçion,
qe ja ses lei non aurai be,
lasse morir, qe noill auon.

V. Pos a midonç no pot valer,
deus ni merces ne.l dreit q'eu ai,
ni.s a lei no ven a plaçer
q'ill m'am, ja mais noll oi dirai,
aissi.m part de lei e.m recre;
mort m'a e per mort li respon;
e vau m'en sella no.m rete
chaitius en esill, non sai on.

VI. Anc no agui de mi poder
ni no fui mes de l'or' en çai
qe.s laiset de mois oillç veçer
en un mirail qe mult mi plai;
mirail, pois me mirei en te,
m'an mort li sospir de preuon;
c'aisi perdei com perdet se
lo bel Narchisus en la fon.

VII. De ço fai femina apparer,
ma dona, per qeu lo recrerai;
qe ço q'om vol no vol voler,
e ço c'om li deveda fai;
chauç sui en mala merce
et ai ben faiç de fols un pon;
ni no sai per qe me d[eve],
mas car poiai trop contra mon.

I despair of women. I will no longer trust them; just as I used to support them, I will abandon them. Since I see that no woman gives me any help against the one who destroys and confounds me, I fear and distrust all of them, for I know very well that they are all alike.

Mercy is lost, in truth, and I never even knew it. For she who ought to have it the most has none at all; and where will I seek it? Ah, whoever sees her with his eyes thinks it ill that she would allow a joyful captive, who without her cannot be well, to die, and not give him aid.

Since none of this is of value to my lady—duty or mercy, or my rights— nor does the fact that I love her bring her pleasure, I will say nothing more to her. So I depart from her and renounce her; she has ended me, and I answer her with an end. And I go away from her who does not detain me, a captive into exile, I don't know where.

I have never had power over myself or been my own, from the hour when she let me look with my own eyes into a mirror that pleases me much. Mirror, since I saw myself reflected in you, sighs from the depths have killed me. Thus I have been lost, like the fair Narcissus was lost in the fountain.

In this she acts just like a woman, my lady, for which I will denounce her. For what a man would want, she does not want to want, and what is forbidden to a man, she does. I have fallen into ill-favor, and I have acted like a crazy man on a bridge; yet I do not know why this happened to me, unless it was because I ascended too high in the world.

VIII. Tristeça no.n aueç de me,	Sorrow, you will have nothing more
e vau m'en mariç non sai on.	from me, and I go away, wretched, I
de chantar me tuoill e.m recre.	don't know where; I deprive myself
e de joi e d'amor m'escon.	of singing and abandon it, and I
	renounce joy and love.

The melody of this song has been transmitted far more widely than any other troubadour melody, and with less difference among the variant readings from beginning to end than in most other songs with multiple readings.[27] Among the striking features of the melody is the return of the music of verse 4 in verse 7, with a variation of the cadence (except in manuscript R, where a lack of variation is perhaps to be expected from the scribe), which descends to the tonal center D in verse 4, but stops on E in verse 7, as if to lead into the final phrase. In the text, the topic of the renunciation of love and of women is expressed in stanza III and reenters in stanza V, where the poet renounces the beloved herself, and again in the *tornada*. The incompleteness of the melody at the end of verse 7 (the ascent to E), moving to the finality on D of verse 8, seems to reflect the text of the final stanza, which expresses bemusement over the poet's finding himself in this unlucky position, followed by the renunciation in the *tornada*.

Another salient musical feature occurs at the end of verse 5, a little over halfway through the melody, with a stark descent of a fifth from D to G (D is decorated in R, again perhaps an editorial intervention). This is the only cadence on G, and it is the widest leap in the melody, from the highest pitch (foreshadowed in verse 3). An arresting point in the poem also comes a little over midway, in stanza V, where the poet declares his intention to abandon his beloved and go into exile—only to return in stanza VI to contemplate her allures through the mirror that is her eyes.[28]

A different kind of *canso*, composed three generations later by Uc de Saint Circ (Example 4–3), poses a series of questions in each stanza. After an introductory *exordium* in stanza I, the poet wonders What shall I do? (stanza II), How shall I endure? (stanza III), How shall I live? (stanza IV), and What shall I say? (stanza V). Unlike the situation with "Can vei la lauzeta mover," the stanza order is consistent in all the manuscripts. In stanza I the poet describes his enemies and his "bad" masters—his eyes and his heart—alternating their descriptions from verse to verse. The questions in the text in stanzas II and III occur on alternate verses, while in stanzas IV and V he breaks the rhythm of alternation by delaying one or another of the queries by a verse.

The melody, extant in only one source, alternates too, beginning with ABAB, repeating B, then CDCD (the two notes beginning verse 8 read D–E in the manuscript; since the rest of this verse is identical to

EX. 4–3. Uc de Saint Circ. PC 457,40. G fol. 82v.

I. Tres enemics e dos mals segnors ai,
c'usqecs pogna noit e jorn con m'aucia;
l'enemic son mei oill e.l cor qi.m fai
voler celei c'a mi no tagneria;
e l'us segnor es amor q.im bailia
ten mon fin cor e mon fin pessamen,
e l'autre vos donna en cui m'enten,
a cui non aus mon cor mostrar ni dir
com m'auciez d'enveia e de desir.

I have three enemies and two evil
lords, each of which stabs me with
death night and day. The enemies are
my eyes and my heart which make me
desire the one who will not agree with
me; and one lord is love who takes my
faithful heart and my faithful thoughts
captive, and the other is you, lady,
whom I love, to whom I dare not bare
my heart, nor tell how you have
murdered me with envy and desire.

II. Qe farai donc donna qe chai ni lai
non puos trobar re ses vos que bo.m
  sia?

So what shall I do, lady, since I cannot
find anything near or far that does me

qe farai eu cui serion esglai
tot autre jois se de vos no.ls avia?
qe farai eu cui chapdella e guia
la vostr'amor e.m fuch e.m sec e.m
    pren?
qe farai eu q'altre joi non aten?
qe farai eu ni con porai gandir
ses vos donna no.m volez retenir?

good except you? What shall I do, I for
whom all other joys become horrors if
they do not come from you? What shall
I do, whom your love rules and guides,
and which flees me and follows me and
seizes me? What shall I do, who await
no other joy? What shall I do, who will
not survive without you, lady, if you do
not wish to preserve me?

III. Com durerai eu qe no pos morir
ni ma vida non es mais malananza?
com durerai eu cui vos faiz languir
desesperaz ab un pauc d'esperanza?
com durerai eu qe ja alegranza
no aurai mais si no me ven de vos?
com durarai donna q'eu sui gelos
de toz home qui vau vas vos ni ven
e de toz cels a cui n'auch dire ben?

How shall I endure, who cannot die,
yet my life is but a torment? How shall
I endure, whom you make languish,
desperate with little hope? How shall I
endure, since I will have no joy if it
does not come from you? How shall I
endure, lady, since I am jealous of all
men who come near you, and all those
of whom I hear good spoken?

IV. Com viurai eu qe tan coral sospir
faz nuoit e jor qe movon de
    pessanza?
com viurai eu qui non pot far ni dir
autra ses vos ren qe.m don
    alegranza?
com viurai eu q'al no port en
    membranza
mas vostres cors e las plaisenz
    faichos
e cortes diz humils e amoros?
com viurai eu qe d'al non prec de me
Deu mas qe.m lais ab vos trobar
    merce?

How shall I live, since I emit such
heartfelt sighs night and day, so moved
by care? How shall I live, for whom
nothing that anyone else does or says,
without you, can give me cheer? How
shall I live, who carry nothing in my
memory except your heart and your
pleasing manners and your courtly,
humble, and lovely utterances? How
shall I live, who ask of God nothing but
that he allow me to find mercy with
you?

V. Qe dirai eu donna, si no.m
    manten
fina merces, sivals d'aitan q'eus
    venza
ab mon fin cor et ab ma leial fe
vostra rictaç e vostra granz valenza?
qe dirai eu si vos no.m faiz sofrenza?
qe dirai eu q'autra non posc vezer
q'en dreit d'amor me posc'al cor
    plazer?
qe dirai eu q'altra el mon non es
qe.m dones joi per nul ben qe.m
    fezes?

What shall I say, lady, if true mercy
does not support me, at least enough so
that I conquer with my true heart and
my loyal faith your nobility and your
great merit? What shall I say if you do
not indulge me? What shall I say, who
cannot see another who can place my
heart in the service of true love? What
shall I say, for whom there is no one
else in the world who gives me joy, she
does me such good?

VI. A la valen comtessa de Proenza,
car son sei faiz de sen de saber,
e.ill dich cortes e.ill semblan de plazer
an ma chanzos, qar cela de cui es
me comandat c'a leis la tramezes.

To the worthy countess of Provence,
for her deeds are full of wisdom, and
her speech courtly and her image
pleasing to my song, for she to
whom it belongs commanded me to
send it to her.

---

verse 6, the first two notes of verse 8 are changed here to conform to the
beginning of verse 6). Phrases A and C are related somewhat, both
having melismas in the same place in the verse, and ending with a
similar cadence. Phrases B and D are related as well: both rise, one to C
and the other to D; the D phrase ends high, however, perhaps emphasizing a push to the end. The intervening B section on verse 5 interrupts the
flow of the melodic structure, and has a different kind of cadence than
most of the other phrases; stanza IV of the text also interrupts the
regularity of the alternating questions and answers, with the postpone-
ment of the final iteration of the question "How shall I live" to verse 8.
The wide range of this melody is characteristic of Uc, suggesting that he
was interested in exploring the outer limits of the musical materials
available to him, just as this poem asks a wide range of questions
concerning the unfairness of love.

The *pastorela*, like the *canso*, is supposed to be about love, but with
a more light-hearted scheme involving the attempted seduction (usually unsuccessful) of a peasant girl by a lord or a knight.[29] The author of
the *Doctrina* uses the term *pastora*, literally "peasant girl," as the name
for the genre itself:

Si vols far pastora, deus parlar
d'amor en aytal semblan com eu te
ensenyaray, ço es a saber: si.t acostes
a pastora e la vols saludar o enquerer
o manar o corteiar, o de qual razo
demanar o dar o parlar li vulles. E
potz li metre altre nom de pastora,
segons lo bestiar que guardara; e
aquesta manera es clara assatz
d'entendre. E potz li fer .vj. o .viij.
cobles, e so novell o so estrayn ia
passat.[30]

If you want to compose a *pastora*,
you must speak of love in the way I
will teach you, thus: if you meet a
shepherdess and wish to greet her or
woo or pursue or court her, or to ask
or give or speak to her about
something, as you wish. And you
can give it a name other than *pastora*,
depending on the animal that she
keeps; and this genre is understood
clearly enough. And you can give it
six or eight stanzas, and a new
melody or a foreign melody that is
no longer current.

Only one Occitan *pastorela* survives with music, a song by the early troubadour Marcabru, "L'autrier just' una sebissa" (Example 4–4).[31] The twelve stanzas and two *tornadas* of this song (far exceeding the limit proposed in the *Doctrina*) are narrated by the *seignor*, who relates a conversation he had with a peasant girl, here called a "vilana," a word that functions as a word-refrain at the end of verse 4 in all the stanzas. All of verse 4 functions as a refrain in alternate stanzas: "Seigner, so.m dis la vilana." The girl resists the lord's advances through ten stanzas, then responds to his offer in stanza XI to "become equals" by agreeing in stanza XII, but cleverly turns the offer around by pointing out that he will become *her* equal, that is, a "vilans." It is a straightforward but witty text, using sophisticated language and structural features. It deals with a tension between upper and lower classes, but all in a courtly idiom— a *grand chant courtois* with rustic subject and characters.

Its melody is similar to others by Marcabru, with conjunct motion, a syllabic texture, phrase repetition, a moderate pitch range, and repeated notes. It is tonally uncomplicated as well: four of the seven verses begin with reiterations of middle C, which is the tune's tonal center (compare his PC 293,35, which also has tonal centers of C and A). The ABABCCD structure of the music mirrors the prominent alternating structure of the poem. The syllabic style allows the poem to move forward quickly, except at the end of the final verse, which is decorated with a short melisma. This lingering at the end of the melody, along with the singular final pitch of A, might reflect the rather unexpected twist at the end of the poem, where the lord escapes in humiliation. As indicated in the diplomatic transcription, the scribe's attempt in manuscript R to use mensural notation for this song possibly reflects the late date of the manuscript.

In the description of the *planh*, the *Doctrina* author allows the use of a preexistent melody, except for that of a *dansa* (see below).[32] We can infer that, with love as its central theme—but specifically the death of a loved one—the same materials can be used as, say, in a *canso*:

Si vols fer plant, d'amor o de tristor deus la raho continuar; e pot[z] lo fer en qual so te vulles, salvant de dança. E atressi potz lo fer d'aytantes cobles con la [un] dels damunt dits cantars, e en contrasembles o en dessemblants. E no.y deus mesclar altra raho sino plahien, si per comp[ar]acio no.y ho podies portar.[33]

If you want to compose a *planh*, the theme must be about love or about sorrow throughout; and you can make it to any tune you wish, except that of a *dansa*. And likewise you can make it with as many stanzas as one of the other songs, corresponding or not [i.e., on same or different rhyme]. And you must not mix in another theme besides mourning, unless you can bring it in through a comparison.

EX. 4–4. Marcabru. PC 293,30. R fol. 5.

1. L'au-trier just' u - na se - bis - sa. 2. tro-bey pas - to - ra mes - tis - sa.

3. de joi e de sen mas-sis - sa. 4. e fon fi - lha de vi - la - na.

5. cap' e go - ne - la pe - lis - sa.

6. vest e ca - mi - za tres - lis - sa.

7. sot - lars e caus - sas de la - na. II. Ves lieys vau

Translation Frederick Goldin, *Lyrics of the Troubadours and Trouvères*, 70.

I. L'autrier just' una sebissa,
trobey pastora mestissa
de joi e de sen massissa;
e fon filha de vilaina,
cap' e gonela pelissa,
vest e camiza treslissa,
sotlars e causas de laina.

The other day, beside a row of hedges, I found a shepherdess of lowly birth, full of joy and common sense. And like the daughter of a woman of the fields, she wore cape and cloak and fur, and a shift of drill, and shoes, and woolen stockings.

II. Ves lieys vau pcr la planissa.
"Toza, fi.m ieu, re faytissa,
dol ay gran del ven qu.eus fissa."
"Senher, so dis la vilayna,
merce Dieu e ma noirissa,
pauc m'o pres si.l ven m'erissa,
c'alegreta soi e sayna."

I came to her across the level ground. "Girl," I said, "beautiful, I am unhappy because the cold is piercing you." "Lord," this peasant's child said to me, "thanks be to God and the woman who nursed me, it's nothing to me if the wind ruffles my hair, because I feel good, and I'm healthy."

III. "Toza, fi.m ieu, cauza pia,
destoutz me soy de la via
per far a·vos companhia;

"Girl," I said, "you're sweet and innocent, I came out of my way to keep you company; for a peasant

car aytal toza vilayna
non pot ses parelh paria
pastoriar tainta bestia
e.l aytal loc tan soldayna."

girl like you should not, without a
comrade near by, pasture so many
cattle all alone in such a place."

IV. "Don, fay sela, qui que sia,
ben conosc sen e folia;
la vostra parelhayria,
Senher, so dis la vilaina,
lay on se tanh si s'estia;
que tal la cui en baylia
tener no.n a mays l'ufayna."

"Master," she said, "whatever I may
be, I can tell sense from foolishness.
Your comradeship, Lord," said this
girl of the fields and pastures, "let it
stay where it belongs, for such as I,
when she thinks she has it for herself,
has nothing but the look of it."

* * * *

* * * *

VII. "Toza, fi.m ieu, gentil fada
vos adastrec can fos nada
d'una beutat esmerada
sobre tot' autra vilayna;
e seria.us be doblada
si.m vezia una vegada
sobiras e vos sotraina."

"Girl," I said, "a gentle fairy endowed
you at birth with your beauty, which
is pure beyond every other peasant
girl. And yet you would be twice as
beautiful if once I saw you under-
neath and me on top."

VIII. "Senher, tan m'avetz lauzada,
[que tota.n seri' enveiada]
pus en pretz m'avetz levada,
so ditz la toza vilayna;
per tal n'auret per soldada
al partir bada, fol, bada,
e la muz' a meliayna."

"Lord, you have praised me so high,
how everyone would envy me! Since
you have driven up my worth, my
Lord," said this peasant girl, "for that
you will have as your reward: 'Gape,
fool, gape,' as we part, and waiting
and waiting the whole afternoon."

* * * *

* * * *

XI. "Toza, tota creatura
revert segon sa natura;
parlem ab paraula pura
fi.m ieu tozeta vilayna;
a l'abric lonc la pastura
que miels n'estaretz segura
per far la cauza dossayna."

"Girl, every creature reverts to its
nature: let us become a couple of
equals, you and I, my peasant girl, in
the cover there, by the pasture, you
will feel more at ease there where we
do the sweet you know what."

XII. "Don, oc, mas segon drechura
serca fol sa folatura,
cortes cortez' aventura,
e.l vilans ab la vilayna;
e mans locs fay so fraytura
que no.y esgarda mezura,
so dis la gen ansiayna."

"Master, yes; but, as it is right, the fool
seeks out his foolishness, a man of the
court, his courtly adventure; and let
the peasant be with his peasant girl.
'Good sense suffers from disease
where men do not observe degrees':
that's what the ancients say."

XIII. "Bela, de vostra figura
non vi autra pus tafura
ni de son cor pus trefayna."

"Girl, I never saw another more
roguish in her face or more false in
her heart."

XIV. "Don, lo m'avetz nos satura.
que tals bad' en la penchura.
c'autre n'espera la mayna."

"Master, that owl is making you a
prophecy: this one stands gaping in
front of a painting, and that one
waits for manna."

Only two *planhs* survive with music, both laments on the death of a lord or patron, which is outside the strict definition of theme given in the *Doctrina*. The melody of Gaucelm Faidit's famous *planh* on the death of Richard Coeur-de-Lion in 1199, "Fortz chauza es que tot lo major dan" (Example 4–5), survives in three of the four main music manuscripts.[34] The three versions of the melody are remarkably concordant in contours, intonations, and cadences. The style in general is similar to that of Gaucelm's other melodies: it is neumatic in texture (although with a few melismas, in contrast to his other melodies), has many thirds and descending triads, is based on D, has a range of about an octave, and has repeated notes at the beginning.

The melody, though, is quite unsettled tonally until the end. The version in manuscripts W and X ends on C, while the other version (including the *contrafacta*) ends on D. This instability might suggest that the melody was not heard as being complete until the final stanza, that a performer might have ended each stanza on C until the final note. A striking melodic feature is the semitone below C that occurs at a structurally prominent point at the end of verse 7, which in stanza I expresses the most poignant sentiment of loss—the B here, followed by a leap up a tritone to F in most versions, seems to express the disharmony of the text directly. Two phrases end by a move upward to a cadence on E, again creating a sense of incompletion. The *caesura* in verse 6 of stanza I, on the words "lo ric valen Richart," is articulated by a drop of a perfect fifth, on which the voice almost by necessity lingers. Something similar occurs in verse 7, where the phrase "es morç" that completes the *enjambement* of verse 6 is followed by the exclamation "a Deus" with a leap of a fourth or a major sixth (depending on the version).[35]

The other extant *planh* with a melody is Guiraut Riquier's "Ples de tristor marritz e doloiros" (PC 248,63), composed on the death in 1270 of Amalric, viscount of Narbonne. Its melody shares some characteristics of Gaucelm's *planh*, including a similar range, a tonal center of D, and a neumatic texture (melismatic and neumatic textures are typical of

EX. 4–5. Gaucelm Faidit. PC 167,22. X fol. 87; G fol. 29v.

I. Fort chausa oiaz e tot lo major dan,
et major dol, las, q'eu anc mais aues,
e so que eu degra dir en ploran,
m'aven a dir en chantan e retraire
qe cil q'era de valors caps e paire,
lo ric valen Richart, rei dels Engles,
es morç, a Deus, qal perda e qal dan
   es;
com estraing mot con salvage ad auzi,
ben a dur cor toz hom qe.l pot soffrir.

II. Morç es lo rei, e son passat mil an
q'anc si grans dol ni fo, ni no vi res,

I have just heard about such a great
loss, alas, and the greatest sorrow
that I have ever had, that I must
speak in song, weeping, and recount
that he who was the chief and father
of valor, the noble, valiant Richard,
king of the English, is dead, oh God,
such a loss and such sorrow! Such a
terrible word, so cruel to hear, that
whoever can bear it has a hard heart
indeed.

The king is dead, and a thousand
years have passed since there has

EX. 4–5. Continued

1. Fort chausa oi - az e tot lo ma - jor dan.

2. et ma - jor dol las q'eu anc mais a - ves.

3. e so que eu de - gra dir en plo - ran.

4. m'a-ven a dire en chan - tan e re - trai - re.

5. qe cil q'e - ra de va - lors caps e pai - re.

6. lo ric va - len Ri - chart rei dels En - gles.

7. es morç. a Deus. qal perda e qal dan es.

8. com es - traing mot con sal - vage ad au - zir.

9. ben a dur cor toz hom qe.l pot sos - frir.

ni ja no er mais hom del seu semblan,
tan larcs, tan rics, tan ardiz, tal
    donaire;
q'Alixandres lo rei qi venqet Daire
non cre qanc tan dones ni tan mises,
ni anc Karle ni Artus tan valgues;
q'a tot lo mond se feç qi vol ver dir,
als un dotar et als autre graçir.

been such a great sorrow, or since
such a thing happened, or indeed
since there was a man like him, so
generous, so noble, so brave, so
meritorious; I don't believe that even
Alexander, who conquered Darius,
was so generous or so giving, nor
was Charlemagne or Arthur so
noble; for throughout the world, in
truth, he made some fear and others
praise.

III. Merueil me q'el fals segle truan
ausa estar savis hom ni cortes

It is a great marvel to me that in this
wicked world there could be a man

pois ren no val beill diç ne faiz presan;
a dunc per que s'esfor chan pauc ni
  gaire,
qe or nos a mostrat morç que pot
  faire
q'a un colp a tut lo meil del mon pres
tota l'amor toz lo prez toz lo bes;
e pois veçem que ren non pot gandir,
ben deuira.m meiz doptat a morir.

* * * *

VII. Ai, Segner Reis, res verais
  Cabdelaire,
vera Vida, vera Lux e Merces,
vos faça cel perdon qe cuiços es,
si qel peçad se oblide el falir,
e menbre vos con vos anet servir.

so wise and so courtly, since he
gained nothing from pretty words or
valorous deeds; which is why I am
enjoined to sing, such as I can, for
now death has shown us what it can
do, in suddenly taking from the
world its best; and since we see that
nothing can stop it, we should well
fear to die.

* * * *

Oh, Lord King, true Knight, true
Life, true Light and Mercy, pardon
him who is in need, if sin caused
him to stumble, and remember him
who wished only to serve you.

Guiraut's music in general; see Chapter 6). In a way similar to the
emphasis on Richard's name in Gaucelm Faidit's *planh*, Guiraut highlights with a melisma the provenance of his song's subject, the word
refrain "Narbona" at the end of verse 5, and articulates the subject's
name, "lo vescomte n'Amalric," syllabically in verse 6.

The *alba* is supposed to fall in the epideictic category of praise
and blame, according to the *Doctrina*, but rather than praise the dawn
itself, as the treatise instructs, the extant *albas* praise or blame the
personages involved—the lady, the lover, the cuckolded husband, or
the watcher:

Si vols far alba, parla d'amor
plazentment; e atressi lauzar la dona
on vas o de que la faras. E bendi
l'alba si acabes lo plazier per lo qual
anaves a ta dona; e si no.l acabes, fes
l'alba blasman la dona e l'alba on
anaves. E potz hi fer aytantes cobles
com te vulles, e deus hi fer so
novell.[36]

If you want to compose an *alba*,
speak pleasantly of love; and so
praise the lady to whom or about
whom you compose it. And praise
the dawn if you have won the
pleasure for which you went to your
lady; and if you do not win it, make
the *alba* censure the lady and the
dawn where you went. And you can
compose it in as many stanzas as
you wish, and it must have a new
melody.

The most famous Occitan *alba* with a surviving melody is Guiraut
de Bornelh's "Reis glorious" (Example 4–6), one of only four melodies

EX. 4–6. Guiraut de Bornelh. PC 242,64. R fol. 8v.

I. Rei glorios, veray lums e clartatz,
totz poderos, Senher, si a vos platz,
al mieu compaynh sias fizels aiuda,
qu'ieu non lo vi pus la nuech fo
   venguda,
et ades sera l'alba.

II. Bel companho, si dormetz o
   velhatz,
no dormas pus, senher, si a vos platz;
qu'en aurien vey l'estela creguda
c'adus lo jorn, qu'ieu l'ay ben
   conoguda;
et ades sera l'alba.

III. Bel companho, en chantan vos
   apel;
non durmas pus, qu'ieu aug chantar
   l'auzel
que vay queren lo jorn per lo boscatie,
et ay paor que.l gilos vos assatie;
et ades sera l'alba.

IV. Bel companho, pos mi parti de vos
yeu no.m durmi ni.m muoc de
   ginolhos,
ans pregieu Dieu, lo filh Santa Maria,

Glorious King, true light and
splendor, almighty God, Lord, if it
please you, be a faithful help to my
companion, for I have not seen him
since the night came on, and soon it
will be dawn.

Fair friend, whether you sleep or
wake, sleep no more, I pray you; in
the east I see the star growing that
brings the day, which I knew well;
and soon it will be dawn.

Fair friend, in song I call you; sleep
no more, for I hear the bird sing,
which I see seeking the day in the
woods, and I fear that the jealous
one will attack you; and soon it will
be dawn.

Fair friend, since I left you I have not
slept or risen from my knees, but I
have prayed that God, the son of
Holy Mary, might return you to me

que.us mi rendes per lial companhia;
et ades sera l'alba.

in loyal friendship; and soon it will
be dawn.

V. Bel companho, issetz al fenestrel
et esgardatz las ensenhas del sel;
conoysiret sieu soy fizel messatie;
si non o faytz, vostres er lo
  dampnatie;
et ades sera l'alba.

Fair friend, go the window and look
at the signs in the sky: you will know
if I am your faithful messenger. If
you do not do this, yours will be the
harm; and soon it will be dawn.

VI. Bel companho, la foras al peiro
me preiavatz qu'ieu no fos dormilhos,
enans velhes tota nueg tro ad dia;
ara no.us platz mos chans ni ma paria;
et ades sera l'alba.

Fair friend, out there by the steps you
begged me not to be sleepy, but to
keep watch through the night until
day; now neither my song nor my
company pleases you; and soon it
will be dawn.

VII. Bel dos companh, tan soy en ric
  sojorn
qu'ieu no volgra mays fos alba ni jorn;
car la genser que anc nasques de
  mayre
tenc et abras, per qu'ieu non prezi
  gaire.
lo fol gilos ni l'alba.

Fair sweet friend, I am in such a
precious situation that I wish no
more for the dawn or day; for I hold
and embrace the most noble woman
that ever was born of a mother, so I
hardly regard the crazy jealous one
or the dawn.

---

of his to survive. The stanzas of this poem are paired by rhyme scheme (*coblas doblas*; see Chapter 5), and as is often the case in such a structure, the contents of the paired stanzas are similar: stanza I is an appeal to God in the manner of an *exordium*; stanza II is an appeal to the lover; stanzas III and IV express warnings and an appeal to trust the messenger; stanzas V and VI restate the warnings and appeals. The final verse of the first six stanzas is a refrain, "et ades sera l'alba." Stanza VII (which may be spurious) departs altogether in its rhyme sounds, its incipit, its speaker (the lover), and its final verse, which retains only the final word, "alba," of the refrain.

    In contrast to Guiraut's other melodies, the structure of this one is much simpler, perhaps because it has only five verses per stanza, as opposed to the eight to ten in his other three poems that survive with music. It is more melismatic than his other melodies, though, especially at the cadences; and its first phrase spans an unusually wide range of a seventh. The pairing of structure and content between the *coblas doblas* is matched by the musical pairing of verses 1 and 2, and of verses 3 and 4: The first two phrases are identical, while verses 3 and 4 are linked by common material that occurs at the beginning of verse 3 (syllables 1–3) and the middle of verse 4 (syllables 5–8). Verse 5, the refrain, begins like verse 4, but ends with a melisma on the word "alba." Stanzas II–VI all begin with the phrase "Bel companho," addressed from the watcher to the lover, stanza VII with "Bel dous companh," spoken by the lover to the watcher; these invocations (which articulate the *caesura*) are highlighted by an upward leap of a fifth. The same leap occurs at the beginning of verse 2, and each of the stanzas has a clear *caesura* here as well, with an imperative in stanzas II, III, and V ("no dormatz plus," "e regardatz") that summarizes the watcher's concern for the lover's safety, and a whine in stanzas IV and VI that invokes the lover's sympathy ("eu no.m dormi," "me preiavatz").

The other extant *alba* melody, which also appears in manuscript R, is the only song by Cadenet whose melody survives (PC 106,14). Its stanzas are longer than Guiraut's, nine verses as compared to five, and the rhyme sounds of the first four verses change with each stanza. While the arrival of the dawn is the recurring theme in all stanzas, the content of this *alba* contrasts with that of Guiraut's song. Instead of the topos of the faithful watcher who warns the lover of the coming of the dawn, here we find a lady unhappily married to "un vilan," who wishes for a "fin amic"—a faithful friend—to whom she can reveal her pain and who will watch with her (while enjoying intimacy) and signal the coming of the dawn. The watcher replies, boasting of his status as the lady's lover, and declares his fidelity. Josef Zemp has noted the aristocratic register of the text, even while it partakes of the low-level topos of the *mal mariée*—even referring to the ill-bred husband as the "mals maritz."[37] This melody's range, tonal center, and overall structure and contour are strikingly reminiscent of Guiraut de Bornelh's *alba*, enough to suggest that Cadenet's melody may have been derived at least partly from Guiraut's.[38] But with four more verses per stanza than in Guiraut's poem, Cadenet's requires more music. Its middle verses explore the higher range, which is avoided in Guiraut's melody, and the musical contrast provided thereby is similar to the poetic contrast in the middle stanzas, whose speaker is the watcher/lover rather than the lady—a contrast missing from Guiraut's poem and melody.

When one sings a *descort*, the *Doctrina* says, "wherever the tune ought to rise, make it low." This suggests that the contour of the melody somehow should reflect the reverse of what the text connotes, to reinforce the discordant *razo*:

Si vols far discort, deus parlar d'amor com a hom qui n'es desemparat e com a hom qui no pot haver plaser de sa dona e viu turmentatz. E que en lo cantar, lla hon lo so deuria muntar, que.l baxes;	If you want to compose a *descort*, you must speak of love, as a man who is separated from it or a man who cannot have pleasure from his lady and is tormented. And when in the song the tune ought to rise, make

e fe lo contrari de tot l'altre cantar. E
deu haver tres cobles e una o dues
tornades e responedor. E potz metre
un o dos motz mes en una cobla que
en altra, per ço que mils sia discordant.[39]

it low; make it do the opposite of all
other songs. And it must have three
stanzas and one or two *tornadas* and a
refrain. And you can put one or two
more words in one stanza than in
another, to make it more discordant.

The *Donatz Proensals* of Uc Faidit includes the word *descort* in its rhyme
lists, with the Latin translation "discordia, vel cantilena habens sonos
diversos" (discord, or a song having different sounds).[40]

One of the three extant *descorts* that have been transmitted with
melodies is "Qui la ve en ditz" by Aimeric de Peguilhan (PC 10,45),[41]
which survives with two different melodies in two different manuscripts. Part of the "disharmony" of Aimeric's song might rest in the
"tortured expressions" made necessary by the structural constraints of
short verses, some of which consist of a single-syllable rhyme word:
"bes," "ges," "es," "res," etc.—a device uncharacteristic of Aimeric.[42]
The subject of the poem is unrequited love, the cruelty and deceit of
Lady Beatriz (of Este), and the despair and bitterness of the lover. R
transmits three stanzas for this poem, W only the first two (to which
were added two additional stanzas, perhaps not by Aimeric).[43] The
melody for this poem that is transmitted in manuscript R has a paired-
versicle structure, AABBBBCCCC (possibly reflecting the propensity of
R's music scribe for regularized structures), but it is strophic, repeated
for all stanzas. This melody does not embody any obvious word- or
phrase-painting that would meet the theorist's requirement of descending where it should rise, or vice versa.[44]

The melody for "Qui la ve en ditz" in manuscript W (Example 4–7)
is much less coherent than the one in R. It is through-composed rather
than strophic, and it has numerous unexpected leaps upwards and
downwards, at the beginnings and ends of phrases, and at different
pitch levels: perfect fourths and fifths D–A, F–C, G–D, F–B♭, and C–G
(ascending and descending); thirds F–A, B♭–D, A–C, G–B♭, and C–A; and
sixths C–A and F–D. Stanza I moves to stanza II with a leap of a minor
seventh. There is no obvious tonal center consistent from phrase to
phrase, and the second stanza includes more added B♭s, which create a
marked modal shift. The texture is almost wholly syllabic; thus the
single-syllable verses have no preparation as they do in R, and would
probably strike the ear as being very abrupt (as they seem to be in the
poem itself). In these senses this melody is certainly "discordant." As in
R, there is no clear-cut word-painting that might conform to the prescription in the *Doctrina*. A striking feature of W's melody is its mensural
notation, which also sets it apart from the melody in R.[45]

A few other genres are defined in the *Doctrina* in some way by their
razos, including the *vers*, *lay*, *estampida*, and *sirventes*, none of which is

EX. 4–7. Aimeric de Peguilhan. PC 10,45, stanza I. W fol. 185/B170.

Translation William P. Shepard and Frank M. Chambers, *Aimeric de Peguilhan*, 215.

I. Whoever has seen her says of her: If God put so many good qualities in Lady Beatrice, there is no mercy in her at all. Her graceful, courtly body is so nobly formed that no pleasure which did not include her would be complete.

Her sweet, bright, cordial glance, flower of the noblest, would give pleasure to obscure words, such is its sweetness. Since her honored honor, raised

EX. 4–7. Continued

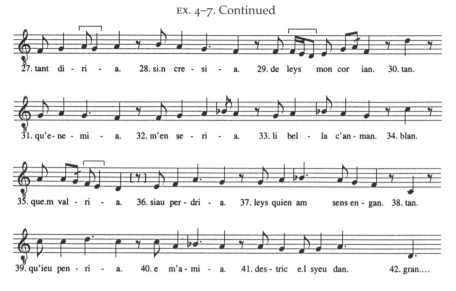

higher than Honor itself, and her graciousness, are equally pleasing, no favor from another would help me much.

If I should believe my own heart, I should say so much about her in my song that the fair lady whom I adore as a lover would be my enemy.

What avail would it be to her, if I should lose her whom I love without guile? I should get thereby great distress of mind and great harm in my love.

---

supposed to be about love specifically. They each draw on the epideictic class of praise and blame, as do a great many love songs as well. The *lay* is distinguished in the *Doctrina* by a didactic or religous theme:

Si vols fer lays, deus parlar de Deu e de segle, o de eximpli o de proverbis, de lausors ses feyment d'amor, que sia axi plazent a Deu co al segle; e deus saber que.s deu far e dir ab contriccio tota via, e ab so novell e plazen, o de esgleya o d'autra manera. E sapies que.y ha mester aytantes cobles com en la canço, e aytantes tornades; e segueix la raho e la manera axi com eu t'ay dit.[46]

If you want to compose a *lay*, you must speak of God or of the world, or of examples or proverbs, of praise without pretense of love, which thus would be pleasing to God as well as the world; and you should know that you must compose and speak always with contrition, and use a new and pleasing melody, or one of the church or another type. And know that it must have as many stanzas as a *canso*, and as many *tornadas*; and follow the theme and manner as I have told you.

The three surviving Old Occitan *lays*, two of which survive with music, however, are love songs. As they are transmitted in manuscript W these two songs are corrupt in both text and melody; the music scribe was hard pressed to enter a coherent melody at some points because of difficulties created by errors in the text.[47] The melodies of these two anonymous songs, the "Lai Markiol" (PC 461,124) and "Lai Non-par" (PC 461,122) have irregular repetition structures that are similar to that of the late sequence; they also foreshadow the later *lai* as it was standardized by Guillaume de Machaut, in that the melody for the first stanza is repeated, with some variation, for the last stanza. Bec asserts that both of these melodies—and perhaps the genre itself—probably had northern origins (and indeed both are found in French sources).[48]

The "Lai Non-par" (stanzas I and III are given in Example 4–8)[49] utters sorrow over the poet's separation from his lady because of his departure for the Holy Land. In expressive language, he addresses the lady, God, and his listeners, but mostly waxes eloquent about his lady's virtues (contrary to the instructions in the *Doctrina*). The melody of this *lai* is simple, conjunct, with many repeated notes, beginning in a recitational style. Besides repeating the music of entire stanzas three times, the author reuses musical material almost formulaically in places; and he often repeats short phrases quickly, perhaps in reflection of the poetic structure.

These examples could be multiplied, but others could be brought forward that do not so easily illustrate the theorist's statements that the melody should serve the *razo* of the text. The point of these examples, though, is that the music and the poem each progressed through time, developing their particular materials in the service of a common subject matter. Sometimes the poetic and musical themes and arguments harmonize in ways that are obvious to us today, but often they do not. The strophic repetition of the melody overlaid on the single iteration of the text provides a multilayered texture to the unfolding of the topoi in the music and those in the poem, and the tension created by the different speeds at which the music and the text reveal their materials helps propel the song forward.

Melody Borrowing

Other considerations entered into the *Doctrina* author's thinking about the role a melody should play in service of a genre. For almost every genre he declares whether one could use a borrowed melody or should compose a new one, suggesting that a preexistent melody by its very nature or because of its origins might or might not enhance the type to which it is transferred. He frowns upon borrowing a tune for a *canso*, *vers*, *retroncha*, *alba*, *estampida*, *dansa*, and *descort*. For other serious types,

EX. 4–8. Anonymous. PC 461,122, stanzas I and III. W fol. 213v–214/ B207v–208.

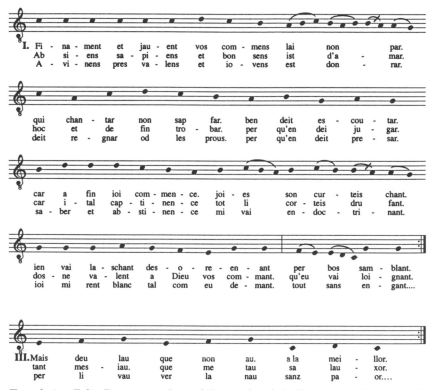

Translation Felip Daumas, in Ismael Fernández de la Cuesta, *Las Cançons dels Trobadors*, 763.

I. With a delicate joy, I begin for you a lay that will be without par. He who does not know how to compose a song must listen carefully for here begins, with delicate joy, a precious melody, a courteous song. I am now leaving straightway.

Along with the men who are wise and knowledgeable and the persons of good sense I quit loving—yes, and making poetry—and thus must I be judged. For all courteous lovers have the same attitude. Honoured dame, I recommend you to God as I am going far away.

Pleasing worth and youth of the heart must reign supreme, along with generosity, among the valiant knights, for they are all the more esteemed for it. Wisdom and abstinence give me their lessons; joy of love is at my service for my request is without treachery.

* * * *

III. But I thank God that I do not hear you; I rejoice so much in the best lady that I celebrate her praise. Thanks to her, I embark without fear.

including the *sirventes, lay, pastora*, and *planh*, however, the theorist says melody borrowing is acceptable, perhaps even expected.

For a *sirventes*, for example, the theorist says that only exceptionally (*specialment*) is the tune newly composed. The poetic modeling that takes place in the composition of a *sirventes* is well known, and this dependence on a preexistent structural scheme is generally thought of as the fundamental generative principle.[50] But the *Doctrina's* wording suggests that the borrowed melody provides the basic structural ingredient for the new *sirventes*, and that the rhyme sounds themselves need not be copied:

Si vols far sirventez, deus parlar de fayt d'armes, e senyalladament o de lausor de senyor o de maldit o de qualsque feyts qui novellament se tracten. E començaras ton cantar segons que usaran aquells dels quals ton serventez començaras; e per proverbis e per exemples poretz hi portar les naturaleses que fan, o ço de que fan a rependre o a lausar aquells dels quals ton serventez començaras. E sapies que.l potz fer d'aytantes cobles co la un d'aquestz cantars que.t he mostratz. E pot[z] lo far en qualque so te vulles; e specialment se fa en so novell, e maiorment en ço de canço. E deus lo far d'aytantes cobles com sera lo cantar de que pendras lo so; e potz seguir las rimas contrasemblantz del cantar de que pendras lo so, o atressi lo potz far en altres rimes.[51]	If you want to compose a *sirventes*, you must speak of feats of arms, and in particular either of praise of a lord or of calumny or of some new deeds. And begin your song following the customs of those with whom you begin your *sirventes*; and by proverbs and examples you can bring in the allegiances they swore, or reprove or praise the deeds of those with whom you begin your *sirventes*. And know that you can make as many stanzas as one of the other songs I discussed. And you can compose it to whatever tune you wish, rarely a new melody, and chiefly that of a *canso*. And you must give it as many stanzas as there are in the song from which you took the melody; and you can follow the rhymes corresponding to the song from which you took the melody, or you can make other rhymes.

A little later the theorist even argues that the very name *sirventes* derives partly from the fact that the new song "is subordinated to" the model song—here implying that the rhymes as well as the melody are in fact adopted in the new song:

Serventetz es dit per ço serventetz per ço com se serveix e es sotsmes a aquell cantar de qui pren lo so e les rimes, e per ço cor deu parlar de senyors o de vassalls, blasman o castigan o lauzan o mostran, o de faytz d'armes o de guerra o de Deu o de ordenances o de novelletatz.[52]	A *sirventes* is so called because it serves and is subordinated to the song from which the melody and rhymes are taken, and because it must speak of lords or of vassals, blame or chastisement or praise or proofs, or of feats of arms or of war or of God or of laws or of justice.

There are at least two notable ideas in these statements. First of all, the *razo* of a *sirventes* is not love, as it is in the *canso*, according to the *Doctrina*, but war, politics, religion, morality, etc. It is not difficult to imagine how structural poetic elements like rhymes and stanza schemes can be used to express such radically different themes, but less obvious how the melody of a love song can be turned to a political or moral purpose. Here again there is not an identifiable musical style that inherently expresses a single *razo*, but musical materials can be assembled in such a way as to enhance the "arguments" of the poem. Further, a progression of topoi in a love song might be reflected in a similar development of topoi in a *sirventes*, so that a single melody can unfold one text as effectively as the other.

Another salient point about the *Doctrina's* discussion is the interdependence of text and melody implied both about the *canso* and the *sirventes*, an interdependence that requires respect for the integrity of both text and melody. The melody not only retains its identity and integrity in the new song but indeed manifests its own flexibility in being able to express the sentiments of a new poem with an altogether different kind of *razo*.

Twenty-five *sirventes* survive with melodies, most of them without extant musical models. One tune occurs twice with different texts in a single chansonnier (manuscript R), separated by 34 leaves (see Example 4–9). Bertran de Born's "Rassa, tan creis e mont' e puoia" (PC 80,37) was used later by the Monge de Montaudon as a model for another *sirventes*, "Fort m'enoja, so auzes dire" (PC 305,10), and both texts use essentially the same melody; the text scribe added a message, presumably to the notator, at the end of the Monk's text: "el so de la Rassa."

This *contrafactum* demonstrates how one troubadour devised a new poem for a borrowed melody, and how creative a poet might be within the prescribed structural bounds. "Rassa" is in spirit a *canso*, although Bertran himself seems not to have differentiated among genres by theme per se.[53] Addressed by its *senhal* to Geoffrey of Brittany, the song has a moralizing tone, while it offers praise of noble women and men who serve love well. The first three stanzas praise the noble lady;[54] stanza IV is a complaint about selfish, ungenerous lords. The final stanza begins with a description of a noble lord and ends with an exhortation to Viscount Aigar V of Limoges to defend his property in the struggles among Richard Coeur-de-Lion, the Young Henry, and the French and Occitanian barons. The Monk's *sirventes* adopts the annoyance that Bertran expresses in stanza IV as the theme for all nine stanzas of his song—complaining of chatterers, slow horses, boasters, flatterers, bad meat, worn-out prostitutes, cold winters, bad fiddle players, etc.—all markedly more sour in tone than Bertran's song.

The melody used for these poems is syllabic, with many repeated

EX. 4–9. Bertran de Born. PC 80,37, R fol. 6v; and Monge de Montaudon,
PC 305,10, R fol. 40.

Text and translation William D. Paden, *Bertran de Born*, 196–203.

I. Rassa, tant creis e mont' e poia
cella q'es de totz engans voia
sos pretz a las autras enoia;
c'una non i a c'alre.i voia.

Rassa, she who is free of all deceits
so grows and rises and ascends that
her merit annoys other women;
there is not a one to whom she must

Qe.l vezers de sa beltat loia
los pros a sos ops, cui que doia.
Qe.l plus conoissen e.il meillor
mantenran ades sa lauzor,
e la tenont per la genssor,
qu'il sap far tan entier' honor:
non vol mas un sol preiador.

concede any advantage. No matter what ladies she teaches a thing or two, the sight of her beauty draws the noblemen into her service. The true connoisseurs and the best will always sound her praise; they consider her the most noble, since she knows how to bestow such undivided honor: she desires one suitor alone.

II. Rassa, als rics es orgoillosa,
et a gran sen a lei de tosa,
qui non vol Peitieus ni Tolosa
ni Bretaigna ni Serragosa.
Anz es de pretz tant enveiosa
q'alz pros paubres es amorosa.
Pois m'a pres per chastiador
prec la qu'il tengua car s'amor,
et am mais un pro vavassor
q'un comt' o duc galiador
que la tengues a desonor.

Rassa, she is proud towards the mighty, and she has a lot of good sense, as young girls do, for she does not want Poitiers or Toulouse or Brittany or Saragossa. But she so values merit that she opens her heart toward the valiant poor. Since she has taken me as her counselor, I pray her to hold dear her love, and to prefer a valiant vavasor to a treacherous count or duke, who might hold her in dishonor.

III. Rassa, dompna q'es fresc' e fina,
coinda e gaia e mesquina,
pel saur ab color de robina,
blanca pel col cum flors d'espina,
coide mol ab dura tetina,
e sembla conil de l'esquina,
e a fina, fresca color,
ab bon pretz et ab gran lauzor,
leu podon triar l'i meillor
aquil qe.is fant conoissedor
de mi, vas cal part q'ieu ador.

Rassa, those who pretend to know about me, and whom I adore, will easily pick her out as the best, a lady who is fresh and fine, pretty and gay and young—golden hair with a ruby sheen, neck as white as a hawthorn bloom, soft arms and firm breasts—and who looks like a rabbit from the spine, and has delicate, fresh color, with a good reputation and high fame.

IV. Rassa, rics hom que ren non
    dona,
ni acuoill ni met ni non sona,
e qui senes tort ochaisona,
e, qui merce.il qier, non perdona,
m'enoia, e tota persona
qe servizi non guizerdona.
E li ric home cassador
m'enoiont, e.il buzatador,
gaban de volada d'austor;
ni ja mais d'armas ni d'amor
non parlaran mot entre lor.

Rassa, a mighty man who gives nothing, who neither entertains nor spends nor invites, and who makes accusations without reason, and does not pardon someone who asks his mercy—this man annoys me, and so does anybody who does not reward service. And the mighty hunters annoy me, and people who hunt with harriers, making fun of the goshawk's flight; none of these will ever say a word of arms or love among themselves.

V. Rassa, aisso.us prec que vos
  plassa:
rics hom que de gerra no.is lassa,
ni no s'en laissa per menassa,
tro c'om se lais que mal no.il fassa,
val mais que ribieira ni cassa,
que bon pretz n'acuoill e n'amassa.
Maurin e n'Agar, son seignor,
ten hom per bon envazidor.
E.l vescoms defenda s'onor,
e.l coms l'apelle per vigor,
e veiam l'ades al pascor.

Rassa, will you agree with this: a
mighty man who does not tire of war,
or give it up for a threat before his
enemies cease to harm him, is worth
more than the falconer on the river-
bank or the hunter, for he gains good
fame and piles it up. People think of
Maurin, and Sir Aigar, his lord, as
good fighters. Let the viscount defend
his fief, and the count demand it with
force, and let's see it now in the
spring.

Text Martín de Riquer, *Los trovadores*, II, 1028–1029.

I. Fort m'enoia, s'o auzes dire,
parliers quant es avols servire;
et hom que trop vol autr'aucire
m'enoia, e cavals que tire;
et enoia.m, si Dieus m'ajut,
joves hom quan trop port' escut
que negun colp no.i a avut,
capellan e monge barbut,
e lausengier bec esmolut.

I am annoyed a great deal, if I dare
say it, by a babbler when he is a poor
servant; and by the man who wants
too much to mistreat others annoys
me, and the horse that balks; and I am
annoyed, God help me, by a young
man who carries around a shield
when he has never received a blow on
it, and a bearded priest and monk,
and a flatterer with a sharp tongue.

II. E tenc dona per enoiosa
quant es paubra et orgoillosa,
e marit qu'ama trop sa sposa,
neus s'era domna de Tolosa;
et enoia.m de cavallier
fors de son pais ufanier,
quant en lo sieu non a mestier
mas sol de pizar el mortier
pebre o d'estar al foguier.

And I consider a lady annoying when
she is both poor and proud, and a
husband who loves his wife too much,
even if it be the lady of Toulouse; and
I am annoyed by the knight who is
pompous outside of his country, when
in his own he has no other occupation
than to crush pepper into powder or
to stay by the hearth.

III. Et enueia.m de fort maneira
hom volpilz quan porta baneira,
et avols austors en ribeira,
e pauca carns en gran caudeira;
et enoia.m, per Saint Marti,
trop d'aiga en petit de vi,
e quan trob escassier mati
m'enoia, e d'orp atressi,
car no m'azaut de lor cami.

And I am annoyed in the strongest
fashion by a cowardly man when he
carries a banner, and a bad goshawk
in a river, and little meat in a large
cauldron; and I am annoyed, by Saint
Martin, by too much water in too little
wine, and when a cripple annoys me
too much in the morning, and
likewise blind men, for they attack me
on their way.

IV. Enoia.m longa tempradura,
e carns quant es mal coita e dura,
e prestre qui men ni.s perjura,
e vielha puta que trop dura;
et enoia.m, per saint dalmatz,
avols hom en trop gran solatz;
e corre quan per via a glatz
e fugir ab cavalh armatz
m'enoia, e.l maldir de datz.

* * * *

And I am annoyed by extended
abstinence, and by meat when it is
badly cooked and hard, and by a
baker who lies and deals falsely, and
by an old prostitute who lives too
long; and I am annoyed, on the holy
vestment, by a wicked man with too
much pleasure; and I am annoyed by
running when the road is icy, and by
fleeing on an armored horse, and by
the curse on dice.

* * * *

pitches, allowing a clear, unencumbered articulation of the words. The stanzas of the Monk's poem are two verses shorter than the stanzas of Bertran's song:

Bertran:	a	a	a	a	a	a	b	b	b	b	b	rhyme
	8'	8'	8'	8'	8'	8'	8	8	8	8	8	syllables
	A	B	C	D	C'	D'	B'	C''	E	F	E'	melody
Monk:	a	a	a	a			b	b	b	b	b	rhyme
	8'	8'	8'	8'			8	8	8	8	8	syllables
	A	B	C	D			B'	C'	E	F	E'	music

The Monk used the same scheme as Bertran, dropping verses 5 and 6 (which continue the a' rhyme). The melody of verses 5 and 6 in Bertran's song are repetitions of verses 3 and 4, except that verse 4 ends on G while verse 6 ends on A—creating an open-closed effect. The adaptation of the melody in the Monk's song omits the musical phrases of verses 5 and 6 and thus eliminates this closure.

There are difficulties with the second part of both melodies, suggesting uncertainty and quite likely error on the part of the scribe (and perhaps also mirroring the shuffling of verses in the b-rhyme portion of the stanzas in this manuscript tradition). There are erasures in both melodies. In verse 7 of the Monk's song the scribe first wrote the melody at the same pitch as Bertran's melody, but then erased the notes and wrote new ones a third lower; the next two phrases are a step lower than in Bertran's melody. The scribe may also have made a mistake in Bertran's melody, whose verse 9 ends with an extra note that might belong to the beginning of verse 10; because there are so many repeated notes, the scribe may have added another A to verse 10 to compensate for the lack of a note. The scribe erased the final note of verse 10 in

Bertran's melody, and since the corresponding place in the Monk's melody is probably at the wrong pitch, it is impossible to be sure what the pitch should be. In any case, it seems reasonable to assume that the melodies *should* be the same here, even if the scribe garbled it in both cases. The two melodies are notated with different clefs and on different locations on the staff, and occasionally have different ligature forms. Clearly the scribe was not copying the melody from fol. 6v onto fol. 40, and may not even have been using a common exemplar for the two melodies.

Another *sirventes* text whose melody survives in manuscript R, Peire Cardenal's "Ricx hom que greu ditz vertat e leu men" (PC 335,49), was modeled on a *canso*, Raimon Jordan's "Vas vos soplei, domna, premieramen" (PC 404,11), whose melody is found in manuscript W (see Example 4–10). Raimon's *canso* addresses the lady, with a typical progression from fear of loss, through devotion, hopelessness, hope, and resignation, to an appeal for mercy and favor. Peire's song is a self-declared *enueg*, contrasting good men to bad, and thematically it seems to bear no relationship at all to the *canso* that was its structural model. Peire evidently simplified the melody, taking out most of the decorative pitches. The melodic structure is the same, although the same kind of pitch variances that can be observed in the Bertran-Monk pair in Example 4–9 occurs here as well, in verses 4, 5, 6, and 8. It seems possible that here also, one scribe or the other (or both) made errors in recording the melodies.

From these two examples one is tempted to suggest that a melody needed to be simple to serve a *sirventes* well. In the first case, the melody was simple to begin with—syllabic, recitational, repetitive. In the second case, the adaptation to a new text was accompanied by a de-coloration of the melody, retaining the same contours but omitting extraneous notes.

Other genres that the author of the *Doctrina* maintains could use borrowed melodies include the *lay*, which he says could use music from a church piece or "another type." Perhaps he had in mind a *lay* such as "Gent me nais" (PC 461,124), which shares its melody with the Latin *lai* "Veritas, equitas, largitas" and whose text appeals to God (although its subject is love). A *pastora* tune can be borrowed as well, according to the *Doctrina*: "so novell o so estrayn ia passat." This reference to a "foreign tune no longer current" may suggest a connection with the French repertoire of *pastourelles*, which is considerably larger than the Occitan body of extant *pastorela* melodies.[55] The phrase also may refer to the genre's popular origins, although in the *art de trobar* it occupied a courtly idiom.

As pointed out earlier, the *Doctrina* says that a *planh* should not borrow the melody of a *dansa*. This exclusion suggests as much about a *dansa* as it does about a *planh*—perhaps that listeners might hear a *dansa*

EX. 4–10. Raimon Jordan. PC 404,11, W fol. 194/B186; and Peire Cardenal, PC 335,49, R fol. 72.

I. Vers vos souple, dosne,
   premieirement,
per que eu fas e commens ma
   chancon;
et s'il vos plas entendez ma raison
c'altre non aus descovrir mon talent
qu'ensinc m'aven quan vei vostre
   facon;
la langue fal, lou cor ai temorouz,
quer qui non tem non ame coralment,
per oc ten car lou vostre seignorage.

II. Eu vos donai per fei et lealment
mon cors e.l cor, dont faites teneison,
et ai grant joi que sab que sui vostre
   hom,

To you I appeal first, lady, for whom
I compose and begin my song; and
please listen to my story, otherwise I
will not dare disclose my desire, just
like when I see your form. My
tongue fails, my heart is fearful, for
he who does not fear does not love
from the heart; for indeed I cherish
your sovereignty over me.

I have given you faithfully and
loyally my body and heart, of which
you have taken possession; and I
have great joy in knowing that I am

c'uns bons espeirs de vos mi ten
  jauzent;
qu'en bon seignor non pert nus
  guerredon.
qui ben la sert, eu vei mainte saison
povre enrichir per bon atendiment.
per oc effors en vers vos mon corage.

III. Tant ai assis mon desir finament
en vos, dosna, se Deus jauzir m'en
  dons
que mieuz vos am servir tot en
  pardons
que de nule altra afar mon
  mandiment;
car si granz jois retrait mon cor vers
  vos
pos que vos vi non fui ainc poderos;
si desirrous sui de vostre cors gent,
conquis m'avez remaig en vostre
  ostage.

IV. Et sab trop ben qu'eu faz fol
  ardimen.
quan eu la prei d'amors ni mot en son;
mas ainc non pos tornar ma
  sonspecon,
et sab trop ben que travaill per neent;
tant a beltas son gent cors orgueillouz
que son ren pres fait puiar soubre toz,
qu'eu desirrans souspir en espervens,
et temeros que non tegne a folage.

V. Et s'eu folei, eu faz a escient;
sabes per quei e.l m'est bel si m'est
  bon;
et dirai vos per quale entention:
bon esperars tient l'ome a salviment;
et s'eu faz ben mout en serai jauzouz,
et s'eu fai mal sufrirai pesancous,
et jausirai ben et mal ensiment;
ensi ferai le connort al salvage.

VI. Bona dosna, merces clam per
  garent,
car sens merces non aten guerredon;
ainz cri merces ou merces venghe ou
  non;
et ja de ce non verrois recredent

your man, for a good hope in you makes me rejoice. For one who serves a good sovereign well does not lack a reward, I have seen many times the poor enriched by good patience; for indeed I reaffirm my devotion to you.

I have fixed my desire in you so completely, lady (God grant me such joy), that I would rather serve you without recompense than any other who might do my bidding. For my heart is drawn with such joy to you that since I saw you I lost all my strength. I am so desirous of your noble body that you have conquered me and I remain your prisoner.

And I know too well that I commit impudent folly when I plead to her for love in word and tune. But I can never relinquish my hope, and I know too well that I work for nothing. Her noble, proud body has such beauty which almost lifts her above all other persons, that I wish to sigh in dismay, and I fear that she will take me for a fool.

And if I become a fool, I do so knowingly; I know why it is proper and good to me. And I will tell you my opinion: good hope brings a man to safety; and if I do well, I will be very happy; and if I do ill, I will suffer grievously, and I will rejoice in good or ill equally; thus I will give hope to the savage.

Good lady, I claim your mercy as surety, for without mercy I do not hope for a reward. So I cry for mercy, whether mercy comes or not, and you will never see me give up, but I will plead for mercy with such

ainz preerei merces tant angoissoz,
que per merces tendrai mes mains
    ansdous
entre vostres et ferai causiment
qu'el mont non sab tan certan
    hommage.

anguish, that in mercy you will take
both my hands in yours and will
take pity, so that the world does not
know such perfect homage.

I. Ricx homs que greu ditz vertat e
    leu men,
e greu vol patz e leu mou occaizo,
e dona greu e leu vol c'om li do,
e greu fa be e leu destray la gen,
e greu es pros e leu es mals als bos,
e greu es francx e leu es ergulhos,
e greu es larcx e leu tol e greu ren,
deu cazer leu d'aut loc en bas estatie.

A powerful man who rarely speaks
the truth but easily lies, and rarely
wants peace but easily picks a fight,
and rarely gives but easily wants
another to give to him, and rarely
does good but easily destroys people,
and rarely is good but easily is bad
toward good persons, and rarely is
generous but easily is proud, and
rarely is generous but easily takes and
rarely returns, must fall easily from a
high place to a low state.

II. De tals en sai que pisson a prezen
et a beure rescondos d'inz maizos,
et al manjar non queron companhos
et al talar queron ni mays de sen,
et a l'ostal son caitieu e renos,
et a tortz far son ricx e poderos,
et al donar son de caitieu prezen,
et al tolre fort e de gran coratie.

I know people who piss out in the
open but go hide in their houses to
drink; and who do not seek friends
when they eat, but when they go out
and destroy, they seek more than a
hundred; and at home they are
miserable and peevish, but to do
injury are rich and powerful; and
when giving they are of mean
offering, but in taking are strong and
of great courage.

III. Malditz es homs que.l be ve e.l
    mal pren,
et e.ls ricx an pres orgohls e trassios;
et an laisat condutz e messios
et an pres dans e grans destruimen;
et an laissat lays e vers e chansos
et an pres plag e novas e tensos;
et an laissat amors e pretz valen
et an pres mal voler e far otratie.

Cursed is the man who sees good and
chooses bad; and the powerful have
chosen pride and treason; and they
have deserted homes and payments
but chosen loss and great destruction;
and they have deserted *lais* and *vers*
and *cansos* but chosen *plag* [questions]
and *novas* [disputes] and *tensos*
[debates]; and they have deserted love
and noble merit but have chosen to
desire evil and to commit outrages.

IV. Aisi can son major an peior sen,
ab mais de tort e ab mens de razo,
ab mais de dan tenir ab menz de pro,

Thus when they are greater they have
less sense, having more mischief but
less reason, harming more but helping

ab may d'orguelh ab mens de
  chauzimen,
ab mais de tolre et ab mens de bels
  dos,
ab mais de mals ab mens de bel
  respos,
ab mais de mietz ab mens
  d'ensenhamens,
ab mais deman ab mens de franc
  coratie.

less, having more pride but less
mercy, taking the most but giving
good things the least, having more
evil but less fair response, having
more worries but less learning, more
demands but less honest courage.

V. Aras digatz, senhors, al vostre sen,
de dos baros cals a melhor razo
can l'un dels dos pot dar e tolre non
l'autre pot tolre dar non pot men?
e dizon motz que.l dar val per un
  dos,
pueys vezem los tolre totas sazos;
a que far doncx van emblan ni tolen,
pus lo donars a dos tans
  d'avantatge.

Now tell me, lords, in your opinion,
of two barons which has more sense,
when one of the two can give and
cannot take, while the other can take
but can give nothing? And they say
that giving makes one worth two, so
we see them taking all the time.
Then why do they go about thieving
and taking, since giving would give
them the advantage of doing it
twice?

VI. Mos chantars es enuetz als
  enveios
et als plazens plazers qui platz
  razos;
tug li dig son plazen et ennos
so cals us platz als autres es salvatie.

My song is annoying to the annoying, and pleasing to the pleasant,
who are pleased by reason. All the
sayings are pleasing and annoying;
what is pleasing to the one is
offensive to the others.

---

tune as too frivolous or simplistic for the somber theme of a lament. It also may imply something about performance: that the social function of a *dansa* would be evoked by its tune, and the ear would thus be offended if it was used for a *planh* text. This late theoretical prescription is credible, if only because it embodies a concept that is familiar even today. The *dansa* as it survives in late sources manifests structural characteristics that appear to have developed only at the end of the era (see below). These particular tunes show no evidence of having been adapted to the text of any extant lament, which is hardly surprising, given that the *planh* as a courtly genre developed long before the functional/structural type that the *Doctrina* describes as a *dansa*.

The *estampida* seems to be a late genre as well, with no traces before the second half of the thirteenth century. The *Doctrina* gives cursory instructions for composing one, saying that its melody should not be borrowed:

Si vols far estampida, potz parlar de
qualque fayt vulles, blasman o
lauzan o merceyan, qui.t vulles; e
deu haver .iiije. cobles e responedor
e una o dues tornades, e so novell.[56]

If you want to compose an *estampida*,
you can speak of whatever you
wish, blaming or praising or
supplicating; and it must have four
stanzas and a refrain and one or two
tornadas, and a new melody.

But one report about the most famous extant Occitan *estampida*, the only one to survive with music (Raimbaut de Vaqueiras' "Kalenda maia," PC 392,9), suggests that its tune was preexistent. A *razo* found in an Italian manuscript dated 1310 (Florence, Biblioteca Medicea-Laurenziana, Pl. 41.42)[57] relates that the melody originated as a French instrumental tune, which Raimbaut adapted to his May song.[58] Raimbaut's poem conforms to the *Doctrina's* definition in its epideictic language of praise and blame, but its structure is unlike the strophic structure with refrain mandated in the treatise. It has no refrain or *tornada*,[59] but has a paired-versicle structure in both text and music that suggests an association with the sequence and the *lai*. Five of the seven surviving Occitan *estampida* texts, including "Kalenda maia," have a multiple-cursus poetic structure, achieved by creating groups of two to six verses. Two others begin with paired groups of verses, but conclude with several unpaired verses.

By asserting that the *estampida* must not use a borrowed melody, the author of the *Doctrina* might have been attempting to make the same sort of distinction that he did in the case of the *planh*, that the character of the song is so distinctive that no other type of song can share its melody. The distinction, though, is perhaps one of function and performance, rather than *razo* (see below).

The *Doctrina's* injunctions on borrowing melodies seem somewhat arbitrary, at least in the case of the *estampida* and perhaps the *pastora*. Because of the scarcity of the musical record it is impossible to discern whether composers really avoided or exploited a practice of melody borrowing in the same way—or for the same reasons—that the theorist proposes. One might observe that the *Doctrina* is addressed to composers rather than to singers, and that there is only indirect evidence at best that a singer might have initiated melody borrowing on his or her own. The poetic modeling on rhyme and verse scheme was a compositional process, and the musical modeling surely was too.[60] Whether a singer would have made the connection of a new song with the melody of the model, without explicit guidance, would depend on whether he or she actually knew the model—something of which we could be certain only if the singer was the composer of the new song. The only possible evidence of a performance practice of borrowing might be seen in the scribal direction at the end of the Monk of Montaudon's *sirventes*, "el so de la Rassa," pointing to Bertran de Born's melody. But it appears more likely that this instruction was addressed by the text scribe to the music scribe, not to a singer.

Function and Performance

The *dansa* and *estampida*, to the author of the *Doctrina*, were distinguished from other genres more by their mode of performance than by their theme or structure. As mentioned above, the theorist considered it inappropriate to use borrowed melodies for either type. He also treated them in the context of an activity in addition to singing: the *dansa* functions as accompaniment to dancing, while the *estampida* perhaps was associated with "counting" (see below).

The theorist says that the *dansa's* subject is love, and that it consists of three stanzas and one or two *tornadas*, plus an optional internal refrain consisting of the last verses of each stanza:

Si vols far dança, deus parlar d'amor be e plasentment, en qualque estament ne sies. E deus li fer dedents .iij. cobles e no pus, e respost, una o dues tornades, qual te vulles; totes vegades so novell. E potz fer, si.t vols, totes les fins de les cobles en refrayn semblan. E aquella raho de que la començaras deu[s] continuar e be servar al començament, al mig, e a la fi.[61]

If you want to compose a *dansa*, you must speak of love well and pleasantly, whatever state you are in. And you must give it three stanzas and no more, and a refrain and one or two *tornadas*, as you wish; every time [it has] a new melody. And you can, if you wish, make all the ends of the stanzas similar, as a refrain. And whatever theme with which you begin, you must continue and make serve well for the beginning, the middle, and the end.

Further, he connects the type specifically with the use of instruments:

Dansa es dita per ço com naturalment la ditz hom dança[n] o bayllan, cor deu [haver] so plazent; e la ditz hom ab esturmens, e plau a cascus que la diga e la escout.[62]

A *dansa* is so called, naturally, because one dances or leaps to it, so that it must [have] a pleasant melody; and one performs it with instruments, and it delights everyone who performs and hears it.

The four extant *dansas* have been identified as such partly because they have a closed ABA melodic structure, which is seen as an incipient *virelai* form. Their *razos* all treat of love, and their language is not overly sophisticated, although their courtly themes can be seen as occupying the "aristocratic register."[63] These four *dansas* are among the additions to manuscript W (discussed in Chapter 2) that were probably copied in the last years of the thirteenth century or perhaps in the early fourteenth. Certainly all of them look toward the fourteenth century in their reliance on a correspondence between poetic and musical structure for their identities. The only one of the four to survive with more than one stanza, Guiraut d'Espanha's "Ben volgra s'esser poges" (Example 4–11) appears to have a textual refrain consisting of four verses with the same rhymes and music as the last four verses of the three stanzas. In the manuscript these verses look like a refrain because the scribe marked them off from the stanza that follows by a long stroke through the staff and a capital letter at the beginning of the first full stanza. Three four-verse *tornadas* at the end (one of which identifies the song as a *dansa*) also match the rhyme scheme of the refrain. A feature that became standard in the fourteenth century, a match between the rhymes and the musical

EX. 4–11. Guiraut d'Espanha. PC 244,1a. W fol. 186–186v/B170*bis*–170*bis*v.

Refrain: Ben volgra, s'esser poges,   I really wish, if possible, that Love
c'amors si gardes d'aytan   would take care not to make a true
que non feses fin ayman   lover choose what pleases Love
chausir en luec que.l plages.   itself.

I. E per que? car per plaser
qu'ieu cresia de vos aver,
donna, vos mi fes chausir
amor, don avia esper
que mi degesses valer
del joy don ieu tant sospir;
ar m'aves a tal punch mes
que tot iorn vauc desiran
la mort don ay dolor gran,
car non faitz so c'amors fes.

And why? Because for the pleasure
that I believed I would have in you,
lady, Love made me choose you, in
whom I hoped that I would partake
of the joy that I so sigh for. But now
you have brought me to such a point
that every day I long for the death
which gives me great pain, for you
do not do as Love does.

II. Amors vos mi fes amar
e chausir vostre cor car
e vostra beutatz plasen
per plaser, mas gens ancar
non ay mas dol e pensar,
e non truep nul garimen;
e pos per plaser ay pres
pena, dolor et affan,
amors meti a mon dan
qu'arebusan a pales.

Love makes me love you and choose
your dear heart and your pleasing
beauty, for pleasure; but yet I have
nothing but sorrow and care, and I
have found no relief. And since
instead of pleasure I have received
pain, sorrow, and torment, I despise
Love, who has openly rebuffed me.

III. E tenray m'ab desamor
et auray gauch e socor
e iay e plaser entier;
e qui si vull' ai' amor,
qu'el viura ab gran dolor
et ieu ab gran alegrier;
e si d'aysso suy repres,
sapcha ma rason enan:
c'amors va.n contrarian,
per so ay.l contrari pes.

And I will keep myself from loving,
and thus I will have joy and relief
and happiness and complete
pleasure. And whoever wants to can
have Love, whoever wants can live
in great sorrow, while I live in great
mirth. And if I am reproached for
this, know my reason: Love has
behaved inconstantly, so I have been
inconstant back.

IV. Mon deliech non vos vuell ges,
mas mon desplaser deman,
e si as el mi coman,
ieu auray tot cant obs m'es.

My delight, I do not want you at all,
but I demand my displeasure, and if
it commands me, I will have all that
I need.

V. E malan puesqu' esser mes
qui amors servira tan,
con a fah, de say enan,
car non fai so que dretz es.

And unhappiness can strike anyone
who serves Love, as it has done, I
know now, for it does not do what is
just.

VI. Dansa, car ieu ay apres
que.l reys Karles fay gent chan,
per aquo as el ti man,
car de fin pres es apres.

Dance, since I have learned that
King Charles composes noble songs,
I send you to him, for he is of true
merit.

structure, does not occur here. If the first four verses are sung at the beginning of each stanza, the rhyme and musical scheme of each stanza would be:

rhymes:	a	b	b	a	c	c	d	c	c	d	a	b	b	a
music:	A	B	C	D	E	F	G	E'	F	G'	A	B	C	D

The stanza proper (after the refrain) can be divided into three sections by both rhyme scheme and musical structure. As noted in Chapter 2, the music notation for Guiraut's song is mensural.

The other three *dansas* with music survive with only one stanza each, but they all manifest the same matching of rhymes and music between the opening three or four verses and the final verses of the stanza; presumably subsequent stanzas would have replicated the scheme. As for a connection of these songs with instruments, Christopher Page has argued that instrumentalists would have found such regularly measured pieces not only easy to play but also familiar as part of a tradition of improvised dance music.[64]

Toward the end of his treatise the author of the *Doctrina* makes one more brief remark about the *estampida*:

Stampida es dita per ço stampida cor pren vigoria en contan o en xantan pus que null autra cantar.[65]	An *estampida* is so called because it is taken vigorously in counting or in singing, more than any other song.

The Occitan verb *estampir* is understood to mean "resound, reverberate," perhaps "make a hubbub."[66] The etymology suggested here evokes an image of raucous performance and perhaps active footwork, which is obviously associated with the dance and perhaps implies a regularity of measure that might explain the term *contar* (to count.)[67]

The author of the *Doctrina* does not connect instruments with the *estampida*, as he does with the *dansa*, although one is reminded of other twelfth- and thirteenth-century texts that do make such an association, notably the passage in Johannes de Grocheio's treatise describing one type of *stantipes* as instrumental: "Stantipes vero est sonus illitteratus, habens sonus difficilem concordantiarum discretionem, per puncta determinatus. . . ."[68] (The *estampie* is a melody without words, having difficult and discrete harmonious sounds, proscribed by *puncta*.) Grocheio also lists it among types of the vocal *cantilena*: "Cantilena, quae dicitur stantipes est illa in qua est diversitas in partibus et refractu tam in consonantia dictaminis quam in cantu. . . ."[69] (The *cantilena* called *estampie* is one that has a diversity of parts, as much in the text rhymes as in the melody.) Grocheio's description of the instrumental *stantipes* invokes the double-cursus structure of "Kalenda maia," the same form as in all the surviving thirteenth-century French *estampies* and four-teenth-century Italian *istanpitte* without text.[70] Pierre Bec has suggested that the Occitan *estampida* was imported from the north in the late twelfth century.[71]

For these two dance types, structure was perhaps an element in their generic definition, but the theorist seems more preoccupied with their performance. Both genres appear to be latecomers to the trouba-dour tradition, perhaps reflecting a move toward regularization.

Structure

In addition to the *dansa*, the *retroncha* and *descort* also are distinguished in the *Doctrina* by certain structural features. The *retroncha* is supposed to have a refrain:

Si vols far retronxa, sapies que deus parlar d'amor, segons l'estament en que.n seras, sia plazen o cossiros; e no.y deus mesclar altra raho. E deus saber que deu haver quatre cobles, e so novell tota vegada. E deus saber que per ço ha nom retronxa car lo refray de cada una de les cobles deu esser totz us.[72]	If you want to compose a *retroncha*, know that you must speak of love, according to the state in which you will be, whether pleasant or anxious; and you must not mix in another theme. And you should know that it must have four stanzas, and a new melody every time. And you should know that it is called *retroncha* because the refrain at the end of one of the stanzas must be used for all of them.

Like the extant *dansa* melodies, the three surviving *retroncha* melodies date from the late thirteenth century (all by Guiraut Riquier), and they reflect the new proclivity toward formal organization by repetition scheme.[73] Each has a textual refrain that makes up the last two verses of each stanza, as prescribed by the *Doctrina*. The music, though, does not have a refrain structure. All the songs are transmitted in manuscript R and have the ABABx musical form that is so common among this codex's melodies:

    PC 248,57:   A B A B C D E F
    PC 248,65:   A B A B C D E F D' D"
    PC 248,78:   A B A B C A' D E F

Example 4–12 gives two of these melodies, which bear some striking motivic resemblances to each other. The style of Guiraut's music in general is very melismatic, and motivic coherence and development are important characteristics of most of his songs. That Guiraut borrowed

EX. 4–12. Guiraut Riquier. PC 248,65 and 248,78. R fol. 111v.

extensively from himself, on both a small and a large scale, becomes evident after even a cursory glance at his music.

As discussed above, the extant Occitan *descorts* have a number of stanzas that are formally independent of one another, and each stanza has an internal structure of two, three, or four sections in which the rhyme scheme is repeated. This sequence-like poetic structure is the same as that associated with the *lay*, which has prompted the argument that there is no substantive difference between the two courtly genres.[74] The *Doctrina*, however, does not refer to such a musical structure in the *descort*, and in fact two of the four extant *descort* melodies are through-composed. J. H. Marshall has observed that in Guillem Augier's descort "Ses alegratge" (stanzas I and II given in Example 4–13)[75] several stanzas end with the same (or similar) cadential phrase, or musical rhyme. He suggests (as he did with the *estampida*) that this might be what "responedor" means in the *Doctrina*;[76] but this allusion does not correspond to the sequence-like musical structure here. It has "open" and "closed" cadences within these stanzas, so that these cadential figures give a sense of finality to the end of each stanza (see Chapter 5 on similar structural features). Marshall points out that no *descorts* were being composed by the late thirteenth century, thus accounting for the inexactitude of the theorists' descriptions.[77]

Every song of the troubadours can be analyzed in terms of its subject matter, structure, arrangement of topics, style of language, and to some extent performing traditions, and these elements can in some respects be associated with various genres. Both text and melody were created during a compositional process that involved making decisions about these elements, and were partially guided by a common intention in the mind of the composer. But an interrelationship between text and melody generally occurs not word by word or note by note, but in different ways for each song. The puzzle of how a poem that is essentially "through-composed" can be served well by a melody that is repeated five or six times in the delivery of the several stanzas of a poem becomes less difficult when one realizes that both melody and poem together should serve the larger rhetorical purpose chosen by the author. The reiteration of the melody reinforces the poem's theme, or *razo*, but here again the different ways in which text and melody serve that *razo* are evident. The poem's structure remains the same in all stanzas, but its words change as they develop and unfold the *razo* to the listener. The melody's notes remain the same, but their impact on the listener changes as they serve as the vehicle for the changing text.

The concept of "genre" can be useful in identifying distinctive features that a song shares with others, but it should be regarded only as a general framework, not as a rigid system of definition. The choice of

EX. 4–13. Guillem Augier. PC 205,5, stanzas I and II. W fol. 186v/B170^bisv.

I. Sens alegrage,   chant per agradage;
follage   faz car mon corage
s'ec lay on s'es   mes.

C'anc plus salvage   reclus de boscage
d'estage   del mieu sennorage
non fon nulz oms pres.

II. C'aysi fos presa
del mal que m'adesa   malmesa.
[cella, cui pauc peza]
car mi fay langir.

Mas on er quesa
merces ni franquesa
pos li plus cortesa
vol sens tort ausir?

Without joy I sing for pleasure; I
commit folly, for my heart lies where
it has placed itself.

For never was any man placed in a
more hostile prison of a forest than
the place of my bondage.

Oh, that she would be captured by
the ill that grips me and wounds me,
she who hardly considers that she
makes me languish.

But where would one seek mercy or
sincerity, since the most courteous
lady wants to kill me without
reason?

theme was the first stage for the composer, but it is not the only decision about the content of a song that he or she made. The "arguments" that would be put forth to develop the *razo*, the modes of expression, and some structural features—the "material style" of a song—enhanced, refined, and amplified aspects of the song's genre. In the chapters that follow, the genre of a song will resurface when it contributes to an understanding of the melody's structure, style, and performance.

FIVE

FORM

The Art of Poetry and Musical Form

The elements of a melody that we associate with its structure are to some extent arbitrary, and they depend on certain conceptual presuppositions. The idea of structure implies unity or coherence, and the elements of a work that constitute its structure are those that in some way are perceived to bring about or contribute to this unity or coherence. Unity of subject matter was of central concern to late medieval poetry theorists, as we have seen, and the arrangement of the materials of a poem—its *dispositio* in rhetoric—was supposed to produce this coherence. The theme of the poem is expressed through certain "arguments" or topics, and as explained in Chapter 4, the arrangement of the melody—its contour, progression of phrases, tonal goals, and so forth—could be seen as serving the same purpose.

In the Ciceronian scheme of rhetoric, *dispositio*, or arrangement, concerned placing the arguments of the oration in a logical and effective order. A classical oration should be arranged in six parts: Introduction, Statement of Facts, Division, Proof, Refutation, and Conclusion,[1] a plan that was clearly useful for subject matter in politics and the law. The order could be modified for particular circumstances, "in accordance with the speaker's judgment," for example, "if our cause seems to present so great a difficulty that no one can listen to the Introduction with patience," in which case it might be omitted.[2]

The theorists of the late medieval arts of poetry, while giving a nod to classical rhetoric, generally reduced a poem's parts to three, as in this passage from Geoffroi de Vinsauf: "Let the poem's beginning, like a courteous attendant, introduce the subject with grace. Let the main section, like a diligent host, make provision for its worthy reception. Let the conclusion, like a herald when the race is over, dismiss it honourably."[3] Geoffroi also echoes the classical authors by allowing changes to the "natural" order, that is, the order that follows the rules, as opposed to an "artificial" arrangement or one that for various reasons is more eloquent. Jean de Garlande expresses these same ideas succinctly, pointing out that the composer arranges the materials mentally before bringing the poem to actuality:

> The next subject after Invention and Selection of subject matter is how to begin and arrange it. Any subject has three aspects: beginning, middle, and end (or commencement, development, and conclusion of the work, and similar labels). These parts should be put straight first of all in the mind, because a word must be in the mind before it may be in the mouth. . . . In poetry, we can launch the subject with either the natural or the artificial beginning. The natural beginning is when a story is told in the order in which it takes place. . . . The artificial beginning is when we start in the middle of the subject or at the end. . . .[4]

But the late medieval poetry theorists, including Occitanian and Catalan ones, soon turned their attention to the technical, elemental aspects of composing a poem, including rhyme, syllable count, accent, and stanza scheme. These pragmatic concerns occupied the rhetorical stage of *elocutio*—expression—which involved the proper use and ordering of words, through syntactical correctness, tropes and figures, and adherence to rules governing meter and rhyme. Jean de Garlande treats rhyme and syllable quantity as one of the rhetorical figures. He first defines rhymed poetry, in contrast to quantitative verse, evoking certain terms from music to make his points:

> The art of rhymed poetry is that which teaches how to compose a rhymed poem, which is in turn defined as follows. A rhymed poem is a harmonious arrangement of words with like endings, regulated not by quantity but by number of syllables. "Harmonious arrangement" serves as the genus; for music is a harmonious arrangement of disparate elements and tones—"discordant concord" or "concordant discord." "Words with like endings" distinguishes it from melody. "By number of syllables" refers to the fact that a rhymed poem consists of some precise number of syllables, be it many or few. "Not by quantity" distinguishes it from the art of quantitative verse. "Regulated" indicates that the words in a rhymed poem should fall in a regular cadence.[5]   .

He then describes how rhymed poetry is similar to quantitative verse, giving examples of various meters, and mentioning Pythagorean proportional relationships in music as having analogs in poetic meters.[6]

Jofre de Foixà and other Occitanian theorists devote most of their attention to grammar and versification. Jofre places rhyme, syllable count, and stanza scheme under the term "measure" (*maneyra*):

Maneyra es que d'aytantes rimes co faras la primera cobla faces les altres, e que les rimes de les cobles sien semblantz en llur loch e pars en sillabes, en axi que la primeyra rima de la primeyra cobla sia semblan a la primeyra rima de la segona cobla, e atressi a la primeyra de totes les altres cobles; e la segona rima de la primera cobla a la segona rima de les altres cobles. E en axi deus apparellar totes les altres rimes. Empero be potz far la primeyra cobla d'unes rimes e cascuna de les cobles d'altres rimes; o potz fer les primeyras duas coblas d'unas rimas e dues altres coblas d'altres rimes, e les altres cobles d'autres rimes. E aço es maneyra, que axi com començaras o perseguesques; pero tota hora deven esser les cobles d'un nombre e en rimes e en sillabes.[7]

Measure is where you give all of the stanzas as many rhymes as the first stanza, and where the rhymes of the stanzas are in the same places and are equal in syllables, so that the first rhyme of the first stanza is the same as the first rhyme of the second stanza, and thus of the first rhyme of all the other stanzas; and the second rhyme of the first stanza is the same as the second rhyme of the other stanzas. And thus you must match all the other rhymes. But you can also give the first stanza one set of rhymes and each of the other stanzas other rhymes; or you can give the first two stanzas one set of rhymes and the next two stanzas other rhymes, and the other stanzas other rhymes. And this is measure, with which thus you begin and continue; but the stanzas must always be of one quantity in rhymes and in syllables.

Here Jofre alludes to the ways stanzas were related to each other by rhyme, describing techniques that later acquired names like *coblas unissonans, singulars*, and *doblas* (see below). The bulk of Jofre's treatise, which follows this passage, is taken up with a discussion of various elements of grammar and of versification, including number, tense, rhyme, accent (in the context of rhyme), definite articles, case, and verbs. Jofre regarded the poetic elements of rhyme, accent, syllables, and stanzas to be as much components of language as were grammatical matters. This is partly because versification had always been seen as a grammatical concern, as one component in the eloquent use of language (see Chapter 3). Furthermore, unlike the way the topics of a song were arranged and imagined in the mind during *inventio* and *dispositio*, the details of versification—especially rhyme, syllable count, and verse schemes—were aural by their very nature, and so were in the realm of the practical and tangible.

As Jofre's text implies, the building blocks of a poem were the verse, which was defined by the number of syllables it encompassed and by the rhyme sound at its end, and the stanza, defined by the number of verses it contained and the pattern in which the verse rhymes occurred. As Jofre's treatise says, all stanzas were identical in their number of verses. Furthermore, all first verses of stanzas were identical in the number of syllables (syllable count), all second verses were identical, all third verses, and so forth. The pattern of rhyme occurrence was generally identical from stanza to stanza as well, although the rhyme sounds themselves might change. The rhyme was distinguished by whether its accent (defined as when one "raises the voice and holds it more on one syllable than on another"[8]) occurred on the final or on the penultimate syllable (what is sometimes called "masculine" and "feminine," or technically, oxytonic and paroxytonic). Rhyme sounds had to match by accent placement as well as by vowel and final consonant sound. A rhyme with an accent on the penultimate syllable had to match vowel and final consonant sounds in both the accented syllable and the unaccented syllable that followed.

The "structure" of a poem is customarily reduced to a graph that expresses three of these fundamental elements of poetic structure— number of syllables per verse, number of verses per stanza, and strophic rhyme scheme: lower-case letters indicate the same rhyme (upper case only in the instance of a verse whose exact words recur in the same position in all stanzas, i.e., a textual refrain), and numbers indicate the number of syllables in each verse (a prime mark usually is used to indicate a paroxytonic rhyme).[9] Verses of six or more syllables might have an internal pause, or *caesura*, which also is defined by whether its accent falls on the penultimate or the final syllable; *caesuras* are not necessarily governed by rhyme, though, and they do not have to recur in identical positions in all stanzas. The portion of a verse before or after a *caesura*—or sometimes more loosely, just the first or second part of a verse—is a *hemistich*.

The traditional system for graphing musical structure in monophonic song is similar, in that it defines musical phrases as coinciding with text verses, and the letters convey the relationships among the musical phrases. Repetition of phrases is designated by the use of the same letter, and slight variations can be indicated by means of prime and double-prime markings. For Friedrich Gennrich, repetition was the chief formal principle in monophonic song.[10] Of the 274 melodies in his catalog of troubadour songs, he counts 96 as "*Kanzone*" (AAB), 53 as *lai/ sequence* types (including *descorts*), seven as *virelais* and *ballades*, three as impossible or too peculiar to classify, and 115 as *oda continua*, or through-composed.[11] At least since Gennrich's ground-breaking work, describing the structure of monophonic vernacular music with reference mainly to repetition or non-repetition of musical phrases has become the norm.

But other musical details give the melodies of the troubadours coherence: they include pitch and interval content, tonal centers, motives, incipits, and cadences. Some researchers have suggested that the ecclesiastical modes, constituting a system of scales with distinct interval content and pitch hierarchy, provide structural boundaries not only for plainchant but also for vernacular monophony. To the extent that church music was part of the aural environment within which the troubadours worked, it influenced the sound of their melodies, at least indirectly. Many troubadour melodies have one or more tonal centers, and features such as range, melodic contour, and beginning and ending formulas can be seen as related to a concept of mode.

Another theory about how troubadours organized their melodies was developed from some ideas of Curt Sachs by Hendrik van der Werf, who suggested that they were based at least in part on interval chains, particularly of thirds and fourths.[12] Analysis of an extant melody along these lines, which other researchers have done also, can provide some insight into its contours and perhaps its important or pivotal pitches.

As discussed in Chapter 2, the extant melodies were shaped to some degree not only by the composers but also by singers and scribes. When two or more versions of a melody survive, they almost always manifest structural differences, not only in the repetition scheme but also in such features as range, tonal centers, interval content, and contour. In many cases it is difficult or impossible to discern what specific structural traits of an extant melody were due to action on the part of the composer, performers, or scribes. But as with other musical elements, if we take into account the date of the composer, the date of the source, and the propensities of the scribe, it is sometimes possible to see how music and poetry interacted on structural levels and to infer the attitudes of composers, singers, and scribes toward musical structure.

Old Occitan Versification

The troubadours devoted meticulous attention to the features of versification, by which means they demonstrated some of their most sensational creativity. A few rhyme/verse combinations were very popular, but the number of schemes that were used only once among the more than 2,500 surviving poems (referred to as poetic *unica*) exceeds 590.[13] Of the 246 poems that survive with melodies, 60 are poetic *unica*, representing about 10 percent of the total number of poetic *unica* extant.

A further 80 share their rhyme scheme, but not the syllable count, with at least one other poem. Thus 140, or 53 percent, of the poems with extant melodies have a unique verse and rhyme structure.

Rhyme scheme, syllable count, and number of verses provide nearly infinite possibilities. Verse lengths could range from one syllable (as in the *descort* discussed in Chapter 4) to twelve; stanzas could be from five to ten or more verses long; rhyme patterns within stanzas could be simple or complex, using both paroxytonic and oxytonic rhymes, and the rhyme sounds themselves were restricted only by the limitations of the language.

Rhyme, syllable count, and verse count are joined by a fourth formal element, relationships among the stanzas, adding a further level of complexity. Stanzaic relationships are not conveyed by the modern graphing system, but are described today using medieval terms found in the fourteenth-century *Leys d'Amors*.[14] The majority of troubadour poems, including those that survive with music, use a device called *coblas unissonans*, literally "stanzas with single sounds," meaning that all stanzas use exactly the same rhyme sounds in the same pattern. But a significant number of poems use devices other than identical rhymes in all stanzas, most of which result in a progression of stanzas that are linked or "enchained" (*encadenadas*) by the rhymes in some fashion; sometimes several different contrivances are used in one poem.

When each stanza in a poem has its own, different rhyme sounds, it is referred to as *coblas singulars*. The stanzas, however, are usually linked by a common pattern of rhymes, even if the sounds themselves change. An example of *coblas singulars* is the famous *estampida* "Kalenda maia" of Raimbaut de Vaqueiras (PC 392,9). A variation on this idea is found in the only song by the Comtessa de Dia that survives with music (PC 46,2; the melody is given in Example 5–8), which is made up of *coblas singulars* except that verses 5 and 7 in all stanzas have the same rhyme sound, -*ens*, as illustrated here by stanzas I and II (this and all other examples cited in this chapter survive with music):

A chantar m'er de so qu'ieu non
   volria,
tant me rancur de lui cui sui amia,
car eu l'am mais que nuilla ren que
   sia;
vas lui no.m val merces ni cortesia
ni ma beltatz ni mos pretz ni mos s*ens*,
c'atressi.m sui enganada e trahia
com degr' esser, s'ieu fos desavin*ens*.

D'aisso.m conort car anc non fis
   faillenssa,

I must sing of what I'd rather not,
I'm so angry about him whose friend
I am, for I love him more than
anything; mercy and courtliness
don't help me with him, nor does
my beauty, or my rank, or my mind;
for I am every bit as betrayed and
wronged as I'd deserve to be if I
were ugly.

It comforts me that I have done no
wrong to you, my friend, through

amics, vas vos per nuilla captenenssa,
anz vos am mais non fetz Seguis
  Valenssa,
e platz me mout que eu d'amar vos
  venssa,
lo mieus amics, car etz lo plus valens;
mi faitz orguoil en digz et en
  parvenssa,
e si etz francs vas totas autras gens.

any action; indeed, I love you more
than Seguis loved Valenssa; it
pleases me to outdo you in loving,
friend, for you are the most valiant;
you offer prideful words and looks
to me but are gracious to every other
person.[15]

Another device used to link *coblas singulars* is to shift the rhyme sounds forward by one verse with each succeeding stanza, as in Peire Vidal's "S'ieu fos en cort que hom tengues drechura" (PC 364,42). Here, each stanza has different rhyme sounds, but those of verses 2 through 6 are taken from the preceding stanza, in the same order; verse 1 always has a new ending:

I:	-ura,	-ella,	-ena,	-ensa,	-ona,	-onha
II:	-iva,	-ura,	-ella,	-ena,	-ensa,	-ona
III:	-ida,	-iva,	-ura,	-ella,	- ena,	-ensa
IV:	-elha,	-ida,	-iva,	-ura,	-ella,	-ena
V:	-ista,	-elha,	-ida,	-iva,	-ura,	-ella
VI:	-era,	-ista,	-elha,	-ida,	-iva,	-ura
VII:	-ina,	-era,	-ista,	-elha,	-ida,	-iva

By stanza VII, none of the rhyme sounds is from stanza I. The three two-verse *tornadas* attached to this poem have the rhymes *-ansa, -ina, -eja, -ansa, -erna*, and *-eja*, none of which is found in any of the preceding stanzas.

Many such poems are also *coblas redondas*, meaning that the rhyme scheme of the final stanza is linked to the rhymes of the first stanza, bringing the verse structure full circle. An example of this procedure is Guiraut Riquier's "Voluntiers faria" (PC 248,85), in which the rhyme sounds of the second and third verse of each stanza become the rhyme sounds of the first and second verse of each successive stanza, and the last stanza is linked in the same way to the first:

I:	-ia,	-ella,	-iva
II:	-ella,	-iva,	-ada
III:	-iva,	-ada,	-ensa
IV:	-ada,	-ensa,	-ida
V:	-ensa,	-ida,	-ia
VI:	-ida,	-ia,	-ella
[I:	-ia,	-ella,	-iva]

In *coblas unissonans* (and *singulars*, where there is no linking from one stanza to the next), the transmission of stanza order from manuscript to manuscript is often unstable. Usually the first and often the last stanzas are found in the same position, but interior stanzas often shift positions or are missing altogether from some sources. This obscures the *dispositio* of the poem's materials, as it might have been intended, and underscores the topical rather than the narrative nature of these lyric poems.[16]

In some poems the rhyme sounds change for every two stanzas (*coblas doblas*) or every three stanzas (*coblas ternas*). Again, all stanzas in such poems have the same pattern of rhymes, but the rhyme sounds themselves change every second or third stanza. This structural feature often reinforces the progression of the poem's topics, where these are expressed by pairs of stanzas (see Examples 4–3, 4–4, and 4–6). In such stanza structures, the transmission of stanza order is more stable than in *coblas unissonans*.

Textual refrains are not as common among troubadour poems as in the trouvère repertoire, but those that survive include refrains that encompass one or more entire verses (which can be indicated in graphs by the use of an upper-case letter), part of a verse (such as a *hemistich*), or a single word. An example of the last is found in Jaufre Rudel's famous "Lan can li jorn son lonc en may" (PC 262,2), in which verses 2 and 4 of every stanza end with the word "lonh" (stanzas I and II from manuscript R are given here):

Lai can li jorn son lonc e may
m'es bel dos chans d'auzels de *lon[h]*
e can mi soi partitz de lay,
remenbran un' amor de *lonh*:
vau de talan enbrons e clis,
si que chans ni flors dels bels pis
no.m val plus que l'yvern in glatz.

Whenever the days are long in May, I like a sweet song of birds from afar, and when I have gone away from there they bring to mind a love from afar. I go bent and bowed with desire, so that neither song nor flower from the beautiful pines is worth more to me than winter in ice.

Ben tenc lo Senhor per veray
que formet sest' amor de *lonh,*
que per un ben que me n'eschay
n'ai dos mals, si be.m soi de *lonh*
ai! car fos ieu lay peleris,
si que [mos fustz e mos tapis]
fos pels sieus bels huelhs remirat[z]![17]

I hold indeed the Lord to be true who formed this love from afar, but for one good thing which befalls me from it I have two griefs, although I am far away. Ah! would that I were a pilgrim there so that [my staff and my cloak] were reflected in her beautiful eyes.

Another song with a word refrain is Marcabru's "Dire vos senes duptansa," (PC 293,30; see Example 4–4). The fourth verse in every stanza is the word "escotatz"; because it constitutes the entire verse it is also a verse refrain. This song also has *coblas doblas*.

Hemistich refrains and refrains of two or three words are more rare, but some examples are found among songs with surviving melodies. Verse 8 of Rigaut de Berbezil's song "Atressi cum Persevaus" (PC 421,3) has ten syllables, and the *senhal* "miels de domna" (best of ladies) occupies the first *hemistich* in all the stanzas; the *tornada* follows the scheme of the last four verses of the stanza, and thus also begins with the refrain phrase (stanzas I and II and the *tornada* are given here):

Atressi con Persavaus	Just like Percival in his day, who was
el temps que vivia,	so stupified by contemplation that
que s'esbait d'esgardar	he could not ask what purpose the
tant qu'anc non saup demandar	lance and the grail served, so am I,
de que servia	best of ladies, when I see your fair
la lansa ni.l grazaus,	body, I likewise forget myself when I
et eu sui atretaus,	regard you, and I think to entreat
miels de dompna, quan vei vostre cors	you, but I don't, instead I dream.
gen,	
qu'eissamen	
m'oblit quan vos remir,	
e.us cug prejar, e non fatz, mais consir.	

Ab uns dous esgartz coraus,	The sweet heartfelt looks—which
que an fag lur via	made their way through my eyes,
per mos oillz ses retornar	without returning, into my heart,
el cor, on los teing tan car	where I hold them so dear—if it
que si.l plasia	would please you, these are my chief
c'aitals fos mos chaptaus	torments and ills from you, best of
dels trebaus e dels maus,	ladies, which I often deal with so
miels de domna, que trac per vos soven	wearily; but I would rather die for
tan greumen,	you than to have joy from any other,
mais am per vos morir	so much do I desire you.
que d'autr'aver nuill joi, tan vos desir.	

* * * *

Miellz de domna, en ren no m'en repen	Best of ladies, I regret nothing if I
s'eu aten	await the joys that will come, for the
lo jois qu'es a venir,	man who serves obtains true love.
que bon' amor gazaingn' om ab	
servir.[18]	

Guiraut Riquier, whose poems are characterized by numerous strophic complexities, used his favorite *senhal* "Bel Deport" as a two-word refrain in verse 6 of his "Los bes qu'ieu truep en amor" (PC 248,53), which also has word refrains at the ends of verses 1 and 2.

Refrains of entire verses are not common among troubadour songs, but they are concentrated in the later generations. Among Guiraut Riquier's works there are three examples of a special type using this device, namely the *retroncha*, whose last verse or verses are repeated exactly in all stanzas (see Example 4–12).

Other linking techniques involve *coblas capcaudadas* (head-to-tail), in which the final verse of each stanza ends with a word or a rhyme sound that is repeated as the word or rhyme sound of the first verse of the following stanza. Usually this device results in an exchange of other rhyme sounds and causes an alternation of stanzas (*alternadadas*), so that every other stanza has the same rhyme sounds. Such is the case in Folquet de Marselha's "Amors, merce, no mueyra tan soven" (PC 155,1), in which the rhyme scheme is as follows:

I, III, V:	-en,	-ire,	-en,	-ire,	-ire,	-os,	-os
II, IV, VI:	-os,	-ire,	-os,	-ire,	-ire,	-en,	-en

A more complex exchange is found in Gaucelm Faidit's "A semblan del rey Tirs" (PC 167,4), with the following alternation:

I, III, V:
-es, -aire, -es, -es, -aire, -ar, -ar, -ansa, -ansa, -ar, -e, -a, -e
II, IV, VI:
-e, -ansa, -e, -e, -ansa, -ar, -ar, -aire, -aire, -ar, -es, -es, -es

A similar device occurs in *coblas retrogradadas*, in which the rhymes or rhyme words are given in reverse order in alternating stanzas, as in Guiraut Riquier's "Fis e verais e pus ferm que no suelh" (PC 248,29):

I, III, V:	-uelh,	-ort,	-ort,	ames,	-or,	-or,	-ans
II, IV, VI:	-ans,	-or,	-or,	ames,	-ort,	-ort,	-uelh

In this song, the rhyme word of verse 4, "ames," is a word refrain in all stanzas.

An even more difficult and ingenious use of *coblas capcaudadas* involves linking not just rhyme sounds, but entire words. Raimon de Miraval used this technique in "Un sonet m'es bel qu'espanda" (PC 406,47). Here the final word of each stanza becomes the rhyme word of the first verse of the following stanza:

I,9 and II,1:	atruanda
II,9 and III,1:	reblanda
III,9 and IV,1:	guaranda
IV,9 and V,1:	desmanda
V,9 and VI,1:	vianda
VI,9 and I,1:	espanda

Note that this is also an example of *coblas redondas*, in that stanza VI is linked by its final rhyme word to stanza I. An even more breathtaking effect is created by the use of the same rhyme words, rearranged, in all stanzas. Perhaps the most famous of such songs is Arnaut Daniel's *sestina* "Lo ferm voler q'el cor m'intra" (PC 29,14), in which every stanza uses the rhyme words "intra," "ongla," "arma," "verga," "oncle," and "cambra," rearranged in what appears at first to be random order (*coblas singulars*), but which actually follows a pattern (123456 = 615243); the rhyme words thus are linked by the technique of *capcaudadas*, since the last word of one stanza becomes the first rhyme word of the next:[19]

I:	intra, ongla, arma, verga, oncle, cambra	abcdef
II:	cambra, intra, oncle, ongla, verga, arma	faebdc
III:	arma, cambra, verga, intra, ongla, oncle	cfdabe
IV:	oncle, arma, ongla, cambra, intra, verga	ecbfad
V:	verga, oncle, intra, arma, cambra, ongla	deacfb
VI:	ongla, verga, cambra, oncle, arma, intra	bdfeca

The three-verse *tornada* of this song uses all of the rhyme words in the order 524361, two rhyme words per verse. It does not follow the pattern established among the stanzas, and hence does not restore the 123456 scheme of stanza I:[20]

Arnautz tramet sa chansson d'*oncle* e d'*ongla*
a grat de lieis que de sa *verga* l'*arma*
son Desirat, cui pretz en *cambra intra*.

Reusing entire words in rhymes, as here, not only functions as a structural device but also reinforces the theme, in that succeeding stanzas are connected by sound as well as by sense. The rhetorical impact of such poems might be more overt, since both the ear and the intellect are led forward by the progression of the stanzas in order.

Another example of resourcefulness is the technique of *rims derivatius*, in which rhyme words are generated by grammatical derivation from other rhyme words. For example, in Guillem de Saint Didier's "Pois tant mi forrs' Amors" (PC 234,16), the rhyme words of the first stanza are built upon the root -*metre*, but with different prefixes (notice here also the rhyme at the *caesuras* of verses 1 and 3):

Pois tant mi forrs' Amors que m'a faich entremetre
c'a la genssor del mon aus ma chansson trametre,
e pois non auz aillors mon fin cor esdemetre,
ben deuri' enplegar mon sotil sen e metre,
si.l plagues qe.m laisses en son servizi metre
cill cui hom liges sui ses dar e ses prometre.[21]

Since with such great strength Love has made me undertake to send my song to the sweetest lady in the world, and since I dare not otherwise let my faithful heart burst forth, I should indeed use and display my keen wit, if it would please her to allow me to enter her service, I who am her liege-man without return and without promise.

The other stanzas of this poem use the same procedure and the same rhyme pattern, but have different root words.

In some poems a stanza has one verse that does not rhyme with any other verses in the stanza, but which rhymes only with the corresponding verses in subsequent stanzas. This device, known as *rims estramps*, can be found in poems with *coblas unissonans, doblas, capcaudadas*, refrains, or other linking features.

One other technique for linking stanzas is the repetition of the final word in each stanza as the first word (not the rhyme word) of the following one: its name, *coblas capfinidas*, meaning literally "head-to-end," describes the effect precisely. Very few poems apply the device this strictly (as it is defined in the *Leys d'Amors*), and many scholars use the term more loosely to include songs in which the final word of a stanza recurs somewhere in the first verse of the following stanza, not necessarily at the beginning.[22] If the word is repeated as the rhyme word, then this is actually a form of *coblas capcaudadas*, as explained above. If it occurs elsewhere in the verse, a technique I prefer to call *quasi-capfinidas*, often the words are derivative, as in Arnaut Daniel's "Chanzon do.l moz son plan e prim" (PC 29,6):

I,9:	broilla
II,1 and 9:	bruoills/orguoilla
III,1 and 9:	orguoills/janguoilla
IV,1:	janglor

The linking does not continue after stanza IV in this song. A very few songs, including Pons de Capduelh's "Us gays conortz me fay gayamen far" (PC 375,27), have a structure that is very close to the definition given in the *Leys d'amors*, with head-to-end connections, here again with derivative word forms:

I,9:	finamen
II,1 and 9:	Fis/humilmen
III,1 and 9	S'umilitatz/razonamen
IV,1 and 9:	razon/chauzimen
V,1:	Chauzimens

The earliest troubadours favored relatively simple verse/rhyme patterns and other fairly straightforward poetic structures, including *coblas unissonans*, word refrains, and *rims derivatius*. The more complex techniques, like *coblas capcaudadas* and *coblas capfinidas, coblas retrogradadas*, and verse refrains, became more and more common after the first quarter of the thirteenth century. The last great troubadour, Guiraut Riquier, reveled in extraordinarily elaborate structural designs, rarely composing a poem that did not use at least two or three enchaining devices at once. As we shall see, his music also is characterized by complexity and imaginative structural schemes. The *dansas* and *retron-chas*, whose poetic and musical structures are more integrated than other types, also do not appear until the second half of the thirteenth century (as we saw in Chapter 4). *Lais* and some *descorts*, as we have also seen, are characterized by a scheme that does not involve stanzas, but instead versicles in groups of two, three, or four.[23]

To what extent poetic structures are related to the genre or theme of a song is not always easy to detect. There is no general rule about the suitability of one poetic device or another to a particular genre, al-though most of the *sirventes* that survive with music are *coblas unis-sonans*, possibly because many *sirventes* were modeled on preexisting poems, and perhaps as a result were more limited structurally.[24]

Graphing Musical Structure

Structure in the melodies of the troubadours, as in their poems, com-prises two areas, the effective arrangement of "arguments" and themes (*dispositio*) and the deployment of notes within schematic boundaries (*elocutio*). Chapter 4 discussed the way a troubadour might have ar-ranged the musical materials in order to complement the order of the poem's topics, which falls in the first domain, *dispositio*. Some of the illustrations offered earlier included large-scale musical features (such as repetition schemes and variation, direction and contour, and tonal centers and goals), which might be seen as corresponding to the poetic process of the ordering of arguments. These features might be linked to the song's genre not only structurally (in the case of the *lai*, *retroncha*, and *dansa*) but also thematically (for example in the *canso*, *sirventes*, or *pastorela*). The more detailed components of versification, like rhyme schemes and refrains, might have parallels in musical features such as incipits, cadences, and motivic relationships. Such correspondences, though, are not usually direct (i.e., rhyme scheme and cadence structure rarely match, even in the *dansas* and *retronchas*) but are complementary, just as the progressions of poetic themes through the stanzas comple-ment but do not overlap the progression of a melody through its contours and tonal goals.

Just as it is impossible to generalize about the structure of the troubadours' poems, because of the myriad of techniques available and the limitless options for mingling them in a poem, it is also hazardous to generalize about musical structures. The troubadours had numerous musical materials at their disposal, and they combined them in ways that were unpredictable and, to modern minds, often inscrutable. The troubadours created as many diverse musical structures as they did poetic; rarely are two musical structures among the extant melodies exactly alike. The composers seem not to have been interested in following systematic musical procedures that are comparable to the poetic rhyme and stanza devices described above.

The traditional graphing system for musical form (described above) is useful in that it illustrates one level of correspondence between music and text—that between whole verses. But the system has its limitations. First of all, the similarities between the poetical graphing system and the musical graphing system, which on the surface appear quite close, are in fact illusive. A graph of text structure conveys the number of verses, the rhyme scheme, and the syllable count of each verse; identity of letter in poetic graphs means the use of the same rhyming sound but not identical text content. In musical graphs, however, identity of letter means not only musical rhyme (cadence identity) but also identical musical content in the entire verse.

This discrepancy between poetic and musical graphs is due at least in part to the superficial relationships between poetic verses and musical phrases. For example, poetic rhyme is rarely mirrored by musical repetition. Furthermore, the poetic techniques for linking stanzas are not usually reflected directly in the music, since the melody is the same for all stanzas. Melodies are given structure by means of devices that are not found in poetry, including verse-length repetition schemes and repeated cadential patterns as well as smaller-scale motives that are repeated and manipulated, tonal centers, and direction and contour—elements that cannot be shown in graphs as easily as nuances of poetic structure can be.

The task of precisely defining the relationships among the melodic phrases of a troubadour melody is rarely easy, because in most cases where there is repetition, it is not exact—there is almost always some variation, ornamentation, or other modification. It becomes necessary to judge whether a phrase is derived from an earlier one, and there are no rules about how extensive the differences can be before two verses are deemed autonomous. Two reasonable people can disagree about whether a song's form is ABCDEF or ABA'CA''D (the first graph is Gennrich's analysis of PC 202,8,[25] the second is mine), depending on how closely related one believes verses 1, 3, and 5 to be. Further, minor variations can appear at the beginning of a phrase or at the middle or end, and sometimes melodic phrases are progressively varied. In such cases, graphs like AA'A''BCB'DE (PC 406,44) or ABB'CDB'B'''E (PC 47,4) indicate a great deal of repetition and variation in these melodies, but they do not show how or where the variations take place.[26] In the many through-composed songs a formal structure expressed as ABCDEFG indicates nothing more about the piece than the absence of repetition of whole musical phrases, although often there is motivic repetition of musical units shorter than a verse. In effect, the traditional system requires the analyst to reduce significant details to a somewhat artificial and arbitrary skeleton, the result of which is often misleading.

All the melodies, including the 259 extant readings that have verse-phrase repetition and the remaining 56 that are purely through-composed, have other traits that are no less central than repetition to their structural coherence, but which are difficult to convey by means of simple graphs. Despite these problems, there is some merit in using the customary system as a starting point, since many of the extant readings involve some repetition of verse-phrases, and I will begin with this type of analysis. Many of my musical graphs are different from other published graphs, and some of these disagreements are due to a more liberal analysis of the musical relationships than a simple identification of repetition.

Phrase Repetition and Variation

Table 5–1 is a catalogue of the large-scale structures of the troubadours' melodies, showing the incidence of repetition of musical material in the extant melodies, repetition that encompasses at least one poetic verse, and in many cases more than one. A form graphed here as AAB, for instance, which Gennrich referred to as *Kanzone*, might involve a melody in which the first two verses as a unit are repeated, followed by several verses that are not repeated, for example, in a melody whose verses follow the pattern ABABCDEF. It might also include a tune in which verses 1 and 2 are the same, and the material that follows contains no repetition, for example, AA'BCDEF. Slightly over a third of the extant troubadour melodies have this large-scale form; and only a few melodies have strict ABABx form, without any variation, in contrast to the large number of such melodies in the trouvère repertoire.

These large-scale graphs do not indicate variation. For the sake of identifying patterns in composition and in transmission, it was neces-

TABLE 5–1. Large-scale Melodic Structures

AAB	121	(38%)
Through-composed with repetition	64	(20%)
ABACx	21	(7%)
ABCBx	10	(3%)
ABBCx	10	(3%)
ABCAx	5	(2%)
Rounded	10	(3%)
Paired-verse	17	(5%)
Through-composed	57	(18%)

sary to decide whether a phrase is essentially the same music as an earlier phrase, even if it manifests some differences. This table indicates roughly the proportions of songs with repetition of some kind, as compared to those that are through-composed. Each of the 315 readings is included as a separate item in this table, whether or not it is concordant with other readings.

Table 5–2 breaks this information down by manuscripts, and some telling patterns emerge. First of all, the percentages for AAB forms and through-composed forms vary significantly among the manuscripts. Manuscript W has the fewest AAB forms proportionately (22 percent), far below the average of 38 percent among all extant readings, while R has a much greater proportion (49 percent) compared to the average. This reinforces some of the observations made in Chapter 2 that the music scribe of R seemed to favor more regular structures, either creating them himself or copying a large proportion of melodies that had them already (e.g., the large collection of Guiraut Riquier songs in R accounts for 38 of the 78 melodies with AAB form in this codex). Manuscript W has a high proportion of rounded forms, made up entirely of the proto-*virelai*-form *dansas* that were discussed in Chapter 4. Manuscript G has a much greater proportion (31 percent) of through-composed melodies than the other manuscripts, again much larger than the average of 18 percent, while R has well below the average (11 percent). The earliest codex, X, also has an above-average number of through-composed melodies (24 percent).

Most melodies that survive in more than one reading share the same large-scale form, as shown in Table 5–3. With the few that do not, the version in manuscript R often diverges in the predictable fashion of being more regular or involving more repetition. Several of these instances were described in Chapter 2.

If we expand these graphs into more traditional profiles, assigning a letter to each verse, and also separate the songs into generations, some details about how specific composers thought about form emerge.

TABLE 5–2. Large-scale Melodic Structures by Manuscript

Form and Average	X	W	G	R	m
AAB (38%)	8 (38%)	11 (22%)	21 (26%)	78 (49%)	
Thr-comp. w/ rep. (21%)	5 (24%)	14 (27%)	14 (17%)	31 (19%)	
ABACx (7%)	2 (10%)	3 (6%)	8 (10%)	9 (6%)	
ABCBx (3%)	0	1 (2%)	4 (5%)	6 (4%)	
ABBCx (3%)	1 (5%)	1 (2%)	3 (4%)	5 (3%)	
ABCAx (2%)	0	1 (2%)	0	4 (2%)	
Rounded (3%)	0	5 (10%)	2 (2%)	3 (2%)	
Paired-verse (5%)	0	4 (8%)	4 (5%)	7 (4%)	2
Through-composed (18%)	5 (24%)	9 (18%)	25 (31%)	17 (11%)	

TABLE 5–3. Concordant Melodic Readings with Different
Large-scale Melodic Structures

PC	Manuscript	Large-scale structure
70,1	W	ABACx
	R	AAB
	G	ABBCx
70,7	W, G	through-composed
	R	ABBCx
167,53	X	through-composed
	R	AAB
167,43	W, R	AAB
	G	ABCBx
364,4	G, X	through-composed
	R	through-composed w/ rep.
364,39	W, G	through-composed
	R	through-composed w/ rep.

Tables 5–4 through 5–10 combine concordant readings unless they have different structures.

In the first generation (Table 5–4), Marcabru and Jaufre Rudel seemed to favor structures that had repetition; Jaufre's melodies (all found in manuscript R) are exclusively in AAB form; Marcabru's are not as predictable. Two of his melodies seem to be mostly through-composed but with the return of some musical material from an early verse in a later one; both of these melodies are found in manuscript W, a large proportion of whose melodies behave in the same way. See Example 5–1, in which verse 7 is a variation of verse 3. Note also in this melody that verse 2 begins with the same intervals as verse 1, transposed up a fifth.

Musical structures in the second generation (Table 5–5) are much more varied (probably because the melodies are more numerous). We find the first examples of paired-verse form and of a rounded form, both among the melodies of Bernart de Ventadorn. In contrast to the earlier generation, AAB structures are decidedly in the minority here—well below the average for such forms throughout the repertoire; Rigaut de Berbezilh and Raimbaut d'Aurenga seem to have avoided them altogether. Three melodies in this generation have no musical repetition at all.

Among the AAB structures in Bernart's melodies, rarely is the repetition without some variation. In Example 5–2, manuscript R's version is without variation, while G and W offer some slight variation,

TABLE 5–4. First Generation (1120–50), 8 Melodies

a. Large-scale Structures

AAB	thr-c/rep.	ABACx	ABCBx	ABBCx	ABCAx	rounded	prd-vers.	thr-c
5	2	1						
63%	25%	13%						

b. Verse Forms

	Mss	PC	Verse form	Large-scale form
Marcabru	R	293,30	A B A B B' B' C	AAB
	W	293,35	A B C D D A' E F G	thr-c/rep.
	W	293,13	A B C D E F C' G	thr-c/rep.
	R	293,18	A B A' C D A"	ABACx
Jaufre Rudel	R	262,6	A A' A A' B C D	AAB
	X, W, R	262,2	A B A B C D B	AAB
	R	262,5	A B A B' C D(B")E	AAB
	R	262,3	A B A B C D	AAB

but in different verses (verse 3 in W and verse 4 in G). Such small differences might reflect a performing practice of ornamentation. Note also that the version in R differs significantly in the intervallic contents of its first four verses—possibly an error of written transmission.

Manuscript X's version of the melody in Example 5–3 features a variation of the B phrase at the end of verse 4 which seems to reinforce the poetic *enjambement* in stanza I (but found in none of the following stanzas):

La dolce vois ai oide
del rosignolet salvage,
qui s'es en mon cor saillide
si que tuit mei desier[27]
e mal trait q'amors mi done
m'adoucist e m'asaizone;
e m'aurie bon mister
l'autrui joi en mon dannage.

I have heard the sweet voice of the wild nightingale, which has so pierced my heart that it has sweetened and softened all the desire and mistreatment that love gives me. And I will very much need another joy in my sorrow.

Earlier (Example 4–1) it was suggested that the progression to a pitch climax from verse 4 to verse 5 in this melody might reflect the thematic development from stanzas I and II to III and IV, where the poet moves from the expression of his oneness with nature to a full-throated utterance of despair and bitterness. On a broad level, then, the melody might be a musical expression of the poem's theme; but on an immediately audible level, at least in stanza I, the melody helps underpin the

EX. 5–1. Marcabru. PC 293,13. W fol. 203v/B195v.

syntactical movement by pushing the range up to B at the end of verse 4, with a smooth transition to C at the beginning of verse 5.

The structures of the two versions of the melody in Example 5–4 differ radically. In manuscript R the structure consists of paired verses, while in manuscript G this form is interrupted at verse 4. While this may be another case of R's scribe's having regularized the structure, I find it more likely that G's scribe—who was not always careful—wrote verse 4 at the wrong pitch level (exactly one step lower than verse 2) and then, thinking that this was a new phrase, carried on the paired-verse structure (making both verses 6 and 8 identical to verse 4) until the end, where he had to create a new musical phrase for the final verse. The rhyme scheme of this poem proceeds in pairs (abababaa), which might argue in favor of the more regular musical structure found in R.

TABLE 5–5. Second Generation (1140–1180), 31 Melodies

a. Large-scale Structures

AAB	thr-c/rep.	ABACx	ABCBx	ABBCx	ABCAx	rounded	prd-vers.	thr-c
9	10	3	1	2		1	2	3
29%	32%	10%	3%	6%		3%	6%	10%

b. Verse Forms

Mss	PC	Verse form	Large-scale form
Rigaut de Berbezilh			
W	421,10	A B C D E B C F	thr-c/rep.
X	421,3	A B C D E F G H G G' H'	thr-c/rep.
X, W, G	421,2	A B A' C D E F C' E' F E"	ABACx
W, G	421,1		thr-c
Peire d'Alvernhe			
R	323,15	A B A' B' C D E	AAB
X	323,15	A B A B C D E	AAB
W	323,4	A B C B' D E F	ABCBx
Raimbaut d'Aurenga			
X	389,36	A B C D B' C' E F	thr-c/rep.
Bernart de Ventadorn			
R	70,1	A B A' B' C D E F	AAB
G	70,17	A B A B' C D E F	AAB
R	70,23	A B A A' C D E F	AAB
W, G, R	70,41	A B A B C D E F	AAB
X	70,23	A B A' B' C D B" E	AAB
R	70,4	A B A' B' C B" D E	AAB
G, R	70,6	A B A' B C C' D E	AAB
G, R	70,12	A B A B' C D B"	AAB
R	70,39	A B B' A' D D E F	thr-c/rep.
W	70,31	A B C D A' C' E F	thr-c/rep.
G	70,31	A B C D A' E F D	thr-c/rep.
X	70,42	A B C D D' E F D"	thr-c/rep.
W, G, R	70,43	A B C D E F D' G	thr-c/rep.
R	70,8	A B C D E F G D'	thr-c/rep.
W	70,24	A B C D E B' F G	thr-c/rep.
W	70,1	A B A' C D E F G	ABACx
G	70,36	A B A' C D C' D C' E	ABACx
R	70,7	A B B' C D B" E F	ABBCx
G	70,1	A B B' C D E F G	ABBCx
R	70,25	A B C B' A B C B' E B" C' D'	rnd.
G, R	70,16	ABCD ABCD'	prd-vers.
R	70,36	AB AB CD CD C'	prd-vers.
W, G	70,7		thr-c
W	70,19		thr-c

EX. 5–2. Bernart de Ventadorn. PC 70,41. R fol. 56v; W fol. 188/B178; G fol 10v.

Peire d'Alvernhe's *tenso* with Bernart de Ventadorn (Example 5–5) presents several dilemmas from a structural point of view. The first four verses appear initially to be quite different from one another, and the melody seems to be through-composed. Verse 4, though, turns out to be similar to verse 2, transposed down a fourth. Verse 3 is not particularly related to verse 1, possibly because of the marked intervallic difference between verses 1 and 2 created by the B♭ added in verse 2, which draws the ear down toward F at the end of the verse. The melody then sinks farther, to its transposition of verse 2 in verse 4—the singer has mutated from the hard to the soft to the natural hexachord over the course of four verses! It is not possible to say whether such a mutation occurred in an actual performance by a singer, or whether a scribe heard it thus in his own ear while writing. It is the only melody of Peire's in manuscript W, and as seen in Example 2–7 above, the transmission of another song of

EX. 5–2. Continued

1. Cant par la flor jus - ta.l verd foil.

2. e vei lo temps clar e se - re.

3. e.l dolç chant dels au - çels pel bruoil.

4. m'a - dol - ça lo cor e.m re - ve.

5. pos l'au - çels chan - ton a lor for.

6. eu q'ai tant de joi en mon cor.

7. deu ben chan - tar qe tuit li mei çor - nal.

8. son joi e chant qe no pes de ren al.

his with different melodies in X and R raises questions about the stability of his music in transmission.

In the third generation (Table 5–6) the large proportion of irregular structures continues, although a number of AAB forms are found, many with variations similar to the ones seen in earlier melodies. In several melodies the repetitions of phrases are exact, particularly among those found in manuscript R. There are no AAB structures among the surviving melodies of Guillem de Saint Didier, Bertran de Born, Folquet de Marselha, Arnaut Daniel, and Gui d'Ussel. Most of the melodies in this generation, in fact, are either entirely through-composed or have one or more repeated phrases among later verses in unpredictable positions.

A melody by Guiraut de Bornelh (PC 242,51) was used later by Peire Cardenal for a *canso* (PC 335,7). Its AAB structure is not as straightforward as in other songs, in that the music of the first three verses recurs,

EX. 5–3. Bernart de Ventadorn. PC 70,23. X fol. 89.

with extra music, in the next four verses. The music of verse 1 is then varied as verse 8, and new music completes the final three verses. Peire's adaptation of this melody retains the same structure, while allowing a few differences in pitches. Both melodies are found in manuscript R, separated by only ten leaves. It is likely that the scribe was cognizant that the same melody served both texts, and since he seems to have paid close attention to musical structure in general, it is not surprising that these two melodies are so similar in overall form, if different in some details. Example 4–9 shows the same scribe's adaptation of a melody by Bertran de Born for a poem by the Monk of Montaudon.

In both of its extant versions, a melody by Gaucelm Faidit (Example 5–6) has internal borrowing of music that is shorter than a verse. It has

EX. 5–4. Bernart de Ventadorn. PC 70,36. R fol. 57v–58; G fol. 20v.

a variegated syllable and rhyme structure: $a_8 b_8 a_8 b_8 b_8 c_8 c_8 c_4 c_4 c_8 d_{10} d_{10}$. In both manuscripts, the first four-syllable verse (verse 8) uses the music of the first *hemistich* of verse 2; in manuscript G, verse 9 uses the notes of that same *hemistich* from verse 2 as a framework for its four syllables and decorates them with several melismas. In manuscript X, verse 9 seems to be new music, and in its contour (continuing the descent to C) it seems almost to complete the phrase begun in verse 8. The scribe of manuscript G borrows material from verse 4 for verse 11 at the end of the song, while in X verse 11 is new music. In X, however, verse 6 is a varied repetition of verse 3. The variation comes at the end of this verse, where the melody rises to C in verse 6 instead of settling on A as in verse 3. This coincides, as in Example 5–3, with a poetic *enjambement* between

EX. 5–5. Peire d'Alvernhe. PC 323,4. W fol. 190v/B180v.

verses 6 and 7. Although this reading in manuscript G does not use the music of verse 3 here, it does have the rise of pitch to C, leading to the high D of verse 7. The kind of internal borrowing seen in both versions seems to be a common compositional (or performing) procedure throughout the troubadour repertoire, but it is impossible in this case to know why the internal borrowing is so different in the two versions.

About half of Folquet de Marselha's melodies are through-composed; the rest have at least one repeated phrase. PC 155,10 falls in the ABBCx category in two of its three versions (manuscripts G and R). In the third version (in manuscript W) the second verse is not repeated immediately, but the last three verses are variations of verses 2 and 3. The text of this reading is a Frenchified version of what occurs as stanza 2 in other manuscripts, and W has no more stanzas, although the scribe allowed space for at least two. Most other sources (including G and R) give five stanzas for this song. The differences that set W's text and melody apart from all other versions suggest that its reading is less reliable.

TABLE 5–6. Third Generation (1160–1210), 87 Melodies

a. Large-scale Structures

AAB	thr-c/rep.	ABACx	ABCBx	ABBCx	ABCAx	rounded	prd-vers.	thr-c
18	28	7	5	4	1	1	2	21
21%	32%	8%	6%	5%	1%	1%	2%	24%

b. Verse Forms

Mss	PC	Verse form	Large-scale form
Jordan Bonel			
W	273,1	A B A B C D E F G	AAB
Guiraut de Bornelh			
R	242,64	A A B C D	AAB
R	242,69	A B A B' C D E F	AAB
R	242,51	A B C A B' D C A" E F	AAB
R	242,45	A B C B' A B D E F B"	ABCBx
Berenguier de Palol			
R	47,3	A B A B C C' D E	AAB
R	47,5	A B A B C D B'	AAB
R	47,7	A B C D B' C' D' B' C" F	thr-c/rep.
R	47,1	A B C D D' E B' B" E' B'	thr-c/rep.
R	47,11	A B C D E C' D'	thr-c/rep.
R	47,12	A B C D E F D' G	thr-c/rep.
R	47,6	A B A' C B' A' C' D	ABACx
R	47,4	A B B' C D B" B''' E	ABBCx
Guillem de Saint Didier			
G, R	234,16	A B C C' D E	thr-c/rep.
Arnaut de Maruelh			
R	30,16	A B A B' C A' D E	AAB
G	30,19	A B C D C' B' E F G H	thr-c/rep.
R	30,15	A B B' C B" D E F G E'	ABBCx
G	30,3		thr-c
R	30,17		thr-c
R	30,23		thr-c
Gaucelm Faidit			
R	167,37	A B A B C D E F	AAB
R	167,53	A B A B C D E F G	AAB
W	167,43	A B A' B' C D E F G H J	AAB
R	167,43	A B A B C C' D E F G B'	AAB
W, G, R	167,30	A B A B' C D C' E F	AAB
G	167,27	A B A B' C D E C C' C" C''' E' F	AAB
X, G, R	167,32	A B C D A' B' C' D' E F G H J J' K L	AAB
X, G, R	167,15	A B C D A' B' E F G A"	thr-c/rep.
X	167,56	A B C D E C' F B' G H J	thr-c/rep.
G	167,56	A B C D E F G B' B" H J	thr-c/rep.

TABLE 5–6. (continued)

Mss	PC	Verse form	Large-scale form
Gaucelm Faidit (continued)			
R	167,4	A B C D E D' F E' G D" H J K	thr-c/rep.
G	167,34	A B C D E F G H J G' F' K F"	thr-c/rep.
G	167,17	A B A C D E B' C' F C"	ABAC*x*
X, G, R	167,52	A B A'C D E F G H J	ABAC*x*
G	167,43	A B C B'D E F G H J K	ABCB*x*
X, W, G	167,22	A B B'C D E F G H	ABBC*x*
X	167,37		thr-c
X	167,53		thr-c
G, R	167,59		thr-c
Bertran de Born			
R	80,37	A B C DC' D' B' C" E C''' E'	thr-c/rep.
Raimon Jordan			
W	404,4	A B A B'C D E C' D	AAB
W	404,11	A B C A'D E C' F	ABCA*x*
Folquet de Marselha			
G, R	155,3	A B C D A' E B' D'	thr-c/rep.
G, R	155,22	A B C D A' E C' F	thr-c/rep.
G, R	155,27	A B C D E C' D' F E' G	thr-c/rep.
W	155,10	A B C D E F C' D'D"	thr-c/rep.
G	155,8	A B C D E F G H J D'	thr-c/rep.
G, R	155,14	A B A'C D E F G B' H	ABAC*x*
G	155,21	A B C B'D E F E'	ABCB*x*
G, R	155,10	A B B'C D E F C' C"	ABBC*x*
R	155,1		thr-c
G	155,1		thr-c
G, R	155,5		thr-c
G	155,11		thr-c
G, R	155,16		thr-c
G, R	155,18		thr-c
W, G, R	155,23		thr-c
Arnaut Daniel			
G	29,6		thr-c
G	29,14		thr-c
Raimbaut de Vaqueiras			
R	392,3	A B A B C D E F G H	AAB
R	392,13	A B C D E A' D' E'	thr-c/rep.
R	392,28	A B C D E C F G	thr-c/rep.
R	392,2	A B C D E F B' G	thr-c/rep.
R	392,18	A B C D E F G H J F' G' H'	thr-c/rep.
R	392,24	ABC A' DB'E A' ABC" A"	rnd
R	392,9	ABCD ABCD A'EA'E' FFGH FFGH'	prd-vers.

Mss	PC	Verse form	Large-scale form
Peire Vidal			
R	364,36	A A' B C D E F G	AAB
R	364,4	A B C D E C' F G	thr-c/rep.
R	364,24	A B C D E E' E" F G H	thr-c/rep.
W	364,49	A B C D E F C D	thr-c/rep.
G	364,40	A B C D E F D'	thr-c/rep.
R	364,39	A B C D E F G B'	thr-c/rep.
G	364,37	A B A'C D B' A" F G	ABACx
R	364,31	A B A'C D E F G	ABACx
R	364,7	A A'A A'B B' C C' D	prd-vers.
X	364,4		thr-c
G	364,4		thr-c
X, G, R	364,11		thr-c
R	364,30		thr-c
W, G	364,39		thr-c
R	364,42		thr-c
Comtessa de Dia			
W	46,2	A B A B C D B	AAB
Gui d'Ussel			
G	194,19	A B C D A' E F G	thr-c/rep.
W	194,8	A B C D E F G H H'	thr-c/rep.
G	194,6	A B C B'D C' E C" F G	ABCBx
G	194,3	A B C B'D E F G F'	ABCBx
Guillem Magret			
W	223,3	A B C D E B' F G C' H	thr-c/rep.
W	223,1	A B A'C D A' B' D' E F A"	ABACx

There is one rounded melodic structure in this generation, in a song by Raimbaut de Vaqueiras (Example 5–7). The music of the first four verses returns, slightly varied, in the last four verses. Two of the intervening four verses are closely related as well, with only verses 5 and 7 providing marked contrast. Two other melodies by Raimbaut have a regular structure, one in AAB form without any variation (PC 392,3), the other the paired-verse form of "Kalenda maia" (PC 392,9). His other four melodies have irregular repetitions of phrases.

A song by Peire Vidal (PC 364,49) illustrates another way of bringing back musical phrases. Here the music of verses 3 and 4 returns without variation in the final two verses. Verses 5 and 6 provide contrast, and the overall structure is actually ABCB—rounded in a certain sense.

The only surviving melody by a *trobairitz*, the Comtessa de Dia

EX. 5–6. Gaucelm Faidit. PC 167,56. X fol. 89v; G fol 22v–23.

EX. 5–7. Raimbaut de Vaqueiras. PC 392,24. R fol. 61v.

(Example 5–8) begins with exact repetition of the first two verses, and the music of verse 2 returns in the final verse as well (once again rounding the melodic shape). The exact repetition of music, obviously, requires the same number of syllables in the verse; when the number of syllables is not the same, often the scribe would make an adjustment by realigning the notes with the syllables, or omitting or adding notes, as we have seen in several examples. In this song, found in manuscript W, however, the music scribe made no adjustment to the melody of verse 7, since its text has the same number of syllables (counting the paroxytonic rhyme) as verse 2. This is curious, however, since all other versions of this poem end with an oxytonic rhyme, "desavinens" instead of "desavinence." This is a Frenchification, which the scribe might have corrected had he entered more than one stanza, and the music then would have needed to be adjusted. Note also that the text scribe gave the masculine form of "amigs" at the end of verse 2, although other manuscripts uses the paroxytonic "amie," for which the music scribe wrote the correct number of notes.[28] It is difficult to tell what the music

EX. 5–8. Comtessa de Dia. PC 46,2. W fol. 204/B196.

might have been, had the text in these two verses conformed to the more common reading. The music scribe did not adjust the melody for verse 2, suggesting that he had a tune either firmly in mind or clearly given in an exemplar. But he did follow the written text of verse 7, suggesting that whatever melody he was remembering or copying, he wrote down a version of it that fit the Frenchified rhyme.

With the fourth generation of troubadours (Table 5–7), the proportion of AAB structures increases dramatically, from 21 percent in the previous generation to 40 percent, while the number of structures with random repetition decreases by a similar proportion (32 to 12 percent). There is also a striking number of paired-verse forms in this generation. The melodies of Aimeric de Peguilhan and Perdigon are somewhat unusual for this period in that most of them are entirely through-composed.

Typical of melodies with AAB structure in this generation is a song by Raimon de Miraval (Example 5–9), in which the second B phrase, on verse 4, is the same as the first until the second *hemistich*, where it ends higher than before, as if to lead into the next phrase. We have seen this in earlier melodies as well (for example, in Bernart de Ventadorn), and the terminology of "open" and "closed" endings comes to mind, although there is no standard way in which such endings manifest themselves. In cases like this one, where the repetition of a phrase ends with a different cadence than before, one that moves in a direction that leads smoothly into the following phrase, the terms "open" and "closed" seem almost backwards—the second ending does not close the first section, but rather links it to the next. Such schemes occur relatively frequently among AAB structures. In this melody, verse 5 stretches to a pitch that is a fourth higher than the melody has reached before, and the ascent at the end of verse 4 helps prepare the ear for the higher tessitura.

One of Pons de Capduelh's melodies (Example 5–10) has the same structure, but here the second B section ends lower than the first, and verse 5 descends even lower—as in Raimon's melody, providing pitch contrast (but here lower) to the earlier verses. While this procedure might fit our conception of "open" and "closed" better (since the drop in pitch to the C—established in earlier verses as a tonal center—has a "final" sound to it; cf. Example 2–5), the context is similar to other examples where the impetus for the variation might be to provide a conjunct transition to the next phrase. Even though the contrast we might expect in the second section is present, the varied B ending does not articulate and set apart the first section so much as it effects a fluid—almost unnoticeable—connection.

An extreme example of phrase variation is found in a melody by the Monk of Montaudon (Example 5–11), whose verses 1, 2, 3, 4, 6, and 8 are built on the same musical material, each with a different ending. Verses

TABLE 5–7. Fourth Generation (1180–1240), 65 Melodies

a. Large-scale Structures

AAB	thr-c/rep.	ABACx	ABCBx	ABBCx	ABCAx	rounded	prd-vers.	thr-c
26	8	5	2	1	1	1	5	16
40%	12%	8%	3%	2%	2%	2%	8%	25%

b. Verse Forms

	Mss	PC	Verse form	Large-scale form
Monge de Montaudon				
	R	305,6	A A' A''A''' B A''''C A''''' D	AAB
	R	305,10	A B C D B'C' E F E'	thr-c/rep.
Peire Raimon de Tolosa				
	G	355,5	A B A' C D E F G E F' H	ABACx
Peirol	X, G	366,12	A B A B' C D E	AAB
	R	366,9	A B A' B' C D E B''	AAB
	G	366,9	A B A' B' C D E E'	AAB
	G	366,11	A B A B' C D E F	AAB
	G	366,14	A B A' B' C D E F	AAB
	R	366,20	A B A B C D E F	AAB
	G	366,6	A B A B' C D E F G	AAB
	R	366,19	A B A B C C'D E	AAB
	G	366,3	A B A' B' C A''	AAB
	G	366,15	A B C D A B C D E F C' D'	AAB
	G	366,29	A B C D B E F G H	thr-c/rep.
	R	366,2	A B C D E F G E'	thr-c/rep.
	G	366,31	A B C D C D' B'	thr-c/rep.
	G	366,33	A B A' C D E F G	ABACx
	G	366,21	A B C D A B' C'	rnd.
	G	366,26	A B A' B' C D C' D'	prd-vers.
	G	366,13		thr-c
	G	366,22		thr-c
Raimon de Miraval				
	R	406,23	A B A B' C D E	AAB
	R	406,24	A B A B C D E F	AAB
	R	406,2	A B A' B' C D E B'' F	AAB
	R	406,47	A B A B C D E C' F	AAB
	G, R	406,13	A B A' B' C D E E'	AAB
	R	406,8	A B A B C D A' A''	AAB
	G, R	406,20	A B A' B C A''D E	AAB
	R	406,44	A A' A'' B C B' D E	AAB
	R	406,14	A B A B C C'D E F	AAB
	G	406,2	A B A B A'C B'' D E	AAB
	R	406,22	A B C D A'E F G	thr-c/rep.
	R	406,15	A B C D D'E F F'	thr-c/rep.
	R	406,9	A B C D E A'C' F	thr-c/rep.

Mss	PC	Verse form	Large-scale form
Raimon de Miraval (continued)			
R	406,18	A B A' C D E F G	ABACx
R	406,31	A B C B' D E D' F	ABCBx
R	406,12	A B C B' D E E B" F	ABCBx
R	406,40	A B B' C D E F G	ABBCx
R	406,42	A B C A B' D C E	ABCAx
G, R	406,7	AB AB' CDB CDB	prd-vers.
R	406,21	A B A B C D C D	prd-vers.
R	406,28		thr-c
R	406,36		thr-c
R	406,39		thr-c
Perdigon G	370,9		thr-c
G	370,13		thr-c
X, G	370,14		thr-c
Aimeric de Peguilhan			
G, R	10,25	A B A' B' C D E D'	AAB
R	10,45		prd-vers.
G	10,12		thr-c
G	10,15		thr-c
G	10,27		thr-c
G	10,41		thr-c
W	10,45		thr-c
Uc Brunenc			
R	450,3	A B A' C D E	ABACx
Pons de Capduelh			
G	375,16	A B A' B' C D E F	AAB
X, R	375,27	A B A B' C D E F G	AAB
W	375,14	A A' A A' B C A' D	AAB
G	375,19		thr-c
Guillem Ademar			
R	202,8	A B A' C A" E	ABACx
Albertet X	16,17a	A B A' B C D E F	AAB
W	16,5a		thr-c
W	16,14		thr-c
Pistoleta X	372,3	A B A B C D E F	AAB
Cadenet R	106,14	A A B C D E C' F G	thr-c/rep.
Guillem Augier			
W	205,5		prd-vers.

EX. 5–9. Raimon de Miraval. PC 406,23. R fol. 87.

2 and 4 end low, on D, while verses 6 and 8 rise to A. The latter two verses lead by conjunct motion to the following verses, which move higher.

Two of the five paired-verse structures from this generation are found in the *descorts* by Guillem Augier and Aimeric de Peguilhan (PC 205,5 and 10,45 in manuscript R; recall that W's melody for Aimeric's *descort* is through-composed; see Example 4–7). The three *cansos* here with this musical form are quite regular; two of them involve some variation while the third has strict repetition. One of the two by Peirol (Example 5–12) features variation of each pair of verses, in the form of ornaments on the pitches rather than modification of the ending, except on the last verse, which rises to G rather than settling on low C as one might expect. This melody was adapted to a French *pastourelle* text (RS 41) by Hue de St. Quentin (fl. c. 1220) and to a *conductus* text which in Notre Dame manuscript F (fol. 356) gives Peirol's melody as the lower of two voices. The melody in all of the *contrafacta* begins on G instead of

EX. 5–10. Pons de Capduelh. PC 375,27. R fol. 55v–56.

C, making the final G seem more suitable as a note leading from the end of one stanza to the beginning of the next. But wide leaps from the last note of one stanza to the first note of the next are not uncommon among the troubadour melodies.

With only six melodies extant from the fifth generation (Table 5–8), it is dangerous to make generalizations. It would appear that the trend toward regularization continues; no through-composed melodies survive from this period. Variation of the same type that we have seen before is found among these melodies. For example, one by Uc de Saint

EX. 5–11. Monge de Montaudon. PC 305,6. R fol. 39v.

Circ (Example 5–13) uses the B music three times: in verse 2 with a rise at the cadence to A in preparation for the high D at the beginning of verse 3; with a descent to low D at the end of verse 4 to lead into an immediate repeat of the phrase in verse 5, beginning on low D; and in verse 5 (which has one more syllable than the others) with the rise to A again, which leads easily to the A at the beginning of verse 6.

The last generation of troubadours (Table 5–9) is dominated by Guiraut Riquier. Probably because of his self-awareness and concern for seeing his works preserved, he is far better represented among the

EX. 5–12. Peirol. PC 366,26. G fol. 46.

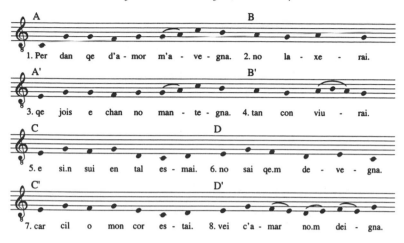

TABLE 5–8. Fifth Generation (1210–1255), 6 Melodies

a. Large-scale Structures

AAB	thr-c/rep.	ABACx	ABCBx	ABBCx	ABCAx	rounded	prd-vers.	thr-c
3	2							1
50%	33%							17%

b. Verse Forms

	Mss	PC	Verse form	Large-scale form
Pons d'Ortaffa				
	R	379,2	A B A B B'C A D	AAB
Aimeric de Belenoi				
	R	9,13a	A B C D D'A' B' F F'	thr-c/rep.
Uc de Saint Circ				
	G	457,3	A B A B C D E F G H	AAB
	G	457,26	A B A B' B''C D E	AAB
	G	457,40	A B A B B'C D C D'	prd-vers.
Blacasset	W	96,2	A B C D E B' F G A'	thr-c/rep.

extant melodies than any other troubadour. Table 5–9a separates out
Guiraut's melodies to show that the AAB structure so prevalent among
his melodies is not the main structure of the few extant melodies by
Peire Cardenal, Daude de Pradas, and Guiraut d'Espanha.

The rounded form in the one extant melody of Guiraut d'Espanha
was discussed as Example 4–11. The ABCA*x* pattern among Peire

EX. 5–13. Uc de Saint Circ. PC 457,26. G fol. 83v.

Cardenal's melodies are both *contrafacta*, one of a melody by Guiraut de Bornelh (PC 242,51 = 335,7), the other of a melody by Raimon Jordan (PC 404,11 = 335,49; see Example 4–10). In both cases Peire respected the basic outline of the borrowed melodies.

Guiraut Riquier's melodies are too numerous to allow extensive study here.[29] Many of the 38 melodies in AAB form entail variation, so often in the guise of motivic development that it will be more appropriate to discuss it along with other such procedures below. Only three melodies are through-composed, and one is in paired-verse form. The remaining six melodies have randomly repeated phrases, usually with some variation, as in PC 248,6, whose verse 4 repeats the music of verse

TABLE 5–9. Sixth Generation (1220–1300), 53 melodies

a. Large-scale Structures

AAB	thr-c/rep.	ABACx	ABCBx	ABBCx	ABCAx	rounded	prd-vers.	thr-c
39	3		2		3	1	1	4
74%	6%		4%		6%	2%	2%	8%

Guiraut Riquier, 48 Melodies

AAB	thr-c/rep.	ABACx	ABCBx	ABBCx	ABCAx	rounded	prd-vers.	thr-c
38	3		2		1		1	3
79%	6%		4%		2%		2%	6%

Without Guiraut Riquier, 5 Melodies

AAB	thr-c/rep.	ABACx	ABCBx	ABBCx	ABCAx	rounded	prd-vers.	thr-c
1					2	1		1
20%					40%	20%		20%

b. Verse Forms

Mss	PC	Verse form	Large-scale form
Peire Cardenal			
R	335,67	A B A B C D B' C'	AAB
R	335,7	A B C A' D E C A' F G	ABCAx
R	335,49	A B C A' D E F G	ABCAx
Daude de Pradas			
W	124,5		thr-c
Guiraut d'Espanha			
W	244,1a	ABCD EFG EFG ABCD	rnd.
Guiraut Riquier			
R	248,33	A B A B C D E	AAB
R	248,46	A B A B' C D E	AAB
R	248,62	A B A B C D E	AAB
R	248,87	A B A' B C D E	AAB
R	248,44	A A' A A'' B C D	AAB
R	248,58	A B A B C D E F	AAB
R	248,63	A B A B C D E F	AAB
R	248,31	A A' A A' B C D E F	AAB
R	248,8	A B A' B' C D E F G	AAB
R	248,68	A B A B C D E F G	AAB
R	248,79	A B A B C D E F G	AAB
R	248,80	A B A B' C D E F G	AAB
R	248,89	A B A B C D E F G	AAB
R	248,27	A B A' B' C D E F G H	AAB
R	248,56	A B A B C D E F B'	AAB
R	248,5	A B A B A' B C D C'	AAB

TABLE 5–9. (continued)

Mss	PC	Verse form	Large-scale form
Guiraut Riquier (continued)			
R	248,82	A B A B' B''C C' D	AAB
R	248,7	A B A B B'C C' D B'' E F E'G H	AAB
R	248,18	A B A B' C A B''	AAB
R	248,29	A B A' B' C A B	AAB
R	248,78	A B A B C A' B' A''D	AAB
R	248,57	A B A B' C D A' E (A'?)	AAB
R	248,12	A B A' B C D A'' B' E F	AAB
R	248,65	A B A B C D C' E D' D''	AAB
R	248,21	A B A B C D E B'	AAB
R	248,30	A B A' B' C D E B''	AAB
R	248,45	A B A' B C D E B'	AAB
R	248,66	A B A B C D E D E F	AAB
		[DE D E F A B A B C	BAA]
R	248,60	A A' B C D E F G	AAB
R	248,2	A B C A B C' D E F G H	AAB
R	248,48	A B C A B C D E F G	AAB
R	248,71	A B C A B' C' D E F G	AAB
R	248,19	A B C A B' D E F G	AAB
R	248,52	A B C A B A' B D E C'	AAB
R	248,26	A B C D A B' C D E F G H C' D'	AAB
R	248,55	A B C D A B C D E F A' G C D'	AAB
R	248,67	A B C D A B C E F G H J	AAB
R	248,69	A B C B'A' C A B C B' A' C D E	AAB
R	248,10	A B C D C'D' A' E	thr-c/rep.
R	248,1	A B C D E F A'	thr-c/rep.
R	248,24	A B C D E F D' F' C' E' F'' G	thr-c/rep.
R	248,6	A B C B' D C' E F	ABCB*x*
R	248,61	A B C B' D E F G	ABCB*x*
R	248,83	A B C A' B' D E F	ABCA*x*
R	248,85	ABC ABC DE DE FG	prd-vers.
R	248,13		thr-c
R	248,23		thr-c
R	248,53		thr-c

2, and verse 6 repeats that of verse 3, both with some modifications—the former by way of ornamentation, the latter as a way of linking the end of verse 6 to the beginning of verse 7.

As mentioned earlier, one of Guiraut's songs (Example 5–14) has a structure unique among extant troubadour songs, which is explained in a rubric in manuscript R:

Canso redonda et encadenada, de motz e so, d'En Gr. Riquier, facha l'an .m.cc.lxxxij. en abril. El so de la cobla segonda, pren se el miehc [sic] de la premiera, e sec se tro la fi. Pueys torna al comensamen, e fenis el mieg aisi co es senhat et aisi canta se la .iiij³. e la vj³. e la tersa e la v³. aisi co la premieira e no y cap retornada.

Canso redonda and *encadenada*, of words and melody, by Guiraut Riquier, made in 1282 in April. For the melody of the second stanza, begin at the middle of the first and stop at the end. Then return to the beginning, and finish at the middle where the sign is. And thus sing the 4th and 6th [stanzas], and sing the 3rd and 5th [stanzas] like the first, not returning to the start.

This canon directs the singer to begin the melody of the second, fourth, and sixth stanzas at a point halfway through, which the scribe marked by a large cross on the staff.[30] The melody is thus divided into two large sections, the first in large-scale AA'B form, which is then reversed to BAA' in alternate stanzas. Two stanzas together then would yield the form AA'BBAA', a very large-scale rounded structure. The rhymes of this song are similarly transposed in succeeding stanzas, although not in such a way as to line up with the retrograde of the melody phrases:

Stanzas I, III, V:									Stanzas II, IV, VI:									
a	b'	a	b'	a	c	d'	c	d'	c	c	d'	c	d'	c	a	b'	a	b'	a	rhymes
A	B	A	B	C	D	E	D	E	F	D	E	D	E	F	A	B	A	B	C	verse form
A		A'		B						B					A		A'			large-scale form

The stanzas are also *capfinidas*, in which not only the last rhyme word, but indeed the entire last verse of each stanza is repeated as the first verse of the following stanza. This melody and its canon are unique in the troubadour repertoire, and indeed in all other medieval monophonic repertoires with which I am familiar.[31]

Of the melodies that survive anonymously (Table 5–10), four are the *dansas* with rounded forms that are discussed in Chapter 4, and two others are the *lais* (Example 4–8). The remaining songs do not depart from the procedures described above.

This survey of the verse forms of the troubadour melodies shows that, even accounting for the variation in transmission and the likelihood of scribal intervention, there was a clear move toward regular repetition structures from the first to the last generations. The early and middle periods saw wide experimentation with repetition and variation, but not in any one large-scale pattern. Through-composed melodies make up a significant proportion of the songs of the third and fourth generations. AAB structures increased dramatically by the end of the twelfth century, while the variety of unpredictable repetition (for example, ABACx) decreased. By the end of the thirteenth century, very

EX. 5–14. Guiraut Riquier. PC 248,66, stanzas I and II. R fol. 108v.

few melodies were through-composed. Paired-verse and rounded forms are found throughout the entire period.

Tonal Centers, Contours, Incipits, and Cadences

Tonal centers, pitch goals and directions, cadences, and incipits can be seen as structural components of a troubadour melody. But the identification of a "final" pitch is problematic. Often the last pitch that a

TABLE 5–10. Anonymous, 13 melodies

a. Large-scale Structures

AAB	thr-c/rep.	ABACx	ABCBx	ABBCx	ABCAx	rounded	prd-vers.	thr-c
3	3					4	2	4
23%	23%					30%	15%	30%

b. Verse Forms

Mss	PC	Verse form	Large-scale form
W	461,197	A B A B C D E	AAB
W	461,150	A B A B C D E F	AAB
W	461,13	A B A' B' C D B"	AAB
W	461,9	A B C D B' E F G H J	thr-c/rep.
W	461,152	A B C D E F G E' HE' J E"	thr-c/rep.
W	461,102	A B C D E F G H E' C'J K	thr-c/rep.
W	461,20a	ABCD EFEF' ABCD	rnd.
W	461,92	ABAB' CDCD' ABAB'	rnd.
W	461,196	ABC DEF DEF' ABC	rnd.
W	461,230	ABAB' CDCD' ABAB'	rnd.
W, m	461,122		prd-vers.
W, m	461,124		prd-vers.
W	461,37		thr-c

manuscript gives for a melody is one that has occurred only rarely, or never, until the end, or is one for which the ear has not been prepared. The number of melodies whose "final" is the same as its initial note, or even the same as the last note of internal cadences, is quite small. One reason for this may be that there were two "final" notes. Because the melodies are strophic, the end of one stanza proceeds immediately to the beginning of the next one. The absolute "final" note heard at the end of a melody is "final" only once, whereas the "final" note of each stanza occurs four or five or times before this, as an intermediate pitch. Because the absolute "final" pitch may not have left as strong an impression in the ear, it may not have made its way into some sources, whereas the intermediate "final" may be the one that was written down.

Furthermore, the intervallic content of many melodies (which is treated in Chapter 6) is not stable, especially in melodies where chromatic inflections are indicated. Without firm reference points, one cannot be sure how long such an inflection should last. And where a tonal center seems to shift, as it does in many melodies, the intervals that are emphasized change—especially whole or half steps and major or minor thirds. In this and in many other respects the extant melodies generally do not behave in the way one would expect if they had been devised with modal features in mind, however much the concepts of tonal center, interval content, and cadential direction might invoke the system of the church modes. It is unlikely that the troubadours consciously strove to design their melodies in accordance with the systemic norms of the modes.[32]

Although there does not seem to be a failsafe way to define the concept of a "tonal center" or apply it uniformly in this repertoire, many melodies do emphasize certain pitches in several ways. Perhaps one of the most important features that gives a melody structure is the direction or directions that it moves among and within phrases. In addition, notes are repeated, or are accentuated by a leap of a fourth or fifth or by location as a peak or low point. The range of a melody, especially if it revolves around or moves toward the high and low notes of an octave, sometimes provides a tonal framework. Incipits or cadences are important articulating devices. Some gravitate to one or two pitches within a melody. The shape of a melody can be influenced by whether an incipit or a cadence ascends or descends; is part of a larger motive; is syllabic, melismatic, or neumatic; involves a leap; or includes repeated pitches. Cadences and incipits are bridges between phrases, and the movement of phrases from one to the next by conjunct or disjunct intervals sometimes plays a structural role, as does the location of various kinds of incipits and cadences within a melody.

While they are in the minority, a few melodies in every generation except the first have identical initial and final notes, and the interior cadences, range, and contours reinforce this note. One of Bernart de Ventadorn's melodies (Example 5–15) begins and ends on low C, four of the verses end on C, and three of them begin on C. The half-step below C, which begins the final two verses, also accentuates the C. The direction of all of the phrases—from low to high to low, or from high to low—leads the ear back to the C, and the small range of a minor sixth (including the B) helps maintain this expectation.

A few of Guiraut Riquier's melodies also have the same initial and final note, including the one in Example 5–16. Here the D is emphasized also by its relationship to the A above, as in verses 2, 4, and 8, where there is a leap between the third and fourth syllables (on a *caesura* in verse 4 of stanza I, but not in verses 2 or 8) from A to D, and in several places where there is a conjunct descent from A to D.

A number of melodies that encompass the range of an octave seem to emphasize both extremes of that octave. A tune by Folquet de Marselha (Example 5–17), which begins on high C and ends on low C in manuscript G, has a B♭ indicated at two points (although whether all the Bs should be flatted is not clear), and several internal cadences end on F. Every phrase except verse 8, though, either moves around the high C or the low C, or features one of the two pitches in the middle of the

EX. 5–15. Bernart de Ventadorn. PC 70,4. R fol. 56v.

contour. The version of this melody in manuscript R has a decidedly different interval content, but the contours are essentially the same in all the phrases. Although it begins on C, its range is D–D, the final pitch is D, and no B♭ is indicated. The interval content is quite distinct, but the emphasis on the octave is the same.

There are far more melodies in which the initial and final pitches are not the same. All the extant melodies from the first generation are in this category, and many of these tunes feature final notes that seem to come unprepared. All of Marcabru's melodies (see Examples 4–4 and 5–1) have this trait. A striking example is in Example 5–18, where the final D—although this pitch occurs earlier in the melody—contrasts with the F that is emphasized by several of the internal cadences. The text of this song has a word refrain that makes up the whole of verse 4, "escotatz,"

EX. 5–16. Guiraut Riquier. PC 248,8. R fol. 105–105v.

an arresting moment in the poem because its imperative case appeals directly to the listener. This word is emphasized in the melody by a descent to C, the lowest note to this point, and the verse that follows continues from the C, as if to retain the listener's attention after demanding it so insistently. The rhyme of the last verse, -atz, matches the rhyme of this word refrain, whereas all the other rhymes change from stanza to stanza (coblas singulars). The music emphasizes the rhymes in these two verses by descending for the first time below the tonal center of F.

One of Raimon de Miraval's melodies (Example 5–19) encompasses

EX. 5–17. Folquet de Marselha. PC 155,27. G fol. 7; R fol. 43.

the octave F–F (touching on low E once in the middle of each of the first four verses). It begins on low F, leaps abruptly from low F to high F in the move from verse 4 to verse 5, descends through the octave in verses 5 and 6, and stays in the lower pentachord in the last three verses. It does not end on F, however, but on G, which is unexpected, especially since B♭ is indicated consistently throughout the melody, perhaps to mitigate any melodic dissonance with the F. This may be one of the melodies in which the "final" G is heard at the end of all of the stanzas except the last, and the singer may have ended the song on F.

EX. 5–18. Marcabru. PC 293,18. R fol. 5v.

Often a melody's contours and pitch goals establish a tonal center, even if this pitch does not occur at the beginning or end. Uc Brunenc's only extant tune (Example 5–20) begins on F, and that pitch seems to be the goal of many of the phrases, including those that are shorter than a verse. Verse 1, for instance, moves from F to B♭ and back to F in the first *hemistich*, to the *caesura*. F figures prominently in several of the melismas, especially as the first or last pitch. The notated B♭ reinforces the prominence of F. The melody ends unexpectedly on D, however; this may have been an intermediate final, and the singer might have concluded the song on F.

In many of the through-composed melodies, even where there is not a clear repetition of phrases, the cadences at the ends of the phrases establish a tonal center. Such is the case in the extant melody by Aimeric de Belenoi (Example 5–21). The song begins on C, and five of its phrases end on C. C is emphasized also as the peak or low point of several of the phrases; it is emphasized as the last note of several of the melismas (verses 1, 3, 6, and 8), and the peak in two melismas (verses 8 and 9). The conclusion on F is a surprise, since that pitch does not appear until the last two verses (see a detailed graph of this melody below).

Many melodies do not focus on a single tonal center in an obvious way. Most of Raimon de Miraval's tunes, for example, have no clear-cut

EX. 5–19. Raimon de Miraval. PC 406,14. R fol. 88v.

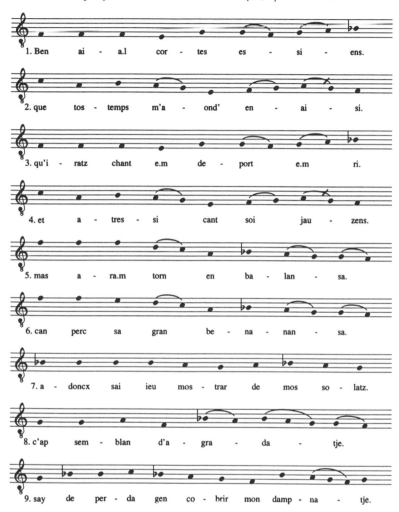

tonal focus. In Example 5–22, the melody begins and ends on F, but internally the cadences move more often to A or D than to F, and high D is sounded abruptly without preparation near the beginning of verse 6. One can almost hear two tonal centers in this melody, F and D. A similar effect is created in PC 406,12, which begins and ends on D but whose internal cadences and contours more often emphasize F or C.

A number of melodies seem to have shifting tonal centers. One notable example is manuscript W's version of a song by Gaucelm Faidit (Example 5–23), in which verses 1 and 3 outline the triad G–B–D, verses 2 and 4 outline the triad F–A–C, verse 5 combines the two triads in more conjunct motion, verse 6 descends to D, verse 7 toys again with the

EX. 5–20. Uc Brunenc. PC 450,3. R fol. 66.

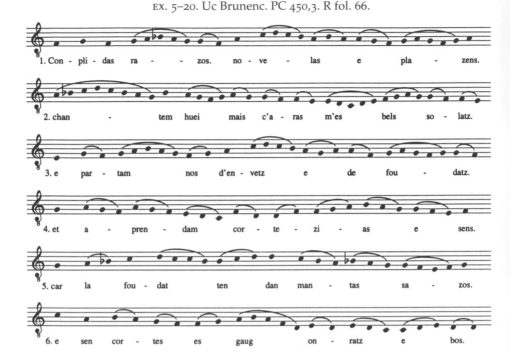

triads on G and F, verse 8 outlines a new triad on D–F–A (extending to the high D), and the final verse stays essentially within this final triad.

Sometimes the internal cadences emphasize a pitch that is neither the initial nor the final note. In a melody in manuscript W by Albertet de Sestaro (PC 16,5a), which begins on F and ends on G, five of the cadences are on A; this is all the more striking because B♭ is consistently notated throughout the piece. This half step above A accentuates the pitch all the more when it comes at a cadence. The scribe added an E♭ toward the end of verse 8, creating a new half-step inflection, this one above D. Although the melody ends on G, it is approached from above as in the other cadences, and one wonders whether a singer would have made his absolute final cadence conform by concluding on A.

In some songs without a clear tonal center, the cadences provide some structure. In manuscript X's reading of one of Rigaut de Berbezilh's songs (Example 5–24), most of the cadences end with a melisma descending through at least a third, some on G, some on F, some on C, some on D; only verse 2 ends by rising. No single pitch stands out as a tonal center, unless one hears the C as "final" because it ends the piece and because the melody is encompassed by the octave C–C. In manuscript W this song has very similar contours and goals, except that it is pitched a fourth higher, and its final note is G rather than

EX. 5–21. Aimeric de Belenoi. PC 9,13a (= PC 392,26). R fol. 89.

C. It has no B♭, so its intervals are different than in manuscripts X and G. Its cadences are nearly identical to those in X and G, however.

Incipits and cadences help articulate the structure in manuscript R's version of a melody by Peirol (Example 5–25). Although in manuscript G this melody is in AAB form, in manuscript R it is somewhat more varied. The incipits of verses 2, 4, 7, and 8 are very similar, rising through a fourth to F. The incipits of verses 3 and 6 descend a third from F to D. The cadences of verses 1, 3, and 6 descend a fourth to C, while those of verses 4 and 8 outline a third around D.

Tonal center and goal do not seem to have been overarching con-

EX. 5–22. Raimon de Miraval. PC 406,8. R fol. 88v.

cerns of the troubadours of any generation, including the last. The troubadours sometimes used pitch hierarchy as a means of unifying a particular melody or giving it coherence, but they did not depend on it consistently. The lack of tonal focus does not necessarily point to a thoughtless disposition of pitches, but rather directs the ear to other features of structure, such as cadential motion, incipit articulation, intervallic content, and motivic manipulation.

Motivic Construction

The troubadour poets manipulated words, rhyme schemes, verse arrangements, strophic connections, and other versification elements by means of such devices as repetition, transformation, derivation, rearrangement, and transposition. Similar manipulative devices appear in

EX. 5–23. Gaucelm Faidit. PC 167,30. W fol. 200/B192.

1. Ja - mais rien tal non por - roit far' a - mor.

2. kiu sie en - nui ne mal - trais ne a - fans.

3. car el m'a fait tant a - vi - nent sou - cors.

4. que res - tau - raz m'a les per - tes e.l dans.

5. qu'a - vi - e fes a dreit per mon fo - la - ge.

6. e si ainc jor de ren m'a fet ma - ri.

7. eu lou par - don lou de - tric e.l da - ma - ge.

8. car tal dos - na fai mon preis a - cuei - llir.

9. qui m'a - men - de tuit que m'a fait su - frir.

the melodies. Derived rhyme finds a musical counterpart in derivation of a cadential figure from a common musical pattern. The telescoping of long poetic verses into shorter ones with the same rhyme might be considered comparable to compressing musical material with the same essential contour into a shorter time span. But this can be achieved in a different way musically than it can poetically, because a musical phrase is not necessarily bound by the length of a verse; thus the musical material of two verse-phrases can be telescoped into the length of a single verse, or of one verse into a *hemistich*. Some of the poetic devices used to unify stanzas of a poem also bear a resemblance to musical

EX. 5–24. Rigaut de Berbezilh. PC 421,2. X fol. 84–84v.

EX. 5–25. Peirol. PC 366,9. G fol. 45v; R fol. 88v.

devices. For instance, the rearrangement of rhyme sounds that occurs in a poem with *coblas retrogradadas* can find a musical equivalent in the rearrangement of motives, incipits, or cadences. And when a musical motive migrates from a location in the first part of one verse to the middle or end of another, one is reminded of the poetic techniques of *coblas capfinidas* and *coblas capcaudadas*.

Such musical techniques might be described as the interconnection and manipulation of motives. Such manipulation includes transposition, sequence, overlapping and linking of motives, musical rhyme, and variation. Frequently the subtle variation of a complete line that effectively transforms the phrase while maintaining its connection with others is a result of ingenious interrelationships among motivic complexes.

A more detailed graphing system would be able to identify motivic materials and show the location of a motive within a verse, its length in syllables, and its connection with other motives; primes could show what motives are varied. No system can show the precise kind and extent of variation, such as transposition or inversion, but it could point out some of the differences between two or more readings of a melody. Elsewhere I have proposed a system in which each letter refers to a complete verse or to a shorter motive that recurs later; repetition of a letter indicates repeated music, whether of a complete verse or of a smaller motive.[33] A subscript number accompanying a letter refers to the number of text syllables encompassed by the motive; when a letter is not accompanied by a subscript number, it refers to a complete verse. Prime marks after a letter indicate slight variation in the verse or motive, while prime marks after a subscript number still refer to a paroxytonic rhyme.

Every troubadour used musical motivic construction to some degree, but in each generation at least one or two composers used it quite extensively. In the first generation, Jaufre Rudel exploited certain motives in several melodies, but manuscript R's version of his most famous song (Example 5–26) uses certain cadential figures over and over.[34] A traditional graph of this structure (from Table 5–4b above) is here superimposed over a detailed graph that shows the motivic structure more clearly:

1	2	3	4	5	6	7
A	B	A	B	C	D	B
A_5B_3	$C_5B'_3$	A_5B_3	$C_5B'_3$	$A'_5B''_3$	D	$C_5B'_3$

B_3 is a cadential motive found in six of the seven verses. Verse 5 contains a transposition of the A_5 and B_3 motives. Only verse 6 has new musical material.

In the second generation, Bernart de Ventadorn was a master of motivic manipulation and used it widely. The melody in Example 5–27 seems to be built upon two small motives, the first ascending C–D–E (often with a descending *plica* on the E), the second descending E–D–C. These particular notes seem almost commonplace, and it might be dangerous to see them as motives rather than simply as notes in a vocabulary of conjunct pitches, were it not for the fact that they occur in such intricate combinations in this melody. In the following graph the letter "x" refers to the first of these motives and "y" to the second:

A	B	C	D	E	F	G	H
$A_1xy_3xy_3$	$xy_5B_{2'}$	C_6y_2	$D_6xy_{1'}$	$y_3E_{4'}$	F_3xy_5	G	$H_6xy_{1'}$

Sometimes the motives occur one after the other without pause, as they do twice in the first verse, across three syllables of text each time, or at

EX. 5–26. Jaufre Rudel. PC 262,2. R fol. 63.

the ends of verses 4 and 8 in a more melismatic configuration across two syllables. At the beginning of verse 2 and in the second *hemistich* of verse 6 they are treated more syllabically, spread across five syllables in each place. The descending motive sometimes appears alone, as at the end of verse 3 and the beginning of verse 5. It is noteworthy that in both Bernart's melody and Jaufre's, the penultimate verse is void of any motivic variation.

Nearly every composer in the third generation used motivic construction plentifully. Gaucelm Faidit was particularly adept in the technique. In all three versions of the melody in Example 5–28 (which gives the reading in manuscript X), motives correspond to the length of either the first or second *hemistich* of a verse, and their reappearance usually involves some variation, indicated here by prime marks after the letters. A_4 serves as an incipit motive, while B_6 occupies the second *hemistich* of two verses:

EX. 5–27. Bernart de Ventadorn. PC 70,19. W fol. 195/B187.

1	2	3	4	5	6	7	8	9	10
A	B	C	D	A'	B'	E	F	G	A"
A	B_{5+6}	$A'_4C_{6'}$	D	$A''_4B'_6$	B"	E	$D'_3F_{7'}$	E'_7G_3	$A'''_4B''_6$

The fourth generation, which began to move heavily toward more regular repetition schemes, used fewer motivic constructions than did earlier composers, but Raimon de Miraval used the technique in combination with variation of full-length phrases to give shape to some of his melodies. In the melody in Example 5–29 he reused the cadence of verse 1 in verse 3, stretched the musical material of the six syllables in verse 4 into eight syllables for verse 5, and then compressed that same material into the cadences of verses 7 and 8. He also began verse 8 with the first part of the music of verse 4:

EX. 5–28. Gaucelm Faidit. PC 167,15. X fol. 85.

1	2	3	4	5	6	7	8
A	B	C	D	D'	E	F	G
A$_{3+3}$	B	C$_3$A$_3$	D	D'$_6$E$_2$	F	G$_6$D''$_4$	D'''$_4$H$_2$D''''$_4$

Among the few melodies extant from the fifth generation, one by
Aimeric de Belenoi (see Example 5–21) provides an example of motivic
construction in which the pitches of the motive are transposed. In this

EX. 5–29. Raimon de Miraval. PC 406,15. R fol. 85v.

case they constitute a five-note melisma followed by a repetition of the last pitch of the melisma, either the pitches D–E–F–E–C,C or A–B–C–B–G,G. In the following graph this motive appears as x_2 or x'_2:

1	2	3	4	5	6	7	8	9
A	B	C	D	D'	A'B'	E	F	F'
A_4x_2	B	$C_1x_2C_3$	D	D_3E_3	$F_2x_2B'_{6'}$	G	$x_2x'_2H_6$	$J_2x'_2J_6$

Notice that the music of verse 6, which has ten syllables, is a combination of variations of the second part of verse 1 and all of verse 2.

Guiraut Riquier was, without a doubt, the master of motivic construction among the troubadours. Very few of his melodies are without internal motives of some sort. One of the most spectacular examples uses the retrograde structure of Example 5–14 on a smaller scale, in which half-verses trade motives back and forth, sometimes in exact repetition, sometimes with some variation. In this *canso* (Example 5–30), except for the end of verse 4 and all of verse 5, the melody is built of two musical phrases, which alternate their order from one verse to the next:

1	2	3	4	5	6	7
A	B	A	B'	C	A	B"
A_4B_6	$B'_4A'_6$	A_4B_6	$B'_4A'_4C_{2'}$	D	A_4B_6	$B'_4A''_6$

The notation accentuates the location of the *caesuras* in verses 1, 3, and 6 with strokes through the staff.

Perhaps more than any other structural device, motivic interrelationships provided coherence as well as variety to the melodies of the troubadours. Many more examples could be presented here. The presence of motives throughout the repertoire suggests that the troubadours were as cognizant of the multifarious possibilities available in their musical materials as in the poetic materials. Far more than verse

EX. 5–30. Guiraut Riquier. PC 248,18. R fol. 105v.

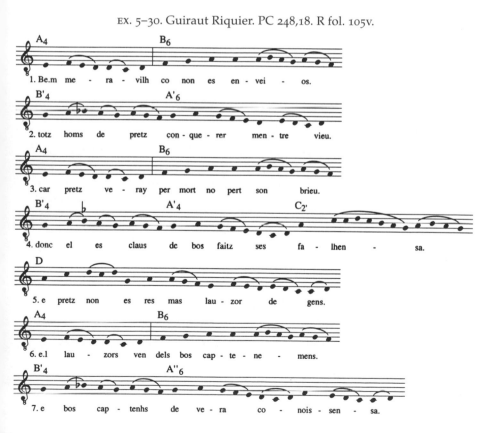

form or tonal organization, the troubadours exploited the techniques of motivic construction, manipulation, development, and linking to give their melodies coherence.

Relationships between Poetic and Musical Structure

The poems of the troubadours contain many structural artifices, and these are very much in the foreground. They can be sophisticated and ingenious, but in the best composers they are not sophistry, since they do not interfere with but enhance the eloquence of the poem and its theme. No matter how complex these devices, they are nearly always audible. *Coblas capcaudadas, capfinidas,* and *retrogradas;* word refrains; verse refrains; and *rims derivatius* all strike the ear almost without fail.

The music sometimes perceptibly reinforces these poetic structural features.[35] Such relationships tend to occur on the level of detail rather than on the level of large-scale schemes, like repetition. A direct concord between specific poetic elements and the musical elements that resemble them—like poetic rhyme and musical cadences—is rare. Music and poetry followed their own rules, and in the area of structure this is particularly true. The devices are similar, but not the same, and are not applied in the same places. The poetic and musical structures sometimes interact, although it is difficult to find such correlations.

The verse, as one of the principal building blocks of the poem, is also one of the principal building blocks of the melody, as can be seen in numerous melodies that repeat musical phrases of verse length. In some melodies the device of *enjambement*, where the syntactic sense of the text spans the end of one verse and the beginning of the next, seems to be reinforced by the direction that the melody follows (see Examples 5–3 and 5–6). And in some instances the melody seems to be broken into units smaller than the verse, coinciding with a *caesura* or *hemistich* (see Examples 5–1, 5–16, 5–20, and 5–30). Sometimes even the notation reflects this, by means of a stroke through the staff.

Rhyme schemes do not usually find a direct parallel in musical structure. A few exceptions include the word refrain in verses 2 and 4 of Jaufre Rudel's PC 262,2 (Example 5–26), which share the same musical cadence. Among the few songs with melodies that use *rims derivatius* (in which rhyme words are grammatically derived from other rhyme words), though, the music of at least one appears to reflect the rhyme relationships. In a song by Bernart de Ventadorn in manuscript W (Example 5–31), the masculine rhymes of the first three verses become feminine words in the next three verses, and the masculine rhyme of verse 7 becomes feminine in verse 8. The verse relationships thus are:

EX. 5–31. Bernart de Ventadorn. PC 70,7. W fol. 190/B180.

1, 4   soleill, soleille
2, 5   rai, raie
3, 6   esmai, esmaie
7, 8   sordei, sordee

In the music, the cadence in each of these pairs of verses moves in the
same direction: 1 and 4 move up, while 2 and 5, and 3 and 6 move
down.[36] Verses 1 and 4 are very closely related throughout, while 3 and
6 share the same cadence.

Because a melody is identical for all stanzas of a poem, there is no
musical counterpart to poetic interrelationships among stanzas. But
even though manipulating words and manipulating notes cannot be

EX. 5–32. Guiraut Riquier. PC 248,58. R fol. 105.

achieved in the same way, a poetic device that has no direct musical counterpart can sometimes be highlighted by a musical device of a different sort. In another melody by Guiraut Riquier (Example 5–32), for instance, in which all the stanzas use the same word rhymes in the same order, all the musical cadences on the last two syllables of the rhyme words have a similar texture: three or four notes followed by one or two notes. The three-verse *tornada* of this song uses all eight rhyme words, three of them at the *caesuras*, which also are marked musically by the same melismatic texture found at the ends of the verses.

Many of the songs with *coblas singulars* (new rhyme sounds for each stanza) are through-composed (new music for each verse), although not enough to call this a rule. Among the songs with *coblas capcaudadas* (in which the rhyme of the last verse of a stanza recurs as the rhyme of the first verse of the following stanza), often the first and last verses of a melody end on the same pitch. Curiously, many of these melodies involve a wide leap from the end of one stanza to the beginning of the next—perhaps to call attention to the rhyme relationship. See, for instance, Example 5–23.

Such examples are difficult to identify, and it is entirely possible that some of the relationships suggested here are coincidental. The structures of the poems and of the melodies appear on the whole to have been conceived separately; yet they are dependent on one another for their definition, certainly in length, and possibly in more subtle ways as well. Without a doubt the composers were as aware of the myriad musical choices in pitches, intervals, motives, contours, and variation as of their options in rhyme, syllable count, verse number, and stanza schemes, and they seem to have capitalized on the wealth of resources in both poetry and music.

CHAPTER
SIX

STYLE

Style in the Art de trobar

The medieval theorists of the art of poetry devoted major portions of their treatises to a discussion of the elements of style, the tangible components of a work, i.e., the words. The poet brought them into being to "embellish" the theme he had invented during *inventio* and the topics he had arranged according to an appropriate material style during *dispositio*.[1] *Elocutio*, the stage of implementation following the creation of the material style and the arrangement of the topics, involved forging words that are dictated by the material style. This process included amplifying or abbreviating the themes and topics by means of stretching or constricting the language used to express them, devising appropriate tropes and figures that give poetry its peculiar eloquence, using grammatical components properly but creatively, and disposing the elements of versification so as to present the words in an effective scheme.

After discussing how the material of a work is chosen and arranged, Geoffroi de Vinsauf explains the next step in the compositional process:

> The way continues along two routes: there will be either a wide path or a narrow, either a river or a brook. You may advance at a leisurely pace or leap swiftly ahead. You may report the matter with brevity or draw it out in a lengthy discourse. . . . The material to be moulded, like the moulding of wax, is at first hard to the touch. If intense concentration enkindle native ability, the material is soon made pliant by the mind's fire, and submits to the hand in whatever

way it requires, malleable to any form. The hand of the mind controls it, either to amplify or curtail.[2]

The poet has created his material and devised the order in which he plans to present his topics. Now, directed by these mental processes, he must "mold" this material, "report the matter" (*rem notare*), that is, give it corporeal shape.

Geoffroi continues with a lengthy description, with numerous examples, of the methods of amplifying or abbreviating the material. The former include such esoteric procedures, most derived from classical rhetoric, as repetition, periphrasis, comparison, apostrophe, personification, digression, description, and opposition; the latter include emphasis, articulus, ablative, avoidance of repetition, implication, asyndeton, and fusion of clauses. These devices encompass a wide variety of ways of manipulating the syntax and the combination and order of words to achieve various levels of sophistication in the language, to convey the material of the poem effectively and eloquently.[3]

In the next section Geoffroi treats tropes and figures, choosing words that ably express the material of the poem, and deploying them strategically to achieve the maximum effect. "Ornamentation" entails certain ways of combining the words in patterns that do not occur in ordinary speech, but which endow poetry with its characteristic expressiveness:

> Do not let the word invariably reside on its native soil—such residence dishonours it. Let it avoid its natural location, travel about elsewhere, and take up a pleasant abode on the estate of another. There let it stay as a novel guest, and give pleasure by its very strangeness. . . .[4]

This introduces a discussion of "difficult ornaments" (*ornatus difficilis*), or "tropes," including such traditional devices as metaphor, onomatopoeia, allegory, metonymy, hyperbole, and synecdoche. While urging their use for an effective expression of the material, Geoffroi warns against excessive obscurity:

> Be weighty in such a manner that your subject is not hidden under a cloud; rather let the words pay fealty to their rightful lord. Words are instruments to unlock the closed mind; they are keys, as it were, of the mind. One who seeks to open what is closed does not set out to draw a cloud over his words. If indeed he has done so, he has done an injury to the words, for he has made a lock out of a key. Be the bearer of a key, then; open up the subject readily by your words. . . . Regard not your own capacities, therefore, but rather his with whom you are speaking. Give to your words weight suited to his shoulders, and adapt your speech to the subject.[5]

The poet can thus use "easy" ornaments (*ornatus facilis*, "of a simplicity that does not shock the ear by its rudeness"[6]), which include "figures
of thought and diction" such as *repetitio, conversio, complexio,* and *tra-
ductio.*

These difficult and easy ornaments do not constitute the three
"styles" (high, middle, and low) that are associated with the material
style of *inventio*, but are ornaments of those styles, details of language.
Any of the styles could use either difficult or easy ornaments.[7] This
concept is important in understanding the specific Occitanian adaptation of difficult and easy ornaments to *trobar clus* and *trobar leu*, which
do not necessarily define the entire style of a work, but can be seen as
specific components of a song.[8]

Geoffroi briefly discusses the way meter in poetry follows special
rules in governing the choice of words and their arrangement:

> Metre is straitened by laws, but prose roams along a freer way, for the
> public road of prose admits here and there wagons and carts, whereas
> the narrow path of a line of verse does not allow of things so inelegant.
> Verse wishes its very words to be graceful in appearance, lest the
> rustic form of a word embarrass by its ungainliness, and bring shame
> to the line. Metre desires to appear as a handmaid with hair adorned,
> with shining cheek, slim body, and peerless form.[9]

As we saw in Chapter 5, Occitanian theorists of the *art de trobar*
discussed versification, including rhyme schemes and stanza structures; to a small extent they also treated other ornaments. But an
extensive treatment of the tropes and figures and other more sophisticated features of *elocutio* did not appear in Occitanian treatises until the
appearance of the treatises of the *gay saber* in the second and third
decades of the fourteenth century. The troubadours themselves, though,
were masters of their language, and in all of these areas—the use of
ornaments of style, amplification and abbreviation, grammar, and versification—they displayed a sophisticated appreciation and understanding of the elements of style at their disposal.

One stylistic feature of the troubadours' poems that the Occitanian
theorists did not discuss is the dichotomy between *trobar leu* and *trobar
clus*, which are viewed as the Occitanian counterparts to the "easy" and
"difficult" ornaments of Latin verse.[10] The word *clus* turns up—along
with *ric, prim, car,* and *naturau*—in the poems themselves, not in treatises. None of the words seem to have referred to a clearly defined
"style," but indicated self-conscious—often ingenious—forays into obscure, unexpected, sometimes strained or almost sophistic uses of
words, rhyme schemes, verse structures, and sound combinations, all of
which seem to be deliberately hermetic. Sometimes entire poems are in
this abstruse style, especially those that are characterized by devices
like derived rhyme schemes, linking devices like *coblas capcaudadas* and

capfinidas, extremely short verses, alliteration, and invented words. Other songs use sophisticated images, especially metaphors, which are often explained in the same poem.

Some poems whose meanings are clear, and hence might fall in the category of *trobar leu*, nonetheless use extraordinarily inventive and unusual structures, words, and turns of phrases. The difference between an impenetrable hermetic style and a sophisticated and creative molding of words is not always easy to define. There are some poems whose meanings are a mystery today but which may have been transparent to their audiences, who were familiar with social, linguistic, or other contexts that have escaped the record of history. For this reason alone, it is hazardous to speculate on the meanings of some of these poems, or on the intentions of the poets, other than what seems to be self-conscious esotericism.

Most deliberate obfuscation in the troubadour repertoire seems to have spent itself by the end of the twelfth century. Peire d'Alvernhe (*trobar clus*), Raimbaut d'Aurenga (*trobar ric*), Guiraut de Bornelh (*trobar sotil* or *clus*), and Arnaut Daniel (*trobar ric*) were the main practitioners of hermeticism, although none of them composed exclusively in this style. Later composers used techniques that were as sophisticated, sometimes the same or similar devices, not for their own sake but as tools of expression.

Features of Musical Style and Their Interaction with Poetic Style

The troubadour Bernart Marti, a contemporary of Guiraut de Bornelh and Arnaut Daniel and an early proponent of *trobar clus*, used a confusing metaphor in one song that seems to suggest "entangling, intertwining, complicating" (*entrebescant*) the words and "refining" (*afinant*) the melody. He followed it with another metaphor that suggests that the words are "interwoven" not only with each other but perhaps also with the melody:

L'esparviers ab bel semblant
va del pueg ves leis volant:
la longua trencada, pren lai sa volada.
En breu m'es [com] fils de lana
lo fortz fres e la capsana
qui que.s grei, so.us autrei,
tota.l rengua ab correi.
C'aisi vauc entrebescant
los motz e.l so afinant:
lengu' entrebescada es en la baizada.

The fine-looking hawk takes flight toward her from the hill-top: the thong severed, it wings toward her. Swiftly the strong curb and the tether are to me as woolen thread, the whole rein and the bridle too, I assure you—whoever may object; for thus I interlace the words and refine the music: the tongue is interlaced in the kiss.[11]

Is the "tongue" (*lengua*) the text and the "kiss" (*baizada*) the melody in this metaphor? If this is ambiguous, at least Bernart is suggesting that as he wove the words he also "refined" the melody, and the metaphor of the tongue and kiss suggests that the style of the words and of the music together comprised the consummation of the material of his song.

In Chapter 4 musical features like contours and directions, incipits and cadences, repetition schemes, and intervals were invoked to support the hypothesis that melodies sometimes reinforced the themes and topics of a poem, expressing its subject matter (hence its genre) and in particular the succession of "arguments" embodied in the topics. Chapter 5 treated repetition and variation, direction and contour, cadences and incipits, and motivic construction as elements of musical structure. But just as medieval theorists treated versification as part of style and expression, these musical ingredients, along with interval content, range, and texture (the number of notes per syllable), can be seen as constituents of musical style.

Sometimes these melodic features interact with poetic elements in ways that are immediately audible. Manipulating the language for sound effect seems to have attracted the attention of some poets, and the audible result of these kinds of poetic devices may have been of interest to the singers as well (see Chapter 7). Peire d'Alvernhe's "Dejosta.ls breus jorns e.ls loncs sers" (Example 6–1) uses *clus* features like alliteration and one-syllable words "to convey orally the impression of wintry chill."[12] The two melodies that survive for this poem are quite different in contours and interval content (see Example 2–7). What the two versions share, though, is a very melismatic style: many syllables carry from two to six notes in both melodies. Such a florid style almost seems to contradict the effect of the monosyllables, the sound of which would be brusque and quick without the melody. If the melismas were sung quickly, their elongating effect would be mitigated. However, a more relaxed performance might in its own fashion reinforce the "harsh consonant clusters" to which Frank Chambers drew attention—words beginning with *b*, hard *j*, and *c*, or ending with fricative *s* and affricative *z* (pronounced *-ts*)—because by articulating the beginnings and ends of these lengthened words the consonants almost seem to be more prominent than if they went by quickly.

Extremely short verses are another transparently audible *clus* device. They sometimes force drastic manipulation of the language to convey the topics. In general such poems are concentrated in the earlier generations, and not many of them from any period survive with their melodies. Because these short verses are articulated by their rhymes, their aural effect is striking. One of the two songs by Arnaut Daniel that survive with melodies (Example 6–2) has five verses with only four syllables each, two with eight syllables, and two with seven plus one unstressed syllable. Aurally, the poem falls into three sections: verses 1–2, each with eight syllables; verses 3–6, three short verses followed by a longer verse with a feminine rhyme; and verses 7–9, two short verses followed by a longer verse with a feminine rhyme. The four-syllable verses are audibly striking because they so abruptly change the flow of the long verses that begin the poem; these verses are set to mainly syllabic music, which facilitates their precipitate delivery. The melody is essentially through-composed, with some reuse of motivic material taken from verse 2 in verses 6 and 9 (the two verses with paroxytonic rhymes). Both paroxytonic rhymes are distinguished by a four-note melisma on the stressed syllable. This poem itself is not considered to be in the *trobar clus* style, but such poetic constraints as short verses nonetheless require great precision from the poet in thought and language.

The reuse of rhyme words in all of the stanzas in Arnaut Daniel's *sestina* (Example 6–3) is a *clus* device that attracted a few imitators. Of this poetic scheme Chambers remarks: "Despite the obvious artificiality of this tour de force, its repetitions produce upon an even moderately sympathetic hearer the effect of an incantation or a litany."[13] The melody is essentially syllabic in texture and through-composed (like Arnaut's other extant melody). The "litany" of the relentless progression of feminine rhyme words, whose final unstressed syllables are assonant on the sound -*a*, can be heard by cadences that descend by step on every verse except the second, and that are articulated by a descending two- or three-note figure on the penultimate stressed syllable in every verse but the first two. It is hard to imagine that a singer would not have lingered briefly on these penultimate syllables, further deemphasizing the unstressed final syllables, which drop in pitch.

Aside from a few such examples, the stylistic traits of the melodies generally do not coincide directly with stylistic traits in the poems, but constitute a separate realm of materials that the composer manipulated to serve whatever purpose he or she had in mind. Like the structural ingredients of a melody, its range, texture, interval content, and motives are comparable to, but not the equivalent of, the verse and rhyme structures, language, and syntactical patterns of the poem.

Toward a Chronology of Style
in the Melodies of the Troubadours

Just as with the musical structures discussed in Chapter 5, it is not possible to draw a uniform picture of the way musical style unfolded from one generation to the next. Melodies certainly may resemble one another in range or interval content, texture, contours of phrases or of the entire melody, incipit and cadence figures, and even musical mo-

EX. 6–1. Peire d'Alvernhe. PC 323,15. X fol. 86; R fol. 6.

tives. And while it seems likely that composers exerted some influence on one another that resulted in the adoption of techniques and the development of new devices out of old, musical borrowing (as distinct from borrowing of entire melodies) is more difficult to establish than poetic borrowing.

One problem in identifying the effect that one troubadour may have had on another is the haphazard way in which the melodies have been preserved. One cannot be sure to what extent a manuscript's reading is a true representation of a troubadour's melodic style or represents a combination of forces from performance and written preservation. The paucity in the musical record, and the fact that the melodies that survive do not completely and accurately chronicle the musical output of the troubadours, hamper our ability to discern clear changes in musical style over time. But the chief reason that such a development is difficult to trace applies also to describing the progression of poetic style through the two centuries during which the troubadours worked: each song is

EX. 6–1. (Continued)

an individualistic expression of a certain idea, and it may or may not have been regarded by the troubadour as related stylistically to any of his or her other works, or to the works of others, past or present. The themes and topics to be imagined were so plentiful, and the poetic and musical tools with which to realize them so varied, it is no wonder that neither poetic nor musical style follows a clear progression from one song to another, let alone from one troubadour to another.

That said, some comparisons of musical style among the works of individual troubadours are possible, as well as among troubadours working at about the same time, perhaps at the same court or under the patronage of the same person. Occasionally one can see similarities and signs of direct or indirect influence, especially in cases where they engaged in a poetic exchange or modeled a poem after that of another troubadour. Certain trends emerge as the twelfth and thirteenth centuries proceed, in the areas of texture, range, tonal orientation, motivic manipulation, interval content, and structure.

EX. 6–2. Arnaut Daniel. PC 29,6. G fol. 73v.

In the first generation, Marcabru and Jaufre Rudel were near contemporaries, and both had contact with the houses of Poitiers and
Angoulême; Marcabru mentioned Jaufre in one poem (see Chapter 2).[14]
Both used repetition in their musical structures, but all of Jaufre's
melodies are in large-scale AAB form (see Table 5–4b, and Example 5–
26), while only one of Marcabru's is—his *pastorela* (Marcabru's more
regular melodies are transmitted only in manuscript R, which may
explain this regularity). Marcabru's melodies are more varied in range
than Jaufre's; the latter generally stay within an octave (two extend to a
ninth), while Marcabru's ranges extend from a major sixth (see Example
5–18) to a major tenth (see Example 5–1). These extremes of range are

EX. 6–3. Arnaut Daniel. PC 29,14. G fol. 73.

found in his two *sirventes* that survive with music. Marcabru's extant melodies are essentially syllabic in texture, while Jaufre's are slightly more florid (see Example 6–4). A striking peculiarity of Marcabru's extant melodies is that they all incorporate a major (as distinct from minor) triad above their initial pitch (either F or C), and all end on a minor third below the initial (D or A). Marcabru's melodies are more triadic in general than Jaufre's.

The second generation is dominated by Bernart de Ventadorn. A variety of form is found in his melodies (see Chapter 5)—from large-scale AAB structures to irregular repetition and variation, to paired-verse, rounded, and entirely through-composed forms (see Table 5–5b). Other musical features in his songs are as diverse, including the initial and final pitches, the ranges, textures, interval content, and contours (see Examples 2–2, 2–4, 2–6, 2–13, 4–1, 4–2, 5–2, 5–3, 5–4, 5–15, 5–27, and 5–31). Even with this variety, however, one is struck by an economy of means, which is perhaps part of what many commentators (both medieval and modern) have meant when they have praised his songs for their straightforwardness and simplicity. Unquestionably the *trobar leu* that characterizes his poetic style is the same aesthetic that guided his musical composition. His textures tend to be syllabic, sometimes

EX. 6–4. Jaufre Rudel. PC 262,3. R fol. 63.

neumatic; a rare melismatic figure occurs, mainly at the ends of verses on the penultimate or final syllable. Bernart did not incorporate wide intervallic leaps often in his melodies, nor did he typically repeat pitches. His ranges tend to stay within an octave, sometimes within a sixth.

Many of Bernart's melodies reveal a creativity in manipulating motivic material that also occurred in some melodies of Jaufre Rudel (see Example 5–26), and which is found increasingly in the melodies of later composers. Bernart used motives to provide structure to the melody in Example 5–27, where he spins out an astonishingly unified through-composed melody by reusing two motives in various positions in almost all the verses. Similarly, in the melody in Example 4–1 he begins almost every phrase with the same rising F–G–A motive. In another typical melody, shown in Example 6–5, he reuses short melodic figures not so much to provide structural articulation but as the musical vocabulary for the song. The descending F–E–D motive recurs in every verse, sometimes in rapid succession, usually in the form of a two-note neume followed by a single note. The figure D–C–B–C occurs often as well, but in varied textures: sometimes as a three-note neume followed by a single note, sometimes as two two-note neumes or a two-note

EX. 6–5. Bernart de Ventadorn. PC 70,12. G fol. 14.

1. Ben m'an per - dut lai en - ves Ven - ta - dorn.

2. tuit mei a - mis pos ma dom - na no m'a - ma.

3. et es ben dreiz qe ja mais lai no torn.

4. c'a - des es - ta vas mi sal - vaz' e gra - ma.

5. ve.z per qe.m fai sen - blan i - raz e morn.

6. car en s'a - mor mi de - leiz en so - jorn.

7. ni de ren als no.s ran - cu - ra ni.s cla - ma.

neume followed by two single notes, sometimes in combination with other notes, sometimes at the cadence, sometimes in the middle of a phrase. One motive emphasizes a semitone–tone progression, while the other reverses the interval order to tone–semitone; the frequent recurrence of both motives amplifies the effect of the semitone.

Rigaut de Berbezilh, Bernart's older contemporary, produced four melodies that survive, none with the large-scale AAB form that Jaufre Rudel favored, but often with repeated phrases that involve slight variation (see Example 5–24). Rigaut's melodies, like Bernart's, generally stay within an octave, although PC 421,10 encompasses a minor tenth. His textures are largely neumatic, with an occasional melisma. He was not nearly as adept at deploying motivic materials in his melodies, although in PC 421,1 and 421,3 (the latter is shown in Example 6–6), two-note neumes of a descending second (whole- and semitone) occur often, especially toward the ends of phrases. Rigaut's melodies have a number of descending and ascending thirds, which are less conjunct than Bernart's and in some respects are more like Marcabru's.

EX. 6–6. Rigaut de Berbezilh. PC 421,3. X fol. 85.

One song that is extant only in manuscript W (PC 461,102), where it is without attribution, has been thought to be by Rigaut, or at least is in imitation of his songs, because its animal subject matter is similar to that of other songs ascribed to him.[15] Van der Werf notes this possibility in his edition, and suggests that "where style and form are concerned, the melody does not differ substantially from the four attributed to him so that his authorship cannot be ruled out for musicological reasons."[16] Its range encompasses an eleventh (A–D'), slightly wider than that of most melodies of this generation, and although its neumatic texture is similar to that found in the melodies attributed to Rigaut, it does not include as many leaps of thirds as his attributed melodies have. It has several prominent and unusual descending leaps of a major sixth, giving this melody a distinctly different sound than the others, and casting doubt on whether Rigaut was the composer.

The other two troubadours in this generation, Peire d'Alvernhe and Raimbaut d'Aurenga, are represented by only four extant melodies, two of them the different versions for one of Peire's poems discussed above as Example 6–1. Both versions are very melismatic and radically different from the music of any earlier or contemporary troubadours; both encompass the wide range of an eleventh. The distinctive character of both versions of this melody may be a reflection of the *trobar clus* elements in the poem. Peire's other extant melody, a *tenso* with Bernart de Ventadorn (see Example 5–5) encompasses only an octave in range. Although it has a few melismas, they are mainly at the ends of phrases, as in the melodies of Bernart de Ventadorn; indeed in many ways this melody resembles Bernart's in style.

Raimbaut's only extant melody (Example 6–7) also resembles this unpretentious style, with a range of a major seventh and conjunct motion; it is mainly syllabic with a few short neumes at the ends of phrases. Like some of Bernart's tunes, this one has a rising figure that begins almost all the verses, usually semitone–tone (B–C–D), once tone–semitone (A–B–C), and once tone–tone (F–G–A). Raimbaut, Bernart, and Peire were probably acquainted with one another, or at least with one another's art, and it is not surprising to find similar features in their melodies.

These three troubadours were known to the next generation also. Guiraut de Bornelh, Gaucelm Faidit, Bertran de Born, Folquet de Marselha, Raimbaut de Vaqueiras, Peire Vidal, the Comtessa de Dia, and Guilhem de Saint Didier crossed paths with them poetically and with each other possibly in person. In general these troubadours began to stretch some boundaries in their music, especially in range and interval content. Melodies commonly extend well beyond the range of an octave in this period, sometimes by as much as a fourth or a fifth. Thirds and triads become increasingly prevalent, and unusual leaps,

EX. 6–7. Raimbaut d'Aurenga. PC 389,36. X fol. 88v–89.

both rising and falling, of fifths, sixths, sevenths, and even tritones appear. In addition, composers found more and more ways to treat their motives creatively, not only by recombining and repositioning them but also by transforming them through transposition and variation.

Although the Comtessa de Dia was reputed to have had a relationship with Raimbaut d'Aurenga (see Chapter 1), her single surviving melody (Example 5–8) is not similar to his (Example 6–7) structurally or in its interval content. While both melodies are essentially syllabic with a few two- and three-note neumes scattered throughout, Raimbaut's emphasizes the major third between G and B and accentuates it by adding the D above to form a triad, while the Comtessa's is mainly confined to the minor triad D–F–A. Her melody employs the same musical thrift that is found in many of Bernart de Ventadorn's melodies and in Raimbaut's. There are only four musical phrases distributed among the seven verses, and the second *hemistich* of verse 6 is essentially the same as the end of verses 1 and 3.

Guiraut de Bornelh's surviving melodies include a *sirventes*, a *tenso*, his famous *alba* "Reis glorios" (Example 4–6), and a *canso*. In the *tenso* (Example 6–8) Guiraut used motivic material in ways that his predecessors and contemporaries did. A three-note descending neume recurs in a number of places, at six different pitch levels (from F, E, D, C, G, and A). As in two of Guiraut's other melodies, the large-scale structure of this one is AAB (see Table 5–6b). Triadic motion is more frequent here than it had been earlier, except in the melodies of Rigaut de Berbezilh and of Marcabru, whose music seems to have been somewhat out of the mainstream.

Only one melody by Bertran de Born (PC 80,37; Example 4–14) and one by Guilhem de Saint Didier (PC 234,16) survive. Guilhem sometimes alluded to Bertran in his poems, and the two shared a similar approach to musical composition. Both extant melodies are syllabic in texture (Guilhem's is slightly more neumatic), are conjunct in motion, and have a range of a ninth, from C to D'. Each melody varies repeated phrases slightly and makes extensive use of repeated pitches, especially at the beginnings of verses. While Bertran's poem has many more verses (eleven as opposed to six), Guilhem's verses have more syllables (twelve as opposed to eight), so the overall textural effect of the two melodies is quite similar.

Gaucelm Faidit, who used the same *senhal* for Raimbaut d'Aurenga ("Linhaure") as did Guiraut de Bornelh, shared Guiraut's fondness for thirds and triads, both ascending and descending, major and minor (see Examples 2–8, 2–12, 4–5, 5–6, 5–23, and 5–28). Fourteen of his poems survive with melodies, several of them with notably different readings. Like Bernart de Ventadorn, Gaucelm used many different structural plans in his melodies and often varied phrases when he repeated them. His textures are primarily neumatic. Many of his melodies encompass a ninth, often from C to D'; sometimes he extended the range to an eleventh, once to a thirteenth (in manuscript W's version of PC 167,43; see Example 2–12). Gaucelm linked phrases in his melodies by means of motives and their variation, often in the cadential position, as in PC 167,17 (Example 6–9). Here the same cadential figure is used at the ends of verses 4, 5, 8, and 10, with the final statement being somewhat more florid. As he did in other melodies, Gaucelm here used leaps of fourths and fifths, ascending and descending (see also Examples 5–6 and 5–28), sometimes almost as a motive. Altogether, Gaucelm's melodies represent something of a departure from those of his predecessors, especially in their interval content, which is a great deal more adventurous than that of earlier composers.

EX. 6–8. Guiraut de Bornelh. PC 242,69. R fol. 8.

Before Folquet de Marselha abandoned the *art de trobar* for service in the church, he produced thirteen poems that survive with melodies. Nearly half of them are through-composed, and none has a large-scale form of AAB (see Chapter 5). Their texture is primarily neumatic, with a few melismas at the ends of phrases (see Examples 2–1, 2–10, and 5–17). Folquet favored C and D' as outer limits for his tunes, although one melody encompasses an octave and a fifth (Example 2–10). Many of his melodies have several repeated As at the beginnings of phrases, similar to Bertran de Born's repeated Cs and As and Guilhem de Saint Didier's repeated Ds. Like Gaucelm, Folquet was not timorous of disjunct motion. He often used thirds, sometimes in a descending chain, as in verses 6 and 8 of Example 2–1, sometimes in rising or descending triads, as in Example 6–10, at the beginning of verse 8. These thirds merely fill in the ninth from C to D' that is outlined in the middle of verse 3. This

EX. 6–9. Gaucelm Faidit. PC 167,17. G fol. 27v–28.

melody also illustrates another of Folquet's propensities, chains of descending seconds reminiscent of similar motion in Rigaut de Berbezilh's and Gaucelm Faidit's melodies. Despite his later chagrin over having been a poet-composer, Folquet was widely admired by his contemporaries and successors, and he received the homage of Peire Vidal, Pons de Capduelh, Aimeric de Peguilhan, and the Monk of Montaudon, among others (see below).

EX. 6–10. Folquet de Marselha. PC 155,11. G fol. 6v.

The Catalan troubadour Berenguier de Palol appears not to have been in direct contact with most of the troubadours of his generation. Scribes took care to record eight of his melodies, however, and some of them use motives in ways that we have seen in the music of other troubadours. In Example 6–11, the descending figure F–E–D occurs in each verse in different positions. The figure occurs on the cadence at verses 1, 2, 3, and 4; at the *caesura* in verses 6 and 7; near the beginning of verse 8; and at various other points in verses 2, 4, 5, 7, and 8. Sometimes it is extended by A–G before, and sometimes then drops the D at the end or continues down to C before rising again. Occasionally the notes are redistributed among the syllables. Because the notes usually appear as a melisma, their prominence as a motive is especially pronounced. Such extensive motivic structuring is one of the elements that give Bernart de Ventadorn's music much of its elegance (see

EX. 6–11. Berenguier de Palol. PC 47,3. R fol. 37v.

1. Ai - tal do - na co yeu say.

2. ri - ca. de be - las fays - sos.

3. ab cors co - vi - nen e jay.

4. ab ditz pla - zen - tiers e bos.

5. si vol - gues precx ni de - man - da so - frir.

6. de - gra m'on - rar. car te - ner e ser - vir.

7. que no.y falh res qu'en bo - na do - na si - a.

8. mas car a - mors y pert sa se - nho - ri - a.

Example 6–5). Berenguier's melodies have a mainly syllabic style with some melismas at the ends of phrases, and his ranges generally stay within an octave.

Raimbaut de Vaqueiras left seven melodies, some of which utilize the motivic interrelationships that have now become a familiar feature of troubadour melodies. He paid homage to Berenguier de Palol by imitating the poetic form in Example 6–11 (PC 392,11 = 47,3) for a *sirventes*; although the rhymes are different, Berenguier's melody could well have served for Raimbaut's poem. This example is the most florid of Berenguier's melodies; in general Raimbaut's textures are more melismatic than Berenguier's, and they sometimes encompassed a wider range, up to an eleventh (see Example 5–7). The motivic constructions found in some of Raimbaut's melodies are illustrated in the crusading song in Example 6–12. The cadences in verses 1, 3, 5, 8, 9, and

EX. 6–12. Raimbaut de Vaqueiras. PC 392,3. R fol. 61v–62.

11 involve melismas at various pitch levels on the last two or three syllables; they begin with an ascending and descending neume of four, five, or six notes followed by a two- or three-note descending neume. This cadential figure is balanced by the incipits of most of the verses, which oscillate around or rise to A. The incipit of the first three syllables of verses 1 and 3 is repeated in verse 4 but with a different distribution over the syllables, stretching into four syllables and avoiding the return to A at the *caesura*; this then introduces the striking leap of a fifth on "de Fransa," emphasizing the phrase "the crusaders *of France*." Other stanzas emphasize phrases such as "et honra" ("and honored," in reference to the marquis to whom the song is dedicated), "el trau" ("the beam" on which Jesus was crucified), and "espaza" (the "sword" with which the troubadour exhorts his listeners to strike the Turks).

Peire Vidal's poetic style is clever but direct, and his fifteen surviving melodies are characterized by a wide variety of techniques (see Example 2–9). Their ranges usually span about a tenth (major or minor). There are frequent leaps of thirds, fourths, and fifths, both ascending and descending. The textures are rarely simply syllabic, but usually involve neumes of two to six notes, which often occur toward the ends of phrases, although they are not infrequent earlier in the phrases as well, even at the beginning.

Example 6–13 illustrates these points. There are frequent thirds and several triads, especially on G–E–C (descending in verses 1 and 3, and ascending in verses 5 and 9), but also on F–A–C (verse 8); there is a very unusual figure in verse 9 of a triad C–E–G that continues to the C above, outlining a full octave. Some of these figures are filled in as variations. For instance, the G–E–C–E triad that ends verse 1 recurs at the end of verse 3 with the last third filled in with a passing tone. The subtle variation of verse 1 that occurs early in verse 3 results partly from the compression of the music for seven syllables into six, and partly from the addition of a D–C neume on the second syllable, which then involves shifting the pitches forward so that the neume on the fifth syllable is one note shorter than in verse 1. Verse 7 develops this further by redistributing the pitches C–D–E–C over the first four syllables before moving on to a different ending to the phrase. Peire alluded to Folquet de Marselha in some poems, and Stronski pointed out that this poem has resonances with one of Folquet's (PC 155,10).[17] Although it is uncertain which song was composed first, their melodies are not entirely unrelated. Both are characterized by triads (especially the version of Folquet's melody in manuscript W), both are somewhat melismatic, and both feature melodic variation among the phrases. It is not entirely implausible that, if one of the poems was composed in response to the other, the melody too was modeled after the earlier one.

Half of Arnaut de Maruelh's melodies are through-composed,

EX. 6–13. Peire Vidal. PC 364,37. G fol. 42v.

while the others involve some kind of repetition and variation. Arnaut favored the octave between C and C', and one of his melodies extends to a fifth above. Like others in his generation, he used leaps freely, especially fourths and fifths both descending and ascending, and the textures are a blend of syllabic and neumatic. One incipit motive that recurs often is a repeated pitch followed by the pitch above, which is also repeated sometimes, as in verses 1 and 2 of Example 6–14. This melody also features some melodic sequencing, whereby a motive is repeated immediately at a lower pitch. In verse 1, the F–G–F–E–D figure on syllables 3, 4, and 5 is followed by (D)-E–F–E–D–C on syllables 6, 7, 8, and 9. The conjunct descent through a fourth that characterizes this

EX. 6–14. Arnaut de Maruelh. PC 30,3. G fol. 31.

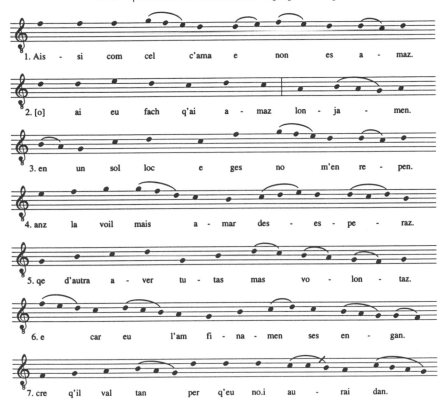

motive reappears several times later, again at different pitches. It occurs
twice in verse 6, on syllables 1 and 2 from F, and on syllables 3 and 4
from D. The final syllables of the song descend through a fourth from C.
The end of verse 3 is a truncation of the musical material of verse 1,
beginning with the descent of a fourth from G as in the first *hemistich* of
verse 1, but then proceeding directly to the cadence taken from the
second *hemistich* of verse 1. Other melodies by Arnaut manifest similar
procedures in their variation of motives.

Arnaut Daniel was a principal proponent of the *trobar clus*, as seen
in the discussion of his two melodies in that context (Examples 6–2 and
6–3). Aside from the ways in which they support the hermetic poetic
features, these melodies are not markedly different in style from those
by some of Arnaut's contemporaries. While PC 29,6 is quite conjunct in
motion, the *sestina* (PC 29,14) features triads that are characteristic of the
melodies of Peire Vidal, Gaucelm Faidit, and others. The textures are
largely syllabic, with some two-, three-, and four-note neumes at the
ends of phrases.

Jordan Bonel and Guilhem Magret both had ties to the court of Alfonso II, as did Peire Vidal, Arnaut de Maruelh, and others. Jordan's only surviving melody contains melodic sequences similar to those in Arnaut de Maruelh's music (Example 6–14), in this case comprising a rising figure of a fourth; it also uses musical rhyme at some of the cadences. His melody is in AAB form, quite conjunct in motion, with some neumatic textures toward the ends of verses and with several repeated notes. In general, though, Jordan's music seems somewhat less venturesome than the melodies of his more famous contemporaries. Guilhem Magret's two extant melodies, on the other hand, are rich in diversity, with much variation of motives and phrases, many unusual leaps, neumatic textures that are not confined to the end of a verse, and the redistribution of motivic material. Example 6–15 illustrates most of these features. Notice the ascending diminished fifth from B to F in verses 1, 3, 6, and 11; the descending thirds at the end of verse 9; the variation of verse 1 in verses 3, 6, and 11 and of verse 2 in verse 7; and the reuse of incipit material from verse 4 at the beginning of verse 5. The diminished fifth is quite prominent, and the question of whether a singer might have altered it by singing a B♭ or an F♯ inevitably arises. But the scribe of W, where this melody is found, was not hesitant elsewhere to indicate a B♭ or an F♯ where it might be needed, and since he made no indication in any of the four places where the leap occurs here, the scribe, at least, probably intended the unusual interval to remain. (See Chapter 7 further on chromatic alterations.)

The melodies of Raimon Jordan are fairly conservative, with a syllabic to neumatic texture, largely conjunct motion, and a range of an octave or slightly more (see Example 4–10). He did use some motivic variation, but not to the extent that some other composers of this generation did. Peire Cardenal later used one of Raimon's extant melodies.

Gui d'Ussel left four melodies, all with some repetition of phrases, but none in AAB form. They all stay within the range of a minor tenth (one is limited to the range of an octave) and have a neumatic texture in general. Gui seems to have remained in the region of Limousin and Auvergne, and may have encountered Gaucelm Faidit at Ventadorn. Like Gaucelm's melodies, Gui's employ numerous thirds and triads, and his phrases are linked by means of motivic transformation and subtle variation, as in Example 6–16. Verse 1 begins with a repetition of A on the first four syllables; verse 3 varies this by oscillating above and below the A before proceeding to a different cadence. Verse 4 modifies the pitches of verse 2 in a similar way before ending with a closely related cadence. Verse 5 begins like verse 4, but ends with a modified version of the cadence of verse 1. Verse 8 is a truncated version of verse 6, to make the same music fit first eight syllables and then six. Verse 9

EX. 6–15. Guillem Magret. PC 223,1. W fol. 201v/B193v.

1. L'ai - gue   pu - ge   con - tre - mont.

2. al   fum   al   niule   et   al   vent.

3. et   quant   est   aut   et   de - scent.

4. et   sa - chent   tuit   cil   del   mont.

5. qu'en - se - ment   pu - ge   va - lors.

6. a   ben   fas   et   ab   en - nor.

7. et   quant   est   aut   de - scen - dri - e.

8. s'on   ben   non   la   sous - te - ni - e.

9. et   de - grem   es - ser   e - nui - ous.

10. del   mar - keis   et   des   al - tres   prous.

11. et   des   on - ras   ric   fas   k'iu   fen.

EX. 6–16. Gui d'Ussel. PC 194,6. G fol. 59v–60.

begins like verse 1, but ends with yet another cadence. These interrelationships among motives and phrases connote a subtle and creative compositional faculty on Gui's part.

The music of this third generation is characterized by a burgeoning interest both in experimenting with the musical materials and with marshalling them to provide coherence and development to a melody. Interval leaps, wider ranges, and more varied textures suggest a propensity toward broadening the musical vocabulary, while the vast creativity in motivic manipulation indicates a deepening concern for unifying this vocabulary into a musical syntax, sometimes for a single song alone, sometimes identifiable throughout a composer's works or among those of several troubadours.

The fourth generation, as demonstrated in Chapter 5, increasingly favored a large-scale AAB melodic structure (see Table 5–7b). Some melodies of this period show signs of a stronger sense of tonal center, especially in the emphasis of a certain pitch by its position at incipits and cadences. As in the preceding period, thirds, triads, fourths, and fifths appear often. A motive that recurs frequently among composers of this generation is an incipit of a rising scale or leap through a third or fourth, or sometimes a fifth—a figure that we saw earlier in the melodies of Bernart de Ventadorn and Raimbaut d'Aurenga.

One of Gui d'Ussel's poems pays homage to a younger contemporary, Cadenet, whose *alba* discussed in Chapter 4 is his only extant melody. This melody is extremely melismatic and conjunct, with an occasional leap of a fourth or a fifth. Its range is conservative, encompassing a ninth, and it has a clear tonal center of D. Its overall contour is similar to that of the famous *alba* by Guiraut de Bornelh ("Reis glorios," Example 4–6), but its style is quite different. In fact, it is more similar in texture to the *trobar clus* song by the early troubadour Peire d'Alvernhe (Example 6–1) than to Guiraut's *alba*. Although Cadenet's poem is not *trobar clus*, it does have some unusual ideas, and perhaps the more ornamental style arises from the interesting twists in the text.

Peire Raimon de Tolosa also paid homage to Cadenet, as well as to Arnaut Daniel. His only extant melody has the more florid style of Cadenet's melody, in contrast to the much less melismatic textures in Arnaut's music (see Examples 6–2 and 6–3). There are also a number of uncommon intervals in Peire's melody, including several wide leaps from the end of one verse to the beginning of the next (a fifth, a minor seventh, a fourth, and an augmented fourth), all concentrated in the first half of the song, and a number of augmented fourths that are outlined either by a triad or joined in conjunct motion. These intervals might be modified by chromatic alteration of either F$\sharp$ or B$\flat$, but no such indication was given by the scribe of manuscript G (see Chapter 7).

Peirol, like Gaucelm Faidit, Peire Vidal, and Raimbaut de Vaqueiras, spent time in Italy. Eighteen melodies of his survive, of which ten have a large-scale AAB form. Like Peire Vidal, Peirol often used leaps of fourths and fifths in his tunes, although the motion in general is conjunct; unusual intervals are rare. Like Raimbaut, Peirol tended to use a conservative range of an octave or a ninth, often between C and D'; as in Gaucelm's music, his textures are syllabic to neumatic (see Examples 5–12 and 5–25). Peirol used a variety of techniques of manipulating motivic materials, although not with the same amount of flexibility found in Gaucelm's music. In Example 6–17, the cadence of verse 3 is the same as that of verse 1, although verse 3 begins differently. Verse 5 begins with a chain of two thirds (C–A–B–G) on the first four syllables, then moves to what begins like a sequential repetition of the chain a step below, B♭–G, but the next third (A–F) is filled in with a G. The cadence at the end of verse 7 is a variation of the cadence of verse 1. The ambiguity between written B♮ and B♭ is not resolved by the directions of the phrases. A singer might flatten the B at the end of verses 1, 3, and 7 since the melody descends immediately to A; but in verse 4 the melody moves up to C, and in verse 5 it has just come down from C, so in these instances B♮ may be appropriate.

Albertet honored Peirol in one of his *tornadas*, and he also paid homage to Gaucelm Faidit and Guilhem Augier. Three melodies by Albertet are extant, and they are in a very conservative style, with a range of no more than a major tenth, essentially conjunct motion with

EX. 6–17. Peirol. PC 366,13. G fol. 43.

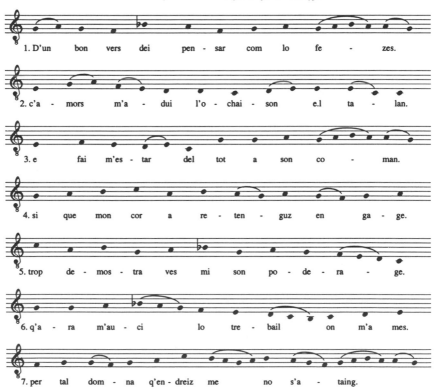

leaps of thirds, fourths and fifths here and there, and a syllabic texture with some melismas toward the ends of phrases. He sometimes linked motives, but not with the imagination of some other composers.

Only one of Guilhem Augier's melodies survives, the *descort* in paired-verse form (Example 4–13). The style of this melody is, like Albertet's, quite conservative in texture, intervallic content, and range.

Aimeric de Peguilhan alluded to Folquet de Marselha in one of his songs, engaged in a poetic exchange with Albertet, and had possible connections with others in Italy; his melodies show some similarities to theirs, but he had a distinctive style. He was somewhat more adventurous than Albertet. Like Folquet, Aimeric favored more neumatic textures, with some melismas on various syllables throughout the verses. His melodies are almost all through-composed (except for the *descort* melody in manuscript R, PC 10,45, which is in paired-verse form), but he linked motives in several of them, providing some structural coherence. Folquet used chains of descending seconds in many of his melodies, as did some others of his generation; Aimeric, on the other hand, often used a rising third at the beginning of phrases, at different pitch levels. In Example 6–18, every verse except the fourth one begins with an ascending scale figure of a third or a fourth (the first of which is augmented unless it is modified by *musica ficta*), starting on F, B, G, D, or C; all but one is filled in with a passing tone. The music of the end of verse 8 is nearly identical to that of the last six syllables of verse 5, except that it is distributed over four syllables.

Pons de Capduelh's four extant melodies are conjunct in motion, although he used triads fairly frequently (see Example 2–5 and 5–10). One of his melodies (Example 6–19) uses the same motive of a rising third that we saw in the melodies of Aimeric de Peguilhan. This tune is marked not only by this incipit motive, but also by a striking similarity in contour among almost all the verses, which rise to a melisma midway in the verse, then descend through a thoroughly neumatic second *hemistich* and cadence on F or sharply rise to C. Verses 1 through 4 are virtually identical except for this difference in the cadence. Only verses 5 and 6 depart from this contour, although the scribe has marked the *caesura* in both by a vertical line that extends all the way through the staff, suggesting a pause at that point that would coincide with the melisma in that position in the other verses. The melismatic character of this melody is reminiscent of the lone surviving melody by Uc Brunenc (see Example 5–20 and below), whom Pons may have known through their mutual connection with Bernart VII of Anduza in Toulouse.

Like Cadenet and Uc Brunenc, Raimon de Miraval and Guilhem Ademar had ties with the court of Toulouse. Raimon is represented in the manuscripts by 22 melodies, nearly half of which have an AAB scheme. His textures are syllabic to neumatic, and the motion is largely

EX. 6–18. Aimeric de Peguilhan. PC 10,41. G fol. 37.

conjunct, although he used thirds, triads, and occasionally a leap of a fourth. He usually stayed within the range of a tenth, often not even venturing beyond an octave (see Examples 2–3, 2–11, 5–9, 5–19, 5–22, and 5–29). He repeated pitches fairly frequently, especially A when the final pitch of a melody is D. Raimon often used a motive of a rising third or fourth figure at the beginnings of phrases—similar to the rising third used by Pons de Capduelh and Aimeric de Peguilhan. One distinctive feature of Raimon's melodies is the extent to which his phrases are varied upon repetition—not so much by transforming motives as by simply changing a few notes, sometimes by redistributing them among the syllables, sometimes by adding notes or moving some of them to a different pitch. In Example 6–20, every phrase begins with a rising third or fourth. Verses 2 and 3 are identical to verse 1 except for the cadence. Verses 4 and 6 begin alike, and indeed in a very similar fashion to verses

EX. 6–19. Pons de Capduelh. PC 375,14. W fol. 202v/B194v.

1 through 3 without the first F, but because verse 6 has four more syllables than verse 4, it stretches the phrase by oscillating around G until the last syllable. Verses 7 and 8 contain new material, but they also begin with the rising third. In this as in many other melodies by Raimon, the final note, F, is also emphasized in other cadences and by its position at the beginnings of several verses, giving the tune a strong sense of tonal center.

Guilhem Ademar, like Peire Raimon de Tolosa, evidently was influenced by the poetic style of Arnaut Daniel, to whom he alluded. One melody by Guilhem is extant (PC 202,8), but a clear derivation from Arnaut's musical style is not evident. Guilhem's phrases are more neumatic in texture throughout than Arnaut's, and in addition to repeating phrases, they contain more motivic manipulation (Arnaut's melodies are through-composed). Although Guilhem did not range

EX. 6–20. Raimon de Miraval. PC 406,44. R fol. 86v.

beyond a ninth in this tune, there is a clearer sense of direction, toward the final D, than in either of Arnaut's melodies.

Uc Brunenc, in addition to his connection with the court of Toulouse, enjoyed the patronage of Dalfi d'Alvernhe (as did Perdigon, Peirol, and the Monk of Montaudon), and he may have known Pons de Capduelh. His one surviving melody (Example 5–20) is extraordinarily melismatic, similar in texture to the *canso* of Peire d'Alvernhe (shown in Example 6–1) and the *alba* of Cadenet. The melismas exhibit certain kinds of variation upon repetition, such as added passing tones and repeated notes, but also a technique of small-scale inversion, for example, the modification of a neume G–F on the fifth syllable of verse 1 to F–G in the comparable place in verse 3, or A–B–A on the eighth syllable of verse 1 to A–G–A in verse 3. There are many thirds and triads in this melody as well, as in many other melodies of this and the previous generation.

Another of Dalfi's beneficiaries was Perdigon, who composed a *tenso* with Raimbaut de Vaqueiras. Perdigon's neumatic textures are similar to those of Raimbaut, although they sometimes have melismas earlier in the verses than in Raimbaut's music. Perdigon used conservative ranges as well, but he does not seem to have borrowed directly from the older composer. His melodies often feature the rising third or fourth at the beginnings of phrases that we have observed in the music of Pons de Capduelh, Raimon de Miraval, and Aimeric de Peguilhan.

Pistoleta was supposed to have been Arnaut de Maruelh's singer, although this has not been corroborated aside from the *joglar's vida* (see Chapter 1). Judging from his single extant melody (PC 372,3), he was a more conservative composer than the older Arnaut, using mostly conjunct motion and syllabic textures. The beginnings of several phrases in this melody outline a rising perfect fifth, either through a triad or by conjunct motion.

The Monk of Montaudon seems to have been well acquainted not only with the works of his own generation but also with those of earlier decades, as evidenced in his satire modeled on Peire d'Alvernhe's famous *sirventes*. The Monk borrowed the extant melody by Bertran de Born for one of his poems (see Example 4–9). The only extant melody evidently by the Monk himself (Example 5–11) is remarkable for its variation of phrases and the use and transformation of motivic material, including a rising fourth or fifth to begin most of the phrases. Unlike the music of some in this generation, it does not end on the note that one has come to expect from the earlier cadences, D, but on G. If such cases indicate an intermediate pitch between stanzas, then the final stanza of this song may have ended as expected on D, like verse 7, of which the last verse is a variation.

The composers of the fourth generation seem to share some musical traits more obviously than did those of earlier generations, such as the proclivity toward triadic motion, especially at incipits of phrases, a clearer tonal focus, and more regular formal schemes. At the same time, several troubadours cultivated a distinctive style, especially Peire Raimon de Tolosa with his melismatic textures and unusual intervallic leaps, Peirol with his creative methods of motivic manipulation, Aimeric de Peguilhan with his through-composed structures, and Raimon de Miraval with his phrase variation.

The fifth generation saw a drastic drop-off in productivity, probably in part due to the aftermath of the Albigensian Crusade. The extant music of these composers does not seem to have the variety, creativity (especially in the manipulation of motives), or tonal or structural coherence of previous generations.

Pons d'Ortaffa, active in Roussillon, may have alluded to Berenguier de Palol in one of his poems, but it is unlikely that he was acquainted with the older Catalan troubadour. The only melody of his to survive (PC 379,2) has a quite frugal style, with an AAB structure (see Table 5–8b) that features exact repetition of phrases without variation (transmitted in manuscript R), an incipit and final pitch of A, which is also the final note of several cadences, a syllabic texture with a few longer neumes toward the ends of verses, and mainly conjunct motion except for the leap of a fifth in the middle of verses 1, 3, and 7.

Aimeric de Belenoi had a poetic exchange with Albertet, and he may have encountered Peirol, Raimbaut de Vaqueiras, and others during his sojourn in Italy. The only extant melody whose poem is now believed to be by Aimeric is shown in Example 5–21. Like Pons's melody, it is conservative, although there is some motivic linking and variation, and its structure is not as regular. Aimeric used the rising-third incipit found in the melodies of other composers of the thirteenth century.

The travels of Uc de Saint Circ throughout Provence, Languedoc, Italy, and northern Spain undoubtedly brought him into contact with a number of other troubadours. His three extant melodies embody a wide assortment of stylistic devices, including numerous leaps of thirds and fifths, melismas in different positions in the verse, and phrase variation (see Examples 4–3 and 5–13). He did not manipulate motivic material as much as did composers in the previous generation. Two of his melodies end on a final pitch that coincides with cadences found earlier in the tune, giving them some tonal coherence.

Blacasset's only extant melody is for the one-stanza *canso* at the end of the Thibaut de Navarre section of manuscript W (see Chapter 2). It is in mensural notation, and the date of its entry may have been the early fourteenth century. The melody shares some features with those of other composers of the mid-thirteenth century, including the rising-fourth incipit, a neumatic texture, variation of phrases, and a tonal center on F articulated at several incipits and cadences and at the end of the melody.

The last generation of troubadours is dominated by the figure of Guiraut Riquier, whose music is quite distinct in style from that of the other troubadours of this generation. The single surviving melody by Daude de Pradas is a simple tune of an octave in range, with a few thirds and triads, a mostly syllabic texture broken by a two-, three-, or four-note neume here and there, and an uncertain tonal center. Daude alluded to Gui d'Ussel in one poem, and his melody seems to have some features in common with Gui's, at least in texture and interval content, but Daude's tune has nothing of the motivic variety found in Gui's music.

Peire Cardenal also left only one melody of his own, but as noted in Chapters 4 and 5, he set one text to a melody by Guiraut de Bornelh (PC 335,7 = 242,51) and another to a melody by Raimon Jordan (PC 335,49 = 404,11; Example 4–10). Peire's own melody (Example 6–21) has the same range, C to D', as those melodies by Guiraut and Raimon, and all three begin on A. Like Guiraut's, Peire's melody ends on D. All three melodies are marked by thirds and triads, with a few leaps of a fourth. The texture of Peire's song is similar to that of Guiraut's as well, mostly syllabic with some melismas toward the ends of phrases, and there is some slight variation in repeated phrases.

Peire Cardenal, Daude de Pradas, and Guiraut Riquier may have

EX. 6–21. Peire Cardenal. PC 335,67. R fol. 69v.

encountered one another in Rodez, but there is no sign that Guiraut d'Espanha was in contact with any of his contemporaries. Guiraut's one extant melody, the *dansa* shown in Example 4–11, is very simple, syllabic, conjunct, and limited to an octave in range.

Guiraut Riquier towers over the end of the thirteenth century largely because so much of his music survives. Many of his melodies have AAB structures (see Table 5–9b), and their melismatic character and remarkable variety in motivic manipulation can be seen in Examples 4–12, 5–14, 5–16, 5–30, and 5–32. He did not explore wide ranges, as some of his predecessors did, but favored the area between C and D'. A large proportion of his melodies end on D, while several others end on G; all of them have a strong sense of tonal direction, reinforced by internal cadences and incipits. The motion is largely conjunct, possibly because many wider intervals are filled in with melismatic figures. One particular motive, an arched figure A–C–D–C–A, occurs in many of his songs, in many different positions throughout the verses, and with several variations. Guiraut often used the same rising-third or -fourth incipit at the beginnings of phrases that composers of the earlier thirteenth century used.

Summary of Style Development

This overview is not intended to be exhaustive or definitive. Any examination of style and structure in this repertoire must above all acknowledge the uncertainties created by the haphazard transmission record. Some compositional traits attributed to a composer in the discussion above could have been due as much to the intervention of scribes or performers as to the troubadour. Where only one or two melodies survive, for example in the cases of Uc Brunenc and Cadenet, the scarce transmission of music prohibits generalizations about their stylistic propensities. Furthermore, the style of a song might be governed by its theme or structure, by the style or structure of the poem, by the demands of performance, or by other undiscernible factors. When the features of a song depart from observable norms we become aware of the extraordinary variety of tools available to the troubadours and of their creativity in exploiting them.

Careful contextualization, though, both of troubadours among their contemporaries and of readings among the manuscripts, allows some interpretation of the data that survive. More thorough study and analysis, especially focused on the relation of musical style to poetic style, and on comparison of features among songs, particularly among composers who were known to have had contact with one another, could

yield a better picture of the development of musical style in the troubadour repertoire. But even from the brief survey presented here several
trends emerge.

By the early thirteenth century, the textures of the troubadour
melodies, largely syllabic in the early generations, become more neumatic or melismatic; and the more florid figures, which at first are found
mainly toward cadences, begin to migrate to other locations in the
verses. Another trend is the move from conjunct motion to more disjunct movement, especially the appearance of leaps of thirds and triads,
along with fourths and fifths, also by the third generation. Composers
developed new ways to transform, combine, and link motivic material
as time went on. Certain motives are found predominantly in some
generations, less so in others, such as the rising third, fourth, and fifth
scale incipit of the fourth generation. Ranges also begin to expand
beyond the octave by the end of the twelfth century. With many exceptions, structures tend to become more regular, and later melodies
(especially after the beginning of the thirteenth century) seem to have a
clearer tonal direction, associated with the incipits, internal cadences,
and final pitches.

Sometimes these features directly interact with or enhance aspects
of the poem: its genre or theme, topics, structure, or language. Sometimes such interaction can be perceived as indirect at best. Most often
the musical style constitutes its own language, distinct from the poetic
style. Terms such as "conservative" and "creative" in the above discussion imply that in every generation some composers challenged the
boundaries in ways that widened the vocabulary available to all composers. For example, although the music of Bernart de Ventadorn is
often seen as direct and unassuming, he was the first composer to use
extensive motivic manipulation in his melodies. Gaucelm Faidit was
one of the earliest to use more disjunct motion, especially leaps of thirds
and triads. Peire d'Alvernhe, Uc Brunenc, Cadenet, and Guiraut Riquier
explored melismatic textures more extensively than did most of the
other composers in their respective generations. The music of other
composers employs a more limited vocabulary, and as the vocabulary
itself expanded, avoidance of the newer techniques can be seen as
conservative.

In the course of analyzing pitch relationships, motives, tonal organization, interval content, and ranges, one realizes that certain performing conventions might force a modification of some interpretations. A
singer who altered pitches chromatically, for instance, could influence
how one hears a tonal center or a motive. Further, the absence of any
indications of rhythmic shape among the notes probably hampers our
perception of a hierarchy of pitches. Were the notation to convey

specific durations of notes, patterns might emerge that would help identify motives and structurally significant notes. It is quite possible that some of the patterns described here on the basis of pitch content alone might not have been heard as patterns at all if they were sung with certain rhythmic shapes. Yet it is also possible that some of these pitch patterns can shed light on what rhythms might have been applied to the notes.

CHAPTER

SEVEN

PERFORMANCE

The songs of the troubadours were intended to be sung aloud to an audience, which was the ultimate step in the art of rhetoric, the author's actual opportunity to persuade the listeners. The final stage in the art of rhetoric, *pronuntiatio*, receives minimal attention from late medieval poetic theorists, but Geoffroi de Vinsauf's comments make clear that public delivery was as important to the work as all of the previous steps:

> In reciting aloud, let three tongues speak: let the first be that of the mouth, the second that of the speaker's countenance, and the third that of gesture. The voice has its own laws, and you should observe them in this way: the period that is spoken should observe its natural pauses, and the word its accent. Separate those words which the sense separates, join those that sense joins. Modulate your voice in such a way that it is in harmony with the subject; and take care that voice does not advance along a path different from that which the subject follows. Let the two go together; let the voice be, as it were, a reflection of the subject. As the nature of your subject is, so let your voice be when you rehearse it: let us recognize them as one.[1]

A number of performance issues confront the modern singer who hopes to recapture the aesthetic of the troubadours' songs. The most disputed issue is rhythm. As for the pitches themselves, there are questions about how much singers might have improvised, or altered notes chromatically; and there is the question of whether they sang to instrumental accompaniment.

Our guides on performance practices include the theoretical materials (poetic and musical), the manuscripts and their illustrations, and references to music and singing in Occitanian literature. All these sources have their limitations. The treatises on poetry and music seem to be addressed to poets and composers rather than to singers, and they allude to performance only incidentally and often cryptically (see Chapters 3 and 4). Music treatises mention only trouvère songs, not those by troubadours. The poetic treatises hint at understood performance customs, such as tempo for certain genres. They also discuss poetic features that may be reflected in musical rhythm, specifically the accent on the rhyme and the *caesura*.

The notation and other paleographical features of the music manuscripts leave many performance questions unanswered, as Chapter 2 demonstrated. Most of the melodies are notated in neumes that do not convey indication of rhythm, although a few late thirteenth- and early fourteenth-century melodies appear in Franconian notation. Some of the music scribes paid close attention to the overlay of music above text, aligning the neumes carefully, marking verse endings and sometimes *caesuras* with vertical strokes through the staff. Some, however, were not consistent in this at all. Chromatic alterations of pitches also are not consistent, either among manuscript readings or within a single melody. Variant readings point to a great deal of fluidity in the pitch content of the melodies, suggesting a lively improvisatory tradition. The poems too display a great deal of instability. All these issues have obvious implications for performance.

The manuscript illustrations that consist of more than simply a "portrait" of a troubadour are few and largely stereotypical.[2] Some of them show troubadours who appear to be singing, some playing an oval-shaped fiddle, a harp, or a mandora (including the *joglar* Perdigo). Others depict troubadours as knights on horseback or wielding swords or spears, holding or reading a book, or conversing with a lady. The illustrations in troubadour chansonniers are neither as numerous nor as diverse as those in trouvère chansonniers. Literary allusions, while numerous and perhaps generally reflective of social conditions, like the illustrations, are not always reliable, since they are subject to considerations of poetic style, structure, and theme.[3]

In certain ways the most useful clues to performance practices are found in the songs themselves—their content, structure, and style, both poetic and musical. We have already seen ways in which the melodies interacted with the poems and ways in which they acted independently, but it is in the area of performance that the interaction between poems and melodies, as well as their independence, becomes most obvious.

The musical performance of a song might have been affected by the poem's topic (hence its genre), structural elements (rhyme, verse, and stanza structure), and style (syntactical phrasing, language, and expression). Most obviously, pronunciation of the language would have direct implications for musical delivery. The most difficult element in the pronunciation of Old Occitan, as in all the Romance languages, is its inflection, not only word accentuation but also the differences between open and closed vowels. A verse or stanza of a poem subsumes the sounds of individual syllables so that their identities become part of the larger whole. The relationship between the melodies and the sonorities of the texts does not reveal any consistent association between particular types of sounds with particular types of melodic figures. Notes with *plicas*, for example, notational symbols which probably evolved from liquescent neumes in plainchant, are no more likely to fall on diphthongs or palatalized sounds (such as *-nh-* or *-gl-*) than on other types of sounds (hence my transcriptions give *plicas* discrete pitch values).[4] Open and closed vowels occur with both single notes and melismas, with high pitches and low.

The element of verse that is more audibly dominant than any other in Occitan poetry is the rhyme accent. In the late thirteenth century theorists began to discuss proper accentuation, of single spoken words and as an element of the structure of poetic verse (see Chapter 5). The treatises explain accent in terms of inflection, which involves raising (*agusa*) the voice, as well as duration, which involves holding (*rete*) the accented syllable. Jofre de Foixà's late thirteenth-century *Regles [de trobar]* defines it this way:

Accen es con hom agusa la votz e la rete pus en una sillaba que en altra, en axi co *conexens*, que en aquell *-xens* qui es derrera sillaba s'agusa pus la votz que en les autres sillabes; o en axi co *benanança*, co en aquell *-nan-*, qui es denan lo *-ça*, s'agusa plus la vots que en les altres.[5]	Accent is when one raises the voice and holds it more on one syllable than on another, as in *conexens*, where on *-xens*, which is the last syllable, the voice is raised more than on the other syllables; or as in *benanança*, where on *-nan-*, which is before *-ça*, the voice is raised more than on the other [syllables].

Jofre does not suggest a specific length of duration, and he suggests that stress is more a vocal than a temporal phenomenon. But he seems not to be concerned with differences between the sound of such inflection when it is spoken and when it is sung to a set of specific pitches. (The author of the *Leys d'Amors*, at least forty years later, remarks specifically that the melody's rise and fall need not coincide with text accent, and that accented syllables do not require more notes to lengthen them.[6]) In the melodies themselves, text accent at the rhyme and the *caesura* is not directly reflected in height or number of pitches. Whether it would have been matched by a specific duration of a single pitch, or coincide with a musical metrical accent, is a complex question that lies at the heart of some theories on rhythm.

Chapters 1 and 2 discussed the performers of the songs, what kinds of skills and training they may have had, the social setting and function of the songs, how singers may have learned the songs, and how that may have affected the transmission of the melodies. This chapter will examine specific performance problems that modern singers encounter, against the background and analyses presented in the preceding chapters. The proposals offered below are based in large measure on personal interpretation as well as application of the ideas presented throughout this book.

Rhythm

The rhythm of the melodies of the troubadours is a conundrum that has intrigued and befuddled scholars and performers since the early twentieth century. Of the various theories so far proposed, none has been proven, none is universally convincing, and all have generated heated debate. No one argues that the melodies were sung with no rhythmic shape at all. The fact that the manuscripts do not indicate rhythm means merely that scribes were disinclined or unable to write the rhythms down.

Most of the modern theories of rhythm approach the problem from the standpoint of prosody, assuming that musical rhythm hinged at least in part on the relationship of the melodies to the texts. These theories emphasize variously the structure of the poem (including its versification), its sound (including accent), or its sense (including the progression of its topics). Some versions of the modal theory assert that musical stress or duration should coincide with the text accentuation, or that the poetic meters that thirteenth-century theorists described in connection with the rhythmic modes of sacred polyphony are found in vernacular lyric as well. The isosyllabic theory proposes that all syllables of the text should receive roughly equal duration. The declamatory theories propose that the melody's rhythm depends on the sonority, syntax, and meaning of the text. Other theories offer some combination of these ideas, but all take account of the centrality of the text in performance.

The modal theories of rhythm in troubadour and trouvère music were first proposed in 1907 by Pierre Aubry and in 1908 by Jean-Baptiste Beck.[7] They observed that French *dupla* in thirteenth-century motets used modal rhythm, and that many of Adam de la Halle's *chansons*, as well as trouvère melodies in other chansonniers (including troubadour manuscript W), were written in mensural notation with modal rhythms. These observations led them to believe that all monophonic French songs were sung in regular patterns of longs and breves, conforming to the rhythmic modes used in *organum*, *discant*, and motets. Assuming that troubadour songs were closely related to the trouvère repertoire in style, content, and performance, they applied the theory to the southern songs as well.

Aubry argued further that the mode mirrors metrical patterns—iambs, dactyls, spondees, etc.—in the texts. Beck rejected this particular argument, noting correctly that neither French nor Occitan poetry is metrical, although the rhymes are defined by accent. He suggested that the durations of the notes (their "quantity") did not have to coincide with the stresses on words in the texts (their "quality"), and that a melody's rhythmic mode could "violate" the tonic syllables on individual words by placing a long note or a melisma on an atonic syllable or a short note on a tonic syllable, just as classical Latin meters sometimes disregard the quantity of individual words. The venerable Friedrich Ludwig added his voice in support of this theory,[8] as did Friedrich Gennrich, whose complete edition of the troubadour melodies with its modal rhythms was for many years the only available modern edition of the entire corpus.[9] None of the studies or editions produced by proponents of the modal theory explain how singers would discern the rhythmic mode, although they all imply that in some respect the text generates it. Many of these editions present interpretations that contradict other published versions.

Most scholars today reject the modal theory out of hand, partly because, as Beck noted, the lyric poetry of the troubadours is neither quantitative nor qualitative, so there are no consistent accentual patterns in the verse other than at the rhyme, and there is no external evidence to support deriving musical rhythmic patterns from the poetry. Furthermore, even though trouvère melodies turn up in polyphonic motets, there is skepticism that outside of that idiom they were governed by the same rhythmic system, especially in view of the different origins, functions, and contexts of liturgically based polyphonic music on the one hand and courtly lyric on the other.[10]

The isosyllabic theory has appeared in various guises. Ugo Sesini, in his study of troubadour manuscript G, pointed out that the notation of troubadour songs is that of late medieval plainchant, and that each syllable is given its own neume.[11] In the nonquantitative Romance languages, each syllable is more or less equal in duration, and each word of more than one syllable has one tonic and one or more atonic syllables, distinguished by more or less "intensification." According to Sesini, poetry, unlike prose speech, moves by a regular pattern of binary or ternary feet which consist of a combination of *arsis* and *thesis*, articulated by intensification (like the *ictus* in the Solesmes interpretation of plainchant). As Beck had pointed out earlier, Sesini argued that the accented beginning of a poetic foot does not always coincide with the accented syllable of a word, and that the natural accent of the word is adapted to the prevailing meter. Unlike the modalists, however, Sesini argued that it is the poetry not the melody that carries this meter. He devoted many pages to outlining the "meters" of Romance verse, based on classical meters. The notes of the music must be adapted to this meter, and the best way to do that is to give each syllable equal duration, no matter how many pitches it encompasses, so that the *arsis* and *thesis* of the text can be articulated. Although Sesini's transcriptions are predicated on isosyllabism, they are characterized by a regular meter, which is ternary in effect.

John Stevens also came to the conclusion that monophonic songs should be sung to isosyllabic rhythm, but he approached it from quite a different, and complex, point of view.[12] He explained how poetic theory of the late Middle Ages describes Latin poetry as "rhythmic" rather than quantitative or qualitative, reliant on syllable count and rhyme rather than on a regular progression of meters. Given the paleographical reality that scribes assigned one neume to each syllable, Stevens agreed that each syllable was of equal duration, but he did not adopt Sesini's complex system of poetic meters. Syllables with one note and those with melismas are of roughly equal duration, with long melismas necessarily being sung with some flexibility. Stevens also distinguished between courtly and more popular genres, suggesting that the latter were more likely to have measured patterns in their melodies.

The declamatory theory, as advanced by Hendrik van der Werf, proposes that the singer "declaim" the text as if reciting it, and that the melody is subservient to this declamatory style of speech.[13] Recently he has emphasized his view that the notes of a melody were of roughly equal duration, allowing for some fluctuation in performance.[14] His theory presupposes that neither the melody nor the text has a "meter" per se, but that the sound, syntax, and structure of the text in any given verse or stanza should generate a rhythm. Like Beck and Sesini, he objects to Aubry's modal theory because it is based on the assumption that poetic stresses must coincide with musical stresses. Instead, individual word stresses can receive intensification in performance (dynamic or rhythmic). Van der Werf says that each pitch would start out being more or less equal in duration, and that the singer might make some syllables shorter or longer, led by shifting elements of the sound, structure, or sense of the text. Each verse and stanza would thus have its own rhythm. He invokes a remark by Johannes de Grocheio, who says that plainchant is not without measure altogether but is "not too precisely measured." Van der Werf believes that the theorist is speaking here also of secular monophony.[15] He also argues that polyphony was a peculiar phenomenon with its own rules; the appearance of French songs in motets necessitated an adaptation of their originally free rhythms into the strict modes, just as the plainchant melodies that made up the tenors were given modal patterns (and different ones in different pieces). He wonders why scribes of the second half of the thirteenth century avoided mensural notation when writing troubadour and trouvère songs, while in some of the same manuscripts they used mensural notation for polyphonic French works.

Like van der Werf, Christopher Page asserts that composers of polyphony in the thirteenth century took old music and forced it into new molds, adding mensural rhythms to previously unmeasured melodies.[16] He maintains that the scribes of the late thirteenth century, in France at least, were concerned chiefly with helping perpetuate and record the new musical style of polyphony, with its notation, which conveyed precise rhythmic patterns. According to Page, using notation that embodies these patterns to write monophony amounted to an anachronistic imposition of a mensural aesthetic that was foreign to the original character of the courtly lyric (see above, Chapter 2). Along with Stevens, Page asserts that Old French and Old Occitan courtly songs in the "High Style," including *cansos*, *complaintes*, and *sirventes*, were originally free and unmeasured, while songs in the "Low Style," including dance songs and *pastourelles*, would have been measured.[17]

Several rhythmic solutions have been offered that produce freer rhythms, but which in certain respects are measured. In the late nineteenth century, Antonio Restori suggested shifting meters, including 2/4, 3/4, and 4/4, frequently treating melismas as ornaments; his interpretations often approach an isosyllabic style but with many exceptions.[18] His transcriptions often align variant readings, and the inflection and structure of the text plays a role in the results. Much later, Raffaello Monterosso suggested a free approach, based loosely but not rigidly on the "ritmo dei versi," allowing for some of the implications of the neumes as well as certain melodic features.[19] His results are similar to Restori's.

In a more thorough-going approach, Ewald Jammers has proposed that text and melody each had a rhythm of its own, but that their two structures interacted to produce a common, broader rhythm.[20] Motives, melismas, repeated pitches, and other musical elements interact with text accents and rhymes to produce a rhythm that is not necessarily patterned (although in his scheme some songs might have a modal rhythm), yet not altogether free. Jammers emphasizes the freedom of the singer in applying this theory, but it is a freedom tempered by internal structural features peculiar to each song.

Gérard Le Vot has offered rhythmic solutions that are self-consciously modern, but are based on close readings of elements in the texts and the music, as well as on manuscript evidence.[21] In recent publications Robert Lug has argued in favor of an interpretation based on readings of the neumes, on certain literary allusions to performance practices, on comparison with folk song, and on word accents in the texts, resulting in the concept of a "Takt-rhythmik" that is somewhat but not strictly measured, allowing for great freedom in detail.[22]

All these theories treat the poems of the songs with great respect, some ascribing primacy to the text over the music, some the music over the text, and some the text and music as equal partners. Some of these ideas presuppose an overarching aesthetic—the existence of a system of metrical patterns that are external to the notes, rhetorical declamation and the predominance of the sound and sense of the text over the music, *arsis* and *thesis* in the poetry, or the concept of "number" in theory and practice—which governed how rhythm or meter (musical or poetic) worked. All troubadours and *joglars* would have known and applied this aesthetic, and it would have determined the rhythmic shape of a song during any performance.

I am skeptical of an *a priori* theoretical or philosophical aesthetic or principle governing all performance. Given the complexity of the elements that make up a troubadour song, a singer's approach to performance might fluctuate from day to day, sometimes centered on the compelling features of versification, sometimes on the theme or mood of the text, sometimes on the motivic relationships in the music, the tonal goals, or other musical features. A performance might be more measured one day, more declamatory the next, more variegated in rhythmic shape the next. If it is true that the songs lived for a specific hearing, then a singer might gauge the audience, the room, and the occasion, and adjust the approach accordingly.[23]

The declamatory theory might be more compelling for the songs of the troubadours than for the trouvère songs. First, whatever connection the troubadours may have had with northern music was certainly less than the trouvères had (there is no evidence, for instance, that troubadours composed motets),[24] so their knowledge of the mensural notational system that accompanied the creation of the motet is difficult to demonstrate. Second, the structural regularity in the repetition of phrases which characterizes so many trouvère melodies is not nearly as common among the troubadours' melodies, which may suggest less rhythmic regularity as well. In addition, the rhetorical variety in the Occitanian poems is in general much greater, more intense, and more colorful, suggesting a need for a rather free musical performance that avoids the imposition of an artificial and external meter.

The drawback of this theory is the rather low regard that it has for the music per se. Notwithstanding van der Werf's recent retreat from his earlier view that the songs are "a poem performed to a simple and unobstrusive melody,"[25] the theory still does not take into account any of the often sophisticated and carefully designed musical features of structure and style that are not generated solely by their relationship with the texts, and which may well shed light on how a singer approached musical rhythm.

The nonmensural notations that transmit the troubadour melodies mean different things to different people. For the modalists, such notation is neutral—it conveys nothing about rhythm, whether measured in some way or not, and it paves the way for a metered interpretation. For Jammers and Lug, the notation is not completely neutral, in that some ligature forms can be interpreted as implying rhythmic shape. Sesini and Stevens argue that the notation, with a single neume for each syllable, is perfectly suited to imply an isosyllabic performance. Van der Werf and Page believe that scribes could have notated courtly songs mensurally had they wished, and the fact that they did not suggests that the songs were not performed with modal or mensural rhythms. Songs with mensural notation, according to this view, do not reflect earlier practices, but demonstrate the influence that polyphony and its special notation had on an older repertoire. This hypothesis has become so widely accepted that it merits some attention here.

Notations of the late Middle Ages and treatises that described them probably followed practice. Longs and shorts existed in polyphony long before notation captured that concept precisely with discrete note forms.[26] The modal system of Parisian polyphony was regulated by patterns that were maintained fairly consistently through a section of music, and which were denoted on the page by a contextual graphing system legendary for its ambiguities. Seeing a certain ligature pattern prompted in the ear of the singer a metrical pattern into which he then fell, continuing until the ligature pattern changed and triggered recognition of a new metrical pattern, as signified by the note groupings. The rhythms of modal music—iambs, dactyls, and so forth—existed orally outside the music itself, and its notation precipitated a response from the ear more than from the eye. Modal notation was in that sense a mnemonic system, a reminder of modes that were part of the oral environment, just as the non-diastematic chant notations of 300 years earlier were reminders of pitches that the singers already knew.

The modal notational system was devised for melismatic music, and it became inadequate after a few decades, when the music began to be more syllabic. It gradually gave way to mensural notation, which was devised toward the middle of the thirteenth century. The increasing complexity and syllabic texture of a type of polyphony—especially motets—required a notational system capable of indicating the durations of individual notes. As the modes waned and the rhythm of music became more flexible, composers and evidently singers began to rely on these discrete and more precise written symbols; the mensural notational system served the eye as much as the ear.

But during the transition from modal to mensural notation, the style of the music had not yet changed radically. A motet could be transmitted both in modal notation (as in Notre Dame manuscripts F and W2) and in mensural notation (in manuscripts Hu and Mo), representing not a difference in style of the music, but a difference in the means of transmitting it. Even when mensural notation became more widespread, it was not always used in pieces where a measured performance was required. In the motet section of troubadour manuscript W (fol. 205–210/B197–203), for example, motet *dupla* with syllabic texts were notated in nonrhythmic chant neumes over melismatic tenors with modal ligatures.

As the more precise notation made transmittal of increasingly complex rhythms possible, the music began to stretch the boundaries of the modal system very quickly. The treatise by Franco of Cologne codifying the mensural notational system did not appear until 1260, or perhaps as late as 1280–85.[27] Thus there was a wide overlap among notational practices (nonrhythmic, modal, and mensural), theory (which followed practice), and oral and written processes for learning music. It is not clear just when performers began to rely on manuscripts to learn rhythms and on treatises to learn notational systems, but the notations and the theories almost certainly postdated the music.

Modal notation was never possible for the vernacular repertoires, because the music is not melismatic enough to allow establishment of the ligature patterns by which the oral patterns of the modes were represented (the same reason that it was not possible or only inconsistently so in the *conductus* repertoire and other *cum littera* music). After the middle of the thirteenth century, when mensural notation began to appear in polyphonic manuscripts, it is possible that some scribes of secular monophony could have been among those experimenting with *longas* and *breves*, but just as not all scribes of motets simultaneously adopted the new notational vocabulary, neither can we assume that scribes of *chansons* did. Mensural notation certainly would not have been part of the vocabulary of any of the scribes of troubadour manuscript X, who used Lothringian plainchant neumes, which were outside the Parisian orbit. The main music scribe of manuscript W probably completed his work before 1280 (see Chapter 2), at a time when mensural notation was still so novel and experimental that he may not have been trained in it.

By the end of the thirteenth century, most northern scribes probably were familiar with Franconian notation, and at least two of them used it in trouvère manuscripts: that of Adam de la Halle (FPn fr. 25566) and the Chansonnier Cangé (FPn fr. 846). If anything, this circumstance reinforces the link between northern polyphony and the French *chanson* repertoire. Whatever it might tell us about the rhythm of trouvère songs, it does not shed light on the aesthetic of the south. In the first place, the Italian and Languedocian scribes of manuscripts G and R may or may not have been trained in mensural notation. And even if they were familiar with northern scribal developments of the period, they may not have seen a use for the system unless they knew that singers would need it or be able to use it. It was suggested in Chapter 2 that the troubadour manuscripts with music were not created with performers in mind. If the singers did not in general use the extant chansonniers, then scribal exactitude when it came to rhythm was unnecessary, nor would it have been necessary if the manuscripts were meant mainly for presentation or preservation. Furthermore, most composers probably were not involved either in the production or use of the manuscripts (except perhaps in the case of Guiraut Riquier and manuscript R), so their control over the rhythmic values indicated by written notation might well have been minimal.

The few instances where mensural notation is used in the troubadour chansonniers are puzzling. Some of the melodies in Franconian notation added to manuscript W (discussed in Chapter 2) appear to be in an early fourteenth-century hand, while others are perhaps of a slightly earlier period. Van der Werf rejects these songs as representative of the troubadour art because he considers them to be "late" additions, representing a later aesthetic.[28] My reasons for including them in this study are given in the Introduction. Their notation is relatively clear-cut, conveying modal patterns.

Manuscript R also contains several songs that use longs and breves. They are written in a hand very similar if not identical to the main notation hand in the manuscript and are probably roughly contemporary with the other melodies and with the texts themselves.[29] The first two songs with melodies in the first gathering (fol. 5 and 5v) are a *pastorela* and a *sirventes* by Marcabru. They represent what Christopher Page has called the "Low Style" and the "High Style" of courtly lyric. Both melodies begin with alternating longs and breves, although neither continues thus in a consistent way to the end.[30] For Page "Low Style" songs like this *pastorela* were more likely to have had measured note values than those in the "High Style." To support this theory he offers the example of two late additions to manuscript W, on fol. 78v/ BXXIv, where the scribe notated a *dansa* in the left column in Franconian notation and a *canso* in the right column in nonmensural neumes.[31] But whatever this late scribe of manuscript W was trying to convey by differentiating the notations of the two melodies, the scribe of R appears not to have shared the same aesthetic. On fol. 5 and 5v, he seems to convey mode 1 in both a "High Style" *sirventes* and a "Low Style" *pastorela*.

Because these are the first songs in the manuscript, it is tempting to infer that this late thirteenth-century music scribe intended from the beginning to indicate mensural rhythms throughout the manuscript, but that he lost heart, interest, or know-how. If he was copying from a manuscript that did not have mensural notation, for instance, he may have found the task of translating the notes into rhythmic values too taxing. The scribe again used measured notation in a *canso* by Bernart de Ventadorn on fol. 57, where the alternation of *longas* and *breves* is consistent, except in the latter portion of each verse where the mode 1 pattern is interrupted by apparently nonmodal ligatures. On fol. 88v (Example 7–1), he used *longas* and *breves* consistently for two verses, gave it up for several more, and made one last attempt at the beginnings of the last two verses. Earlier in the first gathering, where the two songs by Marcabru appear, the inconsistent entry of melodies and the likelihood that there were several music scribes may have discouraged the compiler of the manuscript ultimately from attempting to see that all the melodies were written with mensural notation.

None of this proves whether the presence or absence of mensural notation reflects the actual rhythms of the songs in performance. The example in R seems to suggest that the notation is simply an accident of the process of written transmission, and that the chansonniers were not necessarily intended for use by singers.

Van der Werf and Page have argued that the appearance of mensural notation in late thirteenth-century manuscripts of French and Occitan monophony coincided with the development of a new measured rhythmic style in that period, and that the earlier melodies that were nonmeasured were now transformed by a new notational vocabulary. The same reasoning could argue the opposite: that the repertoires of the troubadours and trouvères had always had some kind of measured rhythms, and that scribes used nonmensural notation (as they did in the majority of cases) to distinguish its aesthetic from that of the Parisian repertoire, perhaps to differentiate graphically between old and new, courtly and sacred, monophonic and polyphonic. We do not know that triple meter did not exist before Leonin, only that it did exist after him.

The troubadours' songs had been around for at least a hundred years by the middle of the thirteenth century. They did not undergo radical stylistic change during the thirteenth century, nor is there any reason to believe that their composers or performers needed a more precise notation. Even if performers used the chansonniers, perhaps the notation of troubadour songs served only as a mnemonic for tunes they already knew. That it should have even occurred to some thirteenth-

EX. 7–1. Peirol. PC 366,9. R fol. 88v.

1. Co - ras   que   mi   fes   do - ler.

2. a - mors   ni.m   do - net   es - may.

3. a - ra.m   ten   a - legr'   e   gai.

4. per   qui   chant   de   mon   pla - zer.

5. car   pus   ric   joi   ai   con - quis.

6. c'a   mi   non   ta - nhi - a.

7. e   ric   cors   cant   s'u - me - li - a.

8. hu - mi - li - tatz   l'en - re - quitz.

century scribes to adapt a new notational system—a mensural one—for an old repertoire is in itself remarkable. Some, like the scribe of R, may have experimented with mensural notation to see if it would convey the rhythms that were already part of the music.

There are other indications that scribes were attempting to provide clues about rhythm. Some syllables have repeated notes, some notes are elongated, and occasionally a note within a ligature is given an extra stem, all suggesting a lengthening of pitch. Some scribes used vertical bars through the staff to coincide with the ends of verses or a *caesura*, or to clarify which notes go with which syllables, to draw attention to a clef change or the presence of a chromatic inflection, or to reflect the textual syntax. Every so often, especially in manuscript R, these vertical bars might suggest a brief pause, especially where the textual syntax might call for it.[32]

Since paleographical clues like these are rare in the troubadour manuscripts, we must look beyond the written melodies for answers, such as to the variant readings. Van der Werf and others have argued that the very existence of significant or numerous variants might suggest that the performances were rhythmically free. But some details in these variants, on the contrary, might be indications of durations, at least of small musical figures. If two versions transmit significant variants on a single syllable, for example, it might be because the syllable was sung quickly and hence its pitches were less stable; pitches that are more consistently transmitted among readings might have been longer and hence more memorable. On the first syllable of Example 7–2, the readings in manuscripts R, X, and G outline three distinct figures, perhaps because this syllable was of short duration; the pitches of the second syllable match exactly except for its last pitch in manuscript R, possibly indicating that singers dwelled on them. The readings disagree somewhat on the third and fourth syllables, again perhaps because they were sung faster; they all agree on the pitch G at the beginning of the fifth syllable, a pitch that might have been transmitted more stably because it was held longer.

Such a close comparison of readings might also lead to the identification of the "essential" pitches of a melody, which may point to rhythmic values common to all versions. As in Example 7–2, two different readings of a melisma on a single syllable might suggest a quick delivery and a consequent instability of pitches. Similarly, a syllable with two different melismas in two versions and only one pitch in a third reading, like the third syllable of Example 7–3, might have been sung quickly, with the melisma treated as an ornament. In cases where the melisma is transmitted consistently, though, for example, the eighth syllable in manuscripts X and W, perhaps the syllable was sung more slowly. The single notes in manuscript G might have reflected these rhythms in the other versions.

Rhythm or measure might have played a positive role during the oral transmission of a melody. A close affinity among the pitches in different readings of a troubadour melody might suggest some overall rhythmic stability. For example, the most widely transmitted troubadour song, Bernart de Ventadorn's "Can vei la lauzeta mover," is remarkably fixed in comparison with most others with multiple readings, perhaps due as much to a certain rhythmic constancy as to its melodic coherence (see Example 4–2). Similarly, Example 7–4 is remark-

EX. 7–2. Peire Vidal. PC 364,11, verse 1. X fol. 87v; R fol. 48; G fol. 40v.

EX. 7–3. Rigaut de Berbezilh. PC 421,2, verse 10. X fol. 84v;
W fol. 195v/B187v; G fol. 63.

ably stable throughout its two readings in manuscripts X and G, more so than many other melodies transmitted by these two sources; a stable rhythmic shape would make such a stable transmission of pitches much easier and more likely.

The text almost certainly played some role in the rhythm of a song. The conceptualization of music as poetic and poetry as musical by contemporary theorists, such as Geoffroi de Vinsauf and Jofre de Foixà, suggests that musical performance reinforces the difference between poetry and prose. Some of the poetic features discussed in previous chapters suggest that the structure of the poetry might call forth some kind of patterned delivery, at least on a large scale, that does not depend entirely on individual word stresses or syntax.

In many works the structure and style of the poem are so compelling as to be impossible to ignore in performance. Many poems with a strongly marked versification scheme cry out for an almost "sing-song" declamation that would find expression in a patterned rhythmic performance, e.g., "Kalenda maia" by Raimbaut de Vaqueiras. [33] In such songs

EX. 7–4. Peirol. PC 366,12. X fol. 88v; G fol. 49v.

with short verses, the persistent rhyme sounds might receive a rhythmic performance that articulates the verse structure (see Chapter 6). As shown in Chapter 4, the genre of a song sometimes affects its speed, and the content and progression of the poem's topics might bear on this as well. As the declamatory theory suggests, some important rhetorical arguments in the poem might call for a more deliberate articulation of the words. *Enjambement* from one verse to another might compel the singer to obscure a verse break that might be observed in other stanzas.

The accent structure of the rhyme and the *caesura* cannot be ignored in performance, since they are the most audible structural features of the poem. In the songs with mensural notation, the disposition of longs and shorts at the rhyme consistently falls into the pattern of long–long on paroxytonic rhymes and short–long on oxytonic rhymes (see Example 7–5). Although I would not argue dogmatically that all rhymes should be articulated this way, I see no reason not to believe that it was quite commonly done. In songs where rhymes are used to link stanzas (*coblas capcaudadas*, etc.) or that have a word or verse refrain or other prominent features of the versification, the melodic rhythm might be used to highlight or emphasize them.

In the final analysis, though, the structure and style of the melodies themselves are our best guides to their rhythms. The very presence of a melody alters the audible effect of a song. The melodies are based on musical principles of structure and style that are not necessarily dependent on the poems, and these structures can be expected to have their own inherent rhythm, even if it is inexact.[34] Music's elements follow rules of their own, regardless of which poetic elements are present.

Many melodic features—including large-scale structure, repetition of phrases and motives, pitch goals and hierarchies, contours, tonal orientation and direction, motivic development, cadences and incipits—add layers of structuring that simply by their presence (whether or not the notes are given precise durations) complicate, obscure, enhance, or complement the elements of the poem. When a singer repeated a set of pitches five, six, or more times for as many stanzas of a poem, with the same contours, same cadences, same tonal goals, same relationships among the verses, same intervals, and same motivic interrelationships (even allowing for some variation of all these features), surely the tune fell into a similar rhythmic structure over all, even if the performer stretched or contracted the pattern here and there (as all singers do, in any repertoire). Such a macrorhythm allows variation on a small scale but maintains consistency on the large scale.

Not only repeated stanzas but also (and perhaps even more so) repeated phrases are likely to have received more or less the same rhythmic shape. I disgree with van der Werf's suggestion that repeated

EX. 7–5. Anonymous. PC 461,37, verses 1–4. W fol. 109/B117.

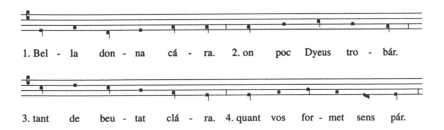

1. Bel - la   don - na   cá - ra.   2. on   poc   Dyeus   tro - bár.

3. tant   de   beu - tat   clá - ra.   4. quant   vos   for - met   sens   pár.

stanzas or verses might have very different rhythms, governed by changing word stresses and rhetorical content.[35] On the contrary, the poetic structure articulated by syllable count and rhyme scheme and the reiteration of the same set of pitches with their own internal coherence (high and low points, motivic identity and interrelationships, cadences, and so forth) were much more compelling audible features than the sound of an individual word or the force of a particular argument. A singer can easily emphasize the changing textual elements of a song within a larger rhythmic framework, and there might have been ways in which the poem was adapted to the melody, rather than the reverse.

We can glimpse how this could have occurred in some extant melodies, where two different versions of a verse have identical (or nearly identical) pitches but differ on the alignment of these pitches with the syllables of text. In a song by Berenguier de Palol (Example 7–6), phrase B of verses 2 and 5, phrase A of verses 3 and 6, and phrase C of verses 4 and 7 share almost exactly the same pitches, but they are distributed slightly differently over the syllables. The repetition of the three distinct series of pitches is surely not accidental, and each continuously recurring pair of musical phrases, with well-defined contours and interval contents repeated stanza after stanza, would probably fall into a more or less similar rhythmic shape. Such a linkage between pitches and rhythms would mean, though, that the syllables of text would shift against the rhythmic framework of each phrase—in other words, that musical rhythm would dominate any otherwise inherent textual rhythm.

Smaller-scale rhythms might be identified also within and among shorter motives, such as in many of the examples discussed in Chapter 5. Further, since composers often developed and manipulated their motivic material, they might have manipulated its rhythmic shape as well. Thus since, in many cases, identical motives probably had identical rhythmic shape, their pitch transformation might have resulted in some rhythmic transformation at the same time.

Clearly we will never discover for certain the rhythms of the songs of the troubadours. But there is less justification for imposing a general fundamental principle on the repertoire, resulting in a universal style of rhythm, than for assuming that each song—each performance, even— had a rhythm of its own. The best way to project what the rhythm of a song might have been is to analyze closely its genre, poetic structure and style, notation, variants, and musical structure and style.

Use of Instruments

Until the 1960s the ubiquitous presence of instruments in literary and artistic works of the twelfth and thirteenth centuries was considered

EX. 7–6. Berenguier de Palol. PC 47,6. R fol. 37v.

adequate evidence that the troubadours (and the trouvères) accompanied their songs. Van der Werf was the first to force scholars and
performers to reevaluate this supposition in light of the very scant
evidence that positively links instruments to the lyric songs themselves.[36] The burden of proof has now fallen on those who believe that
instruments did accompany the songs.

Aside from manuscript miniatures, the only evidence of any direct
connection between instruments and the troubadours is given in literary references in the song texts, in the *vidas* and *razos*, and in didactic,
epistolary, and epic narrative works. While the pictorial evidence shows
certain instruments—fiddle, harp, mandora—it does not give any information on how they might have been used, or indeed why they are

depicted in the hands of troubadours. Literary references, in contrast, use only words, which often have ambiguous meanings, but they are more descriptive about what role instruments had.[37]

The *vidas* and *razos* refer to the instrumental skill of several troubadours and *joglars*. The *joglar* Perdigo was known as a good fiddler: "Perdigons si fo joglars e saup trop ben violar e trobar"[38] (Perdigo was a joglar and he knew very well how to fiddle and to invent songs). Pons de Capduelh was also reputed to be able to play the fiddle: "Ponz de Capduoill . . . sabia ben trobar e violar e cantar"[39] (Pons de Capduelh . . . knew well how to compose and fiddle and sing). Elias Cairel, an early thirteenth-century troubadour and scribe, received an unfavorable report in his *vida*: "Mal cantava e mal trobava e mal violava e peichs parlava"[40] (He sang badly and composed badly and fiddled badly and spoke still worse). The oft-cited *razo* about Raimbaut de Vaqueiras's composition of "Kalenda maia" (see Chapter 4) relates that the troubadour composed words for a tune that he had heard played at court by two northern fiddlers.[41]

Narrative and lyric poetry refer more specifically to the use of instruments in social situations.[42] Often the music of a song is referred to as "son" or "chan," vague words that cannot be isolated to a particular genre, as in this stanza by Bertran de Born:

Gent acuillir e donar ses cor vaire	Noble hospitality and giving
e bel respos e "Ben sias vengut!"	without fickle heart, and fair
e gran hostal pagat e gen tengut,	conversation and warm welcome,
dons e garnirs et estar ses tort faire,	and a great court, well paid and well
manjar ab mazan	kept up, presents and gifts of arms
de viol' e de chan	and living without doing wrong,
e maint compaingnon	eating to the noise of fiddle and
ardit e poissan	song, with many a companion bold
de totz los meillors—	and mighty among all the best—I
tot voill c'om o teingna. . . .	want men to stop it all. . . .[43]

One passage in a mid-thirteenth-century romance depicts the entertainment at a feast by *joglars* playing fiddles, harps, flutes, *giga* and *rota*, bagpipe, shawm, mandora, and psaltery.[44] The fiddlers evidently played specific types of songs:

Qui saup novella violadura,	Whoever knew new fiddle tunes, or
ni canzo ni descort ni lais,	*cansos*, *descorts*, or *lais*, as best he
al plus que poc avan si trais.	could gave it a try.[45]

In a twelfth-century epic work, *Daurel e Beto*, the protagonist "makes" a love song with his fiddle: ". . . e pren sa viola e fai .i. lais d'amor" (. . . and he took his fiddle and performed a love song.)[46] This "lai" might refer to the type of paired-verse song like many Occitan *lais*, but here it is more likely a broad term meaning a love song (the poet could not use the phrase "canso d'amor" or simply "canso" without violating the syllable count).

A lyric song by the early thirteenth-century troubadour Albertet (PC 16,8) ends with the *tornada* "Peirol, violatz e chantatz cointamen/ de ma chanzon los motz e.l son leugier" (Peirol, fiddle and sing my song gracefully, the words and the light melody).[47] The *tornada* to Peire d'Alvernhe's famous satire makes a startling claim, with its rare reference to a wind instrument: "Lo vers fo faitz als enflabotz/ a Puioch-vert tot iogan rizen" (This verse was made to the bagpipe at Puivert, with everyone playing and laughing).[48] Obviously the singer himself could not have played the instrument while singing, so two persons must have been involved.

Because these references are infrequent and often ambiguous, and in any case they appear in manuscripts that cannot be dated much earlier than the middle of the thirteenth century, they are now viewed with some skepticism as clues to performance practices for the entire repertoire. However, their infrequency means that they do not constitute a topos in the literature (or in the manuscript illustrations either, for that matter), and since they refer to the presence of instruments in a variety of situations, without suggesting any impropriety, they surely suggest a widespread acceptance of instruments in the *art de trobar*.

Since there are no music treatises from the Midi of the twelfth and thirteenth centuries, no music theorist refers specifically to the performance of troubadour songs. Johannes de Grocheio mentions the *viella* in relation to the performance of the *cantus coronatus* (the courtly trouvère *chanson*), and it is often assumed that his remarks also apply to the troubadour repertoire. But van der Werf and Christopher Page have each raised serious challenges to Grocheio's reliability as a witness to the performance of the music of either the troubadours or the trouvères.

Page advances two major arguments against the use of instruments in the performance of trouvère and troubadour songs. From his survey of literary and theoretical sources that mention instruments, he concludes that songs in the "High Style"—*chansons, sirventes, planhs*—were elevated above instrumental and popular styles—*dansas, descorts* and *lais, pastorelas*—and that the latter were associated with instruments, while the former were not:

> Our most explicit twelfth-century sources therefore suggest that fiddle-accompaniment was associated with one form which subverts the musico-poetic decorum of the High Style (the *descort*), and another which, at the time we hear of it in relation to the fiddle, may well have been an ephemeral genre which the troubadour ignored, the *dansa*. Thus we have a provisional answer to the question of where instrumental accompaniment belonged in the system of contrasts presented

on p. 16 [which discusses the *dansa* and the *canso* on fol. 78v/BXXIv of manuscript W]. As far as the twelfth century in the South is concerned, the evidence—admittedly very meagre—suggests that instrumental accompaniment did not have a High Style ethos.[49]

Page then suggests that in northern texts, where instruments are sometimes mentioned in connection with songs from the south, possibly including "High Style" songs, "instrumental accompaniment may have been a necessary prop to performances of songs whose words cannot always have been wholly intelligible to northern listeners,"[50] much as in modern performances. Page acknowledges that many *dansas* and epic works (which he suggests do not fall in the "High Style" category either) have texts with the same sorts of courtly themes and language as love *chansons*, but he suggests that the audience for these works came with different expectations:

> Courtliness is not the main issue here, but art. While any simple *dansa* could be as courtly as a High Style troubadour song, its appeal was not to good taste or judgement, but to the feet. In the same way narrative songs, whether in the form of epic or lyric like the *chanson de toile*, catered for a basic human desire—the desire for stories—in a way that the High Style songs of the trouabadours and trouvères resolutely refused to do. If we have uncovered a general principle here it is a very general one and seems to be this: a song was less appropriate for instrumental accompaniment the more it lay claim to self-conscious artistry.
>
> We may be confronting a fundamental characteristic of twelfth- and thirteenth-century string-playing here: instrumental music does not seem to have been associated with the kind of profound creative endeavour which demanded serious and considered attention from the listener.[51]

Page found support for this view in the *Doctrina de compondre dictats*, which he dates around 1300, and in the early fourteenth-century *Leys d'Amors*. As we saw in Chapter 4, the *Doctrina* refers to instrumental performance of *dansas* but does not mention it in connection with other genres. The description of poetic genres in the main version of the *Leys d'Amors* includes some comments about instruments, also in reference to dances, including the *estampida*. Page points out that these comments occur only in marginal glosses, not in the original text.[52] In any case, the lateness of this text (the main text as well as the glosses, no matter how close they are in time to the main text) casts serious doubt on its relevance to performance in the twelfth and thirteenth centuries.

Page's second argument hinges on the view that a radical change of "ethic" occurred after about 1250 in the approach of theorists, scribes, and performers toward music, from a primarily oral to a primarily written world:

In the predominantly notationless world of the troubadours and trouvères before c1250 there existed a courtly tradition of instrumental usage. It was courtly because it rested upon a collective moral and aesthetic apprehension with aristocratic society that it was *courtois* to mix instrumental sound with some kinds of songs but *vilain* to mix it with others.

This austere ethic of instrumental usage—for an ethic it deserves to be called—was vulnerable to abuse by the ignorant who had not the taste to appreciate it, but it was also under threat from the learned and literate who had the manoeuvrability of mind to bypass the tradition and come up with something else. This manoeuvrability was already there in the act of recording courtly songs with neumes and staves, for once a lyric has been written down (as happened to many troubadour and trouvère songs after c1250) it ceases to be an event. It becomes an object and can therefore be objectively perceived. Any moorings which may have tied it to a kind of occasion, or a kind of performance, become loosened.[53]

Thus Johannes de Grocheio's treatise, written around 1300, also is too late a testimony to the courtly repertoire of French and Occitan song, and his allusion to *vielle* accompaniment for the *cantus coronatus* is implausible for performances before the middle of the thirteenth century.

Page treats the issue of rhythm also. He makes the point that instrumental music was more likely to have patterned rhythms, especially because of their association with dances. He postulates that the kind of "accompaniment" of courtly lyric that Grocheio might have known around 1300 was simple note-against-note counterpoint, following the melody in mostly parallel motion. Such counterpoint, Page believes, would force a change on the rhythmic character of the song, because it would require "standardisation of rhythm between singer and instrumentalist":

The free and declamatory rhythm which probably represents the traditional mode of delivery of both troubadour and trouvère songs of the High Style kind is not possible in this context. It has often been suggested that the mensurally notated trouvère monodies are an adaptation of an originally free-rhythm genre to the fixed rhythms which 'Parisian' listeners associated with polyphony. . . . [54]

He then makes the same suggestion for the performance of monophonic Latin *conductus* (although he does not explain why singers might improvise heterophony with parallel motion, when composers and possibly singers during that era were creating sophisticated polyphonic *conductus*, whose predominant contrapuntal texture was contrary, not parallel, motion).

The foundation of Page's arguments is that until about 1250 a general principle, or "ethos," proscribed the use of instruments with courtly lyric. As attractive as this theory is, like those concerning rhythm it has not been proven. As its proponents acknowledge, it is predicated largely on the absence of evidence, rather than the preponderance of it—the absence of mensural notation before the mid-thirteenth century, the absence of extant musical sources before the second half of the century, the absence of overt references to instrumental usage. Such lacunae necessitate explanations *ex silentio* and, as such, cannot lead to conclusive results. Were a source to be discovered that explicitly *prohibited* the use of instruments to play or accompany a *canso*, the case would be compelling indeed. Far from pointing to an "ethic" that "it was *courtois* to mix instrumental sound with ['High Style' songs] and *vilain* to mix it with ['Low Style' songs]," the little evidence we have suggests no such distinction.

More specifically, Page's separation of courtly and narrative poetry into "High Style" and "Low Style" genres conforms to a system that was more fully developed in the fourteenth century than in the thirteenth. As Chapter 4 shows, different styles of poetry in the medieval French and Occitan worlds did indeed occupy different "registers" that might be categorized as "aristocratic" and "popular," but medieval writers did not associate specific genres with these registers until the late thirteenth or early fourteenth century, most importantly in Dante's *De vulgari eloquentia* and in the *Leys d'Amors*. The lateness of this testimony impugns its applicability to a genre system as effectively as it does to a theory of instrumental usage.

As discussed in Chapters 3 and 4, the high, middle, and low styles in the arts of poetry and prose had to do with a complex of ideas including personages, language, and theme in the songs. In the twelfth and thirteenth centuries, the high style depended on subject matter of the loftiest nature, personages of the highest class, and language of the most profound quality. The *chanson de geste* would certainly fall in this category, and Grocheio expresses this ethos by placing the *cantus gestualis* in the preeminent place in his hierarchy of secular music. Evidently ignoring this medieval aesthetic, Page considers the story-telling function of narrative epic works, as well as of *pastorelas* and *lais*, to have appealed to a "basic human desire" for entertainment, which did not engage the head so much as the heart, and since it did not require "serious and considered attention from the listener," the presence of instruments would not detract from its effect. As for the *dansas* and *descorts*, he suggests that the peculiar structural characteristics that help define them as genres also place them in the "Low Style," although again such a classification is not made before the fourteenth century.

Page's other chief argument, that the mid-thirteenth century witnessed a change of ethos from an oral to a written culture, has been buttressed by recent work of Sylvia Huot, who has demonstrated that the emergence of "the book" as literature in the fourteenth century grew out of the practice of collecting autonomous works into anthologies in the thirteenth century.[55] Thus there appeared a major turning point in the development of the literary arts: The thirteenth-century chansonniers were vehicles of the literature; fourteenth-century books were the literature itself—the repositories of the art became the art itself.

But to extrapolate from this that writing music down and notating it with mensural values subverted a traditional ethos of performance, that the "austere ethic" which prohibited using instruments with certain kinds of song "was under threat from the learned and literate who had the manoeuvrability of mind to bypass the tradition," and that "once a lyric has been written down . . . it ceases to be an event" requires a leap of faith that such an ethos existed, and that it completely supplanted whatever ethos preceded it. While such a shift to a literary culture certainly occurred in the later thirteenth century, there is considerable evidence of an earlier written tradition, for the music as well as for the poetry of the troubadours, as suggested in Chapter 2, and there is no reason to believe that the oral ethos of an earlier time disappeared with the appearance of manuscripts. The act of writing down a song did not in and of itself alter its nature or affect its performance or, indeed, reflect anything prescriptive about its performance at all, at least for the southern repertoire.

Having expressed some skepticism about Page's arguments, and while I believe it entirely possible that troubadours used instruments to accompany their songs, like earlier scholars I am unable to find in the small amount of evidence any guidelines about the way instruments might have been used. In the absence of any clear-cut connection between troubadour songs and a polyphonic tradition, I am inclined to believe that an instrumental accompaniment would not resemble the complex contrapuntal texture of northern polyphony and probably would not deviate significantly from the melody itself. Whether it involved the parallel motion that Page suggests is impossible to say. The use of drones is common in performances today, but the evidence in its favor is meagre. Bagpipes, presumably with drones, were known in the south: the "Puivert" mentioned in Peire d'Alvernhe's satire in connection with this instrument ("enflabotz") is south of Carcassonne, and one of the manuscripts of the *cantigas de Santa Maria* features a bagpipe in some illuminations. But unless the air reservoir was filled by bellows under the arm rather than by blowing through an air pipe, performing a song with bagpipes would require two players, the singer and the piper—probably an uncommon occurrence. Further, choosing a specific pitch on which to sound the drone is problematic, given the variability of tonal center in so many of the melodies. The sound of the bagpipe is distinctive, and its drone may have been heard as so much noise rather than as a distinct pitch; there is no reason to assume that the commingled texture of drone and chanter would have been transferred to other instruments, especially gentler ones, such as a fiddle.

Even less compelling would be an inference that the sound and texture of sustained-tone organum of early sacred polyphony was imitated in improvised performances of troubadour song, since the *art de trobar* was so far removed from liturgical style and practice. Even knowing that *organum* was performed in Occitania (according to Jean de Garlande, see Chapter 3), for the troubadours to have emulated that style by sounding drones to their melodies would have involved a creative process that was the opposite of what happened in *organum purum*, where the sustained tenor was the preexistent melody, the moving *duplum* the improvised addition.

Chromatic Inflections

The only sure evidence of chromatic inflection in the troubadour melodies is in the manuscripts. In his excellent survey of this evidence, van der Werf provides a detailed catalogue of the scribal alterations in each of the manuscripts, offers statistical data on the way each scribe used flats and sharps, examines numerous unusual cases, suggests theoretical and functional explanations for the alterations, and extrapolates from the paleographical evidence what the compositional and oral performance practices might have been.[56] He infers that in many cases scribes intended a notated flat or sharp to apply to the pitch that it alters through the end of a staff or a verse. But he catalogs numerous apparent exceptions and concludes that scribes were inconsistent, that no general rule can apply. He proposes that there was a dichotomy between composers and singers on the one hand and notators on the other, and that it is impossible to tell from the manuscripts what alterations the composers intended or the singers sang.

Van der Werf suggests further that not only may scribes have failed to write in chromatic inflections that would have been "appropriate" but also they may have written in flats and sharps that were *not* part of the original compositional intention or the singing practice. He reasons that manuscripts W and X contain more chromatic alterations than do G and R because the former were prepared in the north, where, he suggests, the scribes would have been more influenced by thirteenth-century music theory, which gave specific rules on the modification of pitches through the application of *musica ficta* to the Guidonian gamut. These manuscripts, he says, were further removed from the practice of the troubadours and *joglars* themselves, who "may not have studied Guido's teachings, and they may not have avoided the pitches [that is, chromatic pitches other than B♭] which did not occur in his system."[57] He says that the common assumption that singers knew how to add sharps and flats in appropriate places "has never been proven," and that the notated chromatic inflections in the manuscripts do not support such a conclusion:

> If the persons for whom the written collections were intended were experts on chromatic alterations, the scribes would not have had much reason to write any sharp or flat signs; at most, they might have given them for specifically dubious passages. To the best of my knowledge, this is nowhere the case. Thus, the most prudent approach to our evaluation is to begin with assuming that a scribe marked all the alterations which he considered appropriate.[58]

Citing specific cases, van der Werf concludes that there is no reason to assume that composers or singers applied specific theorists' rules of *musica ficta*, such as the "correction" of a tritone (reached either conjunctly or by leap) and the lowering of a B neighboring tone above A. He also expresses doubt that the repetition of a melodic phrase would necessarily have the same chromatic alterations as its first statement; earlier discussions in his book led him to believe that "it is impossible to determine which melody verses were intended to be identical and which ones were to resemble one another."[59] This uncertainty is even more pronounced in cases where shorter motives are repeated. Yet with all of the discrepancies, apparent contradictions, and ambiguities in the written sources, van der Werf caps his discussion with the comment that "there is no reason to conclude that the general manner of notating (and not writing!) signs of alteration conflicts with medieval [composing and singing] practice."[60] In other words, the few chromatic inflections in the manuscripts should neither be trusted too implicitly nor distrusted too skeptically.

This conclusion is entirely reasonable, yet some specific points merit comment. First, I am not as convinced as van der Werf that northern scribes were necessarily influenced by theories that demanded chromatic alterations. I have already questioned the proposition that scribes "imposed" measured rhythms on secular monophonic melodies, and I regard with the same skepticism the theory that these scribes may also have imposed chromatic inflections in conformance with rules that may have been as foreign to the repertoires as measured rhythm. In the specific case of Lorrainian manuscript X, the scribes may not have known about or been interested in Parisian polyphony or the rules that governed its composition or performance. And if northern scribes of secular monophony were not necessarily concerned with Guidonian theory, southern scribes were even less likely to be so.

At the same time, however, even though the structures, tonal orientation, and combination of intervals in the melodies of the trouba-

dours differ in important respects from the style of polyphony, troubadours and *joglars* may have been familiar with their musical vocabulary.
Many small-scale figures through which troubadour melodies proceed
resemble similar figures in polyphonic melodies, and certainly in plainchant. For instance, as van der Werf points out, B below tenor C (a ninth
below middle C) is never lowered by a scribe in the troubadour
chansonniers, even if the B an octave above is flatted. This could be
because the Guidonian gamut does not include a low B♭, and perhaps
also because in most instances this B occurs as a lower neighbor of C and
might have been heard as *B-mi* to the *C-fa*, what later theory refers to as
a leading tone. Even if troubadours, singers, and scribes did not feel
themselves bound by rules of *musica ficta* (if they knew them at all),
might it not be possible to extrapolate from these cases that a singer or
composer might have raised a lower neighbor because it was part of the
aural musical environment?

Several examples could be cited where this B is approached from
the C above, but the note following is an F, creating a striking diminished fifth leap upwards. As van der Werf says, these leaps also are often
not altered in the manuscripts. In manuscript G's version of PC 155,1,
the upper B is flatted throughout, and the only occurrence of the low B,
in the final verse (Example 7–7), is not altered. The pitch C is a cadential
goal of more than half of the verses, including this final one. The B below
it here has a leading-tone effect aurally, perhaps more compelling even
than the tritone leap. Alteration of either the B to B♭ or the following F to
F♯, as van der Werf points out, would create a new tritone (E–B♭ or C–F♯),
and neither would be as expected by the ear as the B♮ is in the context.
Whether or not it follows solmization rules, this version as written
conforms to what one might expect to hear in contemporary polyphony
or even some plainchants. The reading in manuscript R, while radically
different throughout from the version in G, at this point disagrees only
in the lack of the intermediate tritone between its lowest pitch, G, and
the fifth above it, D (comparable to C–G in manuscript G). If this version
had a lower neighbor F notated, leaping to an intervening C before
reaching D, it seems quite possible that a singer would have raised it to
F♯, retaining the leading-tone sound to the G, which is an even more
persistent cadential goal in the melody in this manuscript than the C is
in manuscript G.

I am more hopeful than van der Werf that the melodies themselves
can provide clues to the chromatic inflections that composers intended,
especially in passages that entail repetition of musical material. Van der
Werf doubts that such instances can give much aid, since he is not
certain that repetition would always have been exact. His edition
suggests chromatic alterations in places where the pitch content in two

EX. 7–7. Folquet de Marselha. PC 155,1, verse 7. G fol. 1v; R fol. 42v.

EX. 7–8. Bernart de Ventadorn. PC 70,6, verses 1–4. G fol. 13v.

verses is exactly the same. Where some pitches change, though, he is much more cautious about adding flats or sharps.

Just as I believe that repeated music would be likely to have similar rhythmic shapes, I think that singers might have altered the same pitches in cases where the repetition is very close even if not exact, not only where the music of an entire verse is repeated or varied but also on smaller figures where the melody seems to be based on motivic interrelationships. In Bernart de Ventadorn's PC 70,6, for instance (Example 7–8), the scribe of G indicated a B♭ in verse 2 but neglected to write one in verse 4, which is exactly like verse 2 except on the final two syllables. Van der Werf does not suggest flatting the B in the second phrase, but I think it likely that a singer would have retained the same interval content in both phrases.

The melodies of Guiraut Riquier are replete with small melismatic motives, and motivic manipulation is inherent to his style (see Chapter 6). In the melody in Example 7–9, the scribe indicated a B♭ at the beginning of verse 2, and again in verse 7; the beginning of verse 4 is the same as verse 2, so it seems to me likely that the B in at least the first *hemistich* of that verse would be flatted as well. Further, in Example 5–30, notes found in the first *hemistich* of verses 2, 4, and 7 form the second *hemistich* of verses 1, 3, and 6; the motivic identity would suggest using B♭ in these places as well. At the end of verse 4, where the melody rises through the hard hexachord above B to a D, the B might remain natural.

EX. 7–9. Guiraut Riquier. PC 248,18. R fol. 105v.

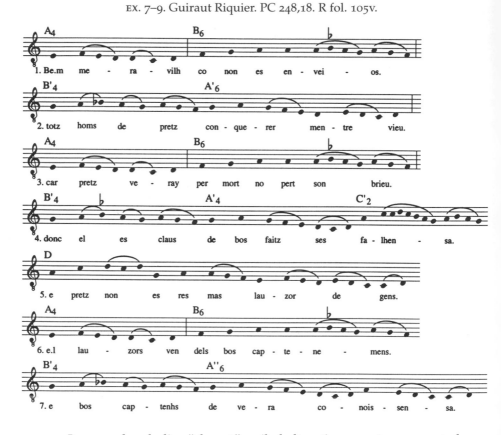

In several melodies "abrupt" scribal alterations create unexpected intervallic shifts.[61] There are many such instances in which chromatic alterations, or the lack of them, created a highly unusual progression of intervals or radically changed the tonal orientation of a melody. Such cases might be evidence of compositional intent and perhaps even of a performance practice. For example, in a melody by Guillem Magret (Example 7–10; the entire melody is given in Example 6–15), a B–F interval in the middle of verses 1, 3, 6, and 11 (in the upper octave) is not altered by the scribe of W, who often added accidentals to the melodies. In each of these verses, B is the lowest note and F the highest. As in Folquet's melody (Example 7–7), C is a chief tonal goal, although this melody descends below B several times. Also, as in Example 7–7, to alter either the B (to B♭) or the F (to F♯) to eliminate the tritone would create new ones, so it seems likely that both the B and the F would remain natural. But in this melody, the B–F leap occurs not once, but four times, making it so predominant that it sounds like a motive that the composer, Guilhem Magret, may have intended.

EX. 7–10. Guillem Magret. PC 223,1, verses 1 and 11. W fol. 201v/B183v.

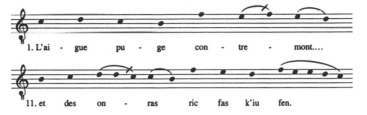

1. L'ai - gue   pu - ge   con - tre - mont....

11. et   des   on - ras   ric   fas   k'iu   fen.

In other melodies, even where repetition of a phrase with a problematic interval occurs, the structural characteristics of the melody
seem to preclude altering any pitches. In a melody by Peire Raimon de
Toloza (Example 7–11) both F and B seem to serve as articulation points
at the beginnings and ends of phrases. Sometimes they occur in succession and cause a leap of an augmented fourth, as between verses 6 and
7, and 9 and 10. There are several other wide leaps between verses in this
melody (the fifth from verse 1 to 2, the sixth from verse 2 to 3, and the
seventh from verse 3 to 4), and a tritone triad is outlined on the second
and third syllables of verse 5; so the augmented fourth leaps are not as
conspicuous as they would be in a more conjunct melody. The more
important point is that both F and B seem to serve structural roles
within the pitch series in this melody, which would be obscured if a
singer altered either pitch.

In summary, I agree in general with van der Werf's conclusions
about the unreliability of the scribal evidence as testimony to a performance practice, although I believe that some melodies demonstrate
enough melodic coherence that the chromatic indications that are
present *or* absent might reflect the composer's preference and perhaps
also a performance practice. When repetition appears to be a clear-cut
imitation of earlier music, whether exact or not, the same chromatic
alteration in all occurrences of the phrase seems likely. To generalize
about the way troubadours and *joglars* might have altered pitches in
performance is dangerous and indeed impossible today, especially
since the melodies do not have either the regularity and predictability of
pitch content or the check of harmonic alignment that characterizes
contemporary polyphony in which the application of *musica ficta* is
somewhat more clear.

Ornamentation and Simplification

As the variety among extant multiple readings of the troubadour
melodies suggests, *joglars* and troubadours certainly were not strictly

EX. 7–11. Peire Raimon de Toloza. PC 355,5. G fol. 52.

limited to some sort of "Urtext" when they sang the songs, and what
was recorded in the extant chansonniers was not the only possible set of
notes for a melody. Extrinsic as well as intrinsic variants of phrases and
motives manifest small-scale differences that probably reflect a performance practice. Some of the variants discussed in earlier chapters
suggest that a singer might have realigned the pitches with the syllables
of text, slightly changed the contour of a phrase, decorated the pitches
by adding to them, or subtracted notes from more florid melodies. Since
the composers were likely to be singers as well, it is not particularly
important to determine who was responsible for these changes in the
shape of a melody. Some intrinsic variants might point to compositional
intent, whereas extrinsic variants certainly represent modifications that
came about during transmission.

The addition of notes to a syllable is quite common and can appear
in several guises. Passing and neighboring tones occur among both
intrinsic and extrinsic variants; they are more common among the latter
and hence perhaps were more part of an oral performing practice than
of a compositional technique. In Bernart de Ventadorn's famous lark
song (Example 7–12), the readings of a verse 8 in manuscripts G and W
differ only slightly. W has passing tones between A and F on the fourth
syllable and between F and D on the final syllable. Note also the "escape
tone" in W at the beginning of the last syllable of the verse, and the
melodic difference on the fifth syllable created by the descending *plica*
in manuscript G, which probably implies a passing tone F. The upper
neighbor figure G–A–G on this syllable in W is different from any other
reading of this melody.

The contours of verses 1 and 6 of a song by Arnaut de Maruelh
(Example 7–13) are the same, even though verse 6 is longer by one
syllable; to lengthen the melody, the F–E on the sixth syllable of verse 1
is split over two syllables in verse 6. At the cadences, the scribe used a
plica in verse 1, but filled in the interval between F and D with an E,

EX. 7–12. Bernart de Ventadorn. PC 70,43, verse 8. W fol 190v/B180v;
G fol. 10.

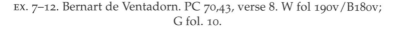

EX. 7–13. Arnaut de Maruelh. PC 30,16, verses 1 and 6. R fol. 52.

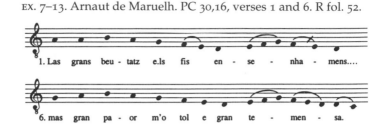

EX. 7–14. Bernart de Ventadorn. PC 70,6, verse 6. R fol. 57v; G fol. 13v.

EX. 7–15. Peire Vidal. PC 364,11, verses 1 and 2. X fol. 87v; G fol. 40v.

suggesting that the *plica* (in manuscript R, at least, but probably in the other troubadour chansonniers as well) was merely scribal shorthand for a specific pitch.

There are many examples where a note is divided into several notes or a figure of several notes is reduced to one or two. In intrinsic variants, it is sometimes possible to determine whether the change was from simple to more decorated or vice versa. Such intrinsic variants are rarer than extrinsic ones, where because it is impossible to know which reading is earlier, we cannot tell whether one version is simplified or the other decorated. For example, in verse 6 of Example 7–14, the fourth and fifth syllables have three notes each in the reading of manuscript R, while in manuscript G they each have only one note. A more complex example is seen in verses 1 and 2 in Example 7–15. The readings of manuscripts X and G are similarly florid. On the fifth syllable of verse 1, X has only one note, while G has four; in verse 2 on the fifth syllable X also has a single note, to three in G. But on the sixth syllable of that verse, X has a melisma of six notes, while G has just two. That neither version represents exclusively a process of decoration or of simplification suggests that neither technique predominated.

Among instances in intrinsic variants where the number of notes on a syllable is different, there is not necessarily a tendency toward more decoration or more simplification upon repetition. For instance, in Example 7–16, verse 3 alters the last two syllables of verse 1 first by adding two notes to the penultimate syllable, then by subtracting notes from the last syllable of the verse (and changing its direction, to lead into verse 5, which begins on C). Sometimes the changes are slight, as in Example 7–17, where the last four syllables of verse 6 add one note to each syllable. In other cases the permutation is more striking, as in Example 7–18, where the melisma is positioned over the fourth syllable in verse 1 but shifted to the third syllable in verse 3, and where the melismatic ending of verse 2 is simplified to only two notes at the end of verse 4. In this and numerous other cases, the modifications might have been calculated by the composer as part of the flow and position of

EX. 7–16. Folquet de Marselha. PC 155,14, verses 1 and 3. G fol. 3v.

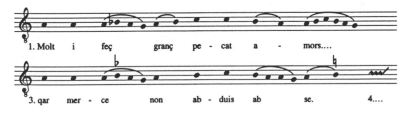

EX. 7–17. Marcabru. PC 293,35, verses 1 and 6. W fol. 194v/B186v.

EX. 7–18. Peirol. PC 366,14, verses 1–4. G fol. 43v.

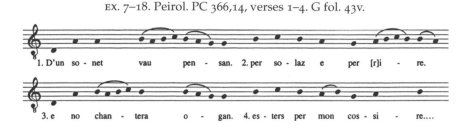

1. D'un so - net   vau   pen - san. 2. per so - laz e   per [r]i - re.

3. e   no   chan - tera   o - gan. 4. es - ters per mon cos - si - re....

EX. 7–19. Peire Vidal. PC 364,37, verses 1 and 3. G fol. 42v.

1. Pois tor - naz sui en   Pro - en - za....

3. ben dei far gai - a   can - zon....

the verses. The melismatic cadence of verse 2 brings the singer and the listeners to a pause, whereas the simplification at the end of verse 4 facilitates the move into the second half of the stanza.

Sometimes the original pitch or pitches disappear upon repetition and are replaced by other notes. In Example 7–19, verse 3 is an elaboration of verse 1, changing the notes on the second, third, and fourth syllables, and adding a note to the fifth syllable. The two readings of Aimeric de Peguilhan's melody exhibit several types of modifications; verse 4 (Example 7–20) includes simplification of the notes over a syllable (syllables one and three), passing tones between syllables (syllables one and two), realignment of notes (syllables five and six), and neighboring tones (syllables nine and ten).

I have not detected specific patterns in such ornamentation within the works of individual composers, or even generations, nor does one manuscript seem to contain more or less ornamentation than the others. Insofar as the thirteenth-century manuscripts represent performance and compositional practices, all the music of the troubadours seems to have enjoyed a lively tradition of improvisation.

Conclusions

Questions about performance cannot be answered without considering the manifold and complex interrelationships among composers, sing-

EX. 7–20. Aimeric de Peguilhan. PC 10,25, verse 4. R fol. 49; G fol. 37v.

ers, and scribes that have been the focus of discussion throughout this book. Because the manuscripts are our only record of the activities of these persons, we must rely on them heavily for evidence. One cannot escape the fundamental question of whom the scribes were targeting with their chansonniers. Other evidence, in the form of theoretical systems (poetic and musical), literary and iconographic records, other contemporary music, and perhaps some kind of overarching "ethic" or aesthetic, can be brought to bear only with great caution. I have expressed doubt that troubadours and *joglars* were affected largely by prohibitions or mandates, or that a monolithic and *a priori* premise dictated composition or performance.

At the same time, I believe that the manuscripts and the melodies they record provide some clues about performance practices. These clues are both paleographical and musical; scribes indicated certain suggestions in rhythm and chromatic inflection, and the style and structure of the melodies themselves point to likely practices as well. Singers no doubt had a great deal of latitude in interpretation, although they may have been constrained somewhat by the norms of the aural world in which they lived. And whatever the scribes and singers did to the songs that they received, some essence of the composers' intentions probably remain in the extant manuscripts, indicating that singers were faithful to what they believed to be the song that the troubadour composed, especially since the troubadours themselves were among those singers. I hope that this discussion will provide an impetus for continuing to explore the multifarious manifestations of human creativity represented in the way the troubadours composed, the scribes preserved, and especially the singers sang, these remarkable songs.

NOTES

Introduction

1. Jean-Baptiste Beck, *La musique des troubadours: Étude critique*.

2. Friedrich Gennrich, ed., *Der musikalische Nachlass des Troubadours*. While van der Werf's edition of 1984 includes several "essays" that offer some musical analysis and a discussion of issues of transmission and performance practices, the book does not undertake an in-depth analysis of the melodies themselves.

3. On the basis of language, it has been argued recently that at least six songs that once were considered part of the troubadour corpus have origins in the North; these six are excluded from the present study. They are PC 420,2; 461,12; and 461,148, which survive with French or hybrid French texts, and 461,146; 461,148a; and 461,170a, all of which have connections with the motet and probably are not southern creations. ("PC" refers in this book to Alfred Pillet and Henry Castens, *Bibliographie der Troubadours*, the standard index of trouba-dour songs.) See Robert A. Taylor, *"L'altrier cuidai aber druda.'"* Two other songs (PC 70,45 and 183,10), whose origins are not are in dispute but whose melodies survive only in fragmentary form, are also omitted from this study. I also exclude PC 461,192a, which appears in a French source with a thoroughly Frenchified text—see Alfred Jeanroy and Pierre Aubry, "Une chanson proven-çale à la Vierge." I include *contrafacta*, both real and supposed, only when they involve exclusively Occitanian texts; French, German, and Latin *contrafacta* have been studied extensively, and I consider them peripheral to the present investigation. The eight melodies in a fourteenth-century manuscript, Rome, Vatican Library, Chigi, C.V.151, present a special problem of contrafacture and are not included here either.

4. See Craig Wright, *Music and Ceremony at Notre Dame of Paris, 500–1500*.

5. See Jacques Chailley, "Les premiers troubadours et les versus de l'école d'Aquitaine" and "Notes sur les troubadours, les versus et la question arabe." See also Wulf Arlt, "Zur Interpretation zweier Lieder: *A madre de Deus* und *Reis glorios*," and "Musica e testo nel canto francese," 179ff. For musical inter-textuality see Margaret Switten, "Modèle et variations: Saint Martial de Li-moges et les troubadours," and "The Voice and the Letter." Gerald Bond, *The Poetry of William VII*, xlii and lxv–lxvi, discusses the educational environment in Poitou in the eleventh and twelfth centuries and its connections with St. Martial.

6. Roger Dragonetti, *La technique poétique des trouvères dans la chanson courtoise*; Page, *Voices and Instruments*.

7. Paul Zumthor, *Essai de poétique médiévale*; Pierre Bec, *La lyrique française au moyen âge (XIIe-XIIIe siècles)*.

8. Stevens, *Words and Music*.

1. Historical Background

1. See the series of volumes on the history of southern France, Philippe Wolff, general editor, *Histoire de la France méridionale* ("Univers de la France": Collection d'histoire régionale), including Charles Higounet, ed., *Histoire de l'Aquitaine*; Edouard Baratier, ed., *Histoire de la Provence*; Philippe Wolff, ed., *Histoire du Languedoc*; and Joaquim Nadal Farreras and Philippe Wolff, eds., *Histoire de la Catalogne*. See also the fifteen-volume classic by Claude de Vic, *Histoire générale de Languedoc*; and René Nelli, *Histoire du Languedoc*. The best general survey of the place of the troubadours in the social and political world of Occitania remains Alfred Jeanroy, *La poésie lyrique des trobuadours*. Other social histories include Archibald R. Lewis, *Medieval Society in Southern France and Catalonia*; E. Carpentier, "Structures féodales et féodalisme dans l'occident"; and Linda Paterson, *The World of the Troubadours*.

2. See David Abulafia, *Commerce and Conquest in the Mediterranean, 1100–1500*.

3. See T. N. Bisson, *The Medieval Crown of Aragon: A Short History*.

4. See Jonathan Riley-Smith, *The Crusades; A Short History*, 89ff. and 139ff. On the troubadours in Spain, see Geneviève Brunel-Lobrichon, "Les troubadours dans les cours ibériques."

5. See a recent study by F. Alberto Gallo, *Musica nel castello: Trovatori, libri, oratori nelle corte italiana dal XIII al XV secolo*.

6. See Martin Aurell, *La vielle et l'epée: Troubadours et politique en Provence au XIIIe siècle*.

7. Among the best studies are Michel Roquebert, *L'Épopée Cathare*, and Jonathon Sumpton, *The Albigensian Crusade*. See also Walter L. Wakefield, *Heresy, Crusade, and Inquisition in Southern France 1100–1250*; René Nelli, *Dictionnaire des hérésies méridionales et des mouvements*, 304ff.; Joseph R. Strayer, *The Albigensian Crusades*; Pierre Belperron, *La Croisade contre les Albigeois*; René Nelli, *Les Cathares du Languedoc*. See further below about the effects of this crusade.

8. See Nelli, *Les Cathares*, 79–94.

9. Stanislaw Stronski, ed., *Le troubadour Folquet de Marseille*, 91.

10. See Etienne Delaruelle, "De la croisade à l'université: la fondation de l'université de Toulouse"; M.-H. Vicaire, "L'École du chapitre de la cathédrale et le projet d'extension de la théologie parisienne à Toulouse (1072–1217)"; and Yves Dossat, "L'Université de Toulouse, Raymond VII, les capitouls et le roi," and "Les premiers maîtres à l'université de Toulouse: Jean de Garlande, Helinand."

11. See Stronski, *La poésie et la réalité aux temps des troubadours*.

12. Jean Boutière and A.-H. Schutz, eds., *Biographies des troubadours* (hereafter BS); Margarita Egan, *The Vidas of the Troubadours*; William E. Burgwinkle, *Razos and Troubadour Songs*. For studies of the reliability of the *vidas* and *razos* see Egan, "'Razo' and 'Novella': A Case Study in Narrative Forms" and "Commentary, *Vitae Poetae* and *Vida*: Latin and Old Provençal 'Lives of Poets'"; Elizabeth W. Poe, "The Meeting of Fact and Fiction in an Old Provençal Razo," "Old Provençal Vidas as Literary Commentary," "Toward a Balanced View of the *Vidas* and *Razos*," and *From Poetry to Prose in Old Provençal*.

13. Excellent summaries of the lives and work of the troubadours, along with current bibliographies, are found in the newly revised *Dictionnaire des lettres françaises: Le Moyen Âge*, eds. Geneviève Hasenohr and Michel Zink.

14. Biographical information was established by Paul Cravayat, "Les origines du troubadour Jaufre Rudel." According to Rupert T. Pickens, ed., *The Songs of Jaufre Rudel*, "princeps" was a local word for "dominus," and both terms imply a low level of authority.

15. See Prosper Boissonnade, "Les personnages et les événements de l'histoire d'Allemagne, de France, et d'Espagne dans l'oeuvre de Marcabru," 228–229.

16. See Carl Appel, "Zu Marcabru." For recent bibliography, see Simon Gaunt and Ruth Harvey, "Bibliographie commentée du troubadour Marcabru; mise à jour."

17. Boissonnade, "Les personnages," 219–220; and R. M. Ruggieri, "Chiose interpretative al Vers del Lavador."

18. François Pirot, *Recherches sur les connaissances littéraires des troubadours occitans et catalans des XIIe et XIIIe siècles*, 150–157; and Martín de Riquer, *Los trovadores: Historia, literaria y textos*, I:206.

19. Boissonnade, "Les personnages," 239–240.

20. Riquer, *Los trovadores*, I:216.

21. Jean-M. L. Dejeanne, ed., *Poésies complètes du troubadour Marcabru*. See Ruth Harvey, "The Troubadour Marcabru and His Public."

22. Rita Lejeune, "Le troubadour Rigaut de Barbezieux." The two modern editors of Rigaut's works, Alberto Varvaro (*Rigaut de Berbezilh: Liriche*) and Mauro Braccini (*Rigaut de Barbezieux: Le canzoni, testo e commento*), remain unconvinced by these dates, but Lejeune reiterated her exposition, buttressed convincingly by stylistic analysis of his poetry, in 1962 ("Analyse textuelle et histoire littéraire: Rigaut de Barbezieux"). See also Jacques Duguet, "L'Identification du troubadour Rigaud de Barbezieux" and Saverio Guida, "Problemi di datazione e di identificazione di trovatori, I. Rigaut de Berbezilh."

23. BS, 595ff. See Varvaro, *Rigaut*, 22–28 and 85–89.

24. Rudolf Zenker, *Die Lieder Peires von Auvergne*, 34.

25. See Rita Lejeune, "Thèmes communs de troubadours et vie de société," 81–88.

26. Zenker, *Peires*, 27–29.

27. Walter T. Pattison, in "The Background of Peire d'Alvernhe's 'Chantarai d'aquest trobadors,'" proposed that this song was composed in conjunction with the grand procession in 1170, from Bordeaux to Tarazona, of Aliénor, daughter of Henry II and of Aliénor of Aquitaine, for her marriage to Alfonso VIII of Castile; this theory has been shown to be improbable, but the date of 1170 is still attached to the poem in various anthologies and other studies. For refutation of the hypothesis, see Rita Lejeune, "La 'Galerie littéraire' du troubadour Peire d'Alvernhe"; and Riquer, *Los trovadores*, I:332–333.

28. Thanks to the thorough study of Walter T. Pattison, *The Life and Works of the Troubadour Raimbaut d'Orange*.

29. Riquer, *Los trovadores*, I:344.

30. Ibid., I:142–147.

31. Ibid., I:343.

32. William D. Paden, "Bernart de Ventadour le troubadour devint-il abbé de Tulle?" based on work by Rita Lejeune, "Le nom de Bernart de Ventadorn."

33. Carl Appel, *Die Singweisen Bernarts von Ventadorn*, offered a transcription of his melodies. Appel also produced a poetic edition, *Bernart von Ventadorn, seine Lieder*, as did Moshé Lazar, *Bernard de Ventadorn, troubadour du XIIe siècle: Chansons d'amour*.

34. BS, 81–84 and 146.

35. Essidolh's church was closely connected with the abbey of St. Martial de Limoges. See Georges Peyrebrune, "Giraut de Bornelh et l'époque limousine d'Excideuil."

36. Adolf Kolsen, ed., *Sämtliche Lieder des Trobadors Giraut de Bornelh*.

37. Terence H. Newcombe, "The Troubadour Berenger de Palazol: A Critical

Edition of His Poems," 54. New edition by Margherita Beretta Spampinato, *Berenguer de Palol, Poesie*.

38. Newcombe, "Berenger de Palazol: A Critical Edition," 55–56; but see Francisco Noy, "Estudio historico sobre el trovador Berenger de Palou," and Martín de Riquer, *Los trovadores*, I:301, who point out that Berengarius' will of 1207 deeds some property to his "nutricii," or his wet-nurse (and her husband?), suggesting that he was still relatively young in 1207 and may not have been active as early as the 1160s.

39. See Félix Lecoy, "Note sur le troubadour Raimbaut de Vaqueiras," which argues that the author of this *sirventes* may have been Raimon de Miraval.

40. "Didier" is the romanized version of Latin "Desiderius." It was mutated to "Lesdier" or "Leidier" in many Occitan sources, including most versions of his *vida* and in rubrics in the chansonniers. See Aimo Sakari, *Poésies du troubadour Guillem de Saint-Didier*, 9.

41. R. C. Johnston, ed., *Les poésies lyriques du troubadour Arnaut de Mareuil*, xvi–xvii.

42. Riquer, *Los trovadores*, II:647 and 1039.

43. Erich Niestroy, ed., *Der Trobador Pistoleta*, 7.

44. See Jean Mouzat, ed., *Les poèmes de Gaucelm Faidit*, 30 n.14.

45. See ibid., 35.

46. Ibid., 37, claims that this is the first song in French composed by a troubadour.

47. William D. Paden, Tilde Sankovitch, and Patricia H. Stäblein, eds., *The Poems of the Troubadour Bertran de Born*. See also Gérard Gouiran, *L'Amour et la Guerre: l'oeuvre de Bertran de Born*, and *Le Seigneur-troubadour d'Hautefort: L'oeuvre de Bertran de Born*, 2d ed.

48. See Hilding Kjellman, ed., *Le troubadour Raimon Jordan, vicomte de Saint-Antonin*.

49. See BS, 161.

50. Stronski, *Folquet*, 3.

51. Thomas Wright, ed., *Johannis de Garlandi: De triumphis ecclesiae*, 92.

52. Henri Gougaud, ed. and trans., *La chanson de la Croisade Albigeoise*.

53. Stronski, *Folquet*, 94–95.

54. Quoted in Riquer, *Los trovadores*, I:585 n.8.

55. Gianluigi Toja, *Arnaut Daniel: Canzoni*. See also James J. Wilhelm, *The Poetry of Arnaut Daniel*, xi–xvii; and Maurizio Perugi, *Le canzoni di Arnaut Daniel*.

56. See Elizabeth Aubrey, "References to Music in Old Occitan Literature," 122–127.

57. See Joseph Linskill, *The Poems of the Troubadour Raimbaut de Vaqueiras*.

58. See D'Arco Silvio Avalle, *Peire Vidal: Poesie*, cxxxii n.1.

59. Ernest Hoepffner, ed., *Le troubadour Peire Vidal, sa vie et son oeuvre*.

60. Called *chansons jumelles* because of their linked subject matter; see Hoepffner, *Peire Vidal*, 79ff.

61. See Janine Monier, "Essaie d'identification de la comtesse de Die," 267–268. For another theory, see William T. Pattison, *Raimbaut d'Orange*, 27–30.

62. Monier, "Essaie," 274–275, based on documents uncovered by Jules Chevalier, "Mémoires pour servir à l'histoire des comtés de Valentinois et de Diois," 125.

63. Gabrielle Kussler-Ratyé, ed., "Les chansons de la Comtesse Béatrix de Dia."

64. BS, 202.

65. Jean Audiau, *Les poésies des quatre troubadours d'Ussel*, 16 and 109. See also

Ernest Hoepffner, "Les troubadours d'Ussel"; and Léon Billet, *Généalogie de la famille d'Ussel*.

66. BS, 205–207.

67. Audiau, *Ussel*, 10.

68. Fritz Naudieth, *Der Trobador Guillem Magret*, 96–97.

69. Félix de la Salle de Rochemaure, *Les troubadours cantaliens*, 248ff.

70. Ibid., 260–262.

71. Michael J. Routledge, ed., *Les poésies du Moine de Montaudon*.

72. Stefano Asperti, "La data di 'Pos Peire d'Alvernh'a cantat.'"

73. See Elizabeth Aubrey, "Genre as a Determinant of Melody in the Songs of the Troubadours and the Trouvères."

74. Alfredo Cavaliere, *Le poesie di Peire Raimon de Tolosa*, viii–ix. See Kurt Lewent, "À propos du troubadour Peire Raimon de Tolosa."

75. Joseph Anglade, "À propos de Peire Vidal," 105–107.

76. Stanley C. Aston, ed., *Peirol, Troubadour of Auvergne*, 9.

77. Ibid., 3 n.3.

78. Ibid., 15.

79. See Leslie T. Topsfield, *Les poésies du troubadour Raimon de Miraval*, 22, 379, and Appendix.

80. The family was in trouble before the crusade, however. Viscount Rogier II of Béziers demanded that a Guilhem de Miraval surrender his possessions in Castres in 1174 for "lawless acts" (ibid., 17, 379).

81. J. Miret i Sans, "Enquesta sobre el trovador Vilarnau amb algunes noves de Guillem de Bergadà, Ramon de Miraval i Guillem de Mur," 264–266.

82. Margaret L. Switten, ed., *The Cansos of Raimon de Miraval: A Study of Poems and Melodies*.

83. See Ernest Hoepffner, "La biographie de Perdigon."

84. See Henry J. Chaytor, *Les chansons de Perdigon*, 39.

85. Hoepffner, "Perdigon," 350.

86. Camille Chabaneau, *Les biographies des troubadours*, 282 n.1. See William P. Shepard and Frank M. Chambers, eds., *The Poems of Aimeric de Peguilhan*.

87. See Riquer, *Los trovadores*, II:963.

88. See Shepard and Chambers, *Aimeric de Peguilhan*, 10–14.

89. Clovis Brunel, "Les troubadours Azémar Jordan et Uc Brunenc," 508.

90. Appel, "Der Trobador Uc Brunec (oder Brunenc)."

91. See Aubrey, "References," 125.

92. See A. Thomas, "L'Identité du troubadour Pons de Chapteuil"; and Stronski, "En Pons de Capduelh."

93. H. H. Lucas, "Pons de Capduoill and Azalais de Mercuor: A Study of the *planh*."

94. Kurt Almqvist, ed., *Poésies du troubadour Guilhem Adémar*. See also A. Serper, "Les troubadours Jaufré Rudel et Guillem Adémar."

95. Almqvist, *Guilhem Adémar*, 15–16.

96. Ibid., 30.

97. Jean Boutière, ed., "Les poésies du troubadour Albertet."

98. Ibid., 18.

99. Erich Niestroy, *Pistoleta*, 7.

100. BS, 491.

101. Niestroy, *Pistoleta*, 8.

102. Ibid., 9–10.

103. Stronski, "Notes sur quelques troubadours et protecteurs des troubadours célébrés par Elias de Barjols," 35ff. See also Niestroy, *Pistoleta*, 3–4.

104. Josef Zemp, ed., *Les poésies du troubadour Cadenet*, 67–68.

105. Chabaneau, *Biographies*, 93.

106. Zemp, *Cadenet*, 76–77.

107. See PC, 172–173; Johannes Müller, "Die Gedichte des Guillem Augier Novella," 48; Guida, "Problemi di datazione."

108. Monica Calzolari, ed., *Il trovatore Guillem Augier Novella*.

109. Müller, "Guillem Augier," 50–52.

110. Edmond de Rivals, "Pons d'Ortaffa," 69, 80–82, 109.

111. Ibid., 80–82.

112. Ibid., 110.

113. Ibid., 108 and 113.

114. Maria Dumitrescu, ed., *Poésies du troubadour Aimeric de Belenoi*.

115. Ibid., 8–12; and Mario Ruffini, *Il trovatore Aimeric de Belenoi*, 8.

116. Dumitrescu, *Aimeric*, 17.

117. Ibid., 13–14 and 36.

118. Ibid., 35–37.

119. Alfred Jeanroy and J.-J. Salverda de Grave, eds., *Poésies de Uc de Saint-Circ*.

120. See BS, ix and xiv; Bruno Panvini, *Le biografie provenzali, valore e attendibilità*, 89–91; Egan, *Vidas*, xiii–xiv and xxiv.

121. Jeanroy and Salverda de Grave, *Uc de Saint-Circ*, xiii and 163.

122. Ibid., xii–xiii and 152–153.

123. Ibid., 155–157; and Nicola Zingarelli, *Intorno a due trovatori in Italia*, 1–23.

124. Otto Klein, ed., *Der Troubadour Blacassetz*.

125. Stronski, "Notes," 40–41.

126. René Lavaud, ed., *Poésies complètes du troubadour Peire Cardenal*, 610–614.

127. Chabaneau, *Biographies*, 163 n.8.

128. A.-H. Schutz, ed., *Poésies de Daude de Pradas*, ix–xvii.

129. Chabaneau, *Biographies*, 352. See O. Hoby, *Die Lieder des Trobadors Guiraut d'Espagne*.

130. See p. xiii for a list of abbreviations and sigla.

131. See Elizabeth Aubrey, "A Study of the Origins, History, and Notation of the Troubadour Chansonnier Paris, Bibliothèque nationale, f. fr. 22543."

132. See Joseph Anglade, *Le troubadour Guiraut Riquier*; J.-M. Petit, "Guiraut Riquier, période narbonnaise et destinée du dernier grand poète de cour."

133. See Vincent Beltràn, "Los trovadores en la Corte de Castilla y León (II): Alfonso X, Guiraut Riquier y Pero da Ponte."

134. Higini Anglès, "Les melodies del trobador Guiraut Riquier" (1926), contains transcriptions of Guiraut's melodies in mensural rhythms.

2. Transmission

1. Ruth Finnegan, in *Oral Poetry*, 17, points out that a poem can be oral in several ways: "(1) its compositon, (2) its mode of transmission, and (3) (related to (2)) its performance." See also Paul Zumthor, *La lettre et la voix*, on the interaction between writing and performing; Walter J. Ong, *Orality and Literacy*, for discussion of the phenomenology of orality and writing and of the changes that writing works on a text; and Brian Stock, *The Implications of Literacy*.

2. See Leo Treitler, "Transmission and the Study of Music History."

3. See Pierre Bec, *La lyrique française au moyen âge*, I:50; François Zufferey, *Recherches linguistiques sur les chansonniers provençaux*, 1–12; D'Arco Silvio Avalle, *La letteratura medievale in lingua d'oc nella sua tradizione manoscritta*; Aubrey, "A Study," 245; Clovis Brunel, *Bibliographie des manuscrits littéraires en ancien provençal*, xv.

4. Gustav Gröber, "Die Liedersammlungen der Troubadours."

5. See Aubrey, "A Study," 231–236, and "The Transmission of Troubadour Melodies," 214. "A Study," Chapter 5, contains a historiography of modern text critical approaches to the songs of the troubadours.

6. Gröber, "Die Liedersammlungen," 342–343.

7. D'Arco Silvio Avalle, *La Letteratura*, 45–48 and passim. See Aubrey, "A Study," 238–239.

8. See, e.g., Dietmar Rieger, "Audition et lecture dans le domaine de la poésie troubadouresque," "'Senes breu de parguamina'? Zum Problem des 'gelesenen Lieds' im Mittelalter," and "'Chantar' und 'faire': Zum Problem der trobadoresken Improvisation." See also Riquer, *Los trovadores*, I:15–19.

9. Notably Jörn Gruber, "Singen und Schreiben, Hören und Lesen als Parameter der (Re-) Produktion und Rezeption des Occitanischen Minnesangs des 12. Jahrhunderts"; and Amelia E. Van Vleck, *Memory and Re-Creation in Troubadour Lyric*. See John M. Foley, *The Theory of Oral Composition*, for a historiography.

10. Paul Zumthor, *Essai de poétique médiévale*.

11. George Wolf and Roy Rosenstein, eds. and trans., *Cercamon and Rudel*, 54–55.

12. See Aubrey, "A Study," and "Transmission."

13. See Agostino Ziino, "Caratteri e significato della tradizione musicale trobadorica," 92–98.

14. BS, 252, emphasis added. See Aubrey, "References," 127.

15. As pointed out in Aubrey, "Troubadour Research and Performing Practice Today," a paper given at the IMS Congress, Bologna 1987, and in more detail in Aubrey, "Literacy, Orality, and the Preservation of French and Occitan Medieval Courtly Songs." See also Wulf Arlt, "The 'Reconstruction' of Instrumental Music: the Interpretation of the Earliest Practical Sources"; for similar indications in the northern repertoire, see Theodore Karp, "The Trouvère MS Tradition."

16. See Hendrik van der Werf, *The Chansons of the Troubadours and Trouvères*.

17. Mary Carruthers, *The Book of Memory*. See Van Vleck, *Memory*, 29–34, for a discussion of scribes' approaches to their texts.

18. Sylvia Huot, *From Song to Book*. Christopher Page bases much of what he says in *Voices and Instruments of the Middle Ages* about genres, rhythm, and instruments on this argument. See also William D. Paden, "The Role of the Joglar in Troubadour Lyric Poetry," 97–99.

19. See discussion of these issues by Wulf Arlt, "Secular Monophony," especially 58–59.

20. See Aubrey, "Literacy."

21. See Aubrey, "Forme et formule dans les mélodies des troubadours."

22. See studies by Jean Rychner, *La chanson de geste*; and Joseph J. Duggan, *The Song of Roland*.

23. Bec, *La lyrique française*, I.20ff.

24. See Van Vleck, *Memory*, which argues that except for the first and last stanzas, the order was not important to the overall theme.

25. See Helmut Hucke, "Der Übergang von mündlicher zu schriftlicher Musiküberlieferung im Mittelalter"; and Leo Treitler, "Homer and Gregory: The Transmission of Epic Poetry and Plainchant" and "'Centonate chant': *Übles Flickwerk* or *E pluribus unus?*"

26. Aubrey, "Forme et formule."

27. Paden, "Role of the Joglar," 97; pp. 104–105 list troubadours who name *joglars* in their poems, including seventeen of the 42 for whom some music survives.

28. See Aubrey, "References," 148–149, on Guiraut Riquier's discussion of this in the late thirteenth century.

29. Christopher Page has supplied evidence that some classes of singers in northern France, especially those who were members of or in some way enjoyed privileges of the aristocracy, were probably able to read plainchant notation. See *The Owl and the Nightingale: Musical Life and Ideas in France 1100–1300.*

30. See Gruber, "Singen und Schreiben," for discussion of such passages.

31. See Aubrey, "References," 126–127.

32. Ibid., 128.

33. See Carruthers, *Memory*; Finnegan, *Oral Poetry*, 56–65; and Paul Zumthor, *Introduction à la poésie orale*, 245–261.

34. See Paden, "Joglar," 93–94.

35. James Grier, "Scribal Practices in the Aquitanian Versaria of the Twelfth Century," is a helpful step toward sorting out the types and causes of musical variants in a medieval repertoire.

36. Zufferey, *Recherches*, 281, insists on a distinction between these chansonniers and ones that were essentially Occitanian manuscripts produced in the north. See L. Gauchat, "Les poésies provençales conservées par des chansonniers français," especially 381–386, for study of the linguistic peculiarities of these texts. See also Manfred and Margret Raupach, *Französierte Trobadorlyrik: Zur Überlieferung provenzalischer Lieder in französischen Handschriften*, 62–79.

37. Facs. ed. by Paul Meyer and Gaston Raynaud, *Le Chansonnier français de Saint-Germain-des-Prés.*

38. The notation was examined by Ian Parker, "Notes on the Chansonnier Saint-Germain-des-Prés," and has been exhaustively catalogued and studied by Robert Lug, *Der Chansonnier de Saint-Germain-des-Prés*. See a summary of the latter in Lug, "Das 'vormodale' Zeichensystem des Chansonnier de Saint-Germain-des-Prés."

39. See Gauchat, "Les poésies provençales," 378–380; Raupach and Raupach, *Französierte Trobadorlyrik*, 113–156.

40. Julius Brakelmann, "Die dreiundzwanzig altfranzösische Chansonniers in Bibliotheken Frankreichs, Englands, Italiens und der Schweiz," 48–49, and *Les plus anciens chansonniers français (XII siècle)*, 81–82, 208. See Madeleine Tyssens, "Les copistes du chansonnier français U"; Eduard Schwan, *Die altfranzösischen Liederhandschriften*, 262; Huot, *From Song to Book*, 53; van der Werf, *Extant Troubadour Melodies*, 23.

41. This Roman numbering is found on the verso side of the leaves. A modern arabic foliation appears in the upper right corner of the recto sides. Because most of the secondary literature does so, this study also will use the newer foliation, despite the fact that it does not coincide with the medieval one.

42. Tyssens, "Les copistes," 391. Mark Everist, *Polyphonic Music in Thirteenth-Century France*, 199–200, argues on paleographical grounds that the manuscript might have been produced as early as c. 1225, which in light of Tyssens' argument seems highly unlikely. He bases his dating on the procedure of writing text "above top line," that is, the top rule drawn by the scribe. This is so only for the first section of the codex; after fol. 91v the scribe wrote below top line. See also Aubrey, "Literacy."

43. Tyssens, "Les copistes," 384.

44. Ibid., 394.

45. See Vincent Pollina, "Troubadours dans le nord," for detailed discussion of the way the scribes of manuscripts X and W approached the southern melodies they received.

46. See Parker, "Notes."

47. Facs. ed. by Jean and Louise Beck, *Les Chansonniers des Troubadours et des Trouvères, 2: Le Manuscrit du Roi, fonds français no. 844 de la Bibliothèque nationale.* An arabic foliation, which ignores the numerous lacunae, was added in the eighteenth century (*Chansonniers*, II:2), before it was realized that the leaves of the codex had been scrambled. The Becks' facsimile edition restores the manuscript to its presumed original order, guided by the Index found in the first gathering, and gives a revised arabic foliation to this restored order, placing the Thibaut manuscript at the end with a roman foliation. This "old" foliation has not been adopted generally in modern literature, but it is given here preceded by the letter "B" to facilitate comparison of the present discussion with the facsimile edition.

48. The manuscript's sobriquet, which it had received by at least the late eighteenth century, may be due to its sumptuous appearance, to its collection of songs of Thibaut, king of Navarre, to its reception in the Bibliothèque du Roi in the eighteenth century, or to its possible connection with Charles d'Anjou. See below, and Beck and Beck, *Chansonniers*, I:ix.

49. Beck and Beck, *Chansonniers*, I:x, and II:18–20 and 90. This theory is disputed, especially by Hans Spanke, "Der Chansonnier du Roi," 101. See the latter for a detailed description of the manuscript's contents. See also Mark Everist, *Polyphonic Music in Thirteenth-Century France*, 184–185.

50. Ibid., 186.

51. Van der Werf excluded all these works except Blacasset's *canso* from his edition, *Extant Troubadour Melodies*.

52. See Aubrey, "Issues in the Musical Analysis of the Troubadour Descorts and Lais," for a discussion of the problems in classifying and analyzing these songs. Judith Peraino, "New Music, Notions of Genre, and the 'Manuscrit du Roi' circa 1300," appeared too late for me to consult.

53. Theodore Karp, in "Three Trouvère Chansons in Mensural Notation," discusses a few late French additions to this manuscript. He suggests that they were added "in the last quarter of the 13th century" (477).

54. Study, modern transcriptions, and incomplete facsimile edition by Ugo Sesini, "Le melodie trobadoriche nel canzoniere provenzale della Biblioteca Ambrosiana (R. 71 sup.)."

55. See Sesini, "Canzoniere," 12; and Giulio Bertoni, *Il canzoniere provenzale della Biblioteca Ambrosiana, R. 71 sup.,* xxi. See Zufferey, *Recherches*, 104, which suggests that the kinship of G with manuscript Q, which was bound with a document that places it in or near Pavia, makes a Lombard provenance for G more likely.

56. Agostino Ziino concludes from this and the other scribal procedures described here that the text scribe was using exemplars without music ("Caratteri," 124–126).

57. See Aubrey, "A Study," for a complete description and discussion of this manuscript. Zufferey, *Recherches*, 105–133, contains an exhaustive study of the linguistic traits of the scribe of R; see also Zufferey, "La partie non-lyrique du chansonnier d'Urfé." Zufferey concludes that the manuscript was produced in the region of Toulouse, not as far south as Carcassonne or Foix, and therefore not in the same region as manuscript C, whose contents are close to those of R. Both manuscripts transmit a large collection of works by Guiraut Riquier, the late Narbonnais troubadour; if Zufferey is correct, manuscript C was probably closer to the troubadour than was R. A more limited study of the scribe's linguistic dialect (Aubrey, "A Study," 91–106) localized it to roughly the same region, but a little broader and farther north than Zufferey (to whom I gladly defer).

58. Zufferey, *Recherches,*130–132, accepts a *terminus ad quem* for the manu-

script of 1326, the date given in a rubric with a small group of songs by Peire Cavalier Lunel de Montech, which were added in a later hand at the end of gathering 16 on fol. 141v–142v. A study of the manuscript's decoration by Geneviève Brunel-Lobrichon, "L'Iconographie du chansonnier provençal R," identifies at least three meridional artists probably working in one atelier in the Toulousain, all of whom manifest a late thirteenth- to early fourteenth-century style.

59. See Pirot, *Recherches*, 214; Zufferey, *Recherches*, 105–133; and Zufferey, "La partie non-lyrique," 13.

60. Zufferey, "La partie non-lyrique," 23, and Brunel-Lobrichon, "L'Iconographie," suggest a northern connection for some sources of R. Zufferey opines that such a connection might explain the presence of music in R, reflecting a northern aesthetic.

61. See Aubrey, "Transmission"; and Antoine Tavera, "La table du chansonnier d'Urfé."

62. See Aubrey, "References," 148–149.

63. Aubrey, "A Study," 39ff.

64. See ibid., 43–45, and "Transmission," 216–221.

65. Aubrey, "A Study," 127–147, and "Transmission," 218–225.

66. Aubrey, "A Study," 258.

67. Ibid., 122–124.

68. See Valeria Bertolucci Pizzorusso, "Il canzoniere di un trovatore: Il 'libro' di Guiraut Riquier"; and Michel-André Bossy, "Cyclical Composition in Guiraut Riquier's Book of Poems." For study of the paleographical characteristics, especially in regard to the music, see Aubrey, "A Study," 86–88, 125, 168, 285, and "Transmission," 227.

69. See Aubrey, "A Study," 166–169. Oddly, manuscript C also transmits this rubric, but there is no music anywhere in this chansonnier. Bertolucci, "Canzoniere," 227–228, 239–240, suggests that the exemplar for C had music.

70. See Aubrey, "A Study," 137–149.

71. See Jean-Baptiste Beck, *Die Melodien des Troubadours*, 36–37; Aubrey, "Transmission," 235–236; Ziino, "Caratteri," 111ff.

72. Zoltán Falvy, "Manuskripte, Herkunft und Verzierung in der Troubadour-Musik," discusses the eighteen melodies that are extant in three or more readings. These represent just five composers, all active in the late twelfth century.

73. Nicoletta Gossen, "Musik und Text in Liedern des Trobadors Bernart de Ventadorn," and Vincent Pollina, "Word/Music Relations in the Work of the Troubadour Gaucelm Faidit," are recent studies that examine variants in text and note alignment, arguing that such differences have an internal logic based upon the relationship between poem and music in a particular source.

74. Van der Werf, in *Extant Troubadour Melodies*, 232*, observes that a note G is erased at the beginning of the next line. The eye might be deceived here, for it is not clear that the note was erased at all; but whether it was or not, another note on "-uelhs," E, was not erased.

75. Ibid., 136*, points out that the same text appears later in R without a melody, attributed to Guilhem de Cabestanh. That the scribe failed to realize that this melody could be used for the later poem suggests that he noticed text concordances only if the composer attributions were identical (and hence it did not occur to him to write in this melody later) or that his musical source was no longer available to him and he did not collate his material.

76. E.g., Switten, *Raimon de Miraval*, 147.

77. See Aubrey, "Issues in the Musical Analysis of the Troubadour Descorts and Lais," 75–77.

78. See a suggested reconstruction by van der Werf, *Extant Troubadour Melodies*, 52*–53*.

3. Poetics and Music

1. See James J. Murphy, *Rhetoric in the Middle Ages*; Charles S. Baldwin, *Medieval Rhetoric and Poetic (to 1400)*, 127ff.; Douglas Kelly, *The Arts of Poetry and Prose*, 41–49.

2. See H. M. Hubbell, ed. and trans., *Cicero: De inventione, De optimo genero oratorum, Topica*, 12–17; and Harry Caplan, ed. and trans., *[Cicero]: Ad C. Herennium, De ratione dicendi (Rhetorica ad Herennium)*, 4–5, and 172ff..

3. Hubbell, *Cicero*, 20–21.

4. Ibid., 180–181 and 386–387. See also Murphy, *Rhetoric*, 16.

5. Hubbell, *Cicero*, 18–19; and Caplan, *Ad Herennium*, 6–7, 184ff.

6. Caplan, *Ad Herennium*, 252–263.

7. Murphy, *Rhetoric*, 20–21; Caplan, *Ad Herennium*, 266–269 and 275ff.

8. Murphy, *Rhetoric*, 29–31, gives a resumé of Horace's treatise.

9. Quoted, ibid., 78.

10. See Kelly, *Arts*, 60, for description of the sources used by medieval poets for study.

11. Useful studies of the late medieval *ars poeticae* include Edmond Faral, *Les arts poétiques du XIIe et du XIIIe siècle*; Kelly, "The Scope of the Treatment of Composition in the Twelfth- and Thirteenth-Century Arts of Poetry," and "Theory of Composition in Medieval Narrative Poetry and Geoffrey of Vinsauf's *Poetria Nova*." See also Margot E. Fassler, "Accent, Meter, and Rhythm in Medieval Treatises 'De rithmis,'" and "The Role of the Parisian Sequence in the Evolution of Notre-Dame Polyphony"; and especially Kelly, *Arts*.

12. Kelly, *Arts*, 65. See also Kelly's definitive work, particularly as it concerns fourteenth- and fifteenth-century literature, *Medieval Imagination: Rhetoric and the Poetry of Courtly Love*; and Jacques Le Goff, *L'Imaginaire médiéval*.

13. Kelly, *Arts*, 71–77.

14. Ulrich Mölk, *Trobar clus trobar leu: Studien zur Dichtungstheorie der Trobadors*.

15. Kelly, *Arts*, 110.

16. Margaret F. Nims, trans., *Poetria nova of Geoffrey of Vinsauf*, 16. Ernest A. Gallo, *The Poetria Nova and Its Sources in Early Rhetorical Doctrine*, 16: "Si quis habet fundare domum, non currit ad actum/impetuosa manus: intrinseca linea cordis/praemetitur opus, seriemque sub ordine certo/interior praescribit homo, totamque figurat/ante manus cordis quam corporis; et status ejus/est prius archetypus quam sensilis. Ipsa poesis/spectet in hoc speculo quae lex sit danda poetis./Non manus ad calamum praeceps, non lingua sit ardens/ad verbum: neutram manibus committe regendam/fortunae; sed mens discreta praeambula facti,/ut melius fortunet opus, suspendat earum/officium, tractetque diu de themate secum./Circinus interior mentis praecircinet omne/materiae spatium. Certus praelimitet ordo/unde praearripiat cursum stylus, at ubi Gades/figat. Opus totum prudens in pectoris arcem/contrahe, sitque prius in pectore quam sit in ore."

17. Nims, *Poetria nova*, 17. Gallo, *Poetria nova*, 16: "Mentis in arcano cum rem digesserit ordo,/materiam verbis veniat vestire poesis."

18. Nims, *Poetria nova*, 55. Gallo, *Poetria nova*, 72: "Proprias igitur ne respice vires,/immo suas, cum quo loqueris. Da pondera verbis/aequa suis humeris, et pro re verba loquaris. . . . In re communi communis, in appropriatis/sit sermo proprius. Sic rerum cuique geratur/mos suus."

19. Nims, *Poetria nova*, 90. Gallo, *Poetria nova*, 124: "Voces quas sensus dividit,

illas/divide; quas jungit, conjuge. Domes ita vocem,/ut non disordet a re, nec limite tendat/vox alio, quam res intendat; eant simula ambae;/vox quaedam sit imago rei."

20. See William G. Waite, "Johannes de Garlandia, Poet and Musician," esp. 181. Waite believed that the grammarian Jean was also the music theorist Johannes de Garlandia, author of one of the most important documents describing Parisian polyphony in the twelfth and thirteenth centuries, although some scholars remain skeptical.

21. Traugott Lawler, ed. and trans., *The Parisiana poetria of John of Garland*, 158–161: "Rithmica est species artis musice. Musica enim diuiditur in mundanam, que constat in proporcione qualitatum elementorum, et in humanam, que constat in proportione et concordia humorum, et in instrumentalem, que constat in concordia instrumentali. Hec diuiditur in mellicam, metricam, et rithmicam. De aliis speciebus nihil ad presens; de rithmica uero ad presens dicetur." See Fassler, "Accent."

22. Lawler, *Parisiana poetria*, 174–175.

23. Thomas Wright, ed., *Johannis de Garlandia, De triumphis*, 92–93. See Stronski, *Folquet de Marseille,*107–108.

24. Lawler, *Parisiana poetria*, 8–9: "Sub inuencione species sunt quinque: vbi, quid, quale, qualiter, ad quid."

25. Ibid., 10–11: "Tria genera personarum hic debent considerari secundum tria genera hominum, que sunt curiales, ciuiles, rurales. Curiales sunt qui curiam tenent ac celebrant, ut Dominus Papa, cardinales, legati, archiepiscopi, episcopi, et eorum suffraganei, sicut archidiaconi, decani, officiales, magistri, scolares. Item, imperatores, reges, marchiones, et duces. Ciuiles persone sunt consul, prepositus, et cetere persone in ciuitate habitantes. Rurales sunt rura colentes, sicut uenatores, agricole, uinitores, aucupes."

26. Ibid., 20–21: "'Quale' ponit qualitatem materie inueniende. . . ."

27. Ibid., 28–31: "De Arte Inueniendi Materiam. Hoc artificio vtendum est in aliis orationibus, quod pueri uolentes ampliare et uariare materiam obseruent, non pretermittentes causas principales quattuor, scilicet causam efficientem, cuiuslibet rei sibi proposite. Ut, si tractet de libro suo, commendet eum uel uituperet per causam efficientem, idest per scriptorem; per causam materialem, idest per pargamenum et incaustum; per causam formalem, ut per libri disposicionem et litterarum protractionem; per causam finalem, considerando ad quid factus est liber, ad hoc uidelicet ut in eo et per eum nescientes scientes reddantur." The examples Jean gives following this passage are all of the *ars dictamini* (letter-writing).

28. Ibid., 20–21: "Qvia dicitur in premissis 'ad quid,' attendendum est quod per hoc denotatur finis inuentoris, scilicet vtilitas et honestas. . . ."

29. Ibid., 10–11: "In personis duo, ut in regibus: bene regnum regere, vel regnum tirannide dilacerare; in prelatis: diuine contemplationi insistere, uel negociis secularibus ociari; in ciuilibus: urbis negocia tractare, rem publicam augere uel dissipare; in ruralibus, contingit circa ruralia desudare uel cessare."

30. See Ibid., 230–231 n.124.

31. Ibid., 78–79: "Item tenor ipsius stili ampliat materiam quando ad grevem stilum graues eliguntur sentencie, ad mediocrem, mediocres, ad humilem, humiles—si tamen ne in humili materia nimis deiecti simus et sine coloribus, ipsius stili elingues. . . ."

32. Ibid., 86–87: "Potest grauis materia humiliari exemplo Virgilii, qui uocat Cesarem Titirum—uel seipsum, Romam fagum; potest et humilis materia exaltari, ut in graui materia coli muliebres uocantur 'inbelles haste'. . . ." See also 237 n.46.

33. Ibid., 254ff., notes.

34. Ibid., 100–101: "nudum sine sepultura carmen, scilicet quod fit de insepultis."

35. Kelly, *Arts*, 98; Fassler, "Accent."

36. The fourteenth-century documents include Raimon de Cornet, *Doctrinal de trobar* (Catalonia, 1324); Guilhem Molinier, *Leys d'Amors*, Version A (Toulouse, 1328–46); *Leys d'Amors*, Version B (Catalonia, 1337–43); Joan de Castellnou, *Compendi de la coneixença dels vicis en els dictats del Gay Saber* (Catalonia, 1337–43); Joan de Castellnou, *Glosari al Doctrinal de Ramon de Cornet* (Catalonia, 1341); Guilhem Molinier, *Leys d'Amors*, Version C (Catalonia, 1355–56). They fall within the tradition spawned by the late development of poetic contests in the north, and they provide evidence mainly of the reception of the art of the troubadours in the fourteenth century. See Kelly, *Arts*, 156–157, 168–174; Gérard Gonfroy, "Les genres lyriques occitans et les traités de poétique."

37. J. H. Marshall, ed., *The "Razos de trobar" of Raimon Vidal and Associated Texts.*

38. J. H. Marshall, ed., *The "Donatz Proensals" of Uc Faidit.*

39. See Marshall, *Razos*, xvi–xxviii, for discussion of the manuscript tradition.

40. Ibid., 2: "voill eu far aqest libre per far conoisser et saber qals dels trobadors an mielz trobat et mielz ensenhat, ad aqelz qe.l volran aprenre, con devon segre la dreich maniera de trobar." See Marshall's commentary, lxxx–lxxxi. See Elizabeth W. Poe, *From Poetry to Prose*, 67–79, and "The Problem of the Prologue in Raimon Vidal's *Las Razos de trobar*."

41. See list in Marshall, *Razos*, xxii–xxiii.

42. They are PC 70,1; 70,6; 70,7; 70,12; 70,25; 70,41; 70,43; 155,3; 155,18; 242,45; 30,23; and 366,21.

43. PC 70,1; 70,7; 70,41; and 70,43.

44. Marshall, *Razos*, xxi–xxviii.

45. Ibid., xxxv–xxli.

46. PC 167,56; 167,59; 70,6; 155,14; and 10,25.

47. PC 167,56.

48. Marshall, *Razos*, xli–xliv.

49. See William D. Paden, "The System of Genres in Troubadour Lyric."

50. Marshall, *Razos*, lxxviii. See lxxv–lxxvi on the paleographical peculiarities of the text.

51. Ibid., xciv–xcv.

52. See Aubrey, "Genre."

53. Ibid.

54. Augustine in *De Musica* (completed A.D. 391), after offering the famous definition of music as "scientia bene modulandi," devoted most of the rest of his tract to a discussion of quantitative metrics.

55. Lawler, *Parisiana poetria*, 158–161. See Kelly, *Arts*, 54, 150–151.

56. See Zumthor, *Poésie orale*, 177–206, for a wide-ranging discussion of this idea.

57. Aristide Marigo, ed., *De vulgari eloquentia*, II.iv.2 (p. 188); "fictio rethorica musicaque poita."

58. See Nan Cooke Carpenter, *Music in the Medieval and Renaissance Universities*; and Jeremy Yudkin, "The Influence of Aristotle on French University Music Texts."

59. For documentation of some of these changes, see Craig Wright, *Music and Ceremony*; and Christopher Page, *The Owl and the Nightingale*, and *Discarding Images*.

60. Kelly, *Arts*, 150ff.

61. See Christopher Page, *Voices and Instruments*. Grocheio's confusing classification system has been subjected to several analyses. It is difficult to match up with surviving pieces and is sometimes simply impenetrable. But we should not be surprised that we cannot find neat analytical details that would help us delineate the elements that constitute secular songs. Providing such details interested Grocheio much less than accounting for the existence of secular music and demonstrating that it is of value within the musical world hitherto dominated, among theorists at least, by sacred music. Grocheio is concerned not so much with describing a *cantus* or a *cantilena* as with justifying it. To do so, he invokes an Aristotelian framework, Ciceronian rhetoric, and Boethian philosophy to ground his discussion in *auctoritas*. See Aubrey, "Genre."

62. Aubrey, "Genre"; and a similar analysis of Grocheio in Christopher Page, *Discarding Images*, 75–76.

63. "But the manner of composing these generally is one and the same, in the manner of [their] nature. For first the texts are prepared in the place of matter, but after this, the melody is introduced in the place of form in proportion to whatever text. I speak, however, of 'in proportion to whatever [text]' because *chanson de geste* or *cantus coronatus* or *cantus versiculatus* [each] has a different [type of] melody, as their descriptions differ, in the manner that was said above. So then concerning musical forms that are performed by the human voice, these have been discussed." Ernst Rohloff, ed., *Die Quellenhandschriften zum Musiktraktat des Johannes de Grocheio*, 134: "Modus autem componendi haec generaliter est unus, quemadmodum in natura. Primo enim dictamina loco materiae praeparantur, postea vero cantus unicuique dictamini proportionalis loco formae introducitur. Dico autem *unicuique proportionalis*, quia alium cantum habet cantus gestualis et coronatus et versiculatus, ut eorum descriptiones aliae sunt, quemadmodum superius dicebatur. De formis igitur musicalibus, quae in voce humana exercentur, haec dicta sint." See Aubrey, "Genre." The reader will recall Jean de Garlande's evocation of Aristotelian causality in reference to inventing subject matter.

64. Quintilian, who speaks freely of musicians and artists, used remarkably similar language along with an analogy from the plastic arts, in speaking of how a work of art comes into being: "A very few critics have raised the question as to what may be the instrument of oratory. My definition of an instrument is that without which the material cannot be brought into the shape necessary for the effecting of our object. But it is not the art which requires an instrument, but the artist. Knowledge needs no instruments, for it may be complete although it produces nothing, but the artist must have them. The engraver cannot work without his chisel nor the painter without his brush. I shall therefore defer this question until I come to treat of the orator as distinct from his art." H. E. Butler, ed. and trans., *The Institutio Oratoria of Quintilian*, I:366–367: "Quaesitum a paucissimis et de instrumento est. Instrumentum voco, sine quo formari materia in id quod velimus effici opus non possit. Verum hoc ego non artem credo egere sed artificem. Neque enim scientia desiderat instrumentum, quae potest esse consummata, etiamsi nihil faciat, sed ille artifex, ut caelator caelum et pictor penicilla. Itaque haec in eum locum, quo de oratore dicturi sumus, differamus."

65. See Mathias Bielitz, "*Materia* und *forma* bei Johannes de Grocheo," for a discussion of other ways in which Grocheio uses these Aristotelian concepts. See also Wulf Arlt, "Musica e testo," 306–308; Margherita Beretta Spampinato, "'Mot' e 'so' nella lirica trobadorica"; and Patricia A. M. Dewitt, *A New Perspective on Johannes de Grocheio's Ars musicae*.

66. "*Cantus coronatus* usually is composed by kings and nobles, and is sung in the court of kings and princes of the land, so that their spirits might be moved to boldness and courage, magnanimity and liberality, which all produce a good government. For this sort of *cantus* concerns delightful and difficult material, like friendship and charity, and is made from all sorts of longs, even perfect [ones]." Rohloff, *Grocheio*, 130: "Cantus coronatus . . . etiam a regibus et nobilibus solet componi et etiam coram regibus et principibus terrae decantari, ut eorum animos ad audiciam et fortitudinem, magnanimitatem et liberalitatem commoveat, quae omnia faciunt ad bonum regimen. Est enim cantus iste de delectabili materia et ardua, sicut de amicitia et caritate, et ex omnibus longis et perfectis efficitur." See Aubrey, "Genre." Recall Jean de Garlande's discussion of classes of persons.

67. See Joan M. Ferrante, "Was Vernacular Poetic Practice a Response to Latin Language Theory?" on the extent to which troubadours were aware of Latin and Occitan grammar; Sarah Spence, *Rhetorics of Reason and Desire*; and Douglas Kelly, "The Poem as Art of Poetry: The Rhetoric of Imitation."

68. Recent studies on reception and intertextuality, such as Jörn Gruber, *Die Dialektik des Trobar* and Maria Luisa Meneghetti, *Il pubblico dei trovatori*, demonstrate the influences that composers had on one another.

69. See Aubrey, "Genre."

70. PC 62,1; Appel, ed., *Bernart von Ventadorn*, 301 (emphasis added). See Aubrey, "References," 112.

71. PC 457,8; Jeanroy and Salverda de Grave, *Uc de Saint-Circ*, #20, verses 1–9.

72. I am grateful to Elizabeth W. Poe for this observation.

4. Genre

1. Hans-Robert Jauss, "Littérature médiévale et théories des genres," 80. See also Pierre Bec, "Le problème des genres chez les premiers troubadours"; and GRLMA.

2. Including the present author. See Aubrey, "Genre."

3. Jauss, "Littérature médiévale," 88–89.

4. Roger Dragonetti, *La technique poétique des trouvères*.

5. Alfred Jeanroy, *La poésie lyrique*, I:132–144.

6. Paul Zumthor, in *Essai de poétique médiévale*, broadened the concept to incorporate "forms of discourse," meaning semantic and linguistic content of the texts, the personal or impersonal relation of the poet to the text, and whether or not the text was sung aloud to a public, all subsumed under the notion of the song's "register." He further explored the idea of a song's orality and its lack of fixity (*mouvance,*) as defining characteristics, in *La lettre et la voix*. Bec, "Problème des genres," 32, offers this definition of a genre: "Une *mouvance typologique*, du registre, qui est une sorte de mouvance thématique ou de dominante isotopique autour de laquelle s'organise le contenu de la pièce," and says that frequency of performance of songs within a certain such register led to "stratification" of a genre.

7. Christopher Page, *Voices and Instruments*. See also Zumthor, *Essai de poétique médiévale*.

8. Friedrich Gennrich's *Grundriss einer Formenlehre des mittelalterlichen Liedes* was useful in bringing to the fore the variety of musical genres and structures extant, but its scheme of classification is now seen as too simplistic and rigid.

9. Pierre Bec, *La lyrique française au moyen âge*.

10. Douglas Kelly, *The Arts of Poetry and Prose*.

11. See, for example, the recent study by Timothy McGee of Grocheio's description of dance forms, "Medieval Dances: Matching the Repertory with Grocheio's Descriptions."

12. See Jauss, "Littérature médiévale"; Zumthor, *Essai;* Bec, "Problème des genres"; Ulrich Mölk, *Trobadorlyrik: Eine Einführung;* Paden, "System."

13. In that regard see Aubrey, "References."

14. See Wulf Arlt, "Musica e testo," who applies some of these ideas to songs by Marcabru, Jaufre Rudel, Folquet de Marselha, and Guiraut de Bornelh.

15. See Amelia E. Van Vleck, *Memory and Re-Creation,* 71–90.

16. See Gérard Gonfroy, "Les genres lyriques," for a recent discussion of these treatises and their treatment of genre.

17. John W. Marshall, *Razos,* 2. See Elizabeth W. Poe, *From Poetry to Prose,* 67–69.

18. Marshall, *Razos,* 6.

19. This *razo* is the same as rhetoric's *materia,* as confirmed in an anonymous treatise of the late thirteenth to mid-fourteenth century, now in Barcelona, the so-called Ripoll treatise, which consistently uses the word "materia" to refer to the subject matter of the poem: "The subject of the canso is love or the praise of ladies. . . ." (La materia de les cancons es de amor o de lahor de dones . . .). Marshall, *Razos,* 101. See also Jörn Gruber, "L'art poétique de Jaufre Rudel," 17–18.

20. Marshall, *Razos,* 22.

21. Ibid., 56–57.

22. Ian Parker, "The Performance of Troubadour and Trouvère Songs," quotes selectively from this and other treatises, as well as from other Occitan and Old French literature, to glean descriptions of performance practices appropriate to various genres.

23. Marshall, *Razos,* 95.

24. Cf. Wulf Arlt, "Secular Monophony," 66.

25. Joan M. Ferrante, "'Ab joi mou lo vers e'l comens,'" 134–137, offers a detailed analysis of another *canso* by Bernart along these lines. See also Leo Treitler, "The Troubadours Singing Their Poems," 26f.

26. See Carl Appel, ed., *Bernart,* 249–250. Van Vleck, *Memory and Re-Creation,* argues that changing the sequence of stanzas was part of the aesthetic of troubadour performance, and that each version extant is a legitimate version of the song.

27. Except for some redistribution of the notes over text in verse 5 of G's version (see van der Werf, *Extant Troubadour Melodies,* 70*). Matthew Steel, in "A Case for the Predominance of Melody over Text in Troubadour Lyric," points out the discrepancy in the rhyme scheme in verses 3 and 4 of manuscript G. This occurs, however, only in stanza 1. The following stanzas have the same scheme as in manuscripts W and R, so the scribe of G simply transposed the two verses in stanza 1.

28. See a different analysis, with somewhat different conclusions, by Leo Treitler, "Troubadours Singing," 27–29. Steel ("Predominance") analyzes R's version of this song, with its different stanza order, in a way that is consistent with my analysis.

29. See William D. Paden, ed., *The Medieval Pastourelle,* I:36.

30. Marshall, *Razos,* 96.

31. See William D. Paden, "Reading Pastourelles," 3–7, for an analysis of this text in the context of the development of the genre.

32. Dietmar Rieger, *Gattungen und Gattungsbezeichnungen der Trobadorlyrik,*

269–301, discusses the poetic style of the *planh*. Marshall (*Razos*, 138 nn.58–60) refers to two cases of melodic borrowing, but he apparently means poetic modeling; the poems he mentions do not survive with melodies, so musical borrowing can only be inferred.

33. Marshall, *Razos*, 96.

34. Its melody later served an Old French *plaint* text, which might mean that the French author heard something in the music that struck him as being appropriate for any lament. See Aubrey, "Genre." Its rhymes were used in 1266 by an unknown author for a lament (PC 461,234) on the death of King Manfred of Sicily, son of Friedrich II.

35. Vincent Pollina, "Word/Music Relations," and "Troubadours dans le nord," 268–273, suggests ways in which different scribes accommodated text to notes in these verses.

36. Marshall, *Razos*, 96. Poe, in "New Light on the *Alba*: A Genre Redefined," identifies eighteen extant poems that meet her definition of the genre.

37. Josef Zemp, *Cadenet*, 249–257.

38. See van der Werf, *Extant Troubadour Melodies*, 77*. See Poe, "La Transmission de l'*alba* en ancien provençal," for the interesting hypothesis that the extant *albas* were collected in a single manuscript that served as an exemplar for the chansonniers that survive. Poe suggests that this collection contained the two melodies by Guiraut and Cadenet. If so, it is curious that this exemplar did not give melodies for any of the other *albas*—perhaps because Guiraut's melody could have been adapted for them as well?

39. Marshall, *Razos*, 97.

40. Marshall, *Donatz*, 230.

41. There is some disagreement about what to call "Qui la ve en ditz." Unlike other *descorts*, it has three stanzas with the same rhyme scheme (albeit not the same rhymes). István Frank, *Répertoire métrique de la poésie des troubadours* (528:1), considered the song to be a *canso*, while both PC and Gennrich, *Der musikalische Nachlass der Troubadours*, label it a *descort*. See Dominique Billy, "Le *descort* occitan: Réexamen critique du corpus," 5. I regard it as a *descort* because of its poetic structure and because double-cursus structure does appear in one version of its melody. See Aubrey, "Issues." The other *descorts* with melodies are PC 205,5 (see below) and 461,37.

42. William P. Shepard and Frank M. Chambers, *Aimeric de Peguilhan*, 216.

43. Ibid., 214–215; Aubrey, "Issues," 75–77.

44. Jean Maillard examines this melody in "Descort, que me veux-tu?...."

45. See Aubrey, "Issues," 76, where it is suggested that Aimeric was not the author of the music in W.

46. Marshall, *Razos*, 95. Such a description applies less accurately to Old Occitan *lays* than to Old French *lais*, many of which are sacred. See Bec, *La lyrique française*, I:197 and 201.

47. See Aubrey, "Issues."

48. Bec, *La lyrique française*, I:204–206.

49. The complete melody, in diplomatic facsimile, is in Aubrey, "Issues."

50. See Frank M. Chambers, "Imitation of Form in the Old Provençal Lyric." For a thorough discussion of the *sirventes* see Rieger, *Gattungen*.

51. Marshall, *Razos*, 95–96.

52. Ibid., 97.

53. See Paden, et al., *Bertran de Born*, 44–48, which points out that Bertran was one of the earliest troubadours to borrow extensively from others and to have inspired imitation of his own works by his contemporaries and successors.

54. Manuscripts R and C contain several verses that are not found in what is

generally considered the central manuscript tradition for this poem; they are enough to form an additional stanza. But in these two sources the verses in the second part of the first four stanzas are combined differently than in the other tradition, making the stanza order difficult to compare between the sources. The text given here is as edited by Paden, et al., *Bertran de Born*, 195–203.

55. See Paden, *The Medieval Pastourelle*. See also Michel Zink, *La Pastourelle: Poésie et folklore au moyen âge*, on the complex traditions of the Occitanian *pastorela*, in contrast with those of the Old French *pastourelle*.

56. Marshall, *Razos*, 97.

57. BS, xvii and 465–468.

58. See Aubrey, "References" and "Genre." The point of Raimbaut's *razo* may not have been to explain a compositional procedure which might have been considered unusual, but to romanticize the state of mind of poor Raimbaut, who was so despondent that he was unable to create his own music and had to borrow another's.

59. Marshall suggests that the "responedor" mentioned in the *Doctrina* refers to some kind of musical rhyme at the ends of verses, as in the *descort* (*Razos*, 139, nn.72–74), but this does not occur in "Kalenda maia." See also Timothy G. McGee, "Medieval Dances," 500ff.; Aubrey, "Genre," nn.61 and 62; and Lloyd Hibberd, "Estampie and Stantipes."

60. See John H. Marshall, "Pour l'étude des *contrafacta* dans la poésie des troubadours."

61. Marshall, *Razos*, 96; see 138 n.52–6.

62. Ibid., 98.

63. Bec, *La lyrique française*, I:239; see Aubrey, "Genre," n.51.

64. Page argues that the explicit connection of dance types with instruments, in the *Doctrina* and other treatises of the late thirteenth century and early fourteenth, along with the silence on instruments in the paragraphs on the more serious genres, is compelling evidence that "High Style" songs were unaccompanied (*Voices and Instruments*, 41–46). It is worth considering, however, as Bec argues, that the extant dance types in Occitan are aristocratic genres in content, at least, and could be interpreted as belonging to the "High Style" (*La lyrique française*, passim). See below, Chapter 7.

65. Marshall, *Razos*, 98.

66. Emil Levy, *Petite dictionnaire provençal-français*, 175; and M. Raynouard, *Lexique romane*, III:201.

67. See Marshall, *Razos*, 141 n.124–5, which suggests that "en contan o en xantan" indicates a scribal hesitation over the reading, and that the author means only "singing." Elizabeth Poe (private communication) suggests that it might mean "recounting" or "telling."

68. Rohloff, *Grocheio*, 136. See Bec, *La lyrique française*, I:241ff.

69. Rohloff, *Grocheio*, 132.

70. See the edition of these pieces by Timothy J. McGee, *Medieval Instrumental Dances*.

71. Bec, *La lyrique française*, I:243–244. See also Patricia W. Cummins, "How Well Do Medieval Treatises Describe Extant Estampies?"

72. Marshall, *Razos*, 96.

73. Ibid., 137 n.40–4.

74. Bec, *La lyrique française*, I:199–206, argues that the term *descort* was peculiar mainly to the south and *lai* to the north, and that the only real difference between them was a closer association in the south of the genre with the courtly *canso*: "La seule différence entre les deux genres—qui n'est pas structurale—est peut-être la plus grande indépendance typologique du lai

français par rapport à la *canso*; alors que le descort occitan, pourtant conçu au départ comme une sorte de repoussoir formel de la *canso*, ne parvient pas à s'en émanciper . . ." (201–202).

75. See Aubrey, "Issues," for a discussion of defects in transmission of this and other *descorts*.

76. Marshall, *Razos*, 140, n.81–6.

77. Ibid. Jean Maillard, "Structures mélodiques complexes au Moyen Âge," should be consulted for a thorough discussion of the music and structures of Occitan and French *descorts*.

5. Form

1. *Exordium* or *principio, narratione, divisione, confirmatione, confutatione,* and *conclusione.* See Harry Caplan, *Ad Herennium,* 8–9, 184ff.

2. Ibid., 186–187: "Si causa nostra magnam difficultatem videbitur habere, ut nemo aequo animo principium possit audire. . . ."

3. Margaret Nims, *Poetria nova,* 18. Ernest Gallo, *Poetria nova,* 18: "Carminis ingressus, quasi verna facetus, honeste/introducat eam. Medium, quasi strenuus hospes,/hospitium sollemne paret. Finis, quasi praeco/cursus expleti, sub honore licentiet illam."

4. Traugott Lawler, *Parisiana poetria,* 52–53: "Post inuentionem et electionem materie sequitur de inchoatione et disposicione ipsius. In qualibet materia considerantur tria: principium, medium, et finis; (vel, principium, progressus, et operis conclusio, etc.). Preordinande sunt iste partes in mente, quia prius debet esse uerbum in mente quam sit in ore. . . . Si continget forsitan materiam esse poeticam, tunc possumus ordiri materiam aut secundum principium naturale aut secundum principium artificiale. Principium naturale est quando res narratur eo ordine quo geritur. . . . Principium artificiale est quando inchoamus a medio materie vel a fine. . . ."

5. Ibid., 160–161: "Rithmica est ars que docet rithmum facere. Rithmus sic describitur: rithmus est consonancia dictionum in fine similium, sub certo numero sine metricis pedibus ordinata. 'Consonancia' ponitur pro genere; est enim musica rerum et uocum consonancia, uel 'concordia discors' vel 'discordia concors.' 'Dictionum in fine similium' ponitur ad differenciam mellice. 'Sub certo numero' ponitur quia rithmi ex pluribus et paucioribus constant sillabis. 'Sine metricis pedibus' ponitur ad differenciam artis metrice. 'Ordinata' dicitur quia ordinate debent cadere dictiones in rithmo."

6. See Margot Fassler, "Accent."

7. John H. Marshall, *Razos,* 57.

8. Ibid., 60.

9. Some rhyme techniques are not apparent from this system, such as *rims derivatius,* the procedure of creating two or more rhyme words from a common root, such as *solelh/solelha, rai/raya, esmai/esmaya, sordei/sordeya* (PC 70,7). Other poetic phenomena also escape indication in this system. See below.

10. Friedrich Gennrich, ed., *Grundriss.*

11. Gennrich, *Der musikalische Nachlass;* he excludes motets and *contrafacta,* but includes the hybrid songs in the St. Agnes drama. Gennrich's system implies that the absence of repetition constitutes a form itself (*oda continua,* a term adopted from Dante).

12. Hendrick van der Werf, *Chansons,* 50–51, and *Extant Troubadour Melodies,* 30–31.

13. See István Frank, *Répertoire.*

14. See Frank Chambers, *Old Provençal Versification*, and Dominique Billy, *L'Architecture lyrique médiévale*.

15. Text and trans. Matilda Tomaryn Bruckner, Laurie Shepard, and Sarah White, *Songs of the Women Troubadours*, 7.

16. But see Amelia Van Vleck, *Memory and Re-Creation*, 71–90.

17. Text of manuscript R, from Rupert Pickens, ed., *Jaufré Rudel*, 178–181, emphasis added.

18. Martín de Riquer, *Los trovadores*, I:293.

19. Margaret Switten, "De la sextine: amour et musique chez Arnaut Daniel," ingeniously demonstrates relationships between the circularity of the poetic structure and certain features of the melody (especially the finals of the verses). The music is given below in Example 6–3. See also Klaus Kropfinger, "Dante e l'arte dei trovatori."

20. James J. Wilhelm, *Arnaut Daniel*, 4.

21. Aimo Sakari, *Guillem de Saint-Didier*, 154.

22. See Wendy Pfeffer, "Guilhem Molinier as Literary Critic," 210.

23. See Aubrey, "Issues."

24. See Chambers, *Versification*.

25. Gennrich, *Der musikalische Nachlass*, II:84. He uses Greek symbols: α β γ δ ε ζ.

26. Gennrich put variation symbols before and after the letter, showing whether the differences were at the beginning or the end of the phrase. But this still does not define the character or the extent of the variation.

27. Sic: other manuscripts read "cosirer" (anxiety).

28. Van der Werf, *Extant Troubadour Melodies*, 21*. See also Pollina, "Troubadours dans le nord," 265–268.

29. See Higini Anglès, "Les melodies del trobador Guiraut Riquier," and especially Chantal Phan, "Le style poético-musical de Guiraut Riquier."

30. See Gennrich, *Der musicalische Nachlass*, II:104; Aubrey, "A Study," 166–169.

31. This song is invoked in Chapter 2, where it is argued that music and text scribes were close collaborators in this section of manuscript R, in contrast to the rest of the codex. The rubric is in the main text hand, and it refers to the sign (*senhat*) in the music, which seems to have been drawn with the same ink as the notes themselves, most likely by the music notator. See also Aubrey, "A Study," 166–169; and Bertolucci, "Canzoniere," 227–240.

32. See Ian Parker, "Troubadour and Trouvère Song: Problems in Modal Analysis"; Hans Zingerle, *Tonalität und Melodieführung in den Klauseln der Troubadours- und Trouvèreslieder*.

33. See Aubrey, "A Study."

34. See Aubrey, "Forme et formule."

35. See similar analyses by Appel, "Uc Brunenc," 54ff. n.4; and Vincent Pollina, "*Canso* mélodique et *canso métrique*: *Era.m cosselhatz, Senhor* de Bernart de Ventadorn." See also Gisela Scherner-van Ortmerssen, *Die Text-Melodiestruktur in den Liedern des Bernart de Ventadorn*; Switten, *Raimon de Miraval*; and Chantal Phan, "Structures textuelles et mélodiques des chansons des troubadours."

36. See Nicolletta Gossen, "Musik und Text," 30–38, for a slightly different interpretation of these interrelationships.

6. Style

1. See Douglas Kelly, *The Arts of Poetry and Prose*, 66–67.

2. Margaret Nims, *Poetria nova*, 23–24. Ernest A. Gallo, *Poetria nova*, 24:

"Curritur in bivio: via namque vel ampla vel arta,/ vel fluvius vel rivus erit; vel tractius ibis,/ vel cursim salies; vel rem brevitate notabis,/ vel longo sermone trahes. . . . / Formula materiae, quasi quaedam formula cerae,/ primitus est tactus duri: si sedula cura/ igniat ingenium, subito mollescit ad ignem/ ingenii sequiturque manum quocumque vocarit,/ ductilis ad quicquid. Hominis manus interioris/ ducit ut amplificet vel curtet."

3. See James J. Murphy, *Rhetoric in the Middle Ages*, 365–374, which defines the figures of thought and diction found in *Rhetorica ad Herennium*.

4. Nims, *Poetria nova*, 43. Gallo, *Poetria nova*, 54: "Noli semper concedere verbo/ in proprio residere loco: residentia talis/ dedecus est ipsi verbo; loca propria vitet/ et perigrinetur alibi sedemque placentem/ fundet in alterius fundo: sit ibi novus hospes,/ et placeat novitate sua. . . ."

5. Nims, *Poetria nova*, 54–55. Gallo, *Poetria nova*, 70–71: "Sic tamen esto gravis ne res sub nube tegatur,/ sed faciant voces ad quod de jure tenentur./ Quae clausum reserent animum sunt verba reperta/ ut quaedam claves animi: qui vult aperire/ rem clausam, nolit verbis inducere nubem;/ si tamen induxit, facta est injuria verbis:/ fecit enim de clave seram. Sis claviger ergo,/ remque tuis verbis aperi. . . . Proprias igitur ne respice vires,/ immo suas, cum quo loqueris. Da pondera verbis/ aequa suis humeris et pro re verba loquaris."

6. Nims, *Poetria nova*, 56; Gallo, *Poetria nova*, 72: "quorum planities turpis ne terreat aures."

7. See Kelly, *Arts*, 79–81.

8. See Kelly, *Arts*; Frank M. Chambers, *Old Provençal Versification*.

9. Nims, *Poetria nova*, 82–83. Gallo, *Poetria nova*, 114: "Legibus arctetur metrum, sed prosa vagatur/ liberiore via, quia prosae publica strata/ admittit passim redas et plaustra; sed arta/ semita versiculi non vult tam grossa, sed ipsas/ voces in forma gracili, ne corpus agreste/ verbi mole sua perturbet et inquinet illum/ vultque venire metrum tanquam domicellula, compto/ crine, nitente gena, subtili corpore, forma/ egregia."

10. The definitive study is by Ulrich Mölk, *Trobar clus, trobar leu*. See also Alfred Jeanroy, *La poésie lyrique des troubadours*, II:13–61; Alberto Del Monte, *Studi sulla poesia ermetica medievale*; Jean Frappier, "Aspects de l'hermétisme dans la poésie médiévale"; Aurelio Roncaglia, "Trobar clus: Discussione aperta"; Erich Köhler, "Trobar clus: Discussion aperta; Marcabru und die beiden Schulen"; Chambers, *Versification*; and Linda Paterson, *Troubadours and Eloquence*.

11. Cited and translated in Paterson, *Troubadours*, 91–92 n.5.

12. Chambers, *Versification*, 99.

13. Ibid., 123.

14. See Jorn Grüber, "L'Art poétique de Jaufre Rudel" for arguments that Jaufre borrowed stylistically from his predecessor Guilhem de Peitieu.

15. See Alberto Varvaro, *Rigaut de Berbezilh*, 217.

16. Hendrik van der Werf, *Extant Troubadour Melodies*, 349*.

17. Stanislaw Stronski, *Folquet de Marselha*, 52*. See also D'Arco Silvio Avalle, *Peire Vidal*, 365–366.

7. Performance

1. Margaret Nims, *Poetria Nova*, 90. Ernest A. Gallo, *Poetria nova*, 124: "In recitante sonent tres linguae: prima sit oris,/altera rhetorici vultus, et tertia gestus./Sunt in voce suae leges, et eas ita serves:/clausula dicta suas pausas, et dictio servet/accentus. Voces quas sensus dividit, illas/divide; quas jungit, conjunge. Domes ita vocem,/ut non discordet a re, nec limite tendat/vox alio,

quam res intendat; eant simul ambae;/vox quaedam sit imago rei; res sicut habet se,/sic vocem recitator habe. Videamus in uno."

2. See Jean-Baptiste Beck, *Musique des troubadours*, plate XI; Joseph Anglade, "Les miniatures des chansonniers provençaux"; Martín de Riquer, *Los trovadores*, I:18–19; Geneviève Brunel-Lobrichon, "L'Iconographie"; Maria Luisa Meneghetti, *Il pubblico*; Sylvia Huot, "Visualization and Memory: The Illustration of Troubadour Lyric in a Thirteenth-Century Manuscript."

3. See Elizabeth Aubrey, "References."

4. See David Hiley, "The Plica and Liquescence," for a catalogue of *plicas* found in manuscript W in songs with French texts, and their coincidence with vowel and consonant combinations.

5. John H. Marshall, *Razos*, 60.

6. See Adolphe-F. Gatien-Arnoult, ed., *Las Flors del Gay Saber, estier dichas Las Leys d'Amors*, I:58.

7. Pierre Aubry, *La rhythmique musicale des troubadours et trouvères*; Beck, *Die Melodien*.

8. Friedrich Ludwig, "Die geistliche nichtliturgische, weltliche einstimmige und die mehrstimmige Musik des Mittelalters bis zum Anfang des 15. Jahrhunderts."

9. Friedrich Gennrich, ed., *Der musikalische Nachlass*.

10. Theodore Karp, in "Three Trouvère Chansons," argues that late trouvères, at least, might have been aware of modal theory as taught by theorists such as Franco of Cologne.

11. Uso Sesini, "Canzoniere," especially 53–101.

12. John Stevens, *Words and Music*.

13. Hendrik van der Werf, *Chansons*.

14. Van der Werf, "The 'Not-so-precisely Measured' Music of the Middle Ages," in which he also backs away from the term "declamatory."

15. "Others, however, divide music into plain, or immeasurable, and measurable [music]; understanding by 'plain' or 'immeasurable,' ecclesiastical [music], which is determined by many tones according to Gregory. By 'measurable' they understand that [music] which is effected by diverse sounds that are sounded and measured simultaneously, as in conductus and motets. But if by 'immeasurable' they understand music that is in no way measured—indeed totally said at will—their understanding is deficient, in that every operation of music and of any art whatever ought to be measured by the rules of that art. If, however by 'immeasurable' they *do not understand 'measured' so precisely*, it seems that this division can remain." Ernst Rohloff, *Grocheio*, 124: "Alii autem musicam dividunt in planam sive immensurabilem et mensurabilem, per planam sive immensurabilem intellegentes ecclesiasticam, quae secundum Gregorium pluribus tonis determinatur. Per mensurabilem intellegunt illam, quae ex diversis sonis simul mensuratis et sonantibus efficitur, sicut in conductibus et motetis. Sed si per immensurabilem intellegant musicam nullo modo mensuratam, immo totaliter ad libitum dictam, deficiunt, eo quod quaelibet operatio musicae et cuiuslibet artis debet illius artis regulis mensurari. Si autem per immensurabilem *non ita praecise mensuratam intellegant*, potest, ut videtur, ista divisio remanere" (emphasis added). See Christopher Page, "Johannes de Grocheio," 20.

16. Christopher Page, *Voices and Instruments*, 73–76.

17. This idea had already been expressed by John H. Marshall in a paper delivered in 1984 (published in 1987), "Une versification lyrique popularisante en ancien provençal," but based on a comparison of versifications in aristocratic and popular types. See 62–65.

18. Antonio Restori, "Per la storia musicale dei trovatori provenzali."

19. Raffaello Monterosso, *Musica e ritmica dei trovatori*.

20. Ewald Jammers, in *Ausgewählte Melodien des Minnesangs*; see also his *Aufzeichnungsweisen der einstimmigen ausserliturgischen Musik des Mittelalters*.

21. See, for instance, Gérard Le Vot, "Notation, mesure, et rythme dans la canso troubadouresque," and Le Vot, Pierre Lusson, and Jacques Roubaud, "La sextine d'Arnaut Daniel: Essai de lecture rythmique."

22. Robert Lug, "Melismen-Untersuchungen am Chansonnier de St.-Germain-des-Prés," "Singen auf dem Pferderücken: Indizien zur Rhythmik der Troubadours," and "Das 'vormodale' Zeichensystem des Chansonnier de Saint-Germain-des-Prés."

23. Cf. Wulf Arlt, "Secular Monophony," 68–72.

24. The "Occitanian" texts that appear in a few motets have been shown to be hybrid-language texts, perhaps the work of northern poets who were trying to evoke the sound of a distant tongue. See the Introduction.

25. Van der Werf, *Chansons*, 45.

26. See Theodore Karp, *The Polyphony of Saint Martial and Santiago de Compostela*, which uses modal rhythms.

27. Gilbert Reaney and André Gilles, eds., *Franconis de Colonia: Ars cantus mensurabilis*, 10.

28. Van der Werf, *Extant Troubadour Melodies*.

29. Aubrey, "A Study."

30. Van der Werf, *Extant Troubadour Melodies*, 225*–226*, gives diplomatic transcriptions of the neumes of these two songs above the staff of his modern transcriptions.

31. Page, *Voices and Instruments*, 17, Figure 2.

32. Pointed out by Carl Appel, *Singweisen*, 4.

33. See Frank M. Chambers, *Versification*, 123 and 129.

34. Cf. Leo Treitler, "Regarding Meter and Rhythm in the *Ars antiqua*," 546–548.

35. Van der Werf, "Not-so-precisely Measured," 49.

36. Van der Werf, *Chansons*, 19–21.

37. See Aubrey, "References."

38. BS, 408.

39. Ibid., 311.

40. Ibid., 254.

41. Aubrey, "References," 128.

42. Ibid., 118–121, 129–132.

43. "Mon chan fenis ab dol et ab maltraire," PC 80,26, stanza 3; William D. Paden et al., *Bertran de Born*, 220–221 (their translation, with minor changes).

44. Aubrey, "References," 129–130.

45. M. J. Hubert and M. E. Porter, *The Romance of Flamenca*, 58.

46. Arthur S. Kimmel, *The Old Provençal Epic "Daurel et Beton,"* line 1180.

47. Jean Boutière, ed., "Albertet," 55. See Joel Cohen, "Peirol's Vielle: Instrumental Participation in the Troubador [sic] Repertory."

48. Alberto del Monte, *Peire d'Alvernha*, 127.

49. Page, *Voices and Instruments*, 25.

50. Ibid., 32.

51. Ibid., 38.

52. Page dismisses the *razo* about Raimbaut's use of a northern fiddle tune for his "Kalenda maia" with the comment that "the combination of a High Style text and a Lower Style melody is part of the wit of the piece—for it is a flamboyantly Lower Style tune, packed with conspicuous and short-range patternings" (ibid., 49).

53. Ibid., 51–52.

54. Ibid., 74.
55. Sylvia Huot, *From Song to Book.*
56. Van der Werf, *Extant Troubadour Melodies,* 38–61.
57. Ibid., 41.
58. Ibid.
59. Ibid., 43.
60. Ibid., 46.
61. Ibid., 42–43.

BIBLIOGRAPHY

REFERENCE WORKS

Anglade, Joseph. *Grammaire de l'ancien provençal ou ancienne langue d'oc.* Paris: Klincksieck, 1921.

Bec, Pierre. *La langue occitane.* 5th ed. Paris: Presses Universitaires de France, 1986.

Brunel, Clovis. *Bibliographie des manuscrits littéraires en ancien provençal.* Paris, 1935; repr. Geneva: Droz, 1973.

Frank, István. *Répertoire métrique de la poésie des troubadours.* 2 vols. Paris: Champion, 1953, 1957.

Grandgent, C. H. *An Outline of the Phonology and Morphology of Old Provençal.* Boston: D. C. Heath, 1905; repr. New York: AMS Press, 1973.

Hamlin, Frank R.; Peter T. Ricketts; and John Hathaway. *Introduction à l'étude de l'ancien provençal; textes d'étude.* 2d ed. Geneva: Droz, 1985.

Hasenohr, Geneviève, and Michel Zink, eds. *Dictionnaire des lettres françaises: Le Moyen Âge.* Paris: Fayard, 1993.

Jeanroy, Alfred. *Bibliographie sommaire des chansonniers provençaux.* Classiques français du moyen âge, 18. Paris: Champion, 1916; repr. 1966.

Levy, Emil. *Petit dictionnaire provençal-français.* 5th ed. Heidelberg: Winter, 1973.
———. *Provenzalisches Supplement-Wörterbuch.* 8 vols. Leipzig: Reisland, 1894–1924.

Mok, Q. I. M. *Manuel pratique de morphologie d'ancien occitan.* Muiderberg: Coutinho, 1977.

Mölk, Ulrich, and Friedrich Wolfzettel. *Répertoire métrique de la poésie lyrique française des origines à 1350.* Munich: Fink, 1972.

Pillet, Alfred, and Henry Carstens. *Bibliographie der Troubadours.* Halle: Niemeyer, 1933.

Raynouard, François-Just-Marie. *Lexique romane, ou Dictionnaire de la langue des troubadours.* 6 vols. Paris: Silvestre, 1838–44.

Schwan, Eduard. *Die altfranzösischen Liederhandschriften: ihr Verhältniss, ihre Entstehung und ihre Bestimmung.* Berlin: Weidmann, 1886.

Smith, Nathaniel B., and Thomas G. Bergin. *An Old Provençal Primer.* New York: Garland, 1984.

Spanke, Hans, ed. *G. Raynauds Bibliographie des altfranzösischen Liedes, erster Teil,* ergänzt mit einer Diskographie und einem Register der Lieder nach Anfangsbuchstaben hergestellt von A. Bahat. Leiden: Brill, 1980.

Switten, Margaret L. *Music and Poetry in the Middle Ages: A Guide to Research on French and Occitan Song, 1100–1400.* New York: Garland, 1995.

Taylor, Robert A. *La Littérature occitane du moyen âge: Bibliographie sélective et critique.* Toronto: University of Toronto Press, 1977.

300 BIBLIOGRAPHY

MUSIC EDITIONS

Appel, Carl. *Die Singweisen Bernarts von Ventadorn, nach den Handschriften mitgeteilt.* Beihefte zur Zeitschrift für romanische Philologie, 81. Halle: Niemeyer, 1934.

Beck, Jean, and Louise Beck. *Les Chansonniers des Troubadours et des Trouvères, 2: Le Manuscrit du Roi, fonds français no. 844 de la Bibliothèque nationale. Reproduction Phototypique publié avec une introduction.* 2 vols. Philadelphia: University of Pennsylvania Press, 1938.

Fernández de la Cuesta, Ismael. *Las cançons dels trobadors.* Toulouse: Institut d'estudis occitans, 1979.

Gennrich, Friedrich, ed. *Der musikalische Nachlass der Troubadours.* 3 vols. Summa Musicae Medii Aevi, 3, 4, 15. Darmstadt and Langen-bei-Frankfurt: Gennrich, 1958–65.

McGee, Timothy J. *Medieval Instrumental Dances.* Bloomington: Indiana University Press, 1989.

Meyer, Paul, and Gaston Raynaud, eds. *Le Chansonnier français de Saint-Germain-des-Prés (Bibl. Nat. fr. 20050): Reproduction phototypique avec transcription.* Paris: Société des Anciens Textes Français, 1892; repr. New York: Johnson, 1968.

Sesini, Ugo. "Le melodie trobadoriche nel canzoniere provenzale della Biblioteca Ambrosiana (R. 71 sup.)," *Studi Medievali,* 12 (1939):1–101; 13 (1940):1–107; and 14 (1941):31–105.

Van der Werf, Hendrik. *The Extant Troubadour Melodies; Transcriptions and Essays for Performers and Scholars.* Rochester, NY: The author, 1984.

TEXT EDITIONS

Almqvist, Kurt. *Poésies du troubadour Guilhem Adémar.* Uppsala: Almqvist & Wiksells, 1951.

Anglade, Joseph, ed. *Las Flors del Gay Saber.* Memòries, Institut d'Estudis Catalans, Secció filològica, 1/2. Barcelona: Institució Patxot, 1926.

———, ed. *"Las Leys d'amors," manuscrit de l'Académie des Jeux Floraux.* 4 vols. Bibliothèque méridionale, 17–20. Toulouse: Privat, 1919–20; repr. New York: Johnson, 1971.

Appel, Carl, ed. *Bernart von Ventadorn, seine Lieder, mit Einleitung und Glossar.* Halle: Niemeyer, 1915.

———, ed. *Der Trobador Cadenet.* Halle: Niemeyer, 1920; repr. Geneva: Slatkine, 1974.

———, ed. "Der Trobador Uc Brunec (oder Brunenc)." In *Abhandlungen Herrn Prof. Dr. Adolf Tobler zur feier seiner fünfundzwanzigjährigen Thätigkeit als ordentlicher Professor an der Universität Berlin von Dankbaren Schülern in Ehrerbietung Dargebracht.* Halle: Niemeyer, 1895. Pp. 45–78.

Aston, Stanley C. *Peirol, Troubadour of Auvergne.* Cambridge: Cambridge University Press, 1953.

Audiau, Jean. *Les poésies des quatre troubadours d'Ussel.* Paris: Delagrave, 1922.

Avalle, d'Arco Silvio. *Peire Vidal: Poesie.* 2 vols. Documenti di filologia, 4. Milan: Ricciardi, 1960.

Beretta Spampinato, Margherita. *Berenguer de Palol, Poesie.* Modena: Mucchi, 1978.

Bertoni, Giulio. *Il canzoniere provenzale della Biblioteca Ambrosiana, R. 71 sup.: Edizione diplomatica preceduta da un'introduzione.* Dresden: Gesellschaft für romanische Literatur, 1912.

Bond, Gerald A., ed. and trans. *The Poetry of William VII, Count of Poitiers, IX Duke of Aquitaine.* New York: Garland, 1982.

Boutière, Jean. "Les poésies du troubadour Albertet," *Studi medievali* 10 (1937):1–129.

Boutière, Jean, and A.-H. Schutz. *Biographies des troubadours*. 2d ed. Paris: Nizet, 1964.

Braccini, Mauro. *Rigaut de Barbezieux: Le canzoni, testo e commento*. Florence: L. S. Olschki, 1960.

Bruckner, Matilda Tomaryn; Laurie Shepard; and Sarah White, eds. *Songs of the Women Troubadours*. New York: Garland Publishing, Inc. 1995.

Burgwinkle, William E., trans. *Razos and Troubadour Songs*. New York: Garland, 1990.

Butler, H. E., ed. and trans. *The Institutio Oratoria of Quintilian*. 4 vols. Loeb Classical Library. Cambridge: Harvard University Press, 1920–1922.

Calzolari, Monica, ed. *Il trovatore Guillem Augier Novella*. Modena: Mucchi, 1986.

Caplan, Harry, ed. and trans. *[Cicero]: Ad C. Herennium, De ratione dicendi (Rhetorica ad Herennium)*. Loeb Classical Library. Cambridge: Harvard University Press, 1981.

Casas Homs, José Maria, ed. *Joan de Castellnou, Obras en Prosa: I. Compendi de la coneixença del vicis en els dictats del Gai Saber; II. Glosari al Doctrinal de Ramon de Cornet*. Barcelona: Fundació Salvador Vives Casajuana, 1969.

Cavaliere, Alfredo. *Le poesie di Peire Raimon de Tolosa (Introduzione, testi, traduzioni, note)*. Biblioteca dell' Archivum romanicum, 22. Florence: Olschki, 1935.

Chaytor, Henry J. *Les chansons de Perdigon*. Classiques français du moyen âge, 53. Paris: Champion, 1926.

Dejeanne, Jean-M. L. *Poésies complètes du troubadour Marcabru*. Bibliothèque méridionale, 12. Toulouse: Privat, 1909; repr. New York: Johnson, 1971.

Del Monte, Alberto. *Peire d'Alvernha: Liriche; testo, traduzione, e note*. Turin: Loescher-Chiantore, 1955.

Dumitrescu, Maria., ed. *Poésies du troubadour Aimeric de Belenoi*. Paris: Société des Anciens Textes Français, 1935.

Egan, Margarita, trans. *The Vidas of the Troubadours*. New York: Garland, 1984.

Faral, Edmond. *Les arts poétiques du XIIe et du XIIIe siècle; recherches et documents sur la technique littéraire du moyen âge*. Paris: Champion, 1924.

Gallo, Ernest A. *The Poetria Nova and Its Sources in Early Rhetorical Doctrine*. The Hague: Mouton, 1971.

Gatien-Arnoult, Adolphe-F., ed. *Las Flors del Gay Saber, estier dichas Las Leys d'Amors*. 3 vols. Monumens de la littérature romane, 1–3. Toulouse: Privat, 1841–43.

Goldin, Frederick. *Lyrics of the Troubadours and Trouvères: An Anthology and a History*. Garden City, New York: Anchor Books, 1973.

Gougaud, Henri, ed. and trans. *La chanson de la Croisade Albigeoise*. Paris: Librairie Générale Française, 1989.

Gouiran, Gérard. *L'Amour et la Guerre: L'oeuvre de Bertran de Born*. 2 vols. Aix-en-Provence: Université de Provence, 1985.

———. *Le Seigneur-troubadour d'Hautefort: L'oeuvre de Bertran de Born*. 2d ed. Aix-en-Provence: Université de Provence, 1987.

Hoby, Otto. *Die Lieder des Trobadors Guiraut d'Espanha*. Freiburg: St. Paulusdruckerei, 1915.

Hoepffner, Ernest. *Le troubadour Peire Vidal, sa vie et son oeuvre*. Paris: Les Belles Lettres, 1961.

Hubbell, H. M., ed. and trans. *Cicero: De inventione, De optimo genero oratorum, Topica*. Loeb Classical Library. Cambridge: Harvard University Press, 1976.

Hubert, M. J., and M. E. Porter, eds. *The Romance of Flamenca: A Provençal Poem of the Thirteenth Century.* Princeton: Princeton University Press, 1962.

Jeanroy, Alfred, and J.-J. Salverda de Grave. *Poésies de Uc de Saint-Circ.* Toulouse: Privat, 1913.

Jeanroy, Alfred; Louis Brandin; and Pierre Aubry. *Lais et descorts français du XIIIe siècle.* Paris: Welter, 1901; repr. New York: AMS Press, 1975.

Johnston, Ronald C. *Les poésies lyriques du troubadour Arnaut de Mareuil.* Paris: Droz, 1935; repr. Geneva: Slatkine, 1973.

Kimmel, Arthur S., ed. *The Old Provençal Epic "Daurel et Beton."* Chapel Hill: University of North Carolina Press, 1971.

Kjellman, Hilding. *Le troubadour Raimon Jordan, vicomte de Saint-Antonin, édition critique accompagnée d'une étude sur le dialecte parlé dans la vallée de l'Aveyron au XIIe siècle.* Upsala and Paris: Almqvist, 1922.

Klein, Otto, ed. *Der Troubadour Blacassetz.* Städtische Realschule zu Wiesbaden, Jahres-Bericht über das Schuljahr 1886/86. Wiesbaden: Carl Ritter, 1887.

Kolsen, Adolf. *Sämtliche Lieder des Trobadors Giraut de Bornelh, mit Übersetzung, Kommentar, und Glossar.* 2 vols. Halle: Niemeyer, 1910–1935; repr. Geneva: Slatkine, 1976.

Kussler-Ratyé, Gabrielle. "Les chansons de la Comtesse Béatrix de Dia," *Archivum romanicum* 1 (1917):161–182.

La Salle de Rochemaure, Félix de. *Les troubadours cantaliens.* 2 vols. Aurillac: Imprimerie Moderne, 1910; repr. Geneva: Slatkine, 1977.

Lavaud, René, ed. *Poésies complètes du troubadour Peire Cardenal (1180–1278).* Toulouse: Privat, 1957.

Lawler, Traugott, ed. and trans. *The Parisiana poetria of John of Garland.* New Haven: Yale University Press, 1974.

Lazar, Moshé, ed. *Bernard de Ventadorn, troubadour du XIIe siècle: Chansons d'amour.* Paris: Klincksieck, 1966.

Linskill, Joseph. *The Poems of the Troubadour Raimbaut de Vaqueiras.* The Hague: Mouton, 1964.

Marigo, Aristide, ed. *Dante Alighieri: De vulgari eloquentia.* Florence: Le Monnier, 1957.

Marshall, John H., ed. *The "Donatz Proensals" of Uc Faidit.* London: Oxford University Press, 1969.

———, ed. *The "Razos de trobar" of Raimon Vidal and Associated Texts.* London: Oxford University Press, 1972.

Mölk, Ulrich. *Guiraut Riquer: Las Cansos.* Heidelberg: Winter, 1962.

Mouzat, Jean. *Les poèmes de Gaucelm Faidit, troubadour du XIIe siècle.* Paris: Nizet, 1965.

Müller, Johannes. "Die Gedichte des Guillem Augier Novella," *Zeitschrift für romanische Philologie* 23 (1899):47–78.

Napolski, Max von. *Leben und Werke des Trobadors Ponz de Capduoill.* Halle: Niemeyer, 1879.

Newcombe, Terence H. "The Troubadour Berenger de Palazol: A Critical Edition of His Poems," *Nottingham Medieval Studies* 15 (1971):54–95.

Naudieth, Fritz. *Der Trobador Guillem Magret.* Halle: Niemeyer, 1914.

Niestroy, Erich. *Der Trobador Pistoleta.* Beihefte zur Zeitschrift für romanische Philologie, 52. Halle: Niemeyer, 1914.

Nims, Margaret F., trans. *Poetria nova of Geoffrey of Vinsauf.* Toronto: Pontifical Institute of Mediaeval Studies, 1967.

Paden, William D., ed. and trans. *The Medieval Pastourelle.* 2 vols. Garland Library of Medieval Literature, A/34–35. New York: Garland, 1987.

Paden, William D.; Tilde Sankovitch; and Patricia H. Stäblein, eds. *The Poems of the Troubadour Bertran de Born*. Berkeley: University of California Press, 1986.

Panvini, Bruno. *Le biografie provenzali, valore e attendibilità*. Biblioteca dell' Archivum Romanicum. Florence: Olschki, 1952.

Pattison, Walter T. *The Life and Works of the Troubadour Raimbaut d'Orange*. Minneapolis: University of Minnesota Press, 1952.

Perugi, Maurizio, ed. *Le canzoni di Arnaut Daniel*. 2 vols. Milan and Naples: Ricciardi, 1978.

Pickens, Rupert T., ed. *The Songs of Jaufre Rudel*. Toronto: The Pontifical Institute of Mediaeval Studies, 1978.

Poli, Andrea. *Aimeric de Belenoi: Saggio di edizione critica*. Naples: Edizioni Scientifiche Italiane, 1993.

Reaney, Gilbert, and André Gilles, eds. *Franconis de Colonia, Ars cantus mensurabilis*. Corpus Scriptorum de Musica, 18. [Rome]: American Institute of Musicology, 1974.

Rieger, Angelica. *Trobairitz: Der Beitrag der Frau in der altokzitanischen höfischen Lyrik. Edition des Gesamtkorpus*. Beihefte zur Zeitschrift für romanischen Philologie, 233. Tübingen: Niemeyer, 1991.

Riquer, Martín de. *Los trovadores: Historia, literaria y textos*. 3 vols. Barcelona: Ariel, 1975.

Rohloff, Ernst, ed. *Die Quellenhandschriften zum Musiktraktat des Johannes de Grocheio, im Faksimile herausgegeben nebst Übertragung des Textes und Übersetzung ins Deutsche, dazu Bericht, Literaturschau, Tabellen und Indices*. Leipzig: Deutscher Verlag für Musik, 1967.

Routledge, Michael J., ed. *Les poésies du Moine de Montaudon*. Montpellier: Centres d'Études Occitanes de l'Université Paul Valéry, 1977.

Ruffini, Mario. *Il trovatore Aimeric de Belenoi*. Turin, 1951.

Sakari, Aimo, ed. *Poésies du troubadour Guillem de Saint-Didier, publiées avec introduction, traduction, notes, et glossaire*. Mémoires de la Société Néophilologique de Helsinki, 19. Helsinki: Société Néophilologique, 1956.

Schutz, A.-H. *Poésies de Daude de Pradas*. Paris: Didier, 1933.

Shepard, William P., and Frank M. Chambers, eds. *The Poems of Aimeric de Peguilhan*. Evanston: Northwestern University Press, 1950.

Stronski, Stanislaw, ed. *Le troubadour Folquet de Marseille; édition critique précédée d'une étude biographique et littéraire et suivie d'une traduction, d'un commentaire historique, de notes, et d'un glossaire*. Cracow: Spolka Widawnicza Polska, 1910.

Switten, Margaret L., ed. and trans. *The Cansos of Raimon de Miraval: A Study of Poems and Melodies*. Cambridge, MA: Medieval Academy of America, 1985.

Toja, Gianluigi, ed. *Arnaut Daniel: Canzoni. Edizione critica, studie introduttivo, commento, e traduzione*. Florence: Sansoni, 1960.

Topsfield, Leslie T. *Les poésies du troubadour Raimon de Miraval, édition critique et traduction française*. Paris: Nizet, 1971.

Varvaro, Alberto. *Rigaut de Berbezilh: Liriche*. Biblioteca di filologia romanza, 4. Bari: Adriatica, 1960.

Wilhelm, James J. *The Poetry of Arnaut Daniel*. New York: Garland, 1981.

Wolf, George, and Roy Rosenstein, ed. and trans. *The Poetry of Cercamon and Jaufre Rudel*. New York: Garland, 1983.

Wright, Thomas, ed. *Johannis de Garlandia, De triumphis Ecclesiae libri octo: A Latin Poem of the Thirteenth Century*. London: Nichols and Sons, 1856.

Zemp, Josef, ed. *Les poésies du troubadour Cadenet*. Berne: Lang, 1978.

Zenker, Rudolf. *Die Lieder Peires von Auvergne, kritisch herausgegeben mit Einleitung, Übersetzung, Kommentar, und Glossar*. Erlangen: Junge, 1900.

STUDIES

Abulafia, David. *Commerce and Conquest in the Mediterranean, 1100–1500.* Brookfield, VT: Variorum, 1993.

Anglade, Joseph. "À propos de Peire Vidal," *Romania* 49 (1923):105–107.

———. "Les miniatures des chansonniers provençaux," *Romania* 50 (1924):593–604.

———. *Le troubadour Guiraut Riquier; Étude sur la décadence de l'ancienne poésie provençale.* Bordeaux: Feret et fils, 1905; repr. Geneva: Slatkine, 1973.

Anglès, Higini. "Les melodies del trobador Guiraut Riquier," *Revista dels Estudis universitaris catalans* 11 (1926):1–78.

Appel, Carl. "Zu Marcabru," *Zeitschrift für romanische Philologie* 43 (1923):403–469.

Arlt, Wulf. "Musica e testo nel canto francese: dai primi trovatori al mutamento stilistico intorno al 1300." In *La Musica nel Tempo di Dante: Ravenna, Comune di Ravenna, Opera di Dante, Musica/Realtà, 12–14 settembre 1986*, ed. Luigi Pestalozza. Milan: Unicopli, 1988. Pp. 175–197 and 306–321.

———. "The 'Reconstruction' of Instrumental Music: the Interpretation of the Earliest Practical Sources." In *Studies in the Performance of Late Mediaeval Music*, ed. Stanley Boorman. Cambridge: Cambridge University Press, 1983. Pp. 75–100.

———. "Secular Monophony." In *Performance Practice: Music Before 1600*, ed. Howard Mayer Brown and Stanley Sadie. New York: Norton, 1989. Pp. 55–78.

———. "Zur Interpretation zweier Lieder: *A madre de Deus* und *Reis glorios*," *Basler Jahrbuch für historische Musikpraxis* 1 (1977):117–130.

Asperti, Stefano. "La data di 'Pos Peire d'Alvernh'a cantat,'" *Studi provenzali e francesi 86/87, Romanica Vulgaria*, Quaderni 10/11 (Rome, 1989):127–135.

Aubrey, Elizabeth. "Forme et formule dans les mélodies des troubadours." In *Actes du Premier Congrès Internationale de l'Association Internationale d'Études Occitanes*, ed. Peter T. Ricketts. London: Westfield College, 1987. Pp. 69–83.

———. "Genre as a Determinant of Melody in the Songs of the Troubadours and the Trouvères." In *Historicizing Genre in Medieval Lyric*, ed. William D. Paden. Champaign: University of Illinois Press, forthcoming.

———. "Issues in the Musical Analysis of the Troubadour Descorts and Lais." In *The Cultural Milieu of the Troubadours and Trouvères: A Symposium at California State University, Northridge, December 7–8, 1990*, ed. Nancy van Deusen. Ottawa: Institute for Mediaeval Music, 1994. Pp. 76–98.

———. "Literacy, Orality, and the Preservation of French and Occitan Medieval Courtly Songs." In *Actas del XV Congreso de la Sociedad Internacional de Musicología, "Culturas musicales mediterráneo y sus ramificaciones," Madrid/ 3–10/IV/1992*, ed. Sociedad Española de Musicología. *Revista de Musicología* 16/4 (1993 [1996]): 2355–66.

———. "References to Music in Old Occitan Literature," *Acta Musicologica* 61 (1989):110–149.

———. "A Study of the Origins, History, and Notation of the Troubadour Chansonnier Paris, Bibliothèque nationale, f. fr. 22543." Ph.D. diss., University of Maryland, 1982.

———. "The Transmission of Troubadour Melodies: The Testimony of Paris, Bibliothèque nationale, f. fr. 22543," *Text* 3 (1987):211–250.

———. "Troubadour Research and Performing Practice Today." In *Atti del XIV Congresso della Società Internazionale di Musicologia: Trasmissione e recezione delle forme di cultura musicale, Bologna, 27 agosto–1 settembre 1987*, II: *Study*

Sessions, ed. Angelo Pompilio, Donatella Restani, Lorenzo Bianconi, and F. Alberto Gallo. Turin: EDT, 1990. Pp. 19–27.

Aubry, Pierre. *La rythmique musical des troubadours et trouvères*. Paris: Champion, 1907.

Audiau, Jean. *La pastourelle dans la poésie occitane du Moyen Âge*. Paris: E. de Boccard, 1923.

Aurell, Martin. *La vielle et l'epée: Troubadours et politique en Provence au XIIIe siècle*. Paris: Aubier, 1989.

Avalle, D'Arco Silvio. *I manoscritti della letterature in lingua d'oc*, ed. Lino Leonardi. Turin: Piccola Biblioteca Einaudi, 1993.

———. *La letteratura medievale in lingua d'oc nella sua tradizione manoscritta: Problemi di critica testuale*. Studi e ricerche, 16. Turin: Giulio Einaudi, 1961.

Baldwin, Charles S. *Medieval Rhetoric and Poetic (to 1400): Interpreted from Representative Works*. New York: Macmillan, 1928; repr. Gloucester, MA: Peter Smith, 1959.

Baratier, Edouard, ed. *Histoire de la Provence*. Toulouse: Privat, 1969.

Baum, Richard. "Les troubadours et les *lais*," *Zeitschrift für romanischen Philologie* 85 (1969):1–44.

Bec, Pierre. *La lyrique française au moyen âge (XIIe–XIIIe siècles). Contribution à une typologie des genres poétiques médiévaux*. 2 vols. Paris: Picard, 1977–1978.

———. "Le problème des genres chez les premiers troubadours," *Cahiers de civilisation médiévale* 25 (1982):31–47.

Beck, Jean-Baptiste. *Die Melodien der Troubadours, nach dem gesamten handschriftlichen Material zum erstenmal bearbeitet und herausgegeben nebst einer Untersuchung über di alteren Notenschrift (bis zum 1250) und das rhythmisch-metrische Prinzip der mittelalterlich-lyrischen Dichtungen*. Strassbourg: Trübner, 1908.

———. *La musique des troubadours; étude critique*. Paris: Laurens, 1910; repr. Geneva: Slatkine, 1976.

Belperron, Pierre. *La croisade contre les Albigeois et l'union de Languedoc à la France (1209–1249)*. Paris: Plon, 1942.

Beltràn, Vincent. "Los trovadores en la corte de Castilla y León (II): Alfonso X, Guiraut Riquier y Pero da Ponte," *Romania* 107 (1986):486–503.

Beretta Spampinato, Margherita. "'Mot' e 'so' nella lirica trobadorica." In *XIV Congresso internazionale di linguistica e filologia romanza, Napoli, 15–20 aprile 1974, Atti, V: Communicazioni*, ed. Alberto Varvaro. Naples: Micchiaroli, 1981. Pp. 279–286.

Bertolucci Pizzorusso, Valeria. "Il canzoniere di un trovatore: Il 'libro' di Guiraut Riquier," *Medioevo romanzo* 5 (1978):216–259.

Bielitz, Mathias. "*Materia* und *forma* bei Johannes de Grocheo; Zur Verwendung philosophischer Termini in der mittelalterlichen Musiktheorie," *Die Musikforschung* 38 (1985):257–277.

Billet, Léon. *Généalogie de la famille "d'Ussel": Les quatre troubadours d'Ussel, leur biographie et celle de la maison d'Ussel*. Tulle: Orfeuil, 1982.

Billy, Dominique. *L'Architecture lyrique médiévale. Analyse métrique et modélisation des structures interstrophiques dans la poésie lyrique des troubadours et des trouvères*. Montpellier: Section Française de l'Association International d'Études Occitanes, 1989.

———. "Le *descort* occitan: Réexamen critique du corpus," *Revue des langues romanes* 87 (1983):1–28.

———. "Les empreintes métriques de la musique dans l'estampie lyrique," *Romania* 108 (1987):207–229.

Bisson, Thomas N. *The Medieval Crown of Aragon: A Short History.* Oxford: Clarendon Press, 1986.

Bogin, Meg. *The Women Troubadours: An Introduction to the Women Poets of 12th-Century Provence and a Collection of Their Poems.* New York: W. W. Norton, 1976.

Boissonnade, Prosper. "Les personnages et les événements de l'histoire d'Allemagne, de France, et d'Espagne dans l'oeuvre de Marcabru (1129–1150)," *Romania* 48 (1922):207–242.

Brakelmann, Julius. "Die dreiundzwanzig altfranzösische Chansonniers in Bibliotheken Frankreichs, Englands, Italiens und der Schweiz," *Archiv für das Studium der neueren Sprachen und Literaturen* 42 (1868):43–72.

———. *Les plus anciens chansonniers français (XII siècle).* Paris: Bouillon, 1870–91.

Brunel, Clovis F. "Les troubadours Azémar Jordan et Uc Brunenc." *Romania* 52 (1926):505–508.

Brunel-Lobrichon, Geneviève. "L'Iconographie du chansonnier provençal R: Essai d'interprétation." In *Lyrique romane médiévale: La tradition des chansonniers, Actes du Colloque de Liège, 1989,* ed. Madeleine Tyssens. Liège: Bibliothèque de la Faculté de Philosophie et Lettres de l'Université de Liège, 1991. Pp. 245–272.

———. "Les troubadours dans les cours ibériques." In *Actes du IV Congrès International de l'Association Internationale d'Études Occitanes, Vitoria-Gasteiz, 22–28 août 1993,* vol. I, ed. Ricardo Cierbide Martinena. Vitoria-Gasteiz, 1994. Pp. 37–45.

Busquet, Raoul; V. L. Bourrilly; and Maurice Agulhon, eds. *Histoire de Provence.* 6th ed. Paris: Presses Universitaires de France, 1976.

Carpenter, Nan Cooke. *Music in the Medieval and Renaissance Universities.* New York: Da Capo Press, 1972.

Carpentier, E. "Structure féodales et féodalisme dans l'Occident méditerranéen (Xe–XIIIe s.)," *Cahiers de civilisation médiévale* 26 (1983):141–146.

Carruthers, Mary. *The Book of Memory; A Study of Memory in Medieval Culture.* Cambridge: Cambridge University Press, 1990.

Chabaneau, Camille. *Les biographies des troubadours en langue provençale.* Toulouse: Privat, 1885.

Chailley, Jacques. "Notes sur les troubadours, les versus et la question arabe." In *Mélanges de linguistique et de littérature romanes à la mémoire d'István Frank.* Annales Universitatis Saraviensis, 6. Saarbrücken: Universität des Saarlandes, 1957. Pp. 118–128.

———. "Les premiers troubadours et les versus de l'école d'Aquitaine," *Romania* 76 (1955):212–239.

Chambers, Frank M. "Imitation of Form in the Old Provençal Lyric," *Romance Philology* 6 (1952–53):104–120.

———. *An Introduction to Old Provençal Versification.* Philadelphia: American Philosophical Society, 1985.

Chevalier, Jules. "Mémoires pour servir à l'histoire des comtés de Valentinois et de Diois," *Bulletin de la Société d'archéologie de la Drôme* 23 (1889):125.

Chickering, Howell, and Margaret L. Switten, eds. *The Medieval Lyric: Commentary Volume.* South Hadley, MA: Mount Holyoke College, 1988.

Cohen, Joel. "Peirol's Vielle: Instrumental Participation in the Troubador Repertory," *Historical Performance* 3 (1990):73–77.

Cravayat, Paul. "Les origines du troubadour Jaufre Rudel," *Romania* 71 (1950):166–179.

Cummins, Patricia W. "How Well Do Medieval Treatises Describe Extant Estampies?" *Neophilologus* 63 (1979):330–337.

Delaruelle, Etienne. "De la croisade à l'université: la fondation de l'université de Toulouse." In *Les Universités du Languedoc au XIIIe siècle,* Cahiers de Fanjeaux, 5. Toulouse: Privat, 1970. Pp. 19–34.

Del Monte, Alberto. *Studi sulla poesia ermetica medievale.* Naples: Giannini, 1953.

De Vic, Claude, and Joseph Vaissette. *Histoire générale de Languedoc, avec des notes et les pièces justificatives.* 15 vols. Toulouse: Privat, 1872–1892.

DeWitt, Patricia A. M. "A New Perspective on Johannes de Grocheio's Ars Musicae." Ph.D. diss., University of Michigan, 1973.

Dossat, Yves. "Les premiers maîtres à l'université de Toulouse: Jean de Garlande, Helinand." In *Les Universités du Languedoc au XIIIe siècle.* Cahiers de Fanjeaux, 5. Toulouse: Privat, 1970. Pp. 179–203.

———. "L'Université de Toulouse, Raymond VII, les capitouls et le roi." In *Les Universités du Languedoc au XIIIe siècle.* Cahiers de Fanjeaux, 5. Toulouse: Privat, 1970. Pp. 58–91.

Dragonetti, Roger. *La technique poétique des trouvères dans la chanson courtoise.* Bruges: De Tempel, 1960.

Duggan, Joseph J. *The Song of Roland: Formulaic Style and Poetic Craft.* Berkeley: University of California Press, 1973.

Duguet, Jacques. "L'identification du troubadour Rigaud de Barbezieux," *Bulletin de la Société des Antiquaires de l'Ouest et des Musées de Poitiers* 9 (1967–1968):537–547.

Egan, Margarita. "Commentary, *Vitae Poetae* and *Vida*: Latin and Old Provençal 'Lives of Poets,'" *Romance Philology* 37 (1983–84):36–48.

———. "'Razo' and 'Novella': A Case Study in Narrative Forms," *Medioevo Romanzo* 6 (1979):302–314.

Eusebi, Mario. "Singolarità del canzoniere provenzale R," *Romanische Forschungen* 95 (1983):111–116.

Everist, Mark. *Polyphonic Music in Thirteenth-Century France: Aspects of Sources and Distribution.* New York: Garland, 1989.

Falvy, Zoltán. "Manuskripte, Herkunft und Verzierung in der Troubadour-Musik," *Studia Musicologica* 27 (1985):193–202.

———. *Mediterranean Culture and Troubadour Music,* trans. Maria Steiner, rev. by Brian McLean. Budapest: Akadémiai Kiadó, 1986.

Faral, Edmond. *Les jongleurs en France au moyen âge.* Paris: Champion, 1910.

Farreras, Joaquim Nadal, and Philippe Wolff, eds. *Histoire de la Catalogne.* Toulouse: Privat, 1982.

Fassler, Margot E. "Accent, Meter, and Rhythm in Medieval Treatises 'De rithmis,'" *The Journal of Musicology* 5 (1987):164–190.

———. "The Role of the Parisian Sequence in the Evolution of Notre-Dame Polyphony," *Speculum* 62 (1987):345–374.

Ferrante, Joan M. "'Ab joi mou lo vers e'l comens.'" In *The Interpretation of Medieval Lyric Poetry,* ed. W. T. H. Jackson. New York: Columbia University Press, 1980. Pp. 113–141.

———. "Was Vernacular Poetic Practice a Response to Latin Language Theory?" *Romance Philology* 35 (1982):586–600.

Finnegan, Ruth. *Oral Poetry: Its Nature, Significance and Social Context.* Bloomington: Indiana University Press, 1992.

Foley, John Miles. *The Theory of Oral Composition: History and Methodology.* Bloomington: Indiana University Press, 1988.

Frappier, Jean. "Aspects de l'hermétisme dans la poésie médiévale," *Cahiers de l'Association Internationale des Études Françaises* 15 (1963): 9–24.

Gallo, F. Alberto. *Musica nel castello: Trovatori, libri, oratori nelle corte italiana dal XIII al XV secolo.* Bologna: Mulino, 1992.

Gauchat, Louis. "Les poésies provençales conservées par des chansonniers français," *Romania* 22 (1893):364–404.

Gennrich, Friedrich. *Grundriss einer Formenlehre des mittelalterlichen Liedes als Grundlage einer musikalischen Formenlehre des Liedes.* Halle: Niemeyer, 1932; repr. with introduction by Werner Bittinger, Tübingen: Niemeyer, 1970.

Gonfroy, Gérard. "Les genres lyriques occitanes et les traités de poétique: de la classification médiévale à la typologie moderne." In *Actes du XVIIIe Congrès International de Linguistique et de Philologie Romanes, Université de Trèves 1986,* vol. 6, ed. Dieter Kremer. Tübingen: Niemeyer, 1988. Pp. 121–135.

Gossen, Nicoletta. "Musik und Text in Liedern des Trobadors Bernart de Ventadorn," *Schweizer Jahrbuch für Musikwissenschaft,* n.s., 4–5 (1984/85):9–40.

Grier, James. "Scribal Practices in the Aquitanian Versaria of the Twelfth Century: Towards a Typology of Error and Variant," *Journal of the American Musicological Society* 45 (1992):373–427.

Gröber, Gustav. "Die Liedersammlungen der Troubadours," *Romanische Studien* 2 (1877):337–668.

Gruber, Jörn. "L'Art poétique de Jaufre Rudel: Analyse philologique, musicologique et herméneutique de la chanson *No sap chantar qui so non di* (262,3)." In *La chanson française et son histoire,* ed. Dietmar Rieger. Tübingen: Gunter Narr, 1988. Pp. 15–25.

———. *Die Dialektik des Trobar: Untersuchungen zur Struktur und Entwicklung des occitanischen und französischen Minnesangs des 12. Jahrhunderts.* Beihefte zur Zeitschrift für romanischen Philologie, 194. Tübingen: Niemeyer, 1983.

———. "Singen und Schreiben, Hören und Lesen als Parameter der (Re-) Produktion und Rezeption des Occitanischen Minnesangs des 12. Jahrhunderts," *Zeitschrift für Litteraturwissenschaft und Linguistik* 15 (1985):35–51.

Guida, Saverio. "Problemi di datazione e di identificazione di trovatori Rigaut de Berbezilh, Sifre e Mir Bernart, Guillem Augier," *Studi provenzali e francezi* 86/87, *Romanica vulgaria,* Quaderni 10/11, L'Aquila (Rome: Japadre, 1989):87–108, 118–126.

Harvey, Ruth E. "*Joglars* and the Professional Status of the Early Troubadours," *Medium Aevum* 62 (1993):221–241.

———. "The Troubadour Marcabru and His Public," *Reading Medieval Studies* 14 (1988):47–76.

Harvey, Ruth E., and Simon Gaunt. "Bibliographie commentée du troubadour Marcabru; mise à jour," *Le Moyen Âge* 94 (1988):425–455.

Haymes, Edward R. "Oral Composition in Middle High German Epic Poetry." In *Oral Traditional Literature: a Festschrift for Albert Bates Lord.* Columbus, OH: Slavica, 1981. Pp. 341–346.

Hibberd, Lloyd. "Estampie and Stantipes," *Speculum* 19 (1944):222–49.

Higounet, Charles, ed. *Histoire de l'Aquitaine.* Toulouse: Privat, 1971.

Hiley, David. "The Plica and Liquescence." In *Gordon Athol Anderson (1929–1981): In Memoriam von seinen Studenten, Freunden und Kollegen,* vol. 2. Musicological Studies 39, ed. Luther Dittmer. Henryville, PA: Institute of Medieval Music, 1984. Pp. 379–391.

Hoepffner, Ernest. "La biographie de Perdigon," *Romania* 53 (1927):343–364.

———. "Les troubadours d'Ussel," *Romance Philology* 9 (1955):138–144.

Hucke, Helmut. "Der Übergang von mündlicher zu schriftlicher Musiküberlieferung im Mittelalter." In *International Musicological Society, Report of the Twelfth Congress, Berkeley 1977,* ed. Daniel Heartz and Bonnie Wade. Kassel: Bärenreiter, 1981. Pp. 180–191.

Huot, Sylvia. *From Song to Book: The Poetics of Writing in Old French Lyric and Lyrical Narrative Poetry*. Ithaca: Cornell University Press, 1987.

———. "Visualization and Memory: The Illustration of Troubadour Lyric in a Thirteenth-Century Manuscript," *Gesta* 31 (1992):3–14.

Jammers, Ewald. *Ausgewählte Melodien des Minnesangs: Einführung, Erläuterungen und Übertragung, Altdeutsche Textbibliothek*. Ergänzungsreihe 1. Tübingen: Niemeyer, 1963.

———. *Aufzeichnungsweisen der einstimmigen ausserliturgischen Musik des Mittelalters*. Paläographie der Musik, I/4. Cologne: Volk, 1975.

———. "Die Rolle der Musik in Rahmen der romanischen Dichtung." In *Grundriss der romanischen Literaturen des Mittelalters*, vol. I, *Généralities*, dir. Maurice Delbouille. Heidelberg: Winter, 1972. Pp. 483–537.

Jauss, Hans-Robert. "Littérature médiévale et théorie des genres," *Poétique* 1 (1970):79–101.

Jeanroy, Alfred. *La poésie lyrique des trobuadours*. 2 vols. Toulouse: Privat, 1934.

Jeanroy, Alfred, and Pierre Aubry. "Une chanson provençale à la Vierge," *Annales du Midi* 12 (1900):67–71.

Karp, Theodore. *The Polyphony of Saint Martial and Santiago de Compostela*. 2 vols. Berkeley: University of California Press, 1992.

———. "Three Trouvère Chansons in Mensural Notation." In *Gordon Athol Anderson (1929–1981): In Memoriam von seinen Studenten, Freunden und Kollegen*, vol. 2. Musicological Studies 39, ed. Luther Dittmer. Ottawa: Institute of Mediaeval Music, 1984. Pp. 474–494.

———. "The Trouvère MS Tradition." In *The Department of Music Queens College of the City University of New York: Twenty-Fifth Anniversary Festschrift (1937–1962)*, ed. Albert Mell. New York: Queens College of the City of New York, 1964. Pp. 25–52.

Kelly, Douglas. *The Arts of Poetry and Prose*. Typologie des Sources du Moyen Âge Occidental, 59. Turnhout: Brepols, 1991.

———. *Medieval Imagination: Rhetoric and the Poetry of Courtly Love*. Madison: University of Wisconsin Press, 1978.

———. "The Poem as Art of Poetry: The Rhetoric of Imitation." In *Historicizing Genre in Medieval Lyric*, ed. William D. Paden. Forthcoming.

———. "The Scope of the Treatment of Composition in the Twelfth- and Thirteenth-Century Arts of Poetry," *Speculum* 41 (1966):261–278.

———. "Theory of Composition in Medieval Narrative Poetry and Geoffrey of Vinsauf's *Poetria Nova*," *Mediaeval Studies* 31 (1969):117–148.

Köhler, Erich. "Trobar clus: Discussion aperta; Marcabru und die beiden Schulen," *Cultura Neolatina* 30 (1970):300–314.

Köhler, Erich; Ulrich Mölk; and Dietmar Rieger, eds. *Grundriss der romanischen Literaturen des Mittelalters*, vol. II: *Les Genres lyriques*, gen. ed. Hans-Robert Jauss, et al. Heidelberg: Winter, 1979–90.

Kropfinger, Klaus. "Dante e l'arte dei trovatori." In *La Musica nel Tempo di Dante: Ravenna, Comune di Ravenna, Opera di Dante, Musica/Realtà, 12–14 settembre 1986*, ed. Luigi Pestalozza. Milan: Unicopli, 1988. Pp. 130–174.

Lecoy, Félix. "Note sur le troubadour Raimbaut de Vaqueiras." In *Études romanes dediées à Mario Roques par ses amis, collègues et élèves de France*. Paris: Droz, 1946. Pp. 31–38.

Le Goff, Jacques. *L'Imaginaire médiéval*. Paris: Gallimard, 1985; trans. by Arthur Goldhammer as *The Medieval Imagination*, Chicago: University of Chicago Press, 1988.

Lejeune, Rita. "Analyse textuelle et histoire littéraire: Rigaut de Barbezieux," *Le Moyen Âge* 68 (1962):331–377.

———. "La 'Galerie littéraire' du troubadour Peire d'Alvernhe." In *Actes et mémoires du IIIe Congrès international de langue et littérature d'Oc et d'études franco-provençales, Bordeaux 1961.* Bordeaux: Université de Bordeaux, 1965. Pp. 35–54.

―――. "Le nom de Bernart de Ventadorn." In *Mittelalterstudien Erich Köhler zum Gedenken,* ed. Henning Krauss and Dietmar Rieger. Heidelberg: Carl Winter, 1984. Pp. 157–165.

―――. "Thèmes communs de troubadours et vie de société." In *Actes et mémoires du IIe Congrès international de langue et littérature du Midi de la France, Aix, 2–8 septembre 1958.* Aix: Centre d'Études Provençales de la Faculté des Lettres d'Aix, 1961. Pp. 81–88.

―――. "Le troubadour Rigaut de Barbezieux." In *Mélanges de linguistique et de littérature romanes à la mémoire d'István Frank.* Annales Universitatis Sara-viensis, 6. Saarbrücken: Universität des Saarlandes, 1957. Pp. 269–295.

LeVot, Gérard. "Intertextualité, métrique et composition mélodique dans les *cansos* du troubadour Folquet de Marseille." In *Contacts de langues, de civilisations et intertextualité, Actes du IIIème Congrès International de l'Association Internationale d'Études Occitanes,* vol. 2, ed. Gérard Gouiran. Montpellier: Université Paul Valéry, 1992. Pp. 637–667.

―――. "Notation, mesure et rythme dans la canso troubadouresque," *Cahiers de civilisation médiévale* 25 (1982):205–217.

―――. "Quelques indices du silence dans la *canso* des troubadours." In *Mélanges de langue et de littérature occitanes en hommage à Pierre Bec.* Poitiers: Université de Poitiers, Centre d'Études Supérieures de Civilisation Médiévale, 1991. Pp. 295–306.

LeVot, Gérard; Pierre Lusson; and Jacques Roubaud. "La sextine d'Arnaut Daniel: Essai de lecture rythmique." In *Actes du Colloque: Musique, Littérature et Société au Moyen Âge,* ed. Danielle Buschinger and André Crépin. Paris: Champion, 1980. Pp. 123–157.

Lewent, Kurt. "À propos du troubadour Peire Raimon de Tolosa," *Romania* 66 (1940): 12–31.

Lewis, Archibald R. *Medieval Society in Southern France and Catalonia.* London: Variorum Reprints, 1984.

Lord, Albert Bates. "Homer as Oral Poet," *Harvard Studies in Classical Philology* 72 (1968):1–46.

―――. *The Singer of Tales.* Cambridge: Harvard University Press, 1960.

Lucas, H. H. "Pons de Capduoill and Azalais de Mercuor: A Study of the *planh,*" *Nottingham Medieval Studies* 2 (1958):119–131.

Ludwig, Friedrich. "Die geistliche nichtliturgische, weltliche einstimmige und die mehrstimmige Musik des Mittelalters bis zum Anfang des 15. Jahrhunderts." In *Handbuch der Musikgeschichte,* vol. I, ed. Guido Adler. Berlin: Max Hesses, 1924. Pp. 155–295.

Lug, Robert. *Der Chansonnier de Saint-Germain-des-Prés (Paris, BN fr. 20050): Edition seiner Melodien mit Analysen zur "vormodalen" Notation des 13. Jahrhunderts und einer Transkriptionsgeschichte des europäischen Minnesangs.* 3 vols. Frankfurt: Lang, 1995.

―――. "Melismen-Untersuchungen am Chansonnier de St.-Germain-des-Prés," *Studia Musicologica Academiae Scientiarum Hungaricae* 27 (1985): 209–221.

―――. "Singen auf dem Pferderücken: Indizien zur Rhythmik der Trouba-dours." In *Soziolinguistik und Sprachgeschichte: Querverbindungen; Brigitte Schlieben-Lange zum 50. Geburtstag von ihren Schülerinnen und Schülern überreicht,* ed. Gabriele Berkenbusch and Christine Bierback. Tübingen: Gunter Narr, 1994. Pp. 229–259.

————. "Das 'vormodale' Zeichensystem des Chansonnier de Saint-Germain-des-Prés," *Archiv für Musikwissenschaft* 52 (1995):19–65.

McGee, Timothy J. "Medieval Dances: Matching the Repertory with Grocheio's Descriptions," *Journal of Musicology* 7 (1989):498–517.

Maillard, Jean. "Descort, que me veux-tu? . . ." *Cahiers de civilisation médiévale* 25 (1982):219–223.

————. *Evolution et esthétique du lai lyrique des origines à la fin du XIV siècle.* Paris: Centre de Documentation Universitaire et SEDES, 1963.

————. "Structures mélodiques complexes au Moyen Âge." In *Mélanges de linguistique et de littérature romanes à la mémoire d'István Frank.* Annales Universitatis Saraviensis, 6. Saarbrücken: Universität des Saarlandes, 1957. Pp. 388–409.

Marshall, John H. "Pour l'étude des *contrafacta* dans la poésie des troubadours," *Romania* 101 (1980):289–335.

————. "Une versification lyrique popularisante en ancien provençal." In *Actes du premier Congrès internationale de l'Association Internationale d'Études Occitanes,* ed. Peter T. Ricketts. London: Westfield College, 1987. Pp. 35–66.

Meneghetti, Maria Luisa. *Il pubblico dei trovatori.* Modena: Mucchi, 1984.

Miret i Sans, J. "Enquesta sobre el trovador Vilarnau amb algunes noves de Guillem de Bergadà, Ramon de Miraval i Guillem de Mur," *Revue hispanique* 46 (1919):264–266.

Mölk, Ulrich. *Trobadorlyrik: Eine Einführung.* Munich: Artemis, 1982.

————. *Trobar clus trobar leu: Studien zur Dichtungstheorie der Trobadors.* Munich: Fink, 1968.

Monier, Janine. "Essaie d'identification de la comtesse de Die," *Bulletin de la Société d'archéologie et de statistique de la Drôme* 75 (1962):265–278.

Monterosso, Raffaello. *Musica e ritmica dei trovatori (con i tavola fuori testo e 28 esempi musicali).* Milan: Giuffrè, 1956.

Murphy, James J. *Rhetoric in the Middle Ages: A History of Rhetorical Theory from St. Augustine to the Renaissance.* Berkeley: University of California Press, 1974.

Nelli, René. *Les Cathares du Languedoc au XIIIe siècle.* Paris: Hachette, 1969.

————. *Dictionnaire des hérésies méridionales et des mouvements, hétérodoxes ou indépendants, apparus dans le Midi de la France depuis l'établissement du christianisme.* Toulouse: Privat, 1968.

————. *Histoire du Languedoc.* Paris: Hachette, 1974.

Newcombe, Terence H. "Berenger de Palozol, troubadour roussillonnais," *Cahiers d'Études et de Recherches Catalanes d'Archives,* 37–38 (1967):194–205.

Noy, Francisco. "Estudio historico sobre el trovador Berenger de Palou," *Boletín de la Real Academia de Buenas Letras de Barcelona* 36 (1975–76):15–104.

Ong, Walter J. *Orality and Literacy: The Technologizing of the Word.* London and New York: Methuen, 1982.

Paden, William D. "Bernart de Ventadour le troubadour devint-il abbé de Tulle?" In *Mélanges de langue et de littérature occitanes en hommage à Pierre Bec.* Poitiers: Université de Poitiers, Centre d'Études Supérieures de Civilisation Médiévale, 1991. Pp. 401–413.

————. "Reading Pastourelles," *Tenso* 4 (1988):1–21.

————. "The Role of the Joglar in Troubadour Lyric Poetry." In *Chrétien de Troyes and the Troubadours: Essays in Memory of the Late Leslie Topsfield,* ed. Peter S. Noble and Linda M. Paterson. Cambridge: Saint Catharine's College, 1984. Pp. 90–111.

————. "The System of Genres in Troubadour Lyric." In *Historicizing Genre in Medieval Lyric,* ed. William D. Paden. Forthcoming.

Page, Christopher. *Discarding Images; Reflections on Music and Culture in Medieval France.* Oxford: Clarendon Press, 1993.

―――. "Johannes de Grocheio on Secular Music: A Corrected Text and a New Translation," *Plainsong and Medieval Music* 2 (1993):17–41.

―――. *The Owl and the Nightingale: Musical Life and Ideas in France 1100–1300.* Berkeley: University of California Press, 1989.

―――. *Voices and Instruments of the Middle Ages: Instrumental Practice and Songs in France 1100–1300.* Berkeley: University of California Press, 1986.

Parker, Ian. "Notes on the Chansonnier Saint-Germain-des-Prés," *Music and Letters* 60 (1979):261–280.

―――. "The Performance of Troubadour and Trouvère Songs," *Early Music* 5 (1977):184–207.

―――. "Troubadour and Trouvère Song: Problems in Modal Analysis," *Revue Belge de Musicologie* 31 (1977):20–37.

Paterson, Linda M. *Troubadours and Eloquence.* Oxford: Clarendon Press, 1975.

―――. *The World of the Troubadours: Medieval Occitan Society, c. 1100–c. 1300.* Cambridge: Cambridge University Press, 1993.

Pattison, Walter T. "The Background of Peire d'Alvernhe's 'Chantarai d'aquest trobadors,'" *Modern Philology* 31 (1933):19–34.

Peraino, Judith Ann. "New Music, Notions of Genre, and the 'Manuscrit du Roi' circa 1300." Ph.D. diss., University of California at Berkeley, 1995.

Petit, Jean-Marie. "Guiraut Riquier, période narbonnaise et destinée du dernier grand poète de cour." In *Actes du 45e Congrès de la Fédération historique du Languedoc méditerranéen et du Roussillon,* vol. II. Montpellier: La Fédération, 1973. Pp. 69–75.

Peyrebrune, Georges. "Giraut de Bornelh et l'époque limousine d'Excideuil," *Lemouzi* 103 (1987):59–74.

Pfeffer, Wendy. "Guilhem Molinier as Literary Critic." In *Studia Occitanica in Memoriam Paul Remy,* vol. I, ed. Hans-Erich Keller. Kalamazoo: The Medieval Institute, 1986. Pp. 210–212.

Phan, Chantal. "Structures textuelles et mélodiques des chansons des troubadours." Ph.D. diss., University of Montréal, 1989.

―――. "Le style poético-musical de Guiraut Riquier," *Romania* 108 (1987):66–78.

Pirot, François. *Recherches sur les connaissances littéraires des troubadours occitans et catalans des XIIe et XIIIe siècles; Les "sirventes-ensenhamens" de Guerau de Cabrera, Guiraut de Calanson et Bertrand de Paris.* Barcelona: Real Academia de Buenas Letras, 1972.

Poe, Elizabeth W. *From Poetry to Prose in Old Provençal: The Emergence of the "Vidas," the "Razos," and the "Razos de Trobar."* Birmingham, AL: Summa Publications, 1984.

―――. "The Meeting of Fact and Fiction in an Old Provençal Razo," *L'Esprit Créateur* 19 (1979):84–94.

―――. "New Light on the *Alba*: A Genre Redefined," *Viator* 15 (1984):139–150.

―――. "Old Provençal Vidas as Literary Commentary," *Romance Philology* 33 (1980):510–518.

―――. "The Problem of the Prologue in Raimon Vidal's *Las Razos de trobar,*" *Res Publica Litterarum* 6 (1983):303–317.

―――. "Toward a Balanced View of the Vidas and Razos," *Romanistische Zeitschrift für Literaturgeschichte* 11 (1987):18–28.

―――. "La transmission de l'*alba* en ancien provençal," *Cahiers de civilisation médiévale* 31 (1988):323–345.

Pollina, Vincent. "*Canso* mélodique et *canso* métrique: Era.m cosselhatz, Senhor de Bernart de Ventadorn." In *Actes du premier Congrès internationale de l'Association Internationale d'Études Occitanes*, ed. Peter T. Ricketts. London: Westfield College, 1987. Pp. 409–422.

———. "Melodic Continuity and Discontinuity in *A chantar m'er* of the Comtessa de Dia." In *Miscellanea di studi romanzi offerta a Giuliano Gasca-Queirazza per il suo 65° compleanno*, vol. 2, ed. Anna Cornagliotti et al. Alexandria: Edizioni dell' Orso, 1988. Pp. 887–895.

———. "Les mélodies du troubadour Marcabru: Questions de style et de genre." In *Atti del Secondo Congresso Internazionale della Association Internationale d'Études Occitanes, Torino, 31 agosto–5 settembre 1987*, vol. 1, ed. Giuliano-Gasca Queirazza. Turin: Departimento di Scienze Letterarie e Filologiche, Università di Torino, 1993. Pp. 289–306.

———. "Structure verbale et expression mélodique dans *Mon cor e mi* du troubadour Gaucelm Faidit." In *Contacts de langues, de civilisations et intertextualité, Actes du IIIème Congrès International de l'Association Internationale d'Études Occitanes*, vol. 2, ed. Gérard Gouiran. Montpellier: Université Paul Valéry, 1992. Pp. 669–678.

———. "Troubadours dans le nord: Observations sur la transmission des mélodies occitanes dans les manuscrits septentrionaux," *Romanistische Zeitschrift für Literaturgeschichte* 9 (1985):263–278.

———. "Word/Music Relations in the Work of the Troubadour Gaucelm Faidit: Some Preliminary Observations on the *Planh*." In *Miscellanea di studi in onore di Aurelio Roncaglia a cinquant'anni dalla sua laurea*, vol. 3. Modena: Mucchi, 1989. Pp. 1075–1090.

Raupach, Manfred, and Margret Raupach. *Französierte Trobadorlyrik: Zur Überlieferung provenzalischer Lieder in französischen Handschriften*. Beihefte zur Zeitschrift für Romanische Philologie, 171. Tübingen: Niemeyer, 1979.

Restori, Antonio. "Per la storia musicale dei trovatori provenzali," *Rivista musicale italiana* 2 (1895):1–22; 3 (1896):231–260 and 407–451.

Rieger, Dietmar. "Audition et lecture dans le domaine de la poésie troubadouresque," *Revue des langues romanes* 87 (1983):69–85.

———. "'Chantar' und 'faire': Zum Problem der trobadoresken Improvisation," *Zeitschrift für romanische Philologie* 106 (1990):423–435.

———. *Gattungen und Gattungsbezeichnungen der Trobadorlyrik: Untersuchungen zum altprovenzalischen Sirventes*. Beihefte zur Zeitschrift für romanischen Philologie, 148. Tübingen: Niemeyer, 1976.

———. "'*Senes breu de parguamina*'? Zum Problem des 'gelesenen Lieds' im Mittelalter," *Romanische Forschungen* 99 (1987):1–18.

Riley-Smith, Jonathan. *The Crusades: A Short History*. New Haven: Yale University Press, 1987.

Rivals, Edmond de. "Pons d'Ortaffa," *Revue des langues romanes* 67 (1933):59–118.

Roncaglia, Aurelio. "Trobar clus: Discussione aperta," *Cultura Neolatina* 29 (1969):5–55.

Roquebert, Michel. *L'Épopée Cathare*. 3 vols. Toulouse: Privat, 1970–86.

Ruggieri, Ruggero. M. "Chiose interpretative al Vers del Lavador," *Cultura Neolatina* 12 (1952):81–101.

Rychner, Jean. *La Chanson de geste: Essai sur l'art épique des jongleurs*. Geneva: Droz, 1955.

Scherner-van Ortmerssen, Gisela. *Die Text-Melodiestruktur in den Liedern des Bernart de Ventadorn*. Forschungen zur romanischen Philologie, 21. Münster: Aschendorff, 1973.

Serper, Arié. "Les troubadours Jaufré Rudel et Guillem Adémar," *Revue des langues romanes* 80 (1973):405–411.

Spanke, Hans. "Der Chansonnier du Roi," *Romanische Forschungen* 57 (1943):38–104.

Spence, Sarah. *Rhetorics of Reason and Desire: Vergil, Augustine, and the Trouba-dours*. Ithaca, NY: Cornell University Press, 1988.
Steel, Matthew C. "A Case for the Predominance of Melody over Text in Troubadour Lyric: Bernart de Ventadorn's 'Can vei la lauzeta mover,'" *Michigan Academician* 14 (1982):259–271.
Stevens, John. *Words and Music in the Middle Ages: Song, Narrative, Dance and Drama, 1050–1350*. Cambridge: Cambridge University Press, 1986.
Stevens, John, and Theodore Karp. "Troubadours, trouvères." In *The New Grove Dictionary of Music and Musicians*, vol. 19, ed. Stanley Sadie. London: Macmillan, 1980. Pp. 189–208.
Stock, Brian. *The Implications of Literacy: Written Language and Models of Interpre-tation in the Eleventh and Twelfth Centuries*. Princeton: Princeton University Press, 1983.
Strayer, Joseph R. *The Albigensian Crusades*. New York: Dial Press, 1971; repr. with a New Epilogue by Carol Lansing. Ann Arbor: University of Michi-gan Press, 1992.
Stronski, Stanislaw. "Notes sur quelques troubadours et protecteurs des trou-badours célébrés par Elias de Barjols," *Revue des langues romanes* 50 (1907):5–44.
———. *La poésie et la réalité aux temps des troubadours*. Oxford: The Clarendon Press, 1943.
———. "Recherches historiques sur quelques protecteurs des troubadours," *Annales du Midi* 18 (1906):473–493.
Sumpton, Jonathon. *The Albigensian Crusade*. London: Faber & Faber, 1978.
Switten, Margaret L. "De la sextine: amour et musique chez Arnaut Daniel." In *Mélanges de langue et de littérature occitanes en hommage à Pierre Bec*. Poitiers: Université de Poitiers, Centre d'Études Supérieures de Civilisation Médiévale, 1991. Pp. 549–565.
———. "Modèle et variations: Saint Martial de Limoges et les troubadours." In *Contacts de langues, de civilisations et intertextualité, Actes du IIIème Congrès International de l'Association Internationale d'Études Occitanes*, vol. 2, ed. Gérard Gouiran. Montpellier: Université Paul Valéry, 1992. Pp. 679–696.
———. "The Voice and the Letter: On Singing in the Vernacular," *Words and Music, Acta, 17*, ed. Paul R. Laird. Binghamton: Center for Medieval and Early Renaissance Studies, SUNY, 1993. Pp. 51–73.
Tavera, Antoine. "La table du chansonnier d'Urfé," *Cultura Neolatina* 52 (1992):23–138.
Taylor, Robert A. "'L'altrier cuidai aber druda' (PC 461,146): Edition and Study of a Hybrid-Language Parody Lyric." In *Studia Occitanica in Memoriam Paul Remy*, vol. I, ed. Hans-Erich Keller. Kalamazoo: The Medieval Insti-tute, 1986. Pp. 189–201.
Thomas, A. "L'identité du troubadour Pons de Chapteuil," *Annales du Midi* 5 (1893):374–379.
Topsfield, Leslie T. *Troubadours and Love*. London: Cambridge University Press, 1975.
Treitler, Leo. "'Centonate' Chant: *Übles Flickwerk* or *E pluribus unus?*" *Journal of the American Musicological Society* 28 (1975):1–23.
———. "Homer and Gregory: The Transmission of Epic Poetry and Plainchant," *The Musical Quarterly* 60 (1974):333–372.
———. "Oral, Written, and Literate Process in the Transmission of Medieval Music," *Speculum* 56 (1981):471–491.
———. "Regarding Meter and Rhythm in the *Ars antiqua*," *The Musical Quar-terly* 65 (1979):524–558.

————. "Transmission and the Study of Music History." In *International Musicological Society, Report of the Twelfth Congress, Berkeley 1977*, eds. Daniel Heartz and Bonnie Wade. Kassel: Bärenreiter, 1981. Pp. 202–211.

————. "The Troubadours Singing Their Poems." In *The Union of Words and Music in Medieval Poetry*, ed. Rebecca A. Baltzer, Thomas Cable, and James I. Wimsatt. Austin: University of Texas Press, 1991. Pp. 14–48.

Tyssens, Madeleine. "Les copistes du chansonnier français U." In *La lyrique romane médiévale: la tradition des chansonniers, Actes du Colloque du Liège, 13–17 décembre 1989*, ed. Madeleine Tyssens. Liège: Bibliothèque de la Faculté de Philosophie et Lettres de l'Université de Liège, 1991. Pp. 379–398.

Van der Werf, Hendrik. *The Chansons of the Troubadours and Trouvères: A Study of the Melodies and Their Relation to the Poems*. Utrecht: Oosthoek, 1972.

————. "The 'Not-so-precisely Measured' Music of the Middle Ages," *Performance Practice Review* 1 (1988):42–60.

Van Vleck, Amelia E. *Memory and Re-Creation in Troubadour Lyric*. Berkeley: University of California Press, 1991.

Vicaire, M.-H. "L'École du chapitre de la cathédrale et le projet d'extension de la théologie parisienne à Toulouse (1072–1217)." In *Les Universités du Languedoc au XIIIe siècle*, Cahiers de Fanjeaux, 5. Toulouse: Privat, 1970. Pp. 35–57.

Wakefield, Walter L. *Heresy, Crusade, and Inquisition in Southern France 1100–1250*. Berkeley: University of California Press, 1974.

Waite, William G. "Johannes de Garlandia, Poet and Musician," *Speculum* 35 (1960):179–195.

Wolff, Philippe, gen. ed. *Histoire de la France méridionale*. Toulouse: "Univers de la France," Collection d'histoire régionale, 1967- .

————, ed. *Histoire du Languedoc*. Toulouse: Privat, 1967.

Wright, Craig. *Music and Ceremony at Notre Dame of Paris, 500–1500*. Cambridge: Cambridge University Press, 1989.

Yudkin, Jeremy. "The Influence of Aristotle on French University Music Texts." In *Music Theory and Its Sources: Antiquity and the Middle Ages*, ed. André Barbera. Notre Dame: Notre Dame University Press, 1990. Pp. 173–189.

Ziino, Agostino. "Caratteri e significato della tradizione musicale trobadorica." In *Lyrique romane médiévale: La tradition des chansonniers: Actes du Colloque de Liège, 1989*, ed. Madeleine Tyssens. Liège: Bibliothèque de la Faculté de Philosophie et Lettres de l'Université de Liège, 1991. Pp. 85–218.

Zingarelli, Nicola. *Intorno a due trovatori in Italia*. Florence: Sansoni, 1899.

Zingerle, Hans. *Tonalität und Melodieführung in den Klauseln der Troubadours- und Trouvèreslieder*. Tutzing and Munich: Hans Schneider, 1958.

Zink, Michel. *La Pastourelle: Poésie et folklore au moyen âge*. Paris: Bordas, 1972.

Zufferey, François. "La partie non-lyrique du chansonnier d'Urfé," *Revue des langues romanes* 98 (1994):1–29.

————. *Recherches linguistiques sur les chansonniers provençaux*. Geneva: Droz, 1987.

Zumthor, Paul. *Essai de poétique médiévale*. Paris: Seuil, 1972.

————. *Introduction à la poésie orale*. Paris: Seuil, 1983; trans. by Kathryn Murphy-Judy as *Oral Poetry: An Introduction*. Minneapolis: University of Minnesota Press, 1990.

————. *La lettre et la voix: de la "littérature" médiévale*. Paris: Seuil, 1987.

————. *La poésie et la voix dans la civilisation médiévale*. Paris: Presses Universitaires de France, 1984.

GENERAL INDEX

accent, 239–44, 252–54
Adam de la Halle, 240, 246
Aigar V of Limoges, 112
Aimeric de Belenoi, 20, 22, 23, 48, 169, 180, 183; and motivic construction, 191–92
Aimeric de Peguilhan, 12, 13, 19, 20, 23, 41–42, 45, 63, 73, 272, 273; and form, 163, 166–67; and genre, 106, 107–8; and style, 215, 227, 228, 231
alba, 10, 21, 78, 86, 102–5, 109, 213, 225, 230, 291n.38
Albertet (de Sestaro), 18, 20, 36, 37, 182, 226–27, 232, 257
Albigensian Crusade, xvi, 3, 5, 10, 13–14, 16–17, 18–19, 23, 27, 45–46, 70, 231. See also Inquisition
Alfonso II (king of Aragón), 10, 11, 13, 15, 17, 19, 21, 222
Alfonso VII (king of Castile), 7
Alfonso VIII (king of Castile), 10, 15, 18, 20, 277n.27
Alfonso IX of León, 15
Alfonso X "el Sabio" (king of Castile), 7, 24, 46
Aliénor of Aquitaine, 1–2, 4, 9, 277n.27
Alphonse-Jourdain of Toulouse, 7
Aquitaine, xvi, 1, 3, 36, 68
Aragón, 2
Aristotle, 71, 76
Arnaut Daniel, xx, 10, 12, 14, 17, 33, 143, 153; and form, 141–42; and genre, 82; and style, 201, 202–3, 206, 207, 221, 225, 229
Arnaut de Maruelh, 10, 11, 17, 20, 48; and performance, 269, 270; and poetry, 72, 73; and style, 220–21, 222
art de trobar, 84, 200; ecclesiastical ties, xvii; and preservation, 5; and rhetoric, xix
arts of poetry and prose, 10, 75, 81, 132–33, 251. See also form, poetic
Aubry, Pierre, xv, 240, 241, 242
Auvergne, 1, 7, 17, 36, 222
Avalle d'Arco, Silvio, 27
Avignon, 9
Azalais of Burlatz, 11

balada, 24
Baldwin of Flanders, 4
Battle of Muret, 3, 5, 18, 19
Baux family, 14
Beatriz de Dia. See Comtessa de Dia
Bec, Pierre, 81, 109, 127

Beck, Jean-Baptiste, xv, 40, 240, 241
Beck, Louise, 40
Berenguier de Palol, 10–11, 48, 216–17, 254, 255
Bernard of Clairvaux, 4
Bernart de la Fon, 78
Bernart de Ventadorn, 8, 9, 12, 45, 51–55, 57–58, 61, 63–64; and form, 148, 152–53, 163, 176, 177; and genre, 82, 87–92; and motivic construction, 188, 190, 265; and musical/poetic relationships, 194–95; and notation, 248, 250; and performance, 269; and poetry, 72, 73; and style, 207–9, 211–13, 216–17, 235
Bernart Marti, 201–2
Bernart VII of Anduza, 19, 227
Bertran Carbonel, 46
Bertran de Born, 10, 12–15, 17, 18, 45, 48, 291n.53; and form, 153, 154; and genre, 112, 122; and performance, 256; and poetry, 72–73; and style, 211, 213, 214, 231
Blacasset, 23, 42, 169, 232
Blacatz, Lord, 20, 21, 23
Boethius, 66–67
Bonifacio I (marquis of Monferrato), 4, 12, 14, 21
Bordelais, 22
borrowing, 23–24, 74, 83, 170, 204, 231, 291n.32; poetic form, 111
Brakelman, Julius, 35
Breviari d'Amor, 24–25
Brunetto Latini, 68

cadence, xxi, 57, 87, 92, 99, 136, 144, 145, 174, 176, 180, 183; internal, 177, 182; and motivic construction, 187, 188; and style, 202, 213, 217, 219, 226, 228, 231, 234
Cadenet, 21, 23, 45, 48, 105, 225, 227, 230, 234, 235
caesura, 99, 105, 135, 180, 193, 194, 197, 216, 219, 238, 239, 252–53
canso, xix, 7–24 passim, 63, 117–20; and form, 144, 166; and genre, 80–87 passim, 292–93n.74; and materia, 78–79; and melody, 109; and motivic construction, 193; and notation, 243, 247, 248; and stanza, 87; and style, 213, 230
cantigas de Santa Maria, 261
cantilena, 126
cantus coronatus, 257, 259, 289n.66
Carcassonne, 18
Castile, 2, 22

59
motivic construction, 184–94, 202, 208, 216, 220–22, 226, 234; graphing, 188; and rhyme, 185–87; and rhythm, 254
mouvance (fluidity), 28, 30, 289n.6
musica ficta, 63, 227, 262–63, 267
music/poetry relationship, 112, 194–95, 198, 201–2, 253–54
music treatises, 75

neumes, 31, 45, 51–52, 55, 64, 208–9, 212, 219, 237, 241, 244, 245, 246
notation: *breve*, 246, 248; clefs, 52; Franconian, 42, 43, 48, 237, 246–47; *longa*, 246, 248; Lothringian neumes, 35, 246; mensural, 48, 63, 232, 240, 243–46, 248, 253, 260, 296n.15; modal, 42, 245–46; neumes, 31; non- diastematic chant, 245; nonmensural, 41, 48, 245, 247; order of entry, 41, 44–45; and performance, 238, 241; and plainchant, 32; rhythmic, 55; semibreve, 42; vertical bars, 249–50

Occitania, xviii, 1, 3, 4, 10
Old Occitan. *See langue d'oc*
oral tradition. *See* transmission
organum, 75, 262
ornamentation, 51, 166, 267–72; difficult (*ornatus difficilis*), 199; easy (*ornatus facilis*), 200; and melody, 270–72; and performance, 61; poetic, 199

Paden, William, 9, 33
Page, Christopher, xv, 81, 126, 243, 247, 248, 257–61
papacy, 3, 14
partimen, 12
passing tones, 51
pastora, 111, 122
pastorela, xx, 7, 24, 31, 78, 260, 292n.55; and form, 144; and genre, 81, 86; and instrumentation, 257; and stanza, 95–96; and style, 206
pastourelle, 81, 117, 166, 243, 292n.55
Pedro II (king of Aragón), 3, 15, 18, 20
Peire d'Alvernhe, 7, 8, 9, 17, 56–57; and form, 152–53, 156; and performance, 257, 261; and style, 201, 202, 211, 215, 225, 230, 235
Peire Cardenal, 21, 23–24, 48, 117–20, 153, 171; and form, 169–70; and style, 222, 233
Peire de Corbian, 46
Peire of Castelnau, 5
Peire Raimon de Tolosa, 17–18, 21, 73, 225, 229, 267, 268
Peire Vidal, 4, 10, 12, 13, 15, 17, 38, 45, 48, 57, 59, 61, 63, 73, 219–20, 221; and form, 159; and performance, 250, 251; and

style, 211, 222, 225
Peirol, 4, 12, 18, 20, 22, 36, 37, 38, 39, 45, 225–26, 248, 249; and form, 166, 169, 183, 187; and performance, 257; and poetry, 73; and style, 230, 232
Perdigon, 12, 18–19, 163, 230, 231, 256
performance, xviii, xxi; aesthetic of, 244; and borrowing, 122–23; and cadences, 182; and chansonniers, 248–49; and genre, 86, 123–27, 238–39; latitude in, 33–34; of melody, 33–34; and notation, 238; and ornamentation, 61; and pitch, 54, 235–36; and rhetoric, 237; sources for, 238; and style, 235–36, 251–52; and text, 251; unconscious changes in, 29. *See also* chromatic inflection; instruments; *musica ficta*; ornamentation; rhythm
Périgord, 1, 7, 36
Philippe II Auguste (king of France), 3, 4, 14
phrase, 59, 176, 233
Pirot, François, 46
Pistoleta, 11, 20–21, 36, 37, 231
pitch, 87, 116–17, 136, 154, 166, 222; and chromaticism, 238, 264–65; goal, xxi, 174–75, 178–79, 182–84, 197, 232; level, 106, 213; and performance, 54, 235–36, 237, 254; and syllables, 250
plainchant, 32, 136, 241–43, 264
planh, xix–xx, 8, 10, 12, 17, 19, 21, 22, 24, 38; and genre, 82, 86, 99–102; and instrumentation, 257; and *materia*, 78, 79; and melody, 96, 111, 117–18, 122
plica, 42, 52, 55, 188, 296n.4
poetry. *See* form, poetic
Poitiers, 7
polyphony, xvii, 242–43, 245–47, 263–64
Pons de Capduelh, 4, 13, 19–20, 36, 37, 38, 39, 54; and form, 142, 163, 167; and performance, 256; and style, 215, 227, 228, 229, 230, 231
Pons d'Ortaffa, 22, 48, 169, 232
preservation, 5, 26, 30, 204
Priscian, 67
pronuntiatio, 67, 68, 77
Provence, 1, 2, 5, 10, 15, 20, 23, 27, 36, 232

quadrivium, 74, 75
Quintilian, 66, 288n.64

Raimbaut d'Aurenga, 7, 8–9, 10, 12, 16, 36, 38, 41; and form, 148; and style, 201, 211–13
Raimbaut de Vaqueiras, 4, 10, 11, 14–15, 22, 33, 48, 122; and form, 137, 159, 161; and performance, 251, 256; and style, 211, 217–19, 225, 231, 232
Raimon V (count of Toulouse), 8, 11, 13, 15, 17

SONG INDEX

ELIZABETH AUBREY

is Professor of Music
at The University of Iowa and author of many
articles on the troubadours and the trouvères.
She also sings and plays medieval and
Renaissance music in
concert.